D0221288

THE COLLECTED LETTERS OF THOMAS HARDY

VOLUME FIVE

1914–1919

Already published

The Collected Letters of Thomas Hardy

Volume One: 1840–1892

Volume Two: 1893–1901

Volume Three: 1902–1908

Volume Four: 1909–1913

THE COLLECTED

LETTERS OF THOMAS HARDY

EDITED BY

RICHARD LITTLE PURDY

AND

MICHAEL MILLGATE

VOLUME FIVE

1914–1919

CLARENDON PRESS · OXFORD

1985

Oxford University Press, Walton Street, Oxford OX2 6DP
London Glasgow New York Toronto
Delhi Bombay Calcutta Madras Karachi
Kuala Lumpur Singapore Hong Kong Tokyo
Nairobi Dar es Salaam Cape Town
Melbourne Auckland
and associated companies in
Beirut Berlin Ibadan Mexico City Nicosia

Oxford is a trademark of Oxford University Press

Published in the United States
by Oxford University Press, New York

The title-page device is reproduced from an engraving by Reynolds Stone

British Library Cataloguing in Publication Data
Hardy, Thomas, 1840–1928
The collected letters of Thomas Hardy.
Vol. 5: 1914–1919
1. Hardy, Thomas, 1840–1928—Biography
2. Novelists, English—19th Century—Biography
I. Purdy, Richard Little II. Millgate, Michael
823'8 PR4753
ISBN 0-19-812622-0

Filmset by Latimer Trend & Company Ltd, Plymouth
and printed in Great Britain
at the Thetford Press, Thetford

CONTENTS

A NOTE ON HARDY'S DRAFTS

FOLLOWING his marriage to Florence Dugdale in February 1914, it became Hardy's regular practice to handle much of his less personal correspondence by drafting replies in his own hand (almost always in pencil) and then passing such drafts on to Mrs. Hardy (or to May O'Rourke, their occasional secretary) to be typed; the draft, generally written on the back or at the foot of the incoming letter, would then be retained as a record. Sometimes Hardy would write in the first person and subsequently sign the typed letter himself; sometimes a first-person letter would be signed 'for Thomas Hardy' by Mrs. Hardy (occasionally using just her first initials, 'F.E.') or by Miss O'Rourke ('M.O'R.'). Often, however, Hardy would draft the letter in the third person, to give the impression that it had actually been composed as well as signed by Mrs. Hardy or Miss O'Rourke. Relatively few of those letters bearing a signature other than Hardy's seem to have survived—for Hardy, indeed, one of the attractions of such procedures lay in the disappointment and deterrence of autograph-hunters—but a large number of the original drafts have been preserved among the files of the Max Gate correspondence now in the Dorset County Museum.

In Volumes 5, 6, and 7 of this edition the editors have drawn selectively upon such materials, choosing most items on grounds of intrinsic interest but including a few simply for the sake of their representativeness—as examples of the kinds of correspondence (requests for autographs or permissions, invitations to lend practical or symbolic support to persons, organizations, or causes) with which Hardy had to deal on an almost daily basis. Typed drafts or drafts written in a hand other than Hardy's have been included only when it was clear, usually from the presence of a correction or annotation in his holograph, that the document had originally been written or dictated by him; other letters signed by Mrs. Hardy and Miss O'Rourke have been omitted, however strong the suspicion (especially in letters containing such phrases as 'I write for my husband') that the wording may in fact have been Hardy's own. When the editors have had available to them both Hardy's draft and the letter as actually sent out over the signature or initials of Mrs. Hardy or Miss O'Rourke they have invariably followed the text of the draft.

Inclusion of these late drafts of Hardy's has not necessitated any change in the established procedures of the edition (see I.xv–xvi), except for the use of four spaced periods ('. . . .') as a standardized representation of the varying numbers of periods or short dashes employed by Hardy to indicate where the person typing the letter should supply a precise date, insert additional information or phraseology, or leave space for a signature.

CHRONOLOGY

THOMAS HARDY 1840–1928

1840	2 June	Born, eldest child of Thomas and Jemima (Hand) Hardy, at Higher Bockhampton, Dorset.
1856	11 July	Articled to John Hicks, Dorchester architect.
1862	17 Apr	Goes to London; soon employed in architectural office of Arthur Blomfield.
1867	20 July	Returns to Dorset because of ill health; again employed by Hicks.
1868	9 June	Completes final draft of 'The Poor Man and the Lady' (later destroyed).
1869	May	Employed by Weymouth architect, G. R. Crickmay.
1870	7 Mar	Goes to St. Juliot, Cornwall, to inspect church; meets Emma Lavinia Gifford for the first time.
1871	25 Mar	*Desperate Remedies* pub. (3 vols.) by Tinsley Brothers.
1872	March	In London lodgings, working for the architect T. Roger Smith.
	June	*Under the Greenwood Tree* pub. (2 vols.) by Tinsley Brothers.
	15 Aug	First instalment of *A Pair of Blue Eyes* in September number of *Tinsleys' Magazine*.
1873	late May	*A Pair of Blue Eyes* pub. (3 vols.) by Tinsley Brothers.
	21 Sept	Suicide of Horace Moule at Cambridge.
	December	First instalment of *Far from the Madding Crowd* in the *Cornhill Magazine*.
1874	17 Sept	Marries Emma Lavinia Gifford at St. Peter's Church, Paddington; honeymoon in France.
	6 Oct	Takes rooms at St. David's Villa, Hook Road, Surbiton.
	23 Nov	*Far from the Madding Crowd* pub. (2 vols.) by Smith, Elder.
1875	22 Mar	Moves to 18 Newton Road, Westbourne Grove, London.
	15 Aug	Moves to West End Cottage, Swanage, Dorset.
1876	early March	Moves to 7 Peter (or St. Peter) Street, Yeovil, Somerset.
	3 Apr	*The Hand of Ethelberta* pub. (2 vols.) by Smith, Elder.
	3 July	Moves to Riverside (or Rivercliff) Villa, Sturminster Newton, Dorset.
1878	22 Mar	Moves to 1 Arundel Terrace, Trinity Road, Upper Tooting.
	4 Nov	*The Return of the Native* pub. (3 vols.) by Smith, Elder.
1880	23 Oct	Beginning of serious illness.
	26 Oct	*The Trumpet-Major* pub. (3 vols.) by Smith, Elder.
1881	25 June	Moves to Lanherne, The Avenue, Wimborne, Dorset.
	early December	*A Laodicean* pub. (3 vols.) by Sampson Low.
1882	late October	*Two on a Tower* pub. (3 vols.) by Sampson Low.
1883	June	Moves to Shire-Hall Lane, Dorchester.
1885	29 June	Moves to Max Gate (designed by himself), just outside Dorchester.

1886	10 May	*The Mayor of Casterbridge* pub. (2 vols.) by Smith, Elder.
1887	15 Mar	*The Woodlanders* pub. (3 vols.) by Macmillan.
	March–April	Visits Italy.
1888	4 May	*Wessex Tales* pub. (2 vols.) by Macmillan.
1891	30 May	*A Group of Noble Dames* pub. by Osgood, McIlvaine.
	late November	*Tess of the d'Urbervilles* pub. (3 vols.) by Osgood, McIlvaine.
1892	20 July	Death of Thomas Hardy, sen.
1893	19 May	In Dublin; first meeting with Florence Henniker.
1894	22 Feb	*Life's Little Ironies* pub. by Osgood, McIlvaine.
1895	4 Apr	First vol. of Wessex Novels edn. pub. by Osgood, McIlvaine.
	1 Nov	*Jude the Obscure* pub. by Osgood, McIlvaine.
1897	16 Mar	*The Well-Beloved* pub. by Osgood, McIlvaine.
1898	December	*Wessex Poems* pub. by Harper & Brothers.
1901	mid-November	*Poems of the Past and the Present* pub. by Harper & Brothers.
1904	13 Jan	*The Dynasts*, Part First, pub. by Macmillan.
	3 Apr	Death of Jemima Hardy.
1906	9 Feb	*The Dynasts,* Part Second, pub. by Macmillan.
1908	11 Feb	*The Dynasts,* Part Third, pub. by Macmillan.
1909	3 Dec	*Time's Laughingstocks* pub. by Macmillan.
1910	June	Receives the Order of Merit.
1912	30 Apr	First two vols. of Wessex Edition pub. by Macmillan.
	27 Nov	Death of Emma Lavinia Hardy.
1913	24 Oct	*A Changed Man and Other Tales* pub. by Macmillan.
1914	10 Feb	Marries Florence Emily Dugdale at St. Andrew's Church, Enfield.
	17 Nov	*Satires of Circumstance* (including 'Poems of 1912–13') pub. by Macmillan.
1915	24 Nov	Death of Mary Hardy, the elder of his sisters.
1917	30 Nov	*Moments of Vision* pub. by Macmillan.
1922	23 May	*Late Lyrics and Earlier* pub. by Macmillan.
1923	15 Nov	*The Famous Tragedy of the Queen of Cornwall* pub. by Macmillan.
1925	20 Nov	*Human Shows, Far Phantasies, Songs, and Trifles* pub. by Macmillan.
1927	21 July	Address at Dorchester Grammar School stone-laying: last public appearance.
1928	11 Jan	Dies at Max Gate.
	2 Oct	*Winter Words* pub. by Macmillan.
	2 Nov	*The Early Life of Thomas Hardy* pub. under the name of Florence Emily Hardy.
1930	29 Apr	*The Later Years of Thomas Hardy* pub. under the name of Florence Emily Hardy.

ACKNOWLEDGEMENTS FOR VOLUME FIVE

IN the course of collecting and editing the letters in this fifth volume the editors have incurred many obligations. Our thanks are due first of all to the authorities of the following institutions for the assistance they have given and for permission to publish manuscripts in their possession:

Aberdeen University; Albert A. and Henry W. Berg Collection, New York Public Library, and Mrs. Lola L. Szladits; University of California, Berkeley, and the Director of the Bancroft Library; University of Birmingham; Bodleian Library; British Library; British Library of Political and Economic Science; Brooklyn Public Library; State University of New York at Buffalo, Lockwood Library Poetry Collection, and Mr. Robert J. Bertholf;

University of California, Los Angeles; Cambridge University Library; Colby College Library, Waterville, Maine, and Dr. J. Fraser Cocks III; Dorset County Museum, Dorchester, and Mr. R. N. R. Peers; University College, Dublin; Duke University; Eton College, School Library, and Mr. Michael Meredith;

Fitzwilliam Museum; Folger Shakespeare Library; Garrick Club; University of Glasgow; Hampshire County Library, Winchester; Thomas Hardy Society, Dorchester; Harvard University, Houghton Library, and Dr. W. H. Bond; Hove Central Library; Huntington Library; University of Illinois Library, Urbana; University of Kentucky, W. Hugh Peal Collection, and Ms. Claire McCann;

University of Leeds, Brotherton Library, and Mr. Christopher Sheppard; Library of Congress; University of London Library; McGill University; Manchester Central Library; Miami University of Ohio; Minnesota Historical Society; National Library of Scotland, and Mr. A. S. Bell; Newberry Library; New York University Library, Fales Library, Bobst Library, and Dr. Theodore Grieder;

University of Pennsylvania Library; Princeton University Library; Rationalist Press Association and Mr. Nicholas Walters; Philip H. and A. S. W. Rosenbach Foundation, Philadelphia; Royal Literary Fund; Royal Society of Literature; University of Texas at Austin, Humanities Research Center, and Mrs. Ellen S. Dunlap; Victoria and Albert Museum; University of Virginia; Wiltshire Record Office; Yale University, Beinecke Library, and Miss Marjorie G. Wynne.

We owe a special debt of gratitude to the following collectors and private owners who have made manuscripts in their possession available to us:

Mr. Frederick B. Adams, Mr. Seymour Adelman, Mr. John Arlott, Mrs. Celia Barclay, Lord Bridges, Miss Dorothy E. Collins, Canon C. P. Cowley, Mr. J. Stevens Cox, Mr. T. R. M. Creighton, Mr. David

Dickinson, Professor C. H. Gifford, Mr. R. Greenland, Mr. David Holmes, Mr. Charles Lock, Mr. Kenneth A. Lohf, Mr. Roger Lonsdale, the Executors of the Estate of Robert Lynd, Mrs. Michael MacCarthy, Mr. Roger Morgan, Mr. Christopher Pope, Miss F. F. Quiller-Couch, Mr. Gordon N. Ray, Mr. J. S. Sample, Mrs. Ethel Skinner, Professor Hisazumi Tagiri, Mr. Robert H. Taylor, Mr. Edwin Thorne, Mr. R. V. Weight, Mrs. Iris Wise.

To the following we offer our grateful thanks for help of many kinds, especially in tracing manuscripts and resolving problems of annotation:

Mr. and Mrs. Frederick B. Adams, Mr. John Antell, Mrs. Celia Barclay, Dr. and Mrs. C. J. P. Beatty, Professor Karl Beckson, Professor Patricia Brückmann, Mr. Alan Clodd, Mrs. Nancy Coffin, Professor Michael Collie, Mrs. Jane Cooper, Professor Pierre Coustillas, Mr. Peter W. Coxon, Mr. Nigel Cross, Miss Helen Garton, Dr. James Gibson, Professor Gordon S. Haight, Mr. David Holmes, Professor Samuel Hynes, Professor Heather Jackson, Professor J. R. deJ. Jackson, Professor W. J. Keith, Professor Martin Kreiswirth, Miss Patience-Anne W. Lenk, Dr. Charles Lock, Mr. Desmond MacCarthy, Mr. Michael Meredith, Professor Jane Millgate, Professor Sylvère Monod, Mr. Stephen R. Parks, Mr. John Pentney, Mr. Charles P. C. Pettit, Mr. Michael Rabiger, Mr. Henry Reed, Professor J. M. Robson, Professor S. P. Rosenbaum, Professor Robert C. Schweik, Mrs. Carola Shephard, Mr. and Mrs. J. P. Skilling, Mrs. Virginia Surtees, Mrs. Lillian Swindall, Professor Kenneth Thompson, Mrs. Ann Thwaite, Dr. Neda M. Westlake, Professor Judith Wittenberg, Miss Marjorie G. Wynne, the Revd. J. M. C. Yates.

Professor Millgate has again been greatly aided in his work on this volume by the generous and sustained support of the Social Sciences and Humanities Research Council of Canada. That support has made available the expert typing of Mrs. Freda Gough and the efficient research assistance of Mr. Edward J. Esche and, especially, Miss Lesley Mann, who has made a substantial contribution to the present volume.

Professor Millgate also particularly acknowledges the researches so willingly and ably undertaken on his behalf by Mr. and Mrs. William Jesty and by the late Mr. Malcolm Tomkins.

Our best thanks, finally, must go to the Trustees of the Thomas Hardy Estate for their grant of an 'exclusive licence' to collect, edit, and publish Hardy's letters, and to Mr. R. N. R. Peers, Curator of the Dorset County Museum and its Hardy Memorial Collection, for assistance of every sort, most generously given.

April 1983

R.L.P.
M.M.

LIST OF ABBREVIATIONS

TH	Thomas Hardy
ELH	Emma Lavinia Hardy
FEH	Florence Emily Hardy
Adams	Frederick B. Adams, private collection
Berg	Berg Collection, New York Public Library
Berkeley	University of California, Berkeley
BL	British Library
Buffalo	State University of New York, Buffalo
Colby	Colby College, Waterville, Maine
DCM	Dorset County Museum
LC	Library of Congress
Leeds	University of Leeds, Brotherton Collection
NLS	National Library of Scotland
NYU	New York University, Fales Library
Taylor	Robert H. Taylor, private collection
Texas	University of Texas at Austin, Humanities Research Center
UCLA	University of California, Los Angeles
D.N.B.	*Dictionary of National Biography*
EL	Florence Emily Hardy, *The Early Life of Thomas Hardy* (London, 1928)
LY	Florence Emily Hardy, *The Later Years of Thomas Hardy* (London, 1930)
Millgate	Michael Millgate, *Thomas Hardy: A Biography* (New York, 1982; Oxford, 1982)
Purdy	Richard Little Purdy, *Thomas Hardy: A Bibliographical Study* (London, 1954, 1968, 1978); where no page is indicated, the reference is to the editor's private collection.
Wessex edn.	Wessex Edition, 24 vols. (London, 1912–31)

For the full names of other private and institutional owners of Hardy letters see Acknowledgements, pp. x–xi.

1914.

To JANE POPHAM

Max Gate | Dorchester. | 4: 1: 1914.

Dear Mrs Popham

I am pleased to make the acquaintance of "The Vineyard", which I had not seen before, & to read your verses in it—in which you have quite caught the spirit of Barnes.

I had not by any means forgotten you, though it must be nearly a quarter of a century since we met. But I had quite forgotten the dead-dog puzzle till you mentioned it. I have not seen Sir George Douglas for more than a year; I heard from him quite lately, & we meet occasionally in London.

My best thanks for your New Year's wishes. I heartily reciprocate them.

Sincerely yours
Thomas Hardy.

P.S. Your father said that he saw the soldiers come on the Down (as described in the 1st Chapter of the Trumpet Major) when he was a boy of 9. T.H.

Text Transcript (in an unidentified hand) DCM.
Popham: Jane Susanna Popham, *née* Gollop (d. 1946), wife of Cecil H. W. Popham of Bournemouth and half-sister of Christina Reeve (see I.149). *spirit of Barnes*: Mrs. Popham's poem 'On Egdon He'th (After the French of Cantacuzéne)', *The Vineyard* (January 1914), is written in Dorset dialect. *dead-dog puzzle*: unidentified. *Douglas*: TH's Scottish friend of many years; see letter of 13 Feb 14 to Douglas. *Your father*: George Gollop (see I.189), who died in 1889 at the age of 97; Mrs. Popham was his daughter by his second marriage. *on the Down*: Bincombe Down, near Weymouth; a Thomas Gollop, farmer, lived nearby during the early years of the 19th century.

To CHRISTINE WOOD HOMER

MAX GATE, | DORCHESTER. | Tuesday. [January 1914?]

Dear Miss Wood Homer,

I am sorry that cat-skins are in request. I have written so lately to the papers about animals that I must not again just yet: but you or your mother might send a line, cautioning people against the theft of their pets.

Sincerely yours
T. Hardy.

Text MS. (correspondence card) Eton College.
Homer: Eleanor Christine Wood Homer (1883–1975), daughter of George and Eliza Wood Homer (see III.123) of Bardolf Manor, near Puddletown, Dorset. *to the papers*: probably a reference to TH's letter, 'Performing Animals', *The Times*, 19 Dec 1913.

To GEORGE MACMILLAN

Max Gate | 7: 1: 1914

Dear Mr Macmillan:

I believe I did give some editor leave to use the poem you mention. Anyhow, it is quite short, & I quite agree with you that permission should be given to the Messrs Longman.

The title of the Poem, by the way, was altered from "The Dead Drummer", to "Drummer Hodge" in later editions of my verses, the former title being that of a poem by another writer. Perhaps, therefore "Drummer Hodge" should be used by the compiler of the volume.

I reciprocate your kind good wishes, & hope you & your household are well.

Sincerely yours
Thomas Hardy.

Text MS. (mourning stationery) BL; TH's wife Emma had died 27 Nov 1912.
Macmillan: George Augustin Macmillan, publisher; see II.108. *Messrs Longman*: Macmillan wrote 6 Jan 14 (Macmillan letterbooks, BL) to ask if TH had already given permission for the inclusion of 'The Dead Drummer' in an anthology to be published by Longman for use in South African schools. *in later editions*: the change was first made in the Wessex edn., 1912. *another writer*: unidentified.

To T. H. TILLEY

MAX GATE, | DORCHESTER. | 9th. January 1914.

My dear Sir.

I am sorry that a sudden and very violent cold in the head (which is now passing off) prevented my seeing you yesterday, when it was at its height, and you might have caught it. I have, however, read a great part of Mr Evans's play, based on "The Woodlanders", with a view of abridging it for the Weymouth performance as you requested. But I find that I could not do this properly without entirely rewriting it—and as it is not my own play I should not care to do this even if I had the time. All I have been able to do has been to mark in yellow pencil certain passages here and there which might, I think, be omitted and materially shorten the play without much injuring it. You will understand, however, that I do not personally wish these passages omitted but merely suggest them for omission if abridgment is absolutely necessary. I could have marked more but as they would mostly have been in the parts of Beaucock, Cawtree and Upjohn, who already have small parts, I do not like to do so.

The play is returned herewith, also the photographs which I examined with much interest. I shall be here next week if there is anything else you would like to see me about.

Yours very truly,
T. Hardy.

P.S. Creedle's part could also be shortened, but in view of his popularity this would probably not be advisable. T.H.

Text MS. (typewritten) DCM.
Tilley: Thomas Henry Tilley, prominent local citizen and leading member of the Dorchester Debating and Dramatic Society; see IV.115. *Woodlanders*": it had been performed in Dorchester 19–20 Nov 1913 and in London 8 Dec 1913; A. H. Evans (see IV.22), the adapter, was now living in London. *Weymouth performance*: on 22 Jan 1914. *photographs*: presumably of scenes from the play. *Creedle's part*: Robert Creedle, Giles Winterborne's servant, was being played by Thomas Pouncy, a Dorchester saddler.

To GEORGE MACMILLAN

MAX GATE, | DORCHESTER. | 14th. January 1914.

Dear Mr Macmillan:

M. Bazalgette did write to me, as he says, in respect of the translation of "Life's Little Ironies", but I omitted to reply, as I get so many letters of the kind, and am not sure if some of the stories have not already been translated. I am, however, replying to him now, to say that he may make the translation. I believe he might have done it without asking, the stories having been published more than ten years.

Enclosures returned herewith.

Yours sincerely,
Thomas Hardy.

Text MS. (typewritten) BL.
Bazalgette: Léon Bazalgette (1873–1929), French translator and critic, known especially for his work on Walt Whitman. *as he says*: Macmillan (13 Jan 14, Macmillan letterbooks, BL) reported Bazalgette as complaining that he had written to TH 'some weeks ago'. *make the translation*: it seems never to have been published, however.

To THE REVD. H. G. B. COWLEY

Max Gate | Jan 15: 1914

Dear Mr Cowley:

Possibly, as the Churchwardens & Major Balfour say, there would have been a difficulty in carrying out our idea of setting up the old font, & I am quite willing to be convinced that it cannot be done; though they seem to misapprehend our notion, which of course was not to "restore" it by designing a detailed base, &c, but merely the joining of the pieces & putting them on a square block for security. The pieces of such a highly interesting, & even valuable, parish asset ought to be made permanent by fixing them to the fabric in some way, loose stones being so apt to be moved hither &

thither & ultimately lost. I trust the objectors do not fancy I have any personal wish about it, which I really have not (I was, by the way, baptized in the present marble one).

As to the date of the font, if I can get a more trustworthy opinion than my own on the point I will do so. It is probably very early Norman, or even Saxon. I think it bears some resemblance to the one at Martinstown (3 miles from here), one of a very rare kind, & very ancient. If you or Mrs Cowley should be driving in that direction any day I should like you to look at it & form an opinion.

Very truly yours
Thomas Hardy.

Text MS. (mourning stationery, with envelope) Canon Cowley.
Cowley: the Revd. Henry Guise Beatson Cowley, vicar of Stinsford; see IV.237. *Major Balfour*: Major Kenneth Robert Balfour (1863–1936), current owner of Kingston Maurward house, in Stinsford parish; he was a generous benefactor of Stinsford Church. *for security*: the old font, broken into seven pieces, had been found buried under rubbish in Stinsford churchyard; it was not in fact preserved as TH here suggests but 'restored' and supplied with a new base, apparently to TH's design. See G. H. Moule, *Stinsford Church and Parish* (Dorchester, 1940) and especially *The Architectural Notebook of Thomas Hardy*, ed. C. J. P. Beatty (Dorchester, 1966), 15. *present marble one*: dating from the early 18th century. *Martinstown*: an alternative name for the village of Winterborne St. Martin.

To G. HERBERT THRING

MAX GATE, | DORCHESTER. | 19th. January 1914.

Dear Sir:

Will you inform me if, under the recent copyright act, a story can be dramatized and put upon the stage without the author's consent? I cannot for the moment find the act.

Yours very truly,
Thomas Hardy.

G. Herbert Thring Esq.

Text MS. (typewritten) BL.
Thring: George Herbert Thring (see III.8), Secretary of the Incorporated Society of Authors, Playwrights, and Composers, of which TH was President. *copyright act*: of 1911. *author's consent*: it is not clear what prompted TH to make such an enquiry at this moment.

To WILLIAM BEAMENT

Jan 21: 1914

My dear Sir,

I have much pleasure in acceding to the unanimous wish of "The Elysians", and to accept the honorary membership of that society of philosophers which of course has read "The Dynasts".

If I can ever be at one of the meetings I shall be glad, but distance is a serious consideration for me now.

Very truly yours
T.H.

Text MS. (pencil draft) DCM.
Beament: William Oliver Beament (1894–1960), a native of Beaminster, Dorset; currently an undergraduate at Selwyn College, Cambridge, he later became an inspector of taxes. *"The Elysians"*: the Selwyn College literary and philosophical society; Beament wrote 18 Jan 14 (DCM) to invite TH to become an honorary member.

To BENJAMIN DE CASSERES

MAX GATE, | DORCHESTER. | 21st. January 1914.

Dear Mr De Casseres:

I have read with interest your article in this month's International Review and also some previous articles that you have sent. I am of course unable to criticize the former, and the others do not require remark.

I am glad to hear that your hands are full of work, since your mind is, no doubt, full of ideas. Wishing you success believe me,

Yours very truly,
Thomas Hardy.

Text MS. (typewritten, with envelope in FED's hand) Brooklyn Public Library.
De Casseres: Benjamin De Casseres, American journalist and author; see III.38. *your article*: presumably the satirical fantasy 'Arcvad the Terrible', *Forum* (New York), January 1914.

To JOHN LANE

MAX GATE, | DORCHESTER. | 21st. January 1914.

Dear Mr Lane:

I have read with interest your letter on bringing Lionel Johnson's book up to date. But I think, with regard to the fortunes of the book itself, that it would be a mistake for Mr Seccombe to talk over with me anything on the subject. The value, whatever that may have been, of Johnson's criticism and estimate lay in its detachment. Everybody admitted it. He had never seen me or heard from me or even knew where I lived when he wrote it, and I feel sure that the same principle should be maintained in its continuation. Mr Seccombe will know that I say this in the interests of the book, as I have of course no objection whatever to seeing him.

Yours very truly,
T. Hardy.

P.S. As the main feature of the continuation will be an appreciation of the poems and "The Dynasts" I will willingly give him any information on facts that may be obscure. T.H.

Text MS. (typewritten) Taylor.
Lane: John Lane, publisher; see I.239. *Johnson's book*: Lionel Johnson, *The Art of Thomas Hardy*, first pub. by Lane in 1894; see II.62. *Mr Seccombe*: Thomas Seccombe, literary critic (see II.269), who had already written on William Barnes; he seems, however, to have withdrawn from participation in the revised edn. of Johnson's book, which eventually appeared in 1923 with an added chapter on TH's poetry by J. E. Barton.

To R. A. SCOTT-JAMES

Max Gate | Dorchester | Jan 25: 1914

Dear Mr Scott James:

I am sending two short poems, but as you probably are aware, it is difficult to find or write verse suitable to the isolation of a periodical. Verses seem to require the weight of a volume, as pills require a draught, to make people swallow them—if they will even then.

As I do not want the trouble of sending them to America I have thought it better to name, say, five pounds for the two, as the inclusive price for serial rights in the two countries. I think you may get the amount entirely from America, if you have time to arrange. If you do, please state that newspaper right only is offered, not copyright.

Many thanks for your book of essays, which I am reading, with great interest, though of course your perspective is different from mine in respect of some features in current literature.

Sincerely yours
Thomas Hardy.

Text MS. (mourning stationery, with envelope) Texas.
Scott-James: Rolfe Arnold Scott-James (see III.310), journalist, editor of the *New Weekly*. *two short poems*: still accompanying this letter are typescripts of 'The Year's Awakening' and 'Before and After Summer', pub. in the *New Weekly* 21 Mar and 4 Apr 1914 respectively. *book of essays*: Scott-James's *Personality in Literature* (London, 1913).

To B. F. STEVENS & BROWN

Jan 25: 1914

Dear Sirs:

In reply to your inquiry of the 24th inst. Mr Hardy desires me to say that the play of "The Three Wayfarers" is not included in the list of his publications, being a dramatization almost word for word of one of his stories. He is not disposed at present to publish it, but he will give the subject his consideration.

I am, dear Sirs,

Yours faithfully
F. D.
Sec. to T. H.

Text MS. (pencil draft) DCM.
& Brown: American library and literary agents, 4 Trafalgar Square, London; TH had dealt

with them previously over the special issue of 'The Convergence of the Twain' (see IV.223). *your inquiry*: the firm had written (24 Jan 14, DCM) to ask if TH would permit Dodd & Livingston of New York to pub. a special first edn. of *The Three Wayfarers* for collectors.

To S. A. DONALDSON

MAX GATE, | DORCHESTER. | 26 Jan: 1914

Dear Dr Donaldson:

Thank you for your very kind reminder that the Pepys commemoration is drawing near apace. Last year, when I was with you, I was full of hopes of being present, but circumstances have altered a little since, & I think I may have to be in Cornwall at that very time, so that I fear I shall not be able to appear at the celebration.

I feel like a distant relation of Pepys since realizing the value & interest of the library that he bequeathed to Magdalene—wise man.

It is a good idea to have Dolmetsch with his contemporary instruments. I heard him a long time ago, & thought that nothing is so powerful in throwing back one's mind into the past as music of the date.

But though I do not see my way to get to Cambridge in February I want to see it again at no distant date, & I hope in summer weather.

My kindest remembrances to Lady Albinia; & with renewed thanks believe me,

Sincerely yours
Thomas Hardy.

Text MS. Purdy.
Donaldson: Stuart Alexander Donaldson, Master of Magdalene College, Cambridge; see IV.260. He had written to TH, as an Honorary Fellow of the college, 24 Jan 14 (DCM). *Pepys commemoration*: the Pepys Dinner, held each year on 23 February, the birthday of Samuel Pepys, the diarist, who attended Magdalene and whose magnificent library was presented to the college after his death. *with you*: for his installation as an Honorary Fellow, November 1913; see *LY*, 158. *Dolmetsch*: Eugene Arnold Dolmetsch (1858–1940), musician and craftsman; *D.N.B.* He was especially famous for reviving early English instrumental music and the instruments on which it was originally played. *Lady Albinia*: Donaldson's wife, a sister of the Earl of Buckinghamshire.

To FLORENCE DUGDALE

MAX GATE, | DORCHESTER. | Thursday [29 January 1914]

My dearest:

I am writing only a line or two, as I expect to see you so soon. Let me know if Saturday or Monday. I will try to meet you—at any rate send carriage.

If anything has happened—I hope not—to prevent your return till I fetch you, let me know that less pleasant news. Of course if you are unwell I will put up with my solitude, as you must not run any risk. A shame to take you away from E!

Katy came in yesterday, & lunched with me in the study. She was going for medicine for Mary. Dr Gowring has visited her, & is doing the best he can. He says the difficulty is the extreme weakness of her stomach.

Wessie goes up into the attics to look for you, but secretly believes you are inside your bedroom, the door of which is kept shut.

The weather here is a warm drizzle from the S.W. I live almost entirely in the study, & the house is very solitary. But I keep well—missing you however, every minute.

Our letters will probably cross, so I will not write more.

Ever your
T.

Your last letter was scarcely fastened. T.

Text MS. (with envelope) Purdy. *Date* From postmark.
Dugdale: Florence Emily Dugdale (see III.179), writer of children's stories; she had just passed her 35th birthday and was to marry TH, as his second wife, on 10 Feb 1914. *meet you*: at one of the Dorchester railway stations, on her return from her home in Enfield, Middlesex. *from E!*: from Enfield. *Katy*: TH's younger sister, Katharine; see letter of 20 Feb 14. *Mary*: TH's elder sister (see letter to her of 29 July 15); she had been ill for some time and died the following year (see letter of 30 Nov 15). *Gowring*: Benjamin Gowring (see IV.260), TH's doctor for many years. *Wessie*: FED's wire-haired terrier Wessex (1913–26); see Millgate, 504, and *LY*, 250–2.

To DOROTHY ALLHUSEN

MAX GATE, | DORCHESTER. | 11: 2: 1914

My dear Dorothy:

I was going to send you a letter to tell you, before the papers had announced it, that I married yesterday Miss Dugdale, an old friend, whom your mother knows, & you may possibly have met at her house. But they got wind of it, although we kept it so quiet.

My wife is a writer of books, like myself, though hers are mostly for children. I hope you will know her some day. I think, if you do, that you will like her.

Ever affectionately
Thomas Hardy.

Your friend "Birdie" has known her a long time. T.H.

Text MS. (correspondence card) Purdy.
Allhusen: Dorothy Allhusen (see I.257), wife of Henry Allhusen, M.P., daughter of Lady St. Helier (see letter of 22 Apr 15) by her first marriage. *"Birdie"*: Helen Lady Ilchester, wife of the 6th Earl; see letter of 2 Nov 16.

To EDWARD CLODD

MAX GATE, | DORCHESTER. | Wedny [11 February 1914]

My dear Clodd:

I wanted to let you know by letter, before you heard of it in any other way, that Miss Dugdale & I were married yesterday at Enfield. But I have been anticipated by telegraph, telephone, & other modern inventions. For reasons which will occur to your mind we thought it best to keep our intention private, & the only way to do this was to tell nobody at all—not even relations. The vicar, who is a friend of Florence's, lent his assistance, & the result was that, though the Church door was wide open, not a soul was present except her father & sister & my brother, & the officiators & contracting parties. We came straight back here, & I am going to put over my study door, "Business as usual during alterations."

Always sincerely
Thomas Hardy.

My dear Mr Clodd:

Of course I wanted you to know before anybody else, but I was under the strictest orders not to tell anyone. I wrote you a long letter but finally decided to be obedient & not send it.

Sincerely yours,
F. H.

Text MS. (with postscript in FEH's hand) BL. *Date* Supplied by Clodd. *Clodd*: Edward Clodd, banker and rationalist author; see I.237. *at Enfield*: the service was at St. Andrew's, the parish church of Enfield. *The vicar*: the Revd. Richard Howel Brown. *her father*: Edward Dugdale; see letter to him of 24 June 14. *& sister*: Margaret Dugdale, the youngest of FEH's four sisters; see letter of 9 May 17. *my brother*: Henry Hardy, TH's younger brother; see I.31.

To SYDNEY COCKERELL

MAX GATE, | DORCHESTER. | Wedny 11: 2: 1914

My dear Cockerell:

How very kind of you & Mrs Cockerell to wire good wishes. I know the words are not a mere form with you. Immediately I got back here last night I was going to write my little story to you that you might learn what had happened directly from me; but I found that in some mysterious way I had been anticipated by the afternoon papers.

We thought it the wisest thing to do, seeing what a right hand Florence has become to me, & there is a sort of continuity in it, & not a break, she having known my first wife so very well.

If I had been able to join you at the Pepys commemoration I should have been delighted. But as I was at Cambridge in November I think I will postpone another visit till the summer.

I quite agree with you about the photographs by Miss Edis.

We have been amused to-day by seeing photographs of my wife in the halfpenny papers. How they got hold of them I cannot tell. Kindest regards to Mrs Cockerell.

Always sincerely
Thomas Hardy.

Text MS. Adams.
Cockerell: Sydney Carlyle Cockerell, director of the Fitzwilliam Museum, Cambridge; see IV.178. He had been on friendly terms with TH since their first meeting in 1911. *my little story*: i.e., of his marriage. *Pepys commemoration*: see letter of 26 Jan 14. *Miss Edis*: Olive Edis, photographer; she had photographed TH the previous December (see IV.331 and *LY*, opp. 156). *halfpenny papers*: e.g., the *Daily Mail*, whose photograph of 'Mr. Hardy's Bride' is attributed to Rodway Gardner.

To EDMUND GOSSE

MAX GATE, | DORCHESTER. | Wedny [11 February 1914]

My dear Gosse:

I was on the point of writing to you & Mrs Gosse when I reached here last night, after marrying my long friend & secretary Miss Dugdale, till I found that in some unforseen way the trifling incident had got into the London afternoon papers, so that I was defeated in my intention of telling you by letter before you could have learnt of it through any other channel.

We thought it better in the circumstances to inform nobody beforehand, not even relations. You will understand all this—as indeed, who should if not you.

I hope Mrs Gosse will let me bring my wife to see her, when we are in London. I send her kindest remembrances.

Sincerely yours
Thomas Hardy.

Text MS. (with envelope) Adams. *Date* From internal evidence.
Gosse: Edmund William Gosse, man of letters, one of TH's oldest friends; see I.110. *Mrs Gosse*: see letter to her of 3 June 15.

To FLORENCE HENNIKER

MAX GATE, | DORCHESTER. | Wedny. 11: 2: '14

My dear friend:

I wanted to tell you by letter before you could have learnt it from the papers that Florence Dugdale & I were married yesterday at Enfield. But somehow, although nobody seemed to know anything of it, the news was telephoned to London immediately. If I had foreseen this I would have written beforehand to you, my best friend. However, we thought it better in the circumstances to inform nobody, not even relations.

Beyond the parties & the officiators there was not a soul present but my brother & her father & sister. And although the church door stood wide open nobody walked in. It was a lovely morning, & the ceremony was over by 8.20!

You do like her I am sure, & I want you to like her better still, if you will be so kind—though as you *always* are kind I needn't have said that, & I am sure you will go on liking her.

Let me hear from you soon. I don't know when we shall go to London. I rather shun it at this time of the year because it gives me such colds. Thank you for your last nice letter. I am glad to know you are on chalk. My experience is that chalk is the healthiest subsoil of any. Believe me

Your always affectte friend
Tho. H.

Text MS. DCM.
Henniker: Florence Ellen Hungerford Henniker, daughter of the 1st Lord Houghton, widow of General A. H. Henniker; see II.11. TH had been in love with her in the 1890s. *do like her*: FED had been friendly with Mrs. Henniker for some years and done secretarial work for her. *last nice letter*: of 17 Jan 14 (transcript, DCM). *on chalk*: in response to an inquiry of TH's she had reported that her cottage at Shoreham (see IV.316) was on 'chalky' soil.

To LUCY CLIFFORD

MAX GATE, | DORCHESTER. | 12: 2: 1914

Dear Mrs Clifford;

Many thanks for the kind present of your charming little book, & for your good wishes on my marriage—so simple & quiet an affair as it was—a course you will see the reasonableness of—though strangely enough it was not, as we expected it might be, humdrum. There were only seven persons, all counted, in the vacant old church, & while the vicar stood waiting for the clock to strike eight people passed by the open door without turning their heads.

I shall not forget to gratify your desire to know my wife better some day when we are in London. Believe me

Sincerely yours
Thomas Hardy.

Text MS. (with envelope) Taylor.
Clifford: Lucy Clifford, novelist, usually known as Mrs. W. K. Clifford; see II.109. *little book*: presumably the new edn. (London, 1914) of her *A Wild Proxy*, first pub. 1893.

To KATE GIFFORD

MAX GATE, | DORCHESTER. | Feb 12. 1914

Dear Miss Gifford:

It is most kind of you & your sister to send such good wishes on my marriage.

I seem to know you very well, though it is possible that we have never met—I cannot quite remember. I wanted to know your father better, but the fates were against me.

If you should ever be anywhere near here I trust that you will let us know. With kind regards to Mrs Ching believe me,

Sincerely yours,
Thomas Hardy.

Text MS. C. H. Gifford.
Gifford: Kate Gifford, ELH's cousin, younger daughter of George Mitchell Gifford of Launceston, Cornwall; she had written to TH 11 Feb 14 (DCM). *your sister*: Edith, who had married Captain Lawrence Ching; see *The Personal Notebooks of Thomas Hardy*, ed. Richard H. Taylor (London, 1978), 24.

To WILLIAM STRANG

MAX GATE, | DORCHESTER. | 12 Feb: 1914

My dear Strang:

Warm thanks from both of us for your kind letter on our very quiet performance.

We regret that your beautiful sketch of my wife could not have been used by the papers as a portrait of her instead of some hideous photographs they got hold of—I don't know how.

Kindest regards to Mrs Strang.

Sincerely yours
Thomas Hardy.

Text MS. Purdy.
Strang: William Strang, painter and etcher; see I.284. He wrote to TH 11 Feb 14 (DCM). *sketch of my wife*: made at Max Gate 26 Sept 1910; it is reproduced in *LY*, opp. 160, and now hangs in the DCM.

To SIR GEORGE DOUGLAS

MAX GATE, | DORCHESTER. | 13: 2: 1914

My dear Douglas:

Sincerest thanks for your good wishes. My wife has so often heard me talk about you as one of my oldest friends, that she would much like to know you, & I trust we may be able to hit off a meeting in London this spring.

Ever yours
T. Hardy.

Of course if you *shd* be in Dorset, that wd be still better.

Text MS. (correspondence card) NLS.
Douglas: Sir George Brisbane Douglas, Bt., Scottish landowner and author, whom TH had known since 1881; see I.166.

To LADY GROVE

MAX GATE, | DORCHESTER. | 13: 2: 1914

My dear Lady Grove:

What a nice letter you write to me. I value good wishes from nobody more than from you. As my wife is a literary woman, whom I have known many years, & a connection of my people (one of the Dugdales who, they say have been in Wareham ever since they landed there from Denmark with marauding intentions) we thought our affair would be rather humdrum, especially as we came straight back here the same evening. But the fine morning, the quiet old church, &c. were not without romance. There were only 7 present.

Yes, do motor over, letting us know beforehand, that we may get you some lunch ready. With kindest regards,

Ever your affectte friend
Thomas Hardy.

Text MS. Purdy.
Grove: Agnes Geraldine Grove, author, wife of Sir Walter Grove, Bt.; see II.92. TH's partly literary, partly romantic friendship with her dated from 1895. *write to me*: on 12 Feb 14 (DCM). *a connection*: the 'pedigrees' of the Hardy and Dugdale families, drawn by TH himself (DCM), show a marriage between a Thomas Dugdale and a Jane Hardy in 1777. *in Wareham*: several Dugdales are mentioned in the Wareham section of John Hutchins, *The History and Antiquities of the County of Dorset*, 3rd edn. (4 vols., Westminster, 1861–73), I.113–14.

To LADY HOARE

MAX GATE, | DORCHESTER. | 13: 2: 1914

Dear Lady Hoare:

I was on the point of telling you in my note of last week. But on account of the press people we decided to tell not even relations, knowing that they & friends generally would understand. An hour after we had left, 26 reporters knocked at my father-in-law's door, so we were well out of it! Please do come at any time, letting us know beforehand, & we will have some lunch ready. My warm thanks for your kind letter. My wife is a literary woman, but not a blue-stocking at all.

Sincerely yours
Thomas Hardy.

Text MS. (correspondence card) Wiltshire Record Office.
Hoare: Alda Hoare, wife of Sir Henry Hoare, Bt., of Stourhead, Wiltshire; see IV.75.

To SIR ARTHUR WING PINERO

MAX GATE, | DORCHESTER. | 13: 2: 1914

Dear Sir Arthur Pinero:

Sincerest thanks to you & Lady Pinero for your telegram of good wishes. Oddly enough it happens that the last play I was present at with the lady now my wife, in which we both were deeply interested, was one of yours. Alas, we don't get them often now.

Always truly yrs
Thomas Hardy.

Text MS. (correspondence card) Purdy.
Pinero: Arthur Wing Pinero, playwright; see I.101. He was knighted in 1909. *one of yours*: probably Pinero's *Playgoers*, first performed 31 Mar 1913.

To HENRY STONE

MAX GATE, | DORCHESTER. | 13: 2: 1914

Dear Mr Stone:

I quite remember you, & thank you sincerely for your good wishes on this occasion, after so long a silence between us. Yes, indeed, hard upon 50 years! I am so glad to hear that you have been fairly fortunate in the profession from which I played truant—not, however, rashly, but because I found I had more power in the other, to which I always inclined by instinct from childhood. Of course I remember John Lee, too, as well as possible, but though I have written once or twice to him in the past, he has not responded. I should be sorry to hear that he is an invalid.

I missed Sir Arthur Blomfield much when he died, as we remained friends to the last, & used frequently to see each other. Believe me

Sincerely yours
Thomas Hardy.

Text MS. (with envelope) Purdy.
Stone: Henry Stone, architect, with an office at 16 John Street, London, W.C.; he had been a colleague of TH's in Arthur Blomfield's architectural office in Adelphi Terrace in the 1860s (see *EL*, 48–9). *Lee*: John T. Lee, 'leading man' in Blomfield's office in the 1860s; see I.3. He subsequently practised in London. *Blomfield*: Arthur William Blomfield, architect; see I.3. He was knighted in 1889 and died in 1899.

To THEODORE WATTS-DUNTON

MAX GATE, | DORCHESTER. | 13: 2: 1914

My dear Watts-Dunton:

How very good of you to write. I need hardly say that your letter has given my wife, too, much pleasure.

As I have known her many years, & she is a Dorset connection of my family, & scribbles like myself, we thought our affair would be as prosy as it was quiet; but it turned out to be otherwise.

I am not at all sure that we shall be much in London. But if we go & stay on as I used to do, we will not forget your kind wish to make my wife's acquaintance.

Always yours
Thomas Hardy.

Text MS. Texas.
Watts-Dunton: Walter Theodore Watts-Dunton, critic, poet, and novelist; see II.216.

To CLEMENT SHORTER

Max Gate: 14: 2: '14

Thanks for photographs returned, which were sent in answer to an urgent telegram from your office, that I understood to come from you.

T.H.

Text MS. (postcard) Berg.
photographs: of FEH; Shorter's 'A Literary Letter', *Sphere*, 21 Feb 1914, was accompanied by a 'hitherto unpublished' photograph of FEH and by a snapshot of her, TH, and Edward Clodd together at Aldeburgh, but these were evidently not the ones supplied by TH.

To FREDERICK WHITEHEAD

FROM THOS. HARDY, | MAX GATE, | DORCHESTER. | Feb 14: 1914

Dear Mr. Whitehead:

Best thanks for your kind letter and good wishes, which we heartily reciprocate.

Sincerely
F. & T. H.

Text Transcript (by Harold Hoffman) Miami Univ. of Ohio.
Whitehead: Frederick W. N. Whitehead (1852–1938), painter; he married Beatrice Case of Dorchester and often painted Dorset scenes.

To THE REVD. J. H. DICKINSON

MAX GATE, | DORCHESTER. | 16 Feb: 1914

Dear Mr Dickinson:

Warmest thanks for your kind letter & good wishes on my marriage, in which I include Miss Dickinson. The step has been so soberly taken, I may even say gravely, that my wife & I hope we shall not be disappointed in it. The romance of S. Juliot abides none the less, & will if I live to be a hundred. Indeed one of the satisfactions of my present position is that my wife was a great friend of my late wife, so that there is no rupture of continuity in my life, which always seems an added sadness in a world that at the best is so transitory & full of severances.

If ever ghosts revisit old scenes I am sure mine will haunt S. Juliot by reason of the experiences I was there blest with before my first marriage, & long before the sadness came that was a result of the slight mental aberration which occasionally afflicted my wife's latter years.

I trust you will have a successful holiday. I suppose I shall never see Rome again. I recall that I was there in the spring of 1887—nearly 27 years ago. With kindest regards to Miss Dickinson, in which my wife joins, I am

Sincerely yours
Thomas Hardy.

Text MS. David Dickinson.
Dickinson: the current rector of St. Juliot, Cornwall; see IV.262. *Miss Dickinson*: Dickinson's sister. *romance of S. Juliot*: i.e., of his meeting his first wife there in 1870. *spring of 1887*: see *EL*, 246–9.

To H. O. LOCK

Max Gate | Feb 16: 1914

Dear Mr Lock:

Best thanks both from my wife & myself for the good wishes you & Mrs Lock send us, & also for the kind & thoughtful present we receive at your hands. By a lucky chance it comes just when I have begun to take a cup—or at least a few sips—of tea before getting up, although I have decried the practice for many years!

We are leaving for a few days, but intend to be back by about to-morrow week, when we hope to have the pleasure of seeing you. With kind regards to Mrs Lock I am

Sincerely yours
Thomas Hardy.

Text MS. Charles Lock.
Lock: Henry Osmond Lock, TH's solicitor; see IV.11. *Mrs Lock*: Lock's mother, widow of Arthur Henry Lock; see IV.241. *present*: evidently a tea-service.

To FREDERIC HARRISON

MAX GATE, | DORCHESTER. | Feb: 17: 1914.

My dear Harrison:

Warmest thanks from both of us for your letter of good wishes. I felt sure the step would not surprise you greatly. Though some of the newspapers treat it (as they mostly do treat such events) gaily, & even jocosely, I can assure you that to us it has been of a sober colour enough. That the union of two rather melancholy temperaments may result in cheerfulness, as the junction of two negatives forms a positive, is our modest hope. It may seem odd to you, but the sense of continuity through her having been attached to my late wife is not the least part of my satisfaction.

We are taking little trips of two or three days each, & later on shall certainly aim to include Bath in one of them. My wife sends kindest regards, & please remember me to Mrs Harrison.

Always sincerely yours
Thomas Hardy.

Text MS. Texas.
Harrison: Frederic Harrison, leading English positivist and a long-standing friend of TH's; see I.134. *your letter*: of 13 Feb 14 (DCM). *include Bath*: Harrison, now living in Bath, had suggested TH might bring FEH there.

To KATHARINE HARDY

Royal Hotel | Teignmouth | Friday night [20 February 1914]

We are staying in a room in the middle of the picture, as you see. Go on to Dartmouth to-morrow.

T.

Text MS. (picture postcard of Teignmouth) Eton College. *Date* From postmark.
Hardy: Katharine Hardy, TH's younger sister; see II.124. *Teignmouth*: a seaside resort in Devon; TH and FEH were taking a brief 'honeymoon' trip. *as you see*: the Royal Hotel appears in the photograph on the postcard and TH has marked one of its rooms with a cross.

To EDEN PHILLPOTTS

Max Gate | 26: 2: 1914

Dear Mr Phillpotts:

How very kind of you to write so hospitably. Our visit to Torquay was the result of a sudden resolve to break our journey home from Dartmouth, &c, where we had sojourned, instead of coming right on: we arrived at noon on Sunday & left early Monday morning. It would have been very pleasant if you & Mrs Phillpotts had chanced to be at home, but we could not reckon on it, dropping down upon you so casually. In spite of the generally wet weather the afternoon at Torquay favoured us with some sun, & after leaving your house we went up to Daddy Hole Plain & had a good view.

My wife *is* a gardener, as you seem to divine, but I have great doubt as to when we can reappear in Torquay & see your flowers. My place here has been so neglected of late years owing to circumstances that it is a perfect wilderness, & she will have enough to do to make it decent.

Many thanks from us both for your very kind invitation, but, as I say, we may not be able to avail ourselves of it. Anyhow I will let you know if we should be that way again.

Always sincerely yours
Thomas Hardy.

Text MS. NYU.
Phillpotts: Eden Phillpotts, novelist and playwright; see II.181. *Torquay*: where Phillpotts lived. *Dartmouth, &c*: see letter of 20 Feb 14. *Daddy Hole Plain*: a picturesque stretch of common just east of Torquay; 'Daddy Hole' = Devil's Hole.

To HARRY POUNCY

FROM THOS. HARDY, | MAX GATE, | DORCHESTER. | 1: 3: 1914

Many thanks. Glad to hear that the M. lecture was a success. Will call to hear the records, as you suggest. Of course produce any of my dialogues in the same way.

T.H.

Text: MS. (postcard) Univ. of London Library.
Pouncy: Harry Pouncy, Dorchester journalist and lecturer; see III.247. *M. lecture*: at Manchester, on 23 Feb 1914, Pouncy gave an illustrated lecture on 'Thomas Hardy and His Wessex' (see *Somerset & Dorset Notes & Queries*, March 1978), presumably under the auspices of The Lecture Agency Ltd. (see IV.1). *records*: evidently recordings of Pouncy's performances of passages from TH's works.

To A. C. BENSON

MAX GATE, | DORCHESTER. | 2 March 1914

Dear Mr Benson:

I feel that I want to write you just a line at least, in answer to your very kind letter, for it touches me much to know that you & my brethren of the College have been interested in my marriage & have shown such good will concerning it. Yes: events seem to prove that I have made a happy choice. There has been nothing precipitate about it at any rate. And so far from that jocundity & forgetfulness of the past, which are conventionally assumed by the lighthearted to accompany such a marriage, being present in our case, we have taken the step soberly, & even gravely. I have known my wife many years, & she was a friend of my first wife as she has been for a long time of my sisters, so that there is not that rupture of continuity in my life by this event which I so much dislike.

My warmest thanks for your good wishes, in which my wife cordially joins.

Believe me,

Yours always sincerely
Thomas Hardy.

Text MS. (with envelope) Eton College.
Benson: Arthur Christopher Benson, man of letters; see I.280. *letter*: of 25 Feb 14 (DCM). *brethren of the College*: Benson was a Fellow (later Master) of Magdalene College, Cambridge, of which TH was an Honorary Fellow.

To FLORENCE HENNIKER

Max Gate | 6: 3: 1914

My dear friend:

I am writing again to you to answer some points on which you say you are curious (as indeed I should have guessed you were), & also because your letter was so kind as to make me wish to write.

It has been a great delight to me all through that you know Florence quite well, & like her. As you say she is very sympathetic—so much so that her own health is largely dependent upon the happiness or otherwise of her friends. One thing you may be sure of—her intense love & admiration of yourself: she often settles points by saying or thinking what *you* would do in the circumstances: assuming invariably that that is absolutely the right thing.

I rather am surprised that *you* were surprised at the step we have taken—such a course seeming an obvious one to me, being as I was so lonely & helpless. I think I told you in my last letter that I am very glad she knew Emma well, & was liked by her even during her latter years, when her mind was a little unhinged at times, & she showed unreasonable dislikes. I wonder if it will surprise you when I say that according to my own experience a second marriage does not, or need not, obliterate an old affection, though it is generally assumed that the first wife is entirely forgotten in such cases.

We are going to London next week, but only for a day or two. I will let you know when we go up later (if we do) for a longer stay, so that we may contrive to see you somehow.

Even now I have not answered your question on what people wrote about our marriage. Well: they all say they foresaw it, except one besides yourself—I forget who. Of course they *might* say so to show their penetration or to claim it. But perhaps they really did. With all affection I am,

Your sincere friend
Tho. H.

I enclose 2 little poems of mine you may like to see. They have appeared in magazines. T.H.

Text MS. DCM.
your letter: of 12 Feb 14 (transcript, DCM). *very sympathetic*: Mrs. Henniker had written of FEH, 'I think she has a beautiful nature,—very full of sympathy, and she combines, (which is perhaps rare—,) the quality of enthusiasm with commonsense'. *my last letter*: see letter to Mrs. Henniker of 11 Feb 14. *answered your question*: TH refers back to the opening sentence of this letter and to Mrs. Henniker's wish to know what Gosse, Shorter, and other 'mutual friends and acquaintances' had said about his marriage. *2 little poems*: one of them, to judge from Mrs. Henniker's letter to TH of 20 Mar 14 (transcript, DCM), was 'Beyond the Last Lamp', first pub. in 1911.

To DOROTHY ALLHUSEN

MAX GATE, | DORCHESTER. | 9: 3: 1914

My dear Dorothy:

How kind of you to remember us, & send this beautiful book. I have never read it, so that I do not on any account wish to exchange it. I suppose & hope we shall have an opportunity of seeing you later on. My wife joins me in thanks & kind regards.

Affectly yours
T.H.

Text MS. (correspondence card) Purdy.
beautiful book: unidentified.

To MAY HANKEY

THE ATHENAEUM, | PALL MALL. S.W. | 13: 3: 1914

Dear Mrs Hankey:

I have been for years a member of the Council of Justice to Animals, in whose name you write, & I am glad to hear that there is to be a public meeting to advance the objects of the Council in Blandford, though unfortunately I shall not be able to attend it. Humane slaughtering has been adopted in so many towns that it is time Blandford took it up. Dorchester butchers, I believe, have done so for a long while, & I hope the cause will be advanced by the meeting.

The conveyance & driving of animals to the slaughter-houses, & their treatment whilst waiting for slaughter, is of little less importance than the actual killing.

Yours very truly
Thomas Hardy.

Text MS. Taylor.
Hankey: May Hankey, *née* Nicholson, wife of the Revd. Basil Hankey, rector of Tarrant Hinton, Dorset, 1911–46. *to Animals*: see IV.143. *public meeting*: it was held at the Town Hall, Blandford Forum, on 30 Mar 1914, with the Revd. Hankey as chairman.

To R. A. SCOTT-JAMES

FROM THO. HARDY, | MAX GATE, | DORCHESTER. | 22: 3: 1914

Dear Scott-James:

I congratulate you on your first number—except a poem called "The Year's Awakening". Gosse's article is excellent. What have you done to offend the blood-puppies of the Daily Express, that they cock up the hind leg over the pages?

Yours truly
T.H.

Text MS. (correspondence card) Texas.
first number: of the *New Weekly*, ed. by Scott-James, 21 Mar 1914. *Awakening*": by TH; see letter to Scott-James of 25 Jan 14. *Gosse's article*: Gosse's 'Old and New', consisting of reflections on changes in the world of letters over the previous 40 years. *Daily Express*: the 'Cabbages and Kings' section of the *Daily Express*, 20 Mar 1914, described the *New Weekly* as 'full of well-known names and excessive amiability' and as containing 'a silly poem by Mr. Thomas Hardy'.

To FREDERIC HARRISON

Max Gate | 23: 3: '14

My dear Harrison:

Our honeymoon—if it could be called such—was & is still being taken in slices, or phases, as I suppose I ought to say: three or four days in Devon; three days in London; &c, &c, between the prosiest of home doings in the way of seeing to repairs, the kitchen garden, getting in manure, & such like. It will take about two years to use up the whole moon at the rate at which we go on at present.

Oddly enough, we also struggled to grasp the meaning of H. J.'s article in the *Times* Supplement of the 19th, & got at it finally only by guessing what he probably was considering. His writing beats Coleridge's talk, with its "objective & sum-jective," quite hollow.

Please don't look at the "New Weekly"—I mean my contribution to it. Scott-James came here one day, & I found that poor pair of stanzas in a drawer & could find nothing else, so I let him have them at his earnest request. Also another little scrap like it, which I hope he won't print.

I read your letter in to-day's Times. Frankly I think Pollard's letter unanswerable as against a Referendum.

Yes, Lady Hoare is a most agreeable woman; warm-hearted & impulsive—which latter quality leads her to write letters in streams.

This is a mere line. I hope Mrs Harrison is well.

Always sincerely
Thomas Hardy.

Text MS. Texas.
in Devon: see letters of 20 and 26 Feb 14. *H. J.'s article*: Henry James's (see letter of 8 Aug 15) 'The Younger Generation', *Times Literary Supplement*, 19 Mar 1914, a signed article on some of the younger novelists; Harrison's letter to TH (21 Mar 14, DCM) described it as 'drivel'. *sum-jective,*": an allusion to the characterization of Samuel Taylor Coleridge in Thomas Carlyle's *The Life of John Sterling* (1851), chap. 8. *"New Weekly"*: see letter of 22 Mar 14. *won't print*: 'Before and After Summer' did, however, appear in the *New Weekly*, 4 Apr 1914. *a Referendum*: in letters pub. in *The Times*, 23 Mar 1914, Harrison argued in favour of a referendum on the issue of Home Rule for Ireland, A. F. Pollard (1859–1944, literary scholar; *D.N.B.*) against. *Lady Hoare*: see letter of 13 Feb 14 to Lady Hoare; Harrison later wrote (26 May 14, DCM) to thank TH for introducing him to the Hoares, describing Lady Hoare as 'a generous, gracious, splendid grande dame'.

To R. A. SCOTT-JAMES

Max Gate | 28: 3: '14

Dear Mr Scott James:

Please use your own judgment as to when you print this. I shall not be likely to publish the volume till after the first or second week in October, even if then. I am not sure about finding another, but if I do I will send it.

Sincerely yours
T. Hardy.

Text MS. Texas.
print this: not, apparently, an additional poem but the proof of 'Before and After Summer'; the text as pub. in the *New Weekly* shows significant revision from the typescript sent to Scott-James 25 Jan 14. *the volume*: TH's *Satires of Circumstance*, not in fact pub. until November 1914, includes 'Before and After Summer'.

To W. M. COLLES

MAX GATE, | DORCHESTER. | 31st. March 1914.

Dear Mr Colles:

I have not written a prose story, long or short, since the last century, nor is there any likelihood of my writing one, though I have written many in verse. Your client's mistake has probably arisen from my having been lately compelled by pirates to reprint some old tales that I would have willingly let die.

Yours truly,
T. Hardy.

Text MS. (typewritten) Adams.
Colles: William Morris Colles, literary agent; see I.241. *Your client's*: unidentified. *old tales*: *A Changed Man and Other Tales*, pub. October 1913; see IV.297.

To CHARLES WATTS

FROM THO. HARDY, | MAX GATE, | DORCHESTER. | 31: 3: 1914

Dear Sir:

Whilst I remember I send on the guinea subscription to Mr Clodd's portrait fund.

Many thanks for your note of yesterday. But I assure you that my declining is no momentary whim, but a real inability which unfortunately is unalterable.

Yours truly
T. Hardy.

Text MS. (correspondence card) Rationalist Press Association.
Watts: Charles Albert Watts (1858–1946), editor and publisher, founder and for many years Vice-Chairman of the Rationalist Press Association, Ltd. *portrait fund*: the portrait, by

the Hon. John Collier (1850–1934; *D.N.B.*), remains in the possession of the Rationalist Press Association. *my declining*: Watts had perhaps invited him to become a member or officer of the Association.

To SYDNEY COCKERELL

MAX GATE, | DORCHESTER. | April 1: 1914

My dear Cockerell:

I have read the obituary notice of Mistral that you kindly forwarded. I now wish I had called round that way when in the south, & had been able to say with you that I once met him.

The worst of publishing casual verse like "The Year's Awakening" in newspapers to oblige editors is that readers turn to it saying to themselves—Ah, let us see so-&-so's latest thoughts on the problem of the universe—when lo—they find some scrap that has been unearthed from a drawer (as in the present case) where it has been lying for years as of no account.

I will faithfully return the Reminiscences of Mistral if you think fit to send it.

We have been to London lately, but nowhere else: yet I forget: we went into Devon for 3 or 4 days: rain all the time. Kind regards to the household.

Always yours
Thomas Hardy.

Text MS. Adams.
Mistral: Frédéric Mistral (1830–1914), the Provençal poet; Cockerell wrote (29 Mar 14, DCM), 'He did for Provence what you have done for Wessex'. *Awakening*": see letters of 25 Jan and 22 Mar 14 to Scott-James; Cockerell had praised the poem. *Reminiscences of Mistral*: Mistral, *Memoirs of Mistral*, trans. Constance Elizabeth Maud (London, 1907; first pub. Paris, 1906, in Provençal).

To NEWMAN FLOWER

MAX GATE, | DORCHESTER. | 2nd. April 1914.

Dear Mr Flower:

I am sorry to say that I have no original writing at hand that would be useful in your proposed Dorset Annual, nor am I likely to have any such, several unfulfilled engagements demanding of me all that I can produce, which is not much nowadays. But I enclose herewith the only poem I can find bearing particularly on Wessex, which I hope may serve your purpose, for though it has already appeared in a volume of mine it is copyright, and is little known.

Yours very truly,
Thomas Hardy.

P.S. I shall, I believe, be here this month, if you are coming to Dorset. T.H.

Text MS. (typewritten) Texas.
Flower: Newman Flower, publisher; see II.164. He had recently taken over the editorship of the *Year-book* pub. by the Society of Dorset Men in London. *poem*: TH's 'Down Wessex Way', *Society of Dorset Men in London: Year-book, 1914–15*; it had previously been pub., as 'The Spring Call', in the *Cornhill Magazine*, May 1906. *P.S.*: the postscript is in TH's hand.

To SIR FREDERICK MACMILLAN

MAX GATE, | DORCHESTER. | April 4: 1914

Dear Sir Frederick:

Many thanks. Please write to the lady translator that she can have the right for one hundred francs per story. You will probably hear no more from her.

The letter I enclose came a few days ago. I do not know if notice should be taken of it. I never heard of "Janet of the Dunes".

Sincerely yours
T. Hardy.

Text MS. BL.
lady translator: Mlle Magdelaine de Lansade, of Paris. *no more from her*: see, however, letter to Macmillan of 24 June 14. *the Dunes"*: it appears from Macmillan's letter of 6 Apr 14 (Macmillan letterbooks, BL) that a Mr. Whitehorn had written to tell TH that a well-known scene from *A Pair of Blue Eyes* had been adapted for inclusion in the 1913 Edison film of Harriet T. Comstock's novel, *Janet of the Dunes* (Boston, 1908).

To AN UNIDENTIFIED CORRESPONDENT

MAX GATE, | DORCHESTER. | 4th. April 1914.

Dear Sir:

In respect of your inquiry as to my sitting for a photograph I intend to be staying on here till the end of this month, and could see your photographer almost any day he would like to name.

After the end of the month I shall probably be in London for a week or more.

Yours very truly,
Thomas Hardy.

Text MS. (typewritten) NYU.

To GEORGE DODDERIDGE

MAX GATE, | DORCHESTER. | April: 1914

Easter offering—

With Mr & Mrs Hardy's compliments

Text MS. (with envelope in FEH's hand) DCM.
Dodderidge: George Dodderidge (d. 1917), for several years a churchwarden at Fordington St.

George, the parish church for Max Gate. *Easter offering*: letter and contents presumably delivered, by hand, shortly in advance of Easter Sunday, 12 Apr 1914.

To LEWIS CHASE

MAX GATE, | DORCHESTER. | 19 April 1914

Dear Mr Chase:

How kind of you to send the oranges. We have already tried them, & find them much to our taste. How I wish I had an orange grove.

Also thanks for the Poe. Any new matter about him will be interesting. My own interest in him is entirely on the poetry side, which America is at last I think beginning to value.

Sincerely yours
Thomas Hardy.

Text MS. (with envelope) LC.
Chase: Lewis Nathaniel Chase, American author and teacher; see IV.166. He had visited Max Gate in the summer of 1911. *the Poe*: Chase's *Poe and His Poetry* (London, 1913).

To SYDNEY COCKERELL

MAX GATE, | DORCHESTER. | Monday: 27: 4: 1914

My dear Cockerell:

You have arranged excellently. The invitation duly came from the Master of St John's, & I answered. We propose to arrive in Cambridge by the 3.0 o'clock from King's Cross on Tuesday the 5th—to-morrow week, & I will write a few days before to the University Arms for a bedroom, which is all, I think, we shall want. Anyhow we can arrange about a sitting-room when we get there, if we find one necessary.

McTaggart has also written, & I will tell him we hope to call, say, Thursday afternoon. He suggests lunch, but a promise to go to them at tea-time will be less binding.

I hope you found everything in order when you got back—no pictures cut from their frames in the Museum, or anything of that sort. We can hardly hope this weather to continue till we get to you.

Always sincerely
Thomas Hardy.

I suppose there will be no speeches at the Johnian dinner? I am as dumb as Zacharias at such times, as you know. T.H.

Of course I shall bring no scarlet—only black cap & gown.

Text MS. Eton College; envelope Adams.
invitation: to attend the 'Porte-Latin' feast at St. John's College, Cambridge; see *LY*, 159. *Master of St John's*: Robert Forsyth Scott (1849–1933), master since 1908. *McTaggart*: John McTaggart Ellis McTaggart, the philosopher; see letter of 31 Dec 19. He wrote on 26 Apr 14 (DCM). *as Zacharias*: in Luke 1: 20–2.

To EDWARD CLODD

FROM THO. HARDY, | MAX GATE, | DORCHESTER. [Late April 1914]

My dear Clodd:

Many thanks for Gissings letters, which I have only just looked into as yet, being rather in a muddle with cleaning & repairs. We think of going to Cambridge in a few days, but scarcely dare hope that this weather will continue. The east wind must have been keen at Aldeburgh.

Sincerely yrs
T.H.

Text MS. (correspondence card) Leeds. *Date* From internal evidence.

Gissings letters: *Letters to Edward Clodd from George Gissing,* of which 30 copies were printed for private circulation by T. J. Wise, 1914; a copy with a presentation inscription by Clodd was in TH's library. For Gissing and TH see I.149. *to Cambridge*: see letter of 27 Apr 14.

To LADY HOARE

FROM THO. HARDY, | MAX GATE, | DORCHESTER. | 29: 4: 1914

I have mentioned *your* tower—"Stourton Tower"—in poem in "The Fortnightly Review" for May.

T.H.

(Am leaving for London.)

Text MS. (postcard) Wiltshire Record Office.

your *tower*: i.e., the tower at Stourhead; it commemorates King Alfred's resistance to the Danes. *in poem*: 'Channel Firing', *Fortnightly Review*, May 1914; see *LY*, 161–2.

To SYDNEY COCKERELL

THE ATHENAEUM, | PALL MALL. S.W. | Sunday [3 May 1914]

My dear Cockerell:

The tobacco-smoke made my head ache, so I went off early, though I had meant to have another talk with you.

I understand that I dine at Jesus Tuesday—& at Magdalene Thursday, D.V. if possible—I will drop a line to Benson, or the Master, of the latter.

I hope *you* did not get a headache.

Ever sincely
T.H.

Text MS. (correspondence card) Taylor. *Date* Supplied by Cockerell.

tobacco-smoke: at the Royal Academy banquet, 2 May 1914 (as noted by Cockerell on the MS.). *Benson*: A. C. Benson. *the Master*: S. A. Donaldson.

To REYMOND ABBOTT

MAX GATE, | DORCHESTER. | May 10: 1914

Dear Abbot:

Your letter arrived while we were away at Cambridge, enjoying the hospitalities of various worthy Heads & Fellows. We met many friends altogether, no doubt some of them known to you; & one afternoon attended the 5 o'clock service in King's Chapel, sitting outside the screen. It was a pleasant visit, tinged of course with some sad memories of those who have "passed down into silence", since I paid a somewhat similar visit more than thirty years ago.

Many thanks for the photographs. I suppose you have returned to Windsor by this time, & address the envelope accordingly. I hope you keep well.

Sincerely yours
Thomas Hardy.

Text MS. (with envelope) Mrs. Michael MacCarthy.
Abbott: James Reymond de Montmorency Abbott, man of cultivated leisure; see III.24. TH, as usual, has misspelled his surname. *into silence*": Psalm 115: 17 reads, 'go down into silence'. *thirty years ago*: an apparent reference to TH's Cambridge visit of 1880 (see I.81 and *EL*, 184) rather than to the occasion, in 1873, of his last meeting with Horace Moule (see *EL*, 123). *photographs*: probably of cathedrals Abbott had visited; see IV.262. *to Windsor*: Abbott was living at 11 Park Street.

To GORDON GIFFORD

Max Gate | 14: 5: '14

Dear Gordon:

If you have nothing better to do, why not come down here for Whitsuntide? We shall be glad to see you, & the change will do you good.

Yr affecte uncle
T. Hardy.

Text MS. (correspondence card) Mrs. Ethel Skinner.
Gifford: Gordon Gifford (1877–1952), ELH's nephew, employed as an architect by the London County Council. *down here*: like his sister Lilian, Gordon Gifford had spent extended periods at Max Gate during his childhood and youth. *Whitsuntide*: in 1914 Whit Sunday fell on 31 May; the invitation was accepted.

To DOROTHY ALLHUSEN

MAX GATE, | DORCHESTER. | 17: 5: 1914

My dear Dorothy:

I received your letter sent from Bruges, & now hear by a side wind that you have returned home, & are likely to come down to Dorset. This is delightful, & I hope I am going to see you.

I wonder what your adventures were in Ghent, Antwerp, Waterloo, Luxembourg & other places you were to visit. I could not guess how long a time you were going to spend in touring—a week, or a month or two. You will now find an increased interest in reading the Third Canto of Childe Harold.

We spent the week before last in Cambridge, & had a lively time in seeing the Colleges & their Dons.

Affectionately yours
Thomas Hardy.

Text MS. Purdy.
of Childe Harold: the Third Canto of Byron's poem contains the famous description of the battle of Waterloo. *in Cambridge*: see letter of 3 May 14 and *LY*, 159–60.

To J. STANLEY LITTLE

MAX GATE, | DORCHESTER. | 20: 5: '14.

Dear Sir:

I have read the proposal you send as to the form the visible memorial to Shelley should take—an arched seat in stone, with bas-relief—& see no objection whatever to such a form of memorial.

Yours truly
Thomas Hardy.

J. Stanley Little Esq.

Text MS. (correspondence card) Princeton.
Little: James Stanley Little, miscellaneous writer; see I.177. *proposal you send*: still accompanying Little's letter to TH of 11 May 14 (DCM) is a copy of a proposal to dispose of the unspent balance of the Shelley Memorial Fund, initiated as far back as 1892 (see I.278–9). *with bas-relief*: the proposal envisaged the erection, near Field Place, Horsham, Sussex (Shelley's birthplace), of a 'Rural Seat in stone' with an arched roof and, at the back or side, 'a representation in permanent form (a bas-relief in bronze, for example), emblematic of some striking incident in the poet's career'.

To NELSON RICHARDSON

MAX GATE, | DORCHESTER. | 22: 5: 1914

Dear Mr Richardson:

Many thanks. I have read the address with much interest, & being behindhand in science I feel now coached up to date.

My wife joins me in also thanking you & Mrs Richardson for your good wishes. Hoping you are both well I am,

Very truly yrs
Thomas Hardy.

Text MS. (correspondence card, with envelope) R. Greenland.
Richardson: Nelson Moore Richardson, president of the Dorset Natural History and Antiquarian Field Club; see II.268. *the address*: Richardson's presidential address to the

annual meeting of the Field Club, delivered 12 May 1914, pub. in the *Dorset County Chronicle*, 14 May 1914. *in science*: Richardson's address dealt largely with recent developments in zoology, botany, geology, astronomy, etc.

To CLEMENT SHORTER

MAX GATE, | DORCHESTER. | 5 June 1914

My dear Shorter:

Thank you much for good wishes. My wife joins me in this. It would indeed be pleasant to dine & meet Clodd on July 1st, but we shall be back here again by that time if our present plans are carried out.

I have just read your Literary Letter (the best you have written for a long time) on the Parnell Life & Letters. I quite agree with you that P.'s divorce case did not affect Home Rule one way or the other, though perhaps I ought not to have an opinion, not having read the book. I speak however from memory.

Very truly yours
Thomas Hardy.

Text MS. Berg.
Parnell Life & Letters: Shorter's 'A Literary Letter', *Sphere*, 6 June 1914, discusses Katharine Parnell, *Charles Stewart Parnell, His Love Story and Political Life* (2 vols., London, 1914).

To W. H. GRATTAN FLOOD

FROM THO. HARDY, | MAX GATE, | DORCHESTER. | 9: 6: 1914

Dear Mr Flood:

Many thanks for sending the score. Any lyrics of mine that you may wish to set to music are at your service.

Yours truly
Thomas Hardy.

W. H. G. Flood Esq. Mus. D.

Text MS. (correspondence card) NYU.
Flood: William Henry Grattan Flood (1859–1928), Irish organist, composer, and historian of music. *the score*: of the ballad beginning 'King Arthur he had three sons', partly quoted in *Under the Greenwood Tree* (Wessex edn., 159); Flood reported (8 June 14, DCM) that he had found the words and music in the British Museum. See I.198–9.

To FLORENCE HENNIKER

MAX GATE, | DORCHESTER. | 11 June 1914

My dear friend:

What a strange thing. This morning when I was dressing it flashed into my mind that I had been going to write to you for several days, & that I would do it this very day: when lo, there was a letter from you. This has happened I think once or twice before in our correspondence. Still I suppose I must knock the romance out of it & say it was only a coincidence.

We intend to be in London from Wednesday to Saturday next week, & we shall I believe be staying at Lady St. Helier's. I was in hopes you were at Stratford Place. I fear there will not be time to run down to you, in the event of her having arranged things to do; but I don't know. I am thinking we may be able, however, to go to London again for a day or two during July, in which case we will make a point of visiting your little orchard. Meanwhile cannot you come here for a week-end or week-middle, just as you choose. I really think you ought to honour Max Gate by sleeping in it just once at any rate. F. will write to you about this.

The vein, or veins, do not trouble me, unless I walk too far. How kind of you to bear in mind that inconvenience of mine. I think bicycling was the original cause.

As you ask what I am doing in poetry I am sending the Fortnightly for May, containing the last thing I published. I have a lot of loose poems in MS. which I must, I suppose, collect into a volume. Of course I shall send you a copy, whenever it comes out.

We are going on very quietly. Florence works at flower-gardening—rather too hard, I think; but she is quite devoted to it. About three weeks ago we motored to Plymouth, partly because I wanted to clear up a mystery as to the Gifford vault there. We came back over Dartmoor. It was cold, & the gradients were high, but the views beautiful.

I, too, have felt uneasy about that physiological Laboratory. But I suppose one must take the words of vivisectors as honest when they assure us that they never torture animals. Altogether the world is such a bungled institution from a humane point of view that a grief more or less hardly counts. Wishing one had never come into it or shared in its degrading organizations is but a selfish thought, as others would have been here just the same. But this sounds gloomy to you I know; & I am after all not without hope of much amelioration.

Ever your affectte friend
Tho H.

P.S. "Wessex", "Wessie", or "Wess" is thriving, but he is pronounced a spoilt dog. He is fond of other dogs, & wd not object to your bringing Milner. T.H.

I enclose something else I have lately printed—quite a trifle as you see.

Text MS. DCM.
letter from you: of 10 June 14 (transcript, DCM). *Lady St. Helier's*: see letter of 22 Apr 15. *Stratford Place*: Mrs. Henniker's London house. *down to you*: at Shoreham, Kent, where she was currently living. *your little orchard*: her Shoreham cottage was called The Little Orchard. *or veins*: TH suffered occasionally from varicose veins. *published*: TH's 'Channel Firing'; see letter of 29 Apr 14. *Gifford vault*: see letter of 15 June 14 to Watson. *that physiological Laboratory*: at Cambridge; Mrs. Henniker had expressed disgust at its being opened by Prince Arthur of Connaught, who had thus identified himself with 'the worst type of vivisector'. *"Wessex"*: see letter of 29 Jan 14. *Milner*: Mrs. Henniker's own dog. *lately printed*: 'Before and After Summer', *New Weekly*, 4 Apr 1914; see letter of 17 July 14.

To SIR SIDNEY COLVIN

MAX GATE, | DORCHESTER. | 14 June 1914

My dear Colvin:

We have been weighing probabilities in the question of the "splendid caverns & grottoes" of Severn, that you write about, & have come to the conclusion that he must mean "Durdle Door", close to Lulworth Cove. (You can get a post-card photograph of it—from Hills & Rowney, Dorchester: there is also an old engraving of it in Hutchins's Dorset.) Why we think it must have been Durdle Door is that it impressed my wife just in the same way when she first saw it as a girl.

To see it from the inside (which would give the impression) they would have landed in the Cove, & have walked over the Cliff to the west, & down behind the "Door". The walk would have taken them only a few minutes.

There is a smuggler's cave in Worbarrow Bay, but it is difficult to find, though in Keats's time it would most likely have been clearer. The only other cave I know about here is Cave Hole, Portland. But that is difficult of access except at low & quiet tides.

I am sending some Keats names that I jotted down when you wrote to the papers. They are useless, I fancy, which is why I did not send them earlier. However here they are. I knew personally all the persons mentioned, & used always to be struck by their resemblance to the poet.

Sincerely yours
Thomas Hardy.

P.S. I assume that Swanage would be too far east. There are, of course, the Tilly-Whim caves near that place. T.H.

Text MS. Fitzwilliam Museum.
Colvin: Sidney Colvin, art and literary critic; see IV.286. *of Severn*: Colvin (13 June 14, DCM) had asked if TH could identify from Joseph Severn's description the part of the Dorsetshire coast visited by John Keats during his voyage from England to Italy in September 1820; see Colvin's *John Keats*: *His Life and Poetry, His Friends, Critics, and After-Fame* (London, 1917), 492. *Hills & Rowney*: of 23 High West Street, Dorchester, picture frame manufacturers. *in Hutchins's Dorset*: Hutchins (see letter of 13 Feb 14 to Lady Grove), I.opp.440. *some Keats names*: those of William Keates (said to have been the 'original' of Reuben Dewy in *Under the Greenwood Tree*) and other members of the Keates family who lived in and near Higher Bockhampton during TH's childhood.

To SIR SIDNEY COLVIN

FROM THO. HARDY, | MAX GATE, | DORCHESTER. [14 June 1914]

I forgot to say in my letter that some 40 years ago my father told me that the K—s of this neighbourhood came of a family of horse-dealers, who lived in the direction of Broadmayne.

T.H.

Text MS. (postcard) Berg. *Date* From postmark.
K—s: Keatses. *Broadmayne*: a village some 4 miles S. of Higher Bockhampton.

To SIR FREDERICK MACMILLAN

MAX GATE, | DORCHESTER. | 15: 6: 1914

Dear Sir Frederick:

I have agreed to let Mr Cecil Palmer of the firm of Frank Palmer compile a Calendar of sentences from my books like the one I enclose. They agree to pay £12, & to give you a *free* advertisement of my works in the Calendar. I thought it was worth while, as the book itself is an advertisement, so I did not trouble you about it. You will see at the end that they have done several, but I know nothing about the firm. However a quotation of single sentences can do no harm.

I hope to see you this week, & am

Sincerely yours
Thomas Hardy.

Text MS. BL.
Calendar of sentences: *The Thomas Hardy Calendar*, comp. C. P. [i.e., H. Cecil Palmer] (London, 1921). *do no harm*: Macmillan (16 June 14, Macmillan letterbooks, BL) concurred in this judgement but said that TH had been right to charge a reasonable fee; the quotations in fact used often amounted to more than a single sentence.

To ANNIE WATSON

Max Gate | Dorchester | 15: 6: 1914

Dear Miss Watson:

I am greatly obliged to you for seeing to the grave. My nephew Gordon Gifford—whom you knew as "Blenny"—thinks of running down from London to Plymouth on his motor-bicycle in August, & he will go & look at it. Probably he will call on you.

There is still a mystery about the Gifford graves. I cannot think where Emma's grandmother lies—of whom she was very fond. I mean the Helen Davie who married Richard Ireland Gifford, & who lived with John Gifford & his family at Bedford Terrace, where she died. Possibly your mother attended the funeral, which was in February 1860, & if so, she may remember. I fear however that the grave was swept away by alterations, as the headstone is against the wall.

Yours very truly
T. Hardy.

P.S. We had a most pleasant journey home across Dartmoor. T.H.

Text MS. Berg.
Watson: Annie Carr Watson, eldest daughter of ELH's first cousin Robert Gifford Watson. *the grave*: that of ELH's parents in Charles Churchyard, Plymouth; see IV.311. *the Gifford graves*: i.e., those of other members of the Gifford family buried in Charles Churchyard; see *The Personal Notebooks of Thomas Hardy*, ed. Richard H. Taylor (London, 1978), 35–6. *your mother*: Ellen Elizabeth Watson, *née* Hill. *alterations*: according to the 'Gifford Pedigree', drawn up by TH himself (DCM), these occurred in 1889. *across Dartmoor*: see letter of 11 June 14.

To EDWARD DUGDALE

MAX GATE, | DORCHESTER. | 24 June: 1914

Dear Mr Dugdale:

The photograph is just what I meant. Many thanks for your trouble in obtaining it.

I think Mrs Dugdale was benefited by her holiday & the change of air. We wish she could have stayed here a little longer.

Florence is going to a bazaar this afternoon. She was asked to open it, & feels that at least she must spend something there. But I am not much inclined for those places.

Sincerely yours
Thomas Hardy.

Text MS. Purdy.
Dugdale: Edward Dugdale (d. 1936), FEH's father; he was headmaster of St. Andrew's National [i.e., Church of England] School for Boys, Enfield, Middlesex. *photograph*: perhaps of FEH as a child or young woman. *a bazaar*: evidently the 'Fordington Fancy Fair' held on 24 and 25 June 1914 in aid of the Fordington St. George restoration fund; FEH's decision against 'opening' the event was perhaps influenced by TH's disapproval of the work being done on the church (see III. 50–1, 235–6).

To SIR FREDERICK MACMILLAN

MAX GATE, | DORCHESTER. | 24: 6: 1914

My dear Macmillan:

I am quite willing to make the abatement you propose in the price to Mlle. de Lansade for printing her translation of stories from "A Changed Man". These ladies who translate often rush into the business in a moment of enthusiasm, & afterwards find themselves in difficulties.

Sincerely yours
Thomas Hardy.

Text MS. BL.
"A Changed Man": Macmillan (23 June 14, Macmillan letterbooks, BL) explained that Mademoiselle M. de Lansade, of 252 Rue de Rivoli, Paris, had translated 'The Committee-Man of "The Terror"' and 'What the Shepherd Saw' but been unable to find an editor willing to pay enough to cover the translation fee of 100 francs per story. A fee of 2 francs per printed page of the English texts was eventually asked, but the fate of the translations remains unknown. See letter to Macmillan of 4 Apr 14.

To LORD BRYCE

MAX GATE, | DORCHESTER. | 26 June: 1914

Dear Lord Bryce:

I feel the honour of being asked to speak at the first meeting for the proposed Commemoration of Shakespeare's Tercentenary. But I fear that a passing attack of rheumatism, from sitting in a draught, may prevent my being present; & in any case I am not able to speak.

The only idea I have on what direction should be given to such a Commemoration is that Shakespeare the man of letters, & not Shakespeare the actor, should be the prime consideration. It has mostly resulted otherwise, the *camaraderie* of actors having been allowed to thrust forward his minor claim on our memory, to the obscuring of his incomparable one.

Very truly yours
Thomas Hardy.

Text MS. Bodleian Library.
Bryce: James, Viscount Bryce (1838–1922), jurist, historian, and statesman; *D.N.B.* *Shakespeare's Tercentenary*: in 1916; Bryce, as president of the British Academy, chaired this organizational meeting, held in London 3 July 1914. TH was not present, although his annotation of a 24 June 15 (DCM) letter from Israel Gollancz (see letter of 29 Oct 15 to Gollancz) indicates that he had originally agreed to attend.

To GORDON GIFFORD

Max Gate | 27: 6: 1914

Dear Gordon:

It is possible that we may be staying at the West Central Hotel, 101 Southampton Row, next Thursday, July 2, and if you have nothing more important to do should be glad to see you there to dinner about ¼ to 7. It is a plain quiet place, so come just as you are. If anything prevents our being there I will let you know.

Miss Watson wrote a week or two ago to tell me that the sexton had finished putting in order your grandfather & grandmother's tomb in Charles Churchyard, as I hired him to do, & that it looks very well. He has taken out all the grass that had grown inside the curb-stone, & laid the space with pounded granite, so if you go there this summer you will be able to see it.

Your affectte uncle
T.H.

Text MS. Mrs. Ethel Skinner.
Miss Watson wrote: see letter of 15 June 14 to her.

To A. M. BROADLEY

FROM THO. HARDY, | MAX GATE, | DORCHESTER. | 28: 6: 1914

Have received page from Guardian and The Ship Beautiful—for each of which thanks. The latter appeals to me less than some of your works. I cannot think how you get through so much work.

Yrs v. truly,
T.H.

Text MS. (postcard) Berg.
Broadley: Alexander Meyrick Broadley, collector and author of historical works; see III.199. *from Guardian*: the *Guardian*, 25 June 1914, 808, reports 'The Crabbe Commem-

oration', held at Trowbridge, Wilts., at which Broadley, as the owner of important Crabbe MSS., had given the address. *The Ship Beautiful*: presumably an article by Broadley, but untraced.

To EDMUND GOSSE

MAX GATE, | DORCHESTER. | 28: 6: 1914

My dear Gosse:

Many thanks. We will certainly give ourselves the pleasure of calling on Mr & Mrs Hanbury as soon as they are settled in. Kingston House is only about a mile from here. Mrs Gifford, my late wife's aunt by marriage, is also Mrs Hanbury's aunt, Ld St Helier's sister Miss Jeune having married Emma's uncle, Archdeacon Gifford.

We were staying at Lady St. Helier's last week, & I should have hunted you up if it had not been that at the only times I might have found you we had to meet several people. Indeed I always imagine you to be practically unapproachable except on a Sunday, when you descend from the clouds of Westminster to the human level of Regent's Park. By the way, I took in to dinner one night Lady Ridley, & I think she lives when in the country somewhere near Philip, does she not? Such a nice woman.

I have a watery eye, owing to sitting by an open window. I am also exercised on what to do with some poems. When I am dead & gone I shall be glad—if I can be anything—for them to have been printed, & yet I don't quite like to print them.

My wife sends her love to Mrs Gosse. I hope you & she are well.

Always sincerely
Thomas Hardy.

P.S. I think I shall be in London next Thursday or Friday, but I am not quite sure. We just run up & down—having taken no house, flat or anything. T.H.

Text MS. (with envelope) BL.
Hanbury: Cecil Hanbury (1871–1937), later M.P. for North Dorset, and his wife Dorothy (see letter to her of 27 Nov 16); they had recently purchased Kingston Maurward House, Stinsford. *Archdeacon Gifford*: Edwin Hamilton Gifford (see I.31) married in 1873, as his second wife, Margaret Symons Jeune, the sister of Francis Henry Jeune, later Lord St. Helier (see I.144), and of John Francis Symons Jeune (see letter of 7 June 16), Mrs. Hanbury's father. *clouds of Westminster*: Gosse was Librarian of the House of Lords. *Regent's Park*: the Gosses lived at 17 Hanover Terrace. *Lady Ridley*: Rosamond, Viscountess Ridley (d. 1947), youngest daughter of the 1st Lord Wimborne. *near Philip*: Gosse's son Philip (see IV.292) was in practice as a doctor at Beaulieu, in the New Forest. *some poems*: those subseqently pub. in *Satires of Circumstance* as 'Poems of 1912–13'.

To AN UNIDENTIFIED CORRESPONDENT

FROM THO. HARDY, | MAX GATE, | DORCHESTER. | 6: 7: 1914

Dear Sir:

"A Changed Man" has recently been added to the definitive Wessex Edition, & can be obtained of the Messrs Macmillan.

My thanks for your letter.

Yours very truly,
T.H.

Text MS. (correspondence card) Colby.
Wessex Edition: it was assigned to the new category of 'Mixed Novels'; see Purdy, 284.

To HENRY HARDY

Stourhead House | Monday [13 July 1914]

Have had a very good time.

Return to-day. F. ascended tower.

Text MS. (pencil, picture postcard of Stourton Tower) DCM. *Date* From postmark.
Stourhead House: TH and FEH were staying with Sir Henry and Lady Hoare; see *LY*, 160–1. *ascended tower*: on the Stourhead estate; see letter of 29 Apr 14.

To SIR FREDERICK MACMILLAN

MAX GATE, | DORCHESTER. | 15th. July 1914.

Dear Sir Frederick Macmillan:

I should much like you to publish the limited edition you write about, and as to royalty, number of copies, style, and other practical details, would agree to the arrangements you suggest.

The only point I have any misgiving about is the omission of the verse, which I confess rather surprises me; for though I have not much feeling on the matter, I fancy that if the "works" are not "complete" purchasers will be shy. There is at present a passion for having *everything* of a writer. It may have been partly the fact that the Bombay edition of Mr Kipling's works included both prose and verse (for the first time I believe) which made it so successful.

My verse has not, of course, a market like the prose, but there is the awkward circumstance that reviewers, scholars, and correspondents consider "The Dynasts" my most important and (as they put it) "greatest book" which will "live longest". America too, which at first, owing to my printing but little of the verse there, almost ignored it, is getting now to be of the same opinion. So that I fear the influence of this opinion, if not the subscribers' own tastes, will make them demand the "epic-drama" if they subscribe at all. There is also a minor difficulty in the prefaces, which refer to verse and prose both.

I imagine you feel compelled to omit the verse because of the number of volumes the whole would run into if it were included, and I have been trying to think of a plan for getting over this contingency without incurring the charge of incompleteness. The following occurred to me:—

1. To print all the verse in smaller type, as a sort of Appendix, so as to get it into two volumes, making also one volume each, of two of the shorter novels to which you have allotted two volumes each. This would still keep the whole number at 28.

(or,)

2. To keep novels under 460 pages in one volume, and only those above 460, which have also long prefaces, in two volumes. The verse in, say, four volumes. This would make 27 volumes altogether.

(or,)

3. To arrange the prose in 28 volumes under one subscription as you propose, and the verse in four or five volumes as a separate subscription, leaving it to subscribers to choose if they will include the latter or not.

By the way, I have enough more verse in M.S. to make a book about as long as "Time's Laughingstocks" whenever you like to print it. But this will go into the set as above reckoned.

I don't know if you have thought of giving the edition a name. Would "The Casterbridge Edition" or "The Mellstock Edition" do?

Very truly yours,
Thomas Hardy.

Text MS. (typewritten) BL.
arrangements you suggest: Macmillan's proposal (13 July 14, Macmillan letterbooks, BL) was to follow up the 'Bombay' edn. of Rudyard Kipling's works with a 28-vol. limited edn. of TH's prose works 'in the same form, same type, and at the same price'. *verse and prose both*: TH refers chiefly to the 'General Preface to the Novels and Poems' included in the first vol. of the Wessex Edn. *without . . . incompleteness*: inserted in TH's hand. *make a book*: see letter of 19 July 14. *Mellstock Edition*": this was the title eventually chosen, but the edition itself, including the verse and totalling 37 vols. in all, was delayed by the First World War and did not appear until 1919–20.

To FLORENCE HENNIKER

MAX GATE, | DORCHESTER. | July 17: 1914

My dear friend:

As you are kind enough to write about that little poem called "Before & after Summer" I remember to tell you that I am collecting the pieces in verse that I have written since the last volume of poetry was published & looking them over with a view of bringing them out some when towards the end of the year. Some of them I rather shrink from printing—those I wrote just after Emma died, when I looked back at her as she had originally been, & when I felt miserable lest I had not treated her considerately in her latter life. However I shall publish them as the only amends I can make, if it were so. The remainder of the book, & by far the greater part of it, will be poems mostly dramatic or personative—many of which have been printed in magazines, &c. (I have let nobody but you & Florence know as yet that I purpose this.)

We are going on calmly enough here as you guess. She is a very tender companion & is quite satisfied with the quietude of life here. But we flit about a little. Last week-end we spent at Sir Henry Hoare's at Stour-head in Wiltshire—a beautiful spot. Lately they have had a visitor by aeroplane: they saw him in the air over their park, & he descended, being unable to get further. He had come from Paris. They gave him a night's lodging, & next morning he flew away, after entering his name in the visitors' book. He was a total stranger, & they think he must be the first entertained in that way & written down as a guest.

The Irish question is perplexing, & gloomy, but I can hardly think there will be bloodshed. I wish Mr Gladstone had never opened it up. The Irish temperament, I fear, will not be satisfied for long with *any* rule, & probably the new rule will work no better than the old.

We had a pleasant time at Lady St. Helier's. She got up a big dinner mainly on our account, & Mr & Mrs Winston Churchill came. I had her next me. He has promised her not to fly again till after a certain event, but he won't promise *never* to fly again.

I am so glad to think you mean to be more in London: I so regretted that you were not there when we were. My impression is that you would have done better by coming to the south coast instead of going to Kent, but probably you don't think so. F. still thinks you the dearest friend she has in the world.

I *may* send you a new magazine later on (if it really comes out) containing a very small poem—two stanzas only—of mine, which I think may interest you, as it refers to so long ago as 1894.

Your neighbours are probably like most country folk—rather stolid. Yet that sort of person does really feel a sincerer regard for one's welfare than town people, I consider.

Ever yr affectionate friend
Tho H.

Text MS. DCM.
write about: in her letter of 11 July 14 (transcript, DCM). *after Summer"*: see letter of 11 June 14. *Irish question*: a Home Rule bill for Ireland (of which Mrs. Henniker's brother had been Lord-Lieutenant; see II.11) had been passed by the House of Commons in 1913 but rejected by the Lords. It could still become law, however, if passed by the Commons in three successive sessions and the Liberal government was pursuing that course in the face of fierce Ulster opposition, including threats of violence and of the establishment of an independent Ulster government. *opened it up*: i.e., the idea of Irish Home Rule, proposed by Gladstone in 1886. *Churchill*: Winston Leonard Spencer Churchill (1874–1965; *D.N.B.*), statesman, currently first Lord of the Admiralty; he married Clementine Hozier in 1908. *a certain event*: the birth of their third child, Sarah (b. 7 Oct 1914). *so long ago as 1894*: possibly 'The Difference', although it seems not to have been pub. prior to its inclusion in *Satires of Circumstance*. *rather stolid*: Mrs. Henniker had described her Shoreham neighbours as '*extraordinarily self-satisfied* and *self-absorbed*'.

To SIR FREDERICK MACMILLAN

MAX GATE, | DORCHESTER. | 19th. July 1914.

Dear Sir Frederick Macmillan:

The plan you think best of those I suggested for including the whole works—to issue prose and verse either separately or together—seems also to me the most advisable, assuming that you cannot, by getting more of the novels into one volume each, bring the complete works into twenty-eight or thereabout.

The signing of 500 additional copies will not I imagine be a formidable business. At any rate I will undertake it.

I gather that the edition will follow exactly the text of the Wessex edition, including classification, prefaces, etc, though in respect of the poetry it will be better no doubt to put "The Dynasts" first, as you have done in the list you send.

I suppose the printers can be depended on for correctness if I don't read the proofs. I have marked a few misprints and oversights in some of the volumes, and can send them in a list whenever they may be wanted, as it will be well to embody them.

In respect of the new volume of verse, I am beginning to go through the MS. to make the pages clear where confused, so as to have less trouble in proof. The title I have thought of is "Satires of Circumstance, Lyrics and Reveries." I shall be glad to know what you think of it. If it seems bad I can easily find another I daresay. I believe I can send up the MS. by the end of the month. Or would it suit you better for me to hunt up the corrections for the Casterbridge edition and send them first?

Yours very truly,
Thomas Hardy.

Text MS. (typewritten) BL.
those I suggested: see letter of 15 July 14. *read the proofs*: Macmillan (13 July 14, Macmillan letterbooks, BL) had suggested that the use of the Wessex edn. text would make this unnecessary. *in a list*: copies of two such lists, dated 18 and 22 June 1919, are in DCM. *Casterbridge edition*: see, however, letter of 15 July 14.

To JOHN READ

MAX GATE, | DORCHESTER. | 25. July 1914

Dear Mr Read:

Many thanks for your volume of dramatic pieces "Wold ways a-gwain" which I have just taken up. You seem to have reproduced the local pronunciation almost phonetically, which is a feat I never attempted. I am not able to do justice to the book for the moment, but shall take it up as a change from dryer matters. Believe me

Sincerely yours
Thomas Hardy.

Text MS. (with envelope) Eton College.
Read: John Read, research chemist and author; see IV.207. *a-gwain*": Read's *Wold Ways A-gwain* (Yeovil, 1914), a collection of dialect pieces.

To SIR SIDNEY COLVIN

MAX GATE, | DORCHESTER. | 29: 7: 1914

My dear Colvin:

"Beautiful grottoes" is certainly rather an exaggerated description of what one finds at Durdle Door, and Stair Hole close by; yet an enthusiastic young Londoner *might* on a first impression use such words. Besides, if not Durdle Door, Stair Hole, &c., what place can it be that Severn meant? The "Door" is an archway in the cliff, as you know: Stair Hole has caves & fissures into which the sea flows, & there is another cave at Bat's Corner, also close at hand.

At any rate I cannot think of another point on the Dorset Coast, easily accessible from a boat, which so well answers the description.

The "Cottages" would be those of the adjoining Lulworth Cove & Village, but they do not, of course, face the "grottoes", as Severn seems to imply. I put that down to his fancy, as such a position would hardly be possible anywhere.

With kind regards

Sincerely yours
Thomas Hardy.

Text MS. Harvard.
exaggerated description: see first letter of 14 June 14. Colvin (28 July 14, DCM) had now quoted more extensively from Severn's description and asked if it tended to confirm TH's suggestion as to the spot where Keats had gone ashore; Severn's phrase was in fact 'splendid caverns and grottoes'. For a comment of TH's on Severn, see *LY*, 260.

To GEORGE MACMILLAN

MAX GATE, | DORCHESTER. | 31st. July 1914.

Dear Mr Macmillan:

It makes no difference to me which I go on with first, so I will now go through the poems, and let you have the MS. as soon as possible.

With kind regards.

Yours sincerely,
Thomas Hardy.

Text MS. (typewritten) BL.
go on with first: Macmillan wrote 20 July 14 to say that Sir Frederick Macmillan had gone on a short holiday and on 28 July 14 (both Macmillan letterbooks, BL) to suggest that TH give priority to his new vol. of verse rather than to the corrections for the limited edn.

To SYDNEY COCKERELL

MAX GATE, | DORCHESTER. | Sunday [9 August 1914]

My dear Cockerell:

I examined the atlas last night, & found it highly interesting, though my glance was but a cursory one. 1603 seems to be the date, which seems now a civilized age by comparison with the present.

Among the other ironies of the time is the fact that all the nations are praying to the same God. There was a gleam of reason in the old nations when they prayed for deliverance each to his own god, but that reasonableness is gone.

My wife will have asked if you & Mrs Cockerell can stay over the night when you come. It will be extremely pleasant to see you. We have 20,000 soldiers at Weymouth, it is said, & there are 5000 in Dorchester, billetted on the inhabitants, but we have none in this house as yet.

With many thanks for the atlas, believe me

Sincerely yours
Thomas Hardy.

Text MS. Seymour Adelman. *Date* Supplied by Cockerell on MS.
atlas: a 1603 edn. of the *Theatrum Orbis Terrarum* of Ortelius; see *Friends of a Lifetime: Letters to Sydney Carlyle Cockerell*, ed. Viola Meynell (London, 1940), 277n. *with the present*: an allusion to the outbreak of war, 4 Aug 1914. *when you come*: they seem, however, to have spent only the afternoon of 10 Aug 1914 at Max Gate.

To GEORGE MACMILLAN

MAX GATE, | DORCHESTER. | 9: 8: 1914

Dear Mr Macmillan:

In view of recent events I am not sure if you expect me to send on the MS. of the poems—which is ready. I will do just as you think best. Believe me

Sincerely yours
Thomas Hardy.

P.S. I should, of course, like them to be printed at some time, even at a loss. T.H.

Text MS. BL.
recent events: i.e., the outbreak of war.

To GEORGE MACMILLAN

MAX GATE, | DORCHESTER. | 10 August 1914

Dear Mr Macmillan:

I have sent off to you by parcel-post the MS. of "Satires of Circumstance" as you suggested I should do. If you decide to print it, it could, of course be published at any favourable time—say, when people get tired of the war, if they do!

Believe me

Sincerely yours
Thomas Hardy.

Text MS. BL.

To EDWARD CLODD

Max Gate | Tuesday [18 August 1914?]

My dear Clodd:

We wonder how you are getting on, & hope satisfactorily, amid the shocks of this dynastic struggle just beginning. Dorchester is teeming with soldiers, mostly drunk, Weymouth & Portland crammed with them, ditches being dug to isolate the latter, & we have 400 German prisoners here. Have they begun to fortify Aldeburgh or the adjoining stretch of coast? So much for 20th century civilization. Mrs Hardy sends kind regards.

Sincerely yours,
Thomas Hardy.

Text MS. Duke Univ. *Date* The date, 11 Aug 14, supplied by Clodd on the MS. appears to be an error for 18 Aug 14, the Tuesday following.
400 German prisoners: this figure, repeated in the letter of 19 Aug 14, seems exaggerated; the *Dorset County Chronicle*, 20 Aug 1914, estimated that 250 prisoners (chiefly merchant seamen trapped by the outbreak of war in British ports) were being held in the Dorchester artillery barracks.

To HARRY POUNCY

MAX GATE, | DORCHESTER. | 18th. August '14

Dear Mr Pouncy:

I am afraid that the continuation of "The Dynasts" into this twentieth century will have to be done by other pens than mine. They will probably not, however, be able to continue it into the twenty first century, all dynasties being likely to be finished by that time.

I should think your lecture on the Dorsetshire regiment would be immensely popular during present events.

I hope there will be a paragraph in the Dorset Chronicle warning landlords against supplying the soldiers with so much liquor.

Yours very truly,
T. Hardy.

Text MS. (typewritten) Taylor.
Dorsetshire regiment: Pouncy lectured on the regiment at Sherborne School in October 1914 and at Portland in November; he also pub. a long two-part article, 'The Dorsets in the Great War', in the 1916–17 and 1917–18 *Year-books* of the Society of Dorset Men in London. *so*

much liquor: Pouncy, as assistant editor of the *Dorset County Chronicle*, was presumably responsible for the item in the issue of 20 Aug 1914 which applauded the 'patriotic action' of the Dorchester publicans in voluntarily agreeing not to serve drink to any man in uniform after 9 p.m.

To GORDON GIFFORD

Max Gate | 19 Aug: 1914

Dear Gordon:

I am glad to find that you were able to get to Wales after all. Possibly you went by train. Anyhow, if you like to call round here on your way back we can put you up for a night or two.

It is interesting to have the inscription on the tomb of my uncle's brother, with whom I used to correspond.

The War Office may not require your services as a dispatch rider yet; but we do not know what may occur, or who may be wanted in the future.

Dorchester is full of soldiers and 400 German prisoners. Weymouth has 20,000 soldiers, & search lights going all night.

Your affectte uncle
T. Hardy.

Text MS. Mrs. Ethel Skinner.
my uncle's brother: the Revd. George Brereton Sharpe (1812–1900), buried at Llanelwedd, Buith, Wales, where he was vicar 1867–1900; he was the elder brother of John Brereton Sharpe (1818–99), who married TH's aunt Martha (his mother's sister) and emigrated with her to Canada. *correspond*: the only survivals from this correspondence seem to be two letters from Sharpe to TH, one dated 21 Sept 1859 (DCM), the other 21 Jan 1868 (Lock collection, Dorset County Library).

To A. G. GARDINER

Max Gate | Dorchester. | 25 Aug. 1914.

Dear Mr Gardiner:

Many thanks for your offer of space in the D.N. for anything I may have to say on the war. But I do not feel impelled to say anything at present, the insufficiency of data apparent in all the newspaper writings on the subject being increased in my case. While as to general opinions & prophecies, they would be laughed at: e.g., such a highly rational one as that all the Churches in Europe should frankly admit the utter failure of theology, & put their heads together to form a new religion which should have at least some faint connection with morality. But as I say, I prefer to write nothing.

My friend Frederic Harrison has just sent me a letter that shows how sadly he, at 83, is affected by events.

Sincerely yours
Thomas Hardy.

P.S. We read the D.N. every day: but for some reason or other it arrives later than the other papers. T.H.

Text Transcript (by Gardiner) British Library of Political and Economic Science. *Gardiner*: Alfred George Gardiner, editor of the *Daily News* 1902–19; see III.307. *D.N.*: the *Daily News*. *affected by events*: Harrison (22 Aug 14, DCM) speaks of his fears for the future and concludes, 'But in this hour of agonising suspense, I can write no more. I feel as if I was waiting for the verdict whilst my son was being tried for murder.'

To EDWARD CLODD

MAX GATE, | DORCHESTER. | 28: 8: 1914

My dear Clodd:

I fear we cannot take advantage of your kind invitation, & pay you a visit just now—much as in some respects we should like to. With the Germans, (apparently) only a week from Paris, the native hue of resolution is sicklied o'er with the pale cast of thought. We shall hope to come when things look brighter.

Trifling incidents here bring home to us the condition of affairs not far off—as I daresay they do to you still more—sentries with gleaming bayonets at unexpected places as we motor along, the steady flow of soldiers through here to Weymouth, & their disappearance across the Channel in the silence of night, & the 1000 prisoners whom we get glimpses of through chinks, mark these fine days. The prisoners, they say, have already mustered enough broken English to say "Shoot Kaiser!" & oblige us by playing "God Save the King" on their concertinas & fiddles. Whether this is "meant sarcastic", as Artemus Ward used to say, I cannot tell.

I was pleased to know that you were so comfortable, when I was picturing you in your shirt sleeves with a lot of other robust Aldeburghers digging a huge trench from Aldeburgh church to the top of those steps we go down to your house, streaming with sweat, & drinking pots of beer between the shovellings, (English beer of course).

Sincerely yours
Thomas Hardy.

P.S. Yes: everybody seems to be reading "The Dynasts" just now—at least, so a writer in the Daily News who called here this morning tells me. T.H.

Text MS. BL.
cast of thought: *Hamlet*, III.i.83–4. *Artemus Ward*: pseudonym of Charles Farrar Browne (1834–67), American humorist. *your house*: Clodd's weekend retreat on the sea-front at Aldeburgh, Suffolk. *in the Daily News*: Robert Lynd (see letter of 30 July 19), presumably sent by Gardiner (see letter of 25 Aug 14). Lynd's letter to TH of 29 Aug 14 (DCM) indicates that he had hoped to persuade TH to write either on the current war or on the Napoleonic period, giving 'just the human nature & spirit of it'.

To SYDNEY COCKERELL

MAX GATE, | DORCHESTER. | 28: 8: 1914

My dear Cockerell:

I hope you have got back to Cambridge without adventure, but I suppose the northern railways are running trains more regularly than ours have been doing.

I certainly hope that you will outlive me for many a long year, & it is very good of you not to mind giving any little attention you can to such literary details of mine that may require looking after. However I think there won't be much: it will be mainly to see that nothing in the way of entries & notes obviously intended as private memoranda should be printed. As I told you I am hoping to jot down some dates, &c., that you may keep them at hand to do what you like with: e.g. to use if any preposterous stories should require contradiction, or as you choose. I do not, in truth, feel *much* interest in posthumous opinions about me, or estimates, & shall sleep quite calmly at Stinsford whatever happens. What I care most about just now is that the poems entitled, "Satires of Circumstance", (they are by no means all satires, but the title seems as good as any) should be brought out by the Macmillans at some time or other. The MS. is already in their hands—I thought it best to let them have it—& they say they think they will at any rate print it now, & perhaps keep it by them for a convenient season.

Curiously enough, a week before the war broke out, they entered into an arrangement with me for publishing an "*edition de luxe*" at about 30 guineas. I shall let this drift till the war is over, as it was to be an exact copy of the Wessex edition lately published, & will have no more value textually than that has.

The newspapers want verses or any other effusions from me, but The Times verse so far is not encouraging. My wife says that in receiving the shock of the war news she did not reckon on the additional infliction of the newspaper poets & prophets.

As for myself, the recognition that we are living in a more brutal age than that, say, of Elizabeth, or of the chivalry which could cry: "Gentlemen of the Guard, fire first!" (far more brutal, indeed: no chivalry now!) does not inspire one to write hopeful poetry, or even conjectural prose, but simply make one sit still in an apathy, & watch the clock spinning backwards, with a mild wonder if, when it gets back to the Dark Ages, & the sack of Rome, it will ever move forward again to a new Renascence, & a new literature. But people would call this pessimistic so I will stop—having inflicted on you a much longer letter than I intended. My wife tells me to give her love to Mrs Cockerell & the children. I am

Always sincerely yours
Thomas Hardy.

Text MS. Colby.
back to Cambridge: Cockerell had last written (see below) from Edinburgh. *require looking after*: TH had asked Cockerell to act as one of his literary executors. *should be printed*: TH

first wrote 'should not be printed'; Cockerell (21 Aug 14, DCM) had already declared that his principal concerns would be to guard TH's literary reputation and prevent publication of 'matter that you have rejected' (see Millgate, 518n). *at Stinsford*: Cockerell was, in the event, largely responsible for the arrangement by which TH's ashes were interred in Westminster Abbey and only his heart in Stinsford churchyard; see Millgate, 574. *keep it by them*: TH first wrote 'keep it in hand'. de luxe": see letters of 15 and 19 July 14. *exact copy*: TH first wrote 'exact reprint'. *Times verse*: *The Times* had recently been publishing a war poem almost every day; on 28 Aug 1914 it printed 'The Kaiser and God' by Barry Pain. *fire first!*": reputed to have been spoken to the French Guard ('Messieurs les gardes françaises, tirez') by Lord Charles Hay at the battle of Fontenoy, 1745.

To GEORGE HARVEY

MAX GATE, | DORCHESTER. | September 1914.

Dear Sir:

If the war had not suddenly displaced intentions for a time I should have written earlier in answer to your letter on the centenary of the North American Review, to say that I am hoping to send some contribution for the number, though it will probably take the shape of verse, as I do not print prose nowadays.

Yours very truly,
Thomas Hardy.

Colonel George Harvey.

Text MS. (typewritten) Harvard.
Harvey: George Brinton McClellan Harvey, editor of the *North American Review* (see III.8); he acquired the title of Colonel while serving on the staff of the governor of New Jersey. *the shape of verse*: TH's poem 'A Hundred Years Since' appeared in the *North American Review*, February 1915.

To EDMUND GOSSE

MAX GATE, | DORCHESTER. | 10: 9: 1914.

My dear Gosse:

I have written to Masterman who, I should think, would be very glad to get you. When I did not see you present at the meeting I thought that, like several, you had not got the notice in time (it was only a few hours before the meeting), or that your official position excluded you—the requests having been restricted to authors who had no governmental connection of any kind.

I think I have not heard from you since the war broke out. The effect of it upon me was for a long while to prevent my doing anything, & is still to a great extent. I was in London only a few hours last week. We have more than 1000 prisoners here—Germans & Austrians; & they have to be separated, the latter fighting the former, & charging them with having made all the trouble.

Always sincerely
Thomas Hardy.

I write in great haste, to catch the morning post for you to get this in the evening. T.H.

Text MS. BL.
Masterman: Charles Frederick Gurney Masterman (1874–1927), historian and politician; *D.N.B.* Currently Chancellor of the Duchy of Lancaster, he was given, on the outbreak of war, special responsibility for propaganda. *the meeting*: at Wellington House, London, 2 Sept 1914. A group of leading writers had been invited to participate in the drafting of a manifesto on British war aims; see *LY*, 163, and letter of 10 Sept 14 to Schuster. *your official position*: as Librarian to the House of Lords. *excluded you*: Gosse had not been invited to the meeting; on 11 Sept 14 (DCM), however, he reported that Masterman had now asked for his co-operation.

To SIR CLAUD SCHUSTER

Sept 10: 1914

Dear Sir Claud Schuster:

In returning the manifesto signed, with every word of which I agree, it occurs to me to ask if the phrase "only half emancipated and still struggling to the light" as applied to Russia is *politic* at the present moment, considering that the document is sure to be translated into Russian; & whether the words might not be deleted without weakening the argument, though they are, of course, quite true.

Yours faithfully
T.H.

Text MS. (pencil draft) DCM.
Schuster: Sir Claud Schuster (1869–1956), senior civil servant; *D.N.B.* *the manifesto*: Schuster (9 Sept 14, DCM) enclosed the draft manifesto drawn up following the 2 September meeting (see letter of 10 Sept 14 to Gosse) by Anthony Hope Hawkins, Gilbert Murray, and Sir Owen Seaman. The final printed statement, 'The War: Declaration of British Authors' (copy, DCM), was signed by TH and 51 others; it appeared in *The Times*, 18 Sept 1914. *be deleted*: a telegram from Schuster to TH (10 Sept 14, DCM) asks him to consider the paragraph on Russia as already omitted.

To CLEMENT SHORTER

FROM THO. HARDY, | MAX GATE, | DORCHESTER. | 10: 9: 1914

My dear Shorter:

Just a hasty line (that you may get it this evening) to say that certainly you have permission to print the 12 copies of the poem that you speak of. Ah, when the war is over, you say! Echo answers When.

Faithfully yours
T. Hardy.

Text Facsimile in Shorter's privately printed pamphlet of *Song of the Soldiers* (1914).
the poem: TH's 'Song of the Soldiers', later retitled '"Men Who March Away" (Song of the Soldiers)', was pub. in *The Times*, 9 Sept 14, together with a statement that copyright in the poem was not reserved. Shorter followed up this first privately printed pamphlet of TH material with six others, until TH refused to give further permissions; see Purdy, 349–50, and letter of 6 May 16. *Echo answers When*: adapted from the last line of Canto XXVII of Byron's *Bride of Abydos*.

To SYDNEY COCKERELL

Max Gate | 11: 9: 1914

My dear Cockerell:

I am glad the song pleased you. In writing for the many there is always of course the difficulty of avoiding banality without losing popularity, except in a dialect song.

You may possibly have suspected the "Friend with the musing eye" to be the author himself.

I am sorry to hear of the missing undergraduates.

Always sincerely
T.H.

Text MS. Taylor; envelope Adams.
"Friend . . . eye": the second line of the second stanza of 'Song of the Soldiers'; cf. *LY*, 246. *missing undergraduates*: presumably from Jesus, Cockerell's Cambridge college.

To ARTHUR SYMONS

Max Gate | 13 Sept 1914

My dear Symons:

I am glad to hear that you liked the verses, though I fear they were not free from some banalities which it is difficult to keep out of lines which are meant to appeal to the man in the street, & not to "a few friends" only. The army badly wants some new marching songs, being at present compelled to fall back on those that have no bearing on circumstances. There are, of course, good *old* military songs, but they are unknown to the modern Tommy.

Sincerely yours
Thomas Hardy.

Text MS. Colby.
Symons: Arthur Symons, poet and critic (see II.90); TH had corresponded with him since the 1890s. *"a few friends"*: perhaps an allusion to Abraham Cowley, 'The Mistress, or Love Verses', 'May I a small house, and large garden have!/And a few friends, and many books, both true, . . .'

To EDGAR LANE

MAX GATE, | DORCHESTER. | 14th. September 1914

Dear Mr Lane:

Use it certainly. There is no copyright. In my previous reply I thought non-copyright matter would not serve the purpose. I enclose corrections of two oversights.

Yours very truly,
T. Hardy.

Stanza 3, line 5:—
for, "set us rueing," read, "leave us rueing".
Stanza 4, line 5:—
for, "March we," read "Press we".

Text MS. (typewritten) Texas.
Lane: Edgar Alfred Lane, Dorchester musician and composer; see III.23. *Use it*: TH's 'Song of the Soldiers' (see letter of 10 Sept 14 to Shorter); Lane's setting was pub. in London ('E. Ashdown, for the Author') later in 1914, with a dedication to FEH.

To NEWMAN FLOWER

FROM THO. HARDY, | MAX GATE, | DORCHESTER. | 18: 9: 1914

Many thanks. Hope the Dorset Annual will be a success.

T.H.

Text MS. (correspondence card) Texas.
Dorset Annual: see letter of 2 Apr 14.

To CLEMENT SHORTER

MAX GATE, | DORCHESTER. | 22nd. September 1914.

My dear Shorter:

The song of the soldiers—"Men who march away"—has been set to music by a composer,—Mr Edgar Lane—who has a school of music in this town, and gives concerts, etc. in the county. I think the tune a very catching one, which may possibly be popular if known. Soldiers' Songs are badly wanted in the army, and I should like this to be published. Before asking elsewhere I (by agreement with the composer) write to know if you would like to issue the music and words in the pages of the Sphere or Tatler, in the way songs are printed in the Queen and other papers. The object being to get it known I can offer it you for serial use free of charge.

Believe me,

Yours sincerely,
Thomas Hardy.

P.S. Many thanks for the reprint of the song, which I ought to have acknowledged before.

Text MS. (typewritten) BL.
set to music: see letter of 14 Sept 14. *Sphere or Tatler*: Shorter, as editor of these magazines, seems not to have adopted TH's suggestion. *reprint*: see letter to Shorter of 10 Sept 14.

To CLEMENT SHORTER

FROM THO. HARDY, | MAX GATE, | DORCHESTER. | Thursday. [24 September 1914]

Many thanks for letter. The music will reach you by this post.

T.H.

Text MS. (postcard) Univ. of Kentucky. *Date* From postmark.
The music: see letter of 22 Sept 14.

To EDWARD CLODD

Max Gate | Friday. [25 September 1914?]

My dear Clodd:

Best thanks for letter & good opinion of the Song. It has been set to music, & may possibly be published.

We are continually getting evidences of the war, if we go outside our gate, & even if we don't. Two days ago we were motoring in a district near here that used to be absolutely secluded, & we came upon "Kitchener's army" of recruits in camp. Some thousands marched past us on their way back from bathing in Lulworth Cove. They were in large part young miners from the north. When will this ghastly business come to an end!

Always sincerely
Thomas Hardy.

Text MS. BL.
published: i.e., as a song with a musical setting; see letter of 22 Sept 14. *"Kitchener's army"*: Field Marshal Lord Kitchener (1850–1916; *D.N.B.*), currently Secretary of State for War with responsibility for mobilizing the British army.

To SYDNEY COCKERELL

MAX GATE, | DORCHESTER. | 26: 9: 1914

My dear Cockerell:

Many thanks for sending Cramb's book, which we have now finished reading. He had evidently an inordinate admiration for the German idea of power, though he tries to be a good Englishman. What a dreamer he seems to have been. His attempts to elevate the vulgar ambition of German Junkers to the height of a noble national aspiration shows this: also his blindness to Napoleon's true character.

If facts bore out his theories the book would be a weighty discourse. But it seems to me that Nietzsche, Treitske, Cramb, & all of the school (if it can be called a school) insanely regard life as a thing improvable by force to immaculate gloriousness, when all the time life's inseparable conditions allow only clumsy opportunities for amelioration by plodding compromises & contrivances.

By the by it is rather rough on Kant, Schopenhauer, &c., to be swept into one net of condemnation with Nietzsche, &c, when those philosophers & the latter are as poles asunder; though I see this done by Christian writers in the papers. The truth is that in ethics Kant, Schopr &c. are nearer to Christianity than they are to Nsche.

We have had a few motor rides during the late magnificent weather. Kind regards.

Sincerely yours
Thomas Hardy.

Text MS. Taylor.
Cramb's book: John Adam Cramb (1862–1913), historian; author of *Germany and England* (London, 1914). *Nietzsche*: Friedrich Wilhelm Nietzsche (1844–1900), German philosopher; see *LY*, 160. *Treitske*: TH presumably means Heinrich von Treitschke (1834–96), German historian. *Kant*: Immanuel Kant (1724–1804), German philosopher. *clumsy*: TH wrote 'clumsly'. *Schopenhauer*: Arthur Schopenhauer (1788–1860), German philosopher. *motor rides*: see *LY*, 163–4; the Hardys did not own a car but hired the one owned by Hermann Lea (see letter of 6 Mar 15), with Lea himself as driver.

To HARLEY GRANVILLE BARKER

[27] Sept . . . 1914

Dear Mr Granville Barker:

I should be much interested in your producing The Dynasts at your theatre. Of course, at first, I never contemplated the possibility of staging it, or any part of it, though many people have written from time to time since it came out to suggest that it might be done. And since the war broke out people write & say, "It's The Dynasts over again!".

I am quite willing to leave the abridgement & arrangement to you, & will examine any copy you may have marked for the purpose. I suppose that the Spirits would simply be heard singing and speaking in large hollow voices from the sky. If instead of sending the scheme you are preparing you would like to come down here & stay over the night with us to talk it over we should be delighted. Or I could run up to London for a few hours any day, should you prefer that, as I often do so.

Nothing certainly could be more apt than The Dynasts at the present time. And whatever the virtues or defects of its adaptation, the public and the papers would probably regard its production as so timely and patriotic that they would feel bound to make it a success. However, we will not anticipate.

Yours very sincerely

P.S. My wife says that if Mrs Barker would like also to run down with you she would be much pleased—as should I.

Text MS. (pencil draft) DCM. *Date* From transcript of same letter in DCM.
Barker: Harley Granville Barker, actor, producer, dramatist, and critic; see III.257. He wrote to TH 25 Sept 14 (DCM). *at your theatre*: the Kingsway Theatre, London; Barker's production of *The Dynasts* opened there on 25 Nov 1914 and ran for 72 performances. See *LY*, 164–5. *marked for the purpose*: TH subsequently agreed to participate directly in the

adaptation; see letters of 4 and 9 Oct 14. *of its adaptation*: the DCM transcript reads 'of it, or its adaptation'. *Mrs Barker*: Lillah McCarthy, the actress; see IV.100.

To F. A. DUNEKA

Sept 28. 1914

Dear Mr Duneka:

In reply to your inquiry: The song "Men who march away" (of which I enclose a correct copy as you may like to see one) is intended to appear in a new volume of poems of mine that Messrs Macmillan propose to bring out this autumn. It will be the last in the book, so will naturally follow the others, being last in date. This volume will of course be added to every set of my books. I do not quite see how you can put this song into any other volume; but perhaps I mistake your meaning.

Since correcting a year ago a part of "The Dynasts" for your Wessex edition of my collected works in prose and verse I have not heard from you of the progress of the edition or seen any copy of it.

[Space of a line]

It is a great solace to us in England that the American people are so clear-sighted in respect of the prime-movers and aggressors in the present war. You will know what a man of peace I am, & how ugly a thing war at its best is to me; but events proved to me with startling rapidity that there was no other course for us but to fight. The transparent falsity of the charge that we purposed war, and might otherwise have prevented it, is shown in a dozen ways—not the least of which was our being so unprepared.

Yours truly

Text MS. (pencil draft) DCM.

Duneka: Francis A. Duneka, American publisher, general manager of Harper & Brothers; see IV.254. *new volume*: *Satires of Circumstance*; Duneka (15 Sept 14, DCM) had asked in which vol. of his 'collected set' TH would like to have the new poem included. *your Wessex edition*: Harper & Brothers' version of the English Wessex edn. was the limited signed 'Autograph Edition' of 1915; see Purdy, 286. [*Space of a line*]: TH's words and square brackets. The second paragraph of Duneka's letter spoke of the American people as united in their sympathy with the British, and TH was here instructing FEH, as typist, to separate the business part of his own letter from what he clearly thought of as the 'propaganda' part, to which Duneka might conceivably give wider circulation.

To HARLEY GRANVILLE BARKER

MAX GATE, | DORCHESTER. [Late September 1914]

It has occurred to me that the Spirits & Choruses *might* be visible figures, if that would help the scenes, & relieve the monotony of invisible voices. But I have not thought this out.

T.H.

Text MS. (correspondence card) McGill Univ. *Date* See letter of 27 Sept 14.

To R. A. SCOTT-JAMES

Max Gate | 2: 10: '14

Dear Mr Scott James:

Herewith receipt. Many thanks for the trouble you took about American rights.

I was sorry you had to close down; but who wd have expected such a war to come so suddenly. If you start again, please try another title. I never cared for the one you adopted.

Sincerely yrs
T. Hardy.

Text MS. Texas.
American rights: see letter to Scott-James of 25 Jan 14; it is not clear whether TH's two poems were in fact separately pub. in the United States. *close down*: the last issue of the *New Weekly* was dated 22 Aug 1914.

To HARLEY GRANVILLE BARKER

Max Gate | Oct 4: 1914

My dear Mr Barker:

I send back the Forescene and Scene 1, modified as I fancy you wished, with a new Prologue to connect your patriotic effort with the present war. Please make any changes you like.

I will send the ensuing scenes as I get through them.

Sincerely yours
Thomas Hardy.

P.S. About the length. Shall I make cuts in speeches where it can be done without harm? T.H.

Text MS. Adams.
patriotic effort: Barker's production of *The Dynasts*; see letter of 27 Sept 14. *get through them*: Barker had evidently sent TH a typed transcription (see letter of 15 Oct 14) of the scenes which he had selected and which TH had undertaken to adapt to stage purposes.

To HARLEY GRANVILLE BARKER

Max Gate | 9: 10: 1914

Dear Mr Granville Barker:

I am sending along the sheets up to the end of Part II.

You will of course write in details of exits, entrances, & business generally.

At first I wrote the second part of the cellar scene as if viewed from without, with Napoleon &c., visible, & the fugitives looking out through the window. But I altered it. I am glad you think of having him seen after all.

Sometimes I am not clear whether the curtain of each scene rises before the Reader begins to explain circumstances, or after. Please correct any errors on this account.

Sincerely yours
Thomas Hardy.

P.S. I have received Mr Drinkwater's letter on business arrangements, & am answering it. It is quite satisfactory. T.H.

Text MS. Adams.
the sheets: see letter of 4 Oct 14. *the Reader*: introduced into the stage version as a linking device; the part was played by Henry Ainley. *Mr Drinkwater's*: manager of the Kingsway Theatre; see letter to him of 10 Nov 14.

To RHODA SYMONS

MAX GATE, | DORCHESTER. | 12 Oct 1914

Dear Mrs Symons:

I fear that "The Dynasts" is rather a frail reed in the circumstances, even if it should really be produced. The object being mainly a patriotic one the actors are to be asked to take merely nominal salaries, & neither manager nor author thinks of making money by it. I will however tell Mr Barker what you say. Believe me

Yours sincerely
Thomas Hardy.

Text MS. Kenneth A. Lohf.
Symons: Rhoda Symons (see III.353), wife of Arthur Symons; she had asked TH to try and get her a part in Barker's production.

To HARLEY GRANVILLE BARKER

FROM THO. HARDY, | MAX GATE, | DORCHESTER. | 14 Oct '14

Dear Mr Barker:

I send particulars of the Dynasts required by Thring. Any further information can be got from the Macmillans.

Sincerely yrs
T.H.

Thring's letter returned.

The Dynasts

Part I printed and published 1904 simultaneously in England and America by the Messrs Macmillan, so that copyright was secured.

Part II (1906) and Part III (1908) issued in America, but not printed there, it having been considered that copyright in Part I would be sufficient protection.

No transfer of any right to stage the drama has been made in America—or in England till now to Mr Granville Barker.

It would probably be well to copyright the play as adapted, by simultaneous acting.

Text MS. (correspondence card) Yale; enclosure (pencil draft) DCM.
Thring: of the Incorporated Society of Authors; see letter of 19 Jan 14.

To HARLEY GRANVILLE BARKER

Max Gate, | Dorchester. | 15th. October 1914.

Dear Mr. Barker:

I send a few lines to link the two "Victory" scenes; but please alter as you choose, as I am a child at this adaptation.

Also as to the other scenes—cut where you wish, for it would never do to make the play boring.

I also send the pages so far as I have got, and am now at a halt—not understanding your notes on typescript as to the battle of Waterloo—(page 501 book)—that "one narrative should connect these scenes".

Are they to be separated scenes as in the book, or is the battle to be one scene in which French and English enter alternately? When I know this I will resume and soon finish.

I enclose what I fancy would be a proper form for the announcements to take.

Always sincerely,
T. Hardy.

Why not go back to the old style, and have long playbills in consideration of the number of characters? T.H.

Text Typed transcript DCM.
"Victory" scenes: *The Dynasts,* Part First, Act V, Scenes 2 and 4. (*page 501 book*): i.e., p. 501 of the 1-vol. edn. of *The Dynasts*.

To HARLEY GRANVILLE BARKER

MAX GATE, | DORCHESTER. | 21st. October 1914.

Dear Mr Barker:

I am sending back the conclusion, which I have gone through. You will have to twist and chop it about pretty much, I imagine, before it will do.

If you don't consider "abridged and adapted" quite correct, you might say "abridged and arranged"—which is quite true. I have been much struck by the ingenuity you have shown all through.

I don't think it would be well or in the interests of the production to publish an acting edition, even if it were practicable. It would be better and more attractive I think to sell to the audience a synopsis of the arrangement—giving the scenes *seriatim*, and some of the reader's words perhaps, with the photographs you speak of.

Always sincerely yours,
Thomas Hardy.

Text Typed transcript DCM.
and arranged": TH is discussing the form in which Barker's part in the adaptation of *The Dynasts* should be recorded in the playbill.

To HARLEY GRANVILLE BARKER

28 Oct. 1914

Concerning The Dynasts

Dear Mr Barker:

I Sent yesterday:

1. The few additional lines you asked for, to fill up time, and link scenes. With one or two other notes.
2. The music of the two songs "Budmouth Dears" and "My Love's gone a-fighting".

The other songs, viz: "Buonaparty" (the marching song of the soldiers when the coach overtakes them), and "The Night of Trafalgar"—both in Part I, can be bought at Boosey's, 295 Regent Street—so I don't send copies of them. The published titles are:

1. "Buonaparty." Song. Words by T.H. Music by Ralph Vaughan Williams.
2. "Song of Trafalgar". Words by T. H. Music by Cyril Scott.

If you cannot get them there, I could send my copy of them; but I suppose you will be able to.

I think that the more songs you have the better, & if you like I can send the music of "Men who march away!"—the Song of the Soldiers that appeared in "The Times" the other day. It might perhaps be sung between the Parts, or at the end. However you know best.

The realities of the present war are very distressing. I think you are doing the best you can in the circumstances.

Our kind regards to Mrs Granville Barker.

Sincerely yours

Text MS. (pencil draft) DCM.
Concerning The Dynasts: TH probably added this heading at a later date. *I Sent*: TH seems originally to have begun 'Sent yesterday'. *"Budmouth Dears"*: from *The Dynasts*, Part Third, II.i; it had been set to music by the Dorchester composer Boynton Smith. *a-fighting*": from Part Third, V.vi; it is not clear what setting TH supplied. *Williams*: for both the song and the composer see III.358. *Scott*: Cyril Meir Scott (1879–1970), composer; *D.N.B.* *be able to*: Barker seems largely to have disregarded TH's specifications as to the music to be used; the playbill of the production states that the songs were 'set to folk-airs selected and adapted by Cecil Sharp'.

To LADY HOARE

MAX GATE, | DORCHESTER. | 28: 10: 1914

My dear Lady Hoare:

I have just heard from my wife that Harry has gone to the war, & I sympathize so much with you & Sir Henry that I must write a line to tell you so. It is really terrible to see what is going on around us—all wrought by the madness of one man: at least, that's how it seems to me, but it will be 50 years before we get to the bottom of the matter to the true cause.

However, there is no reason for despair, & doubtless we shall see H. marching about the grounds at Stourhead again in good time.

Sincerely yours
Thomas Hardy.

Text MS. Wiltshire Record Office.
from my wife: FEH was in frequent correspondence with Lady Hoare. *Harry*: Henry Colt Arthur Hoare (1888–1917), the Hoares' only child. *of one man*: i.e., the German Kaiser. *in good time*: see, however, the letter of 26 Dec 17.

To DOROTHY ALLHUSEN

MAX GATE, | DORCHESTER. | 30: 10: 1914

My dear Dorothy:

I have heard from the Kingsway Theatre to-day that "The Dynasts" is to be produced between the 12th and the 21st of November, if all's well. The exact day I will let you know later on. I have no active hand in the production, everything being arranged by Mr Granville Barker, but I shall be able to get seats for you & Lady St Helier the first night, & should like to do so, if she will go. I myself shall not be there, but I expect my wife will.

I am not sure you will care for it, as it will be unlike an ordinary play.

Ever affectly
Thomas Hardy.

We have more than two thousand German prisoners here, & the town is full of soldiers still. We are not allowed to have Belgians, this being a prohibited area. T.H.

Text MS. Garrick Club.
if all's well: the first night was, in fact, put back to 25 Nov 1914. *Lady St Helier*: her mother. *my wife will*: FEH did go; see letter of 22 Nov 14 to Drinkwater. *to have Belgians*: Mrs. Allhusen was characteristically active in the cause of refugees from the German invasion of Belgium.

To CLEMENT SHORTER

MAX GATE, | DORCHESTER. | 6th. November 1914.

Dear Shorter:

I cannot very well formally authorize you to reprint letters that I hurriedly wrote for the moment only on matters on which one's opinion is liable to be modified by new information, although of course you can reprint the letters if you wish to. I therefore ask you to take out the sentence deleted. For the same reason I cannot correct the proof.

I hope you will not be disappointed with Barker's adaptation of scenes from The Dynasts. I do not quite see how he is going to manage the job. I don't suppose I shall be at the production.

Sincerely yours
Thomas Hardy.

Text MS. (typewritten) Adams.
if you wish to: a few days later Shorter did pub. *Letters on the War*, a privately printed pamphlet comprising two letters by TH on the German bombardment of Rheims Cathedral which had previously appeared in the *Manchester Guardian*; see Purdy, 159–60. *sentence deleted*: presumably a statement in the colophon to the effect that TH had authorized publication of the pamphlet.

To HARLEY GRANVILLE BARKER

FROM THO. HARDY, | MAX GATE, | DORCHESTER. | 8 Nov. 1914

This song might be useful in filling an interval. It has not yet been published (except the words in The Times).

T.H.

Text MS. (correspondence card) Texas.
This song: 'Song of the Soldiers' (see letter of 10 Sept 14 to Shorter); TH also supplied Edgar Lane's setting (see letter of 22 Nov 14 to Lane).

To HARRY POUNCY

FROM THO. HARDY, | MAX GATE, | DORCHESTER. [8 November 1914]

Many thanks. I thought you once said you had a MS. of some kind which ought to be destroyed, which is why I mentioned it.

T.H.

Text MS. (postcard) Gordon N. Ray.
MS. of some kind: perhaps of the inductions which TH had written in 1907 for Pouncy's dramatization of scenes from *Far from the Madding Crowd*; see III.281.

To A. E. DRINKWATER

MAX GATE, | DORCHESTER. | 10th. November 1914.

Dear Mr Drinkwater:

I hear that the play is maturing, so if you could let me have three tickets for friends, as you kindly offered to do, I should feel obliged.

It has occurred to me that if stalls were sent to Mrs Asquith she might come—and possibly the Prime Minister. Anyhow I leave you and Mr Barker to judge.

I hope to be at the rehearsal on Monday next—if you will let me know the hour.

Yours very truly,
Thomas Hardy.

Text MS. (typewritten) Colby.
Drinkwater: Albert Edwin Drinkwater (1852–1923), actor and playwright, currently general manager for Harley Granville Barker and Lillah McCarthy of the Kingsway, Court, and Little Theatres. *Mrs Asquith*: Margot Asquith, active in letters and politics; see III.131. *the Prime Minister*: her husband, Herbert Henry Asquith; see III.353. He did go to see *The Dynasts*; see letter of 23 Dec 14.

To SIR FREDERICK MACMILLAN

MAX GATE, | DORCHESTER. | 10th. November 1914

Dear Sir Frederick:

I am pleased at hearing news of the book. I do not, of course, expect a large sale at this critical time, but it may be well for you to have brought it out, as it will secure it in your list, and, if anything should happen to me, you will then be able to include it with my collected works without difficulty.

I send a few names and addresses to which I should feel obliged to you for sending copies.

I don't know what arrangements you have made for America, but as some of the poems are already copyright there (having been printed in American Magazines) I suppose the volume is secured.

You may have seen paragraphs in the papers stating that some scenes from "The Dynasts" are to be presented at the Kingsway Theatre by Granville Barker. It seems that it was a question of producing something martial, bearing on English victories; or shutting the theatre altogether, and throwing many poor people out of employment. As nobody expects to make money out of a play at present, and the actors have agreed to take half-salaries, the royalty to author is nominal, even in the event of success.

However, it struck me that such a production might send people to the book, and I agreed to his doing it, although I confess I don't quite see how he is going to get over some of the difficulties of a drama which I stated in the preface to the book *could not* be acted! Certain plans for accomplishing it which he has invented, and explained to me, are highly ingenious, and unlike anything seen on the English stage hitherto. I daresay you know Mr and Mrs Barker, and I hope they will send you tickets. Anyhow I should like you to see it, if you can. The first night is Nov. 20 or 21. If you should be going away perhaps George or Maurice might go?

I don't know if Mr Barker has asked you to let them have some copies of the book for sale in the theatre. He thought of doing so.

Believe me,

Yours very truly,
Thomas Hardy.

Text MS. (typewritten) BL.
the book: TH's *Satires of Circumstance*, pub. by Macmillan 17 Nov 1914. *sending copies*: those receiving copies direct from the publisher seem to have included John Masefield, Lord Crewe, A. C. Benson, and A. E. Housman. *for America*: Macmillan reported (12 Nov 14, Macmillan letterbooks, BL) that the American market would be supplied through his firm's New York office, as in the case of *Time's Laughingstocks*. *highly ingenious*: in the event, however, the production did not meet with TH's approval; see *LY*, 165. *if you can*: Macmillan did go, expressing his enjoyment in a letter to TH of 29 Nov 14 (DCM). *George*: George Macmillan. *Maurice*: Maurice Macmillan; see letter of 16 June 15.

To EDMUND GOSSE

MAX GATE, | DORCHESTER. | Nov 11: 1914

My dear Gosse:

I am sorry that I was prevented writing yesterday.

It is extremely good & hospitable of you to ask me to dine. It will be an interesting occasion I am sure. But I, alas, see no prospect of being able to be in London at that date. I used to go up specially for any attractive gathering like this of yours, but I find I cannot now stand it in winter, having been more & more troubled with a weak throat which gets caught by the London air & leads to all sorts of ills.

I shall be sending you something in a few days.

Have you seen in the papers that Granville Barker is going to produce at the Kingsway Theatre next week scenes from "The Dynasts"? It is all his own doing, & I don't know what the result will be. I have no supervision of the rehearsals. You probably know Mr Barker & may go to see it, but I do not guarantee anything in it, though it will certainly be curious, he having thought of some very ingenious arrangements.

Always sincerely
Thomas Hardy.

Text MS. BL.
sending you something: a copy of *Satires of Circumstance* (Adams) inscribed 'To / Edmund Gosse: / the mixture as before, of unstable / fancies, conjectures, & contradictions: / from / Thomas Hardy. / Nov: 1914'.

To HARLEY GRANVILLE BARKER

FROM THO. HARDY, | MAX GATE, | DORCHESTER. | 13: 11: '14

Would it be advisable to print the Prologue on the playbill, so that it would be quoted by papers & the object of the Play made clear to the public. No answer necessary as you must be worked to death.

T.H.

Text MS. (correspondence card) Texas.
on the playbill: TH's suggestion was adopted; see Purdy, 173.

To FLORENCE HARDY

Max Gate | Sat. 2.30 [14 November 1914]

Dearest best:

Your letter came by the mid-day post, & I am writing to get this off by the afternoon clearing, or you will not have it till Monday morning. I also had your telegram last night.

I was so glad to know that your journey was comfortable. It was very dismal after you had gone: the rain increased & kept on till late in the afternoon. I went with Wessie to Froom Hill, & he behaved with perfect honour: afterwards Amy & Hester took him to Dorchester. He wanders about the house into the West bedroom & up to the attic looking for you.

I have had a pleasant letter from Sir Courtenay Ilbert, Clerk to the House of Commons, about ballotting for the Militia in old times. Hermann Lea called this morning, but did not stay long. Mrs Sutro writes & hopes we will call.

How strange that you should have met Mrs Allhusen. We are thinking of lighting the conservatory stove to-night, as it is colder. I have heard nothing from the theatre. Don't get wet to-morrow. K. has written to say she has such a bad cold she cannot come out of doors, so she will not be here to tea. Kind love to them all.

Ever your affectte husband
T.

I have posted on to you three letters. T.

Text MS. (with envelope) Purdy. *Date* From postmark.
your journey: to Enfield, to visit her family. *Wessie*: i.e., Wessex, FEH's dog. *Amy & Hester*: servants at Max Gate. *Ilbert*: Sir Courtenay Peregrine Ilbert (1841–1924), clerk to the House of Commons 1902–21; *D.N.B.* Ilbert had a special responsibility for the drafting of parliamentary legislation, and it appears from his letter (12 Nov 14, DCM) that the government was considering the use of balloting procedures for the purposes of war-time recruitment. *Lea*: see letter of 6 Mar 15. *Mrs Sutro*: Esther Sutro, painter, wife of Alfred Sutro, playwright (see II.250); she wrote from London. *K.*: TH's sister Katharine.
them all: FEH's parents and sisters.

To SIR SIDNEY COLVIN

MAX GATE, | DORCHESTER. | 20: 11: 1914

My dear Colvin:

We return here to find your kind invitation awaiting us. I have attended one or two rehearsals of "The Dynasts"—or rather scenes therefrom—since Granville Barker wished me to do so; but shall probably not go up again: otherwise it would have been very pleasant to call on you & Lady Colvin. The fact is, Barker is doing it entirely in his own way, & I have no responsibility. I must admit that his method is most ingenious & interesting.

Sincerely yours
Thomas Hardy.

Text MS. (correspondence card) Berg.

To DOROTHY ALLHUSEN

MAX GATE, | DORCHESTER. | 22: 11: 1914

My dear Dorothy:

You may have seen in the papers that the first performance of "Scenes from the Dynasts" is on Wednesday night next, the 25th, & I have told Mr Granville Barker's manager to send two tickets to your mother at Portland Place, one for her & one for you. I thought this would be a safer plan than to send them here for me to send on to you. I hope this will be carried out all right, & that you & she will be able to go.

My wife may possibly be there, not far from you, though this weather in London half kills me, & I doubt if I shall be able to go.

Ever affectionately
Thomas Hardy.

Text MS. Texas.
Barker's manager: see letter of 22 Nov 14 to Drinkwater.

To HARLEY GRANVILLE BARKER

MAX GATE, | DORCHESTER. | 22nd. November '14.

Dear Mr Barker:

In the extreme uncertainty as to when we shall get to London—or if at all—occasioned by this cold weather, which, in London, gives me an ulcerated throat, we think it best not to accept your kind invitation to dine with you and Mrs Barker this week. I think there is no train that would take us up to tomorrow's rehearsal, but if we should be there Tuesday we will appear about seven for the evening rehearsal you mention. You have the whole thing so well in hand that my being there is not absolutely necessary, though I should like to see the performance,

Yours very sincerely,
Thomas Hardy.

Text MS. (typewritten) Yale.
evening rehearsal: TH did attend rehearsals of *The Dynasts* (see letter of 20 Nov 14 and *LY*, 164), but it is not clear that he was present on this occasion.

To A. E. DRINKWATER

MAX GATE, | DORCHESTER. | 22nd November 1914.

Dear Mr Drinkwater:

The idea of arranging for carrying out cinema productions in the way you mention seems a good one, if such should be required. Should any application of the kind be made to me I will refer them to you as requested.

I promised two seats to two old friends of mine—Lady St. Helier and her daughter Mrs Allhusen. If you could kindly send them direct to Lady St. Helier (52 Portland Place) it would save time. I am not sure what I shall be doing. In case I cannot be there could Mrs Hardy have the next seat to them?

Yours sincerely
Thomas Hardy.

Text MS. (typewritten) Colby.
a good one: Drinkwater had suggested (18 Nov 14, DCM) that the scenes of the production might be filmed and shown in theatres with actors present to speak the lines of the Reader and the two Chorus figures; see, however, letter of 6 Nov 15. *next seat to them?*: FEH went up to London by herself for the first night of *The Dynasts*; according to her letter of 1 Dec 14 (Colby) to Rebekah Owen (see letter of 15 Oct 15), she sat next to John Masefield (see letter of 15 Sept 16) and his wife—and found some of the scenes 'too harrowing'.

To EDGAR LANE

MAX GATE, | DORCHESTER. | 22nd. November '14.

Dear Mr Lane:

I am much pleased to hear that your music to "Men who March Away" has been published, and will be sung at the Patriotic Concert. I have sent it up in MS. to the Kingsway Theatre in London, with your name as composer, (where they are going to produce on Wednesday an arrangement of "The Dynasts") asking them to sing it during an interval in the play, if they can. I don't know whether they will do so or not.

Yours sincerely,
Thomas Hardy.

Text MS. (typewritten) DCM.
published: see letter of 14 Sept 14. *Patriotic Concert*: held in Dorchester 24 Nov 1914 to raise money for the Dorset Regiment's 'Comforts Fund'. *sent it up*: see letter of 8 Nov 14 to Barker.

To KATE GIFFORD

MAX GATE, | DORCHESTER. | 23 Nov: 1914

Dear Miss Gifford:

I am sending you my new volume of poems—not because I think you will care for a large number of them, but because it contains some that relate to Emma. From what I have found among her memoranda I see that she had a great affection for you & your sister. In later years an unfortunate mental aberration for which she was not responsible altered her much, & made her cold in her correspondence with friends & relatives, but this was contrary to her real nature, & I myself quite disregard it in thinking of her. She was, as you know, most childlike & trusting formerly. You may be able to perceive some of her characteristics in the poems about her.

I forget if I informed you that I have put up a tablet to her memory in St Juliot Church. I have not been able to go & see it, but they tell me it looks well. If you ever go to Boscastle you may be inclined to go up the valley to the church & see it yourself.

With kindest regards

Sincerely yours
Thomas Hardy.

Text MS. C. H. Gifford.
relate to Emma: notably the section of *Satires of Circumstance* entitled 'Poems of 1912–13'. *memoranda*: neither Miss Gifford nor her sister is mentioned by name in ELH's *Some Recollections*, ed. Evelyn Hardy and Robert Gittings (London, 1961), but their mother, ELH's aunt, is said to have 'loved to have the children, cousins of the family, to come together at her house and know each other' (29); other diaries and papers of ELH's, however, were destroyed after her death. *her real nature*: Miss Gifford replied (25 Nov 14, DCM) that it must have been 'very sad' for TH that ELH's mind 'became so unbalanced latterly', although she did not think that any of the Giffords had 'resented her not keeping up a correspondence after she married'. *a tablet*: see *LY*, 156, and IV.275.

To EDWARD CLODD

Max Gate | Monday [30 November 1914]

My dear Clodd:

Many thanks for your letter about the poems.

As for The Dynasts, or rather scenes from it, I have had very little to do with its production, the selection of the episodes shown, passages, arrangement, &c. being all Granville Barker's, & I am glad for his sake that the press has been so appreciative, for it was a courageous & patriotic venture of his to do it at a time when theatrical affairs are at such a low ebb that many managers think they must close their doors, & they would but for the distress among the poorer actors. On account of this I did not send a single complimentary ticket to friend or relative.

I am just recovering from a bad cold, which prevented my seeing the performance. It depends upon the length of its run whether I shall be in Town soon enough to see it at all.

Always sincerely
Thomas Hardy.

Text MS. Leeds. *Date* Supplied by Clodd on MS.
the poems: TH had sent him a copy of *Satires of Circumstance*. *so appreciative*: e.g., *The Times*, 19 Nov 1914, and *Athenaeum*, 28 Nov 1914; some of the later reviews were more critical. *to friend or relative*: see, however, letters of 10 and 22 Nov 14 to Drinkwater; TH is seeking to excuse his failure to send a ticket to Clodd himself.

To A. E. DRINKWATER

MAX GATE, | DORCHESTER. | 30th. November 1914.

Dear Mr Drinkwater:

I received today the box office returns for the two Saturday performances, but those you speak of for the three previous days as having been sent have not arrived.

I am glad that you think hopefully of the general result. I, myself, was prepared for any slackness on the part of the public owing to the times. My great wish is that Mr Barker should not suffer any pecuniary loss through his spirited and patriotic venture.

Please send the summaries on any day that may be convenient to you.

I, of course, hope to see the play as soon as possible. All the people who have written to me whose judgment is worth much are deeply impressed by the method of presentation.

With kind regards,

Yours sincerely,
Thomas Hardy.

Text MS. (typewritten) Colby.
the summaries: presumably the consolidated figures for box office returns to date.

To EDMUND GOSSE

MAX GATE, | DORCHESTER. | Dec 1: 1914

My dear Gosse:

As my wife will have told you, we were much interested in your going to the play. It was really generous of you & Mrs Gosse to insist on paying. I only hope G. Barker will not lose on the production, but it seems that almost all the theatres are starving under the present blight.

I return the playbill with the Prologue signed as you wished. (The cold I had last week gave me rheumatism in the shoulder & arm, which made writing painful: it has now gone off I am happy to say). I am afraid the lines were hardly worth signing, having nothing to do with the drama as a whole, & being just an effusion for the nonce to help the performance of what was staged mainly for patriotic & practical objects.

It is, indeed, rather a comical result of the good Barker's abridgement that I am made to appear thereby as orthodox as a church-warden, although he has, as you remark, been most loyal to the text & characterization in the parts selected. He has a wonderfully artistic instinct in drama.

Your letter on the poems was inspiriting. Certainly quote lines from the Swinburne one if you think them appropriate. I will see if I have any letters of his worth sending you.

Some—even many—of the pieces in the volume do not precisely express my attitude to certain matters nowadays—or rather they express what I would now prefer to leave unexpressed. They had, however, been printed in periodicals in past years, & I could hardly leave them out of the book, though they seem to myself harsh beside the others. There is too, in me, a little of Pilate's feeling: "What I have written I have written."

And so few of the critical trade recognize what you know well—a poem expresses a mood that sometimes ends with the very writing of it, & not a scientific conviction.

Always sincerely yours
Thomas Hardy.

I am *so* glad you like the 1912–1913 section. T.H.

Text MS. BL.
the Prologue: see letter of 13 Nov 14. *letter on the poems*: Gosse wrote 25 Nov 14 (DCM) to thank TH for sending *Satires of Circumstance* (see letter of 11 Nov 14) and to praise his 'imaginative kinship with Donne'. *quote ... Swinburne one*: Gosse had asked if he might quote the final stanza of 'A Singer Asleep' in his forthcoming biography of Swinburne (pub. 1917). *letters of his*: Gosse also asked if TH had any letters from Swinburne; for TH and Swinburne see I.165. *harsh beside the others*: TH is referring chiefly to the group of 'Satires of Circumstance'. *have written."*: John 19: 22.

To EDWIN STEVENS

MAX GATE, | DORCHESTER. | 2nd. December 1914.

Dear Mr Stevens:

I am afraid that the only opinion of any value to your friend on his literary work is that of a publisher's reader or magazine editor, if he wants to get it published. Mine would be given, however long a time I devoted to its consideration, from a point of view which is quite unlikely to be that of the general public. But as you say it is printed, perhaps it has already been published. If you send the book, or whatever it may be, I will endeavour to look it over.

Yours very truly,
T. Hardy.

Text MS. (typewritten) David Holmes.
Stevens: Edwin John Stevens, Dorchester civil servant and amateur actor; see IV. 190. *your friend*: unidentified, although Stevens may have been inquiring on his own behalf.

To AMY LOWELL

MAX GATE, | DORCHESTER. | 6 Dec. 1914

My dear Miss Lowell:

We were so glad to hear that you & Mrs Russell got back home so smoothly & comfortably. We talked of you frequently before you wrote, & wondered if you grew more uncomfortable as the noise of war waxed louder. It is evident now that you did not. The car, too: I hope its adventures were as mild as your own.

I fear I am late in thanking you for your kind gift of "Sword Blades & Poppy Seed," my correspondence having become fitful by the incidence upon all our lives here of this hideous European tragedy, the sinister feature of which is the barbarousness of the German methods, which seem to put the clock of civilization centuries back. It does not express the German nation at all, as I have imagined that people, who seem to be the victims of an unscrupulous military oligarchy. The whole thing is a mystery to thoughtful Englishmen.

However: of the poems I like those called "Music" & "A Lady". The Browningesque tragedies "The Foreigner" & "After hearing a Waltz" are arresting: the latter holds one from the first syllable to the last, & the metre & rhythm keep up the beat of the waltz admirably. This piece reminds me to say that, but for the difference of sex, critics might be asking you when you committed the murder—that is, if they are such geese as some of them are here, who in my case devoutly believe that everything written in the first person has been done personally.

I also like "The Captured Goddess", "The Tree of Scarlet Berries", & "Clear with Light". Whether I should have liked them still better rhymed I do not know.

The subject of "The Book of Hours" seems to me (I may not be right) somewhat too slight to support a poem of that length—charming fancy as it is—& would have had increased beauty if shorter.

But you will not require any criticism from me, even if I could make it real & well-balanced, which I cannot.

We trust that you feel by this time no sort of inconvenience from the accident at the hotel. My wife sends her kindest regards, & unites with me in wishing you & Mrs Russell a happy Christmas.

Sincerely yours
Thomas Hardy.

Text MS. (with envelope) Harvard.
Lowell: Amy Lowell (1874–1925), American poet and critic. *Mrs Russell*: Miss Lowell's friend Ada Russell, well-known as an actress under her maiden name of Ada Dwyer. *waxed louder*: they had visited Max Gate on 1 Aug 1914, just as the war in Europe was beginning, and anticipated difficulty in getting back to the United States; see *LY*, 190, and S. F. Damon, *Amy Lowell* (Boston, 1935), 240–1. *The car*: Miss Lowell had brought with her to England 'her maroon automobile, and one of her two chauffeurs with his maroon livery'; the moment England entered the war, 'with remarkable foresight, she had her automobile crated and sent home on the very next boat, so that it would not be commandeered' (Damon, 226, 242). *Poppy Seed,"*: Miss Lowell's *Sword Blades and Poppy Seed* (New York,

1914). *a Waltz*": i.e., 'After Hearing a Waltz by Bartók'. *with Light*": i.e., 'Clear, with Light Variable Winds'. *of that length*: 'The Book of Hours of Sister Clotilde' occupies some 20 pages of the first edn. *accident*: resulting in a sprained ankle.

To LASCELLES ABERCROMBIE

MAX GATE, | DORCHESTER. | 9: 12: 1914

Dear Mr Abercrombie:

I have a book of my poems waiting for you here, but I am not sure where to address it to you. So I send this note first, at a venture, to find you out.

You may remember calling on me unexpectedly, & my thinking you an interviewer!

A post-card with your abode on it will be sufficient. I have no directory.

Sincerely yours
Thomas Hardy.

Text MS. Texas.
Abercrombie: Lascelles Abercrombie (1881–1938), poet and critic; *D.N.B.* His *Thomas Hardy: A Critical Study* was pub. in 1912.

To GEORGE DEWAR

MAX GATE, | DORCHESTER. | 9 Dec. 1914

Dear Mr Dewar:

I raked together all the verses I could find to fill up my late volume—a heterogeneous lot!—& I fear I must pass over in silence the transit into next year, the times being too uncertain to inspire the right message—at least in one of my age who has just been through a bad cold. I hope that we shall see light ahead before long.

Warmest thanks for the generous review of the poems & criticism of the play, & with best wishes I am

Sincerely yours
Thomas Hardy.

Text MS. John Arlott.
Dewar: George Albemarle Bertie Dewar, currently editor of the *Saturday Review*; see IV.139. *review of the poems*: unsigned review of *Satires of Circumstance, Saturday Review*, 21 Nov 1914. *criticism of the play*: John Palmer's notice of *The Dynasts, Saturday Review*, 5 Dec 1914.

To GORDON GIFFORD

Max Gate | Sunday Dec 20. [1914]

Dear Gordon:

If you would like to see The Dynasts at the Kingsway Theatre present the enclosed card at the Box Office about 10 minutes before the performance. Evening performances at 8—matinées Wednesdays &

Saturdays at 2.30. The theatre is, as you probably know, just off Kingsway, in Great Queen Street, not far from the Holborn Restaurant.

We are expecting Lilian next Thursday. I hope you are well. Thanks for telegram of war news.

Yr affectte uncle
T. Hardy.

Text MS. Mrs. Ethel Skinner. *Date* From internal evidence.
expecting Lilian: Gordon Gifford's sister, ELH's niece; she spent Christmas at Max Gate, as did one of FEH's sisters.

To THE EDITORS OF THE *NORTH AMERICAN REVIEW*

MAX GATE, | DORCHESTER. | December 20th. 1914.

Dear Sirs:

I send herewith some verses on the Centenary of the North American Review which I hope may be of a character suited to its celebration; and I remain

Yours very truly,
Thomas Hardy.

The Editors, | North American Review.

Text MS. (typewritten) Harvard.
some verses: TH's 'A Hundred Years Since', *North American Review*, February 1915; see letter of Sept 14 to Harvey and Purdy, 317.

To CALEB SALEEBY

MAX GATE, | DORCHESTER. | Dec 21: 1914

Dear Sir:

I have read with much interest the lecture on "The Longest Price of War" that you kindly send: & its perusal does not diminish the gloom with which this ghastly business on the Continent fills me, as it fills so many. The argument would seem to favour conscription, since the inert, if not the unhealthy, would be taken, I imagine.

Your visits to The Dynasts show that, as Granville Barker foretold, thoughtful people would care about it. My own opinion when I saw it was that it was the only sort of thing likely to take persons of a musing turn into a theatre at this time.

I have not read M. Bergson's book, & if you should not find it troublesome to send your copy as you suggest, please do.

The theory of the Prime Force that I used in the Dynasts was published in Jan: 1904. The nature of the determinism embraced in the theory is that of a *Collective* Will; so that there is a proportion of the total will in each part of the whole, & each part has therefore, in strictness, *some* freedom, which would, in fact, be operative as such whenever the remaining great mass of will in the universe shd happen to be in equilibrium.

However, as the work is intended to be a poetic drama & not a philosophic treatise I did not feel bound to develope this.

The assumption of unconsciousness in the driving force is, of course, not new. But I think the view of the unconscious force as gradually *becoming* conscious: i.e. that consciousness is creeping further & further back towards the origin of force had never (so far as I know) been advanced before The Dynasts appeared.

But being only a mere impressionist I must not pretend to be a philosopher in a letter, & ask you to believe me

Sincerely yours
Thomas Hardy.

Dr Saleeby.

Text MS. (with envelope) Adams.
Saleeby: Caleb Williams Saleeby (1878–1940), doctor, eugenist, and reformer. *of War"*: it is not clear whether the lecture had been published or simply printed (or otherwise duplicated) by Saleeby himself. *favour conscription*: the 'Price' in Saleeby's title referred to the cost to the nation of losing so many of its finest men, all of them (at this stage of the war) volunteers; see also letter to Saleeby of 16 Mar 15. *unhealthy*: TH wrote 'unheathy'. *visits to The Dynasts*: mentioned in Saleeby's letter of 16 Dec 14 (DCM). *M. Bergson's book*: Saleeby asked if TH had read Henri Bergson's (1859–1941) *Creative Evolution*, Bergson's conception of the *élan vital* seeming to be very close to TH's idea of the Immanent Will; see letter to Saleeby of 7 Jan 15 and letter of 2 Feb 15.

To FLORENCE HENNIKER

MAX GATE, | DORCHESTER. | 23 Dec. 1914

My dear friend:

I have not written till now to thank you for your letter about the volume of poems, & I am glad that I combine with it by my delay a Christmas greeting which I wanted you to have from me. I sent the poems through the publishers because by doing so you received them 2 or 3 days sooner than they would have reached you if they had come here first. Of course I will write your name in them when I have opportunity.

At first I thought I would not send any copy to any friend owing to the harsh contrasts which the accidents of my life during the past few years had forced into the poems, & which I could not remove, so many of them having been printed in periodicals—those in fact that I liked least. And unfortunately they are the ones the papers have taken most notice of. My own favourites, that include all those in memory of Emma, have been mentioned little. The one to Florence was written when she was a mere acquaintance: I think she likes it. I am so glad that you like, "When I set out for Lyonnesse". It is exactly what happened 44 years ago.

We went to London last week to see The Dynasts. I had not seen it till then, except in an early rehearsal. It is much more impressive than I thought it would be: perhaps the present war makes one feel it more. Some people have been three times, they tell me. The actors themselves are very keen about it, & there are understudies 2 or 3 deep, on the chance of their being required. "Wessex" has developed a tendency to fight other dogs, quite to our surprise. We fancy he will get a nip from a big dog who lives near here, which will make him less bumptious.

Gosse's poem was among the few good ones that have been brought out by the war. At night here the sky is illuminated by the searchlights in Portland Roads, so we are kept in mind of the slaughter in progress. Mr Asquith went to The Dynasts one afternoon, & liked it much. I hope you keep well, & will have a cheerful Christmas.

Yr affectionate friend,
Tho H.

F. has gone to see my sisters, she wd send her love if she were here I know, & good Christmas wishes. T.H.

Text MS. DCM.
your letter: of 28 Nov 14 (transcript, DCM). *liked least*: i.e., the series of 'Satires of Circumstance'. *one to Florence*: 'After the Visit'; Mrs. Henniker said she liked it '*very* especially'. *44 years ago*: i.e., when TH left Higher Bockhampton for St. Juliot early in the morning of 7 March 1870; see *EL*, 86. *Gosse's poem*: 'To Our Dead', *The Times*, 20 Oct 1914. *Portland Roads*: the waters just off Portland and the naval dockyard at Weymouth. *Mr Asquith*: the Prime Minister; see letter of 10 Nov 14 to Drinkwater. *my sisters*: Mary and Katharine Hardy were now living, with their brother Henry, at Talbothays Lodge, West Stafford, 2 miles east of Max Gate.

To THE REVD. E. C. LESLIE

Max Gate | 25 Dec. 1914

Dear Mr Leslie:

It was a great pleasure to get a Christmas letter from you, for we often talk of you, & wonder how life is proceeding with you at Brighton. Above all is the question if the air of the place suits you after Came: it is wise of you, I think, to be a little up from the sea. I prefer that part to the water-front.

At this time of the year you have the advantage over us in point of Society, Brighton being so cheerful & bustling in winter. I am in great doubt as to when we shall see the place again, though I like it. Whenever we do we shall not forget you.

It was strange that you should have gone & just got settled there when the war came. I question however, if that would have made any difference to your plans, had you known that it was coming.

We go to London occasionally on brief visits, but do not care about it in the winter, particularly now that it is so dark there. Dorchester is more or less full of soldiers & German prisoners, & I suppose this sort of thing will go on for a long time yet, for I see no prospect of any conclusion to the war. A newspaper editor asked me to send him a Christmas greeting for his readers, & I told him the puzzle was too hard for me, seeing that present times are an absolute negation of Christianity.

As my wife is writing I will enclose this in her envelope, & with kindest regards to Mrs Leslie, & good wishes for you both for the coming year I am

Sincerely yours
Thomas Hardy.

Text MS. (with envelope) Adams.
Leslie: the Revd. Edward Charles Leslie (1858–1924), who had recently left William Barnes's (see I.120) old living of Winterborne Came for a new parish in Brighton; his wife Margaret was the eldest child of TH's late friend Henry Joseph Moule (see I.121). *up from the sea*: TH wrote to Leslie at 63 Dyke Road, Brighton. *newspaper editor*: George Dewar of the *Saturday Review*; see letter of 9 Dec 14 to Dewar.

To FORD MADOX HUEFFER

FROM THO. HARDY, | MAX GATE, | DORCHESTER. | Dec 27: 1914

Many thanks. Verses quite beautiful in their spontaneity.

T.H

Text MS. (postcard) Univ. of Kentucky.
Hueffer: Ford Madox Hueffer (later Ford), novelist and critic; see III.327. *Verses*: presumably Hueffer's *Antwerp* (London, 1914), which he seems to have used as a Christmas card.

To A. C. BENSON

MAX GATE, | DORCHESTER. | Dec 30: 1914

Dear Mr Benson

Just a line to wish you a happy new year & to thank you for your very kind remarks on the Poems—which I rather dreaded publishing, & am now relieved to look upon as past productions. The difficulty lay in those very "Satires" that you mention. I did not like them—particularly in the same volume with those written at a later date when my thoughts had been set on quite another track by painful events. But they had already appeared (years ago) in a prominent periodical, & people are so fond of raking up one's old work that I decided to take the bull by the horns, & do it myself. It was the publishers who thought it better to use them for the title than to call the book merely Poems, or Lyrics.

It is sad to hear how the young men around you are thinning away. To me the war seems only beginning. What we shall be doing next year this time I cannot surmise. However I will repeat my wish, & ask you to believe me

Always yours
Thomas Hardy.

My wife sends kindest regards.

Text MS. (with envelope) Berkeley.
remarks on the Poems: Benson had acknowledged the gift of *Satires of Circumstance* 27 Nov 14 (DCM), praising the 'Poems of 1912–13' as 'extraordinarily moving & beautiful' but describing the 'Satires of Circumstance' as 'too strong for me'.

To SYDNEY COCKERELL

Max Gate | Dec 30: 1914

My dear Cockerell:

I am writing just this line to wish you & Mrs Cockerell a happy New Year & to thank you for your remembering us at Christmas. I cannot say that there is the cheeriness in my wish that there (I suppose) ought to be, for really I do not recollect the end of any year which has been so full of uncertainty & gloom. To look forward to February, as we have hints to do, as the time when fighting will be renewed on a large scale, is not exhilarating.

Thank you much for taking the trouble to read those poems. I may have told you that if I could have had my wish I should have kept the Satires & those akin to them in a separate book, as I think they injured the others that I cared most about—particularly as they (the satires) seem to be the *only* ones read by most people, which is what always happens. However they will probably shake down with the rest as past performances.

I daresay you are in the midst of soldiers in training. We have just helped to give a Christmas tree & presents to 550 soldiers' children.

My wife asks me to include her in this letter, & to tell you to give her love to Mrs Cockerell & the children.

Always sincerely yrs
Thomas Hardy.

Text MS. Taylor; envelope Adams.
soldiers' children: TH and FEH were among those present at an entertainment for soldiers' and sailors' wives and children held in the Corn Exchange, Dorchester, on 29 Dec 1914.

1915

To HAMO THORNYCROFT

MAX GATE, | DORCHESTER. | Dec [January] 1. 1915

My dear Thornycroft:

Warm thanks for your good wishes for the new year, which we reciprocate. Would that there were more confidence in my wishes in these troublous times. However I wish them.

The Dynasts is to some extent *sculpturesque* (as represented, I mean) & I hope therefore you will like it. Barker has managed very cleverly in some of the difficulties, but of course I never contemplated the putting of it on the stage.

Always sincerely
Thomas Hardy.

Text MS. DCM. *Date* Corrected on basis of internal evidence.
Thornycroft: William Hamo Thornycroft, sculptor, whom TH had known for many years; see III.137. *on the stage*: Granville Barker's production of *The Dynasts* ran until 30 Jan 1915; Thornycroft had seen it by the time he wrote to TH 5 Jan 15 (DCM).

To LADY HOARE

[7 January 1915]

"Chuzzlewit" is, I agree, ahead of "Dombey & Son."

I certainly do not rate "Dombey & Son" as the highest of Dicken's works.

I think "David Copperfield" his best.

The Curiosity Shop is excellent in the grotesque parts relating to the wax-work, but little Nell I don't care for much—(I hate her—F.H.) Jingle is the best in the Pickwick. The much lauded Sam does not seem to me to be nearly so funny as Jingle. Pickwick would be Dickens's best if its humour did not miss fire occasionally & fall flat—at least to my sense.

I am rather shocked that you do not like Scott—though I like him in what would be called the wrong way—that is I prefer his poetry to his prose, & Kenilworth to his Scotch novels. I simply adore (*can* that be T. H. speaking? FH.) Marmion,, I mean as a poem, & "The Eve of St John" has more interest than the much praised "Antiquary"—the humour of which I think forced.

Text Transcript in FEH's hand (incorporated into her letter of 7 Jan 15 to Lady Hoare) Wiltshire Record Office.

I agree: it appears from FEH's letter that she had read a letter of Lady Hoare's aloud to TH, that he had jotted down his reply, point by point, on a 'nasty scribbled little scrap of paper', and that she was copying out his comments in order to make them more readable. *Marmion, . . . of St John"*: see *EL*, 64, 313.

To CALEB SALEEBY

FROM THO. HARDY, | MAX GATE, | DORCHESTER. | 7: 1: 1915

Thanks for N.P. Cutting, which I have read. Am reading the book you kindly sent, but not in a hurry, which you will not mind.

T.H.

Text MS. (postcard) Adams.
N.P. Cutting: newspaper cutting, identified in Saleeby's letter of 28 Dec 14 (DCM) as a *Sunday Times* report of a lecture Saleeby had given on *The Dynasts*. *the book*: Bergson's *Creative Evolution*; see letter of 21 Dec 14. *not in a hurry*: for TH's eventual response see letter of 2 Feb 15.

To EDMUND GOSSE

Max Gate | 13: 1: 1915

My dear Gosse:

We have just finished reading (aloud) the article, & are going to hunt up the various pieces you allude to. Thanks for waking us up to them. Really people are extraordinarily ignorant of what was done by the poets of those days—even their better work—such as the Waterloo stanzas of the Childe, which are now so slighted through having I suppose become so hackneyed, as if that were their fault & not their misfortune.

I fear the Tibbald's Row School of rhymeless youngsters who think poetry was all wrong till they discovered the true art at the beginning of the present King George's reign, is responsible for some of this, or rather that the newspaper critics who follow that school are responsible.

Ever sincerely
Thomas Hardy.

Text MS. (with envelope) Leeds.
the article: Gosse's 'The Napoleonic Wars in English Poetry', *Edinburgh Review*, January 1915. *the Childe*: i.e., Byron's *Childe Harold*. *Tibbald's Row School*: i.e., of contemporary and especially 'Georgian' poets, earlier referred to as 'the new ugly school of poetry' (IV.300). TH's allusion, though not entirely clear, is evidently to Pope's attack in *The Dunciad* upon what he considered the dulness and pedantry of 'piddling Tibbald', Lewis Theobald (1688–1744; *D.N.B.*), editor of Shakespeare.

To CLEMENT SHORTER

FROM THO. HARDY, | MAX GATE, | DORCHESTER. | 14: 1: 1915.

Best thanks. A review of insight, & only wrong in that the writer does not know that the sequence was the other way: i.e. verse written first (1864 to 1870): then, for practical reasons, novels.

T.H.

Text MS. (postcard) Taylor.
review of insight: unidentified.

To DOROTHY ALLHUSEN

MAX GATE, | DORCHESTER. | 20: 1: 1915

My dear Dorothy:

Many thanks for your kind letter. It was a cold & very harsh cough that I had, but they are quite gone, & I am going about as usual.

I am glad that you thought well enough of The Dynasts to go again. All the intellectual people go—to judge from many letters I get—& the frivolous people don't. Unfortunately there are many more of the latter than of the former.

I have been appealing to the Americans for the Belgians who are still in Belgium, but likely to starve. I enclose the lines since you may not have seen them. They have appeared in all the American papers. One lady writes in hurt terms to say that America has already given a great deal, & cannot be expected to give more; but I think they can, as it is very deep to the bottom of their dollars.

When you are coming again do let us know.

Ever affectionately
Thomas Hardy.

Text MS. Purdy
your kind letter: of 19 Jan 15 (DCM). *the lines*: TH's poem 'An Appeal to America on behalf of the Belgian Destitute', pub. in *New York Times*, 4 Jan 1915, and in other newspapers in the United States; see Purdy, 191–2.

To VIRGINIA WOOLF

MAX GATE, | DORCHESTER. | 20 Jan. 1915

Dear Mrs Woolf:

I am much pleased to hear that you like the lines I wrote in recollection of your father, & that the imperfect picture I gave of him as editor, in Professor Maitland's book, brought him back to you. He had a peculiar attractiveness for me, & I used to suffer gladly his grim & severe criticisms of my contributions & his long silences, for the sake of sitting with him.

As to what I am doing now, I often wonder what he would say to it. I find that most of the present-day critics read it very superficially, & often miss one's intention, in a way that he certainly never did.

Believe me, with best wishes,

Sincerely yours
Thomas Hardy.

Text MS. (with envelope) Berg.
Woolf: Adeline Virginia Woolf, *née* Stephen (1882–1941), novelist and critic; *D.N.B.* She married Leonard Sidney Woolf (1880–1969; *D.N.B.*) in 1912. *lines . . . of your father*: TH's sonnet, 'The Schreckhorn', first pub. with TH's recollections of Leslie Stephen in F. W. Maitland's *The Life and Letters of Leslie Stephen* (London, 1906); V. Woolf (17 Jan 15, DCM) had been prompted to write by the reappearance of the poem in *Satires of Circumstance*. See *The Letters of Virginia Woolf,* II, ed. Nigel Nicolson (London, 1976), 58. *back to you*: V. Woolf described the poem and reminiscences as 'incomparably the truest & most imaginative portrait of him in existence'.

To EDMUND GOSSE

Max Gate | 22: 1: 1915

My dear Gosse:

It came into my head in the middle of the night that you asked me for any letters from Swinburne. I have found two, & send them on.

Always yrs
T.H.

Text MS. Leeds.
letters from Swinburne: see letter of 1 Dec 14; the two letters TH sent were pub. in *The Letters of Algernon Charles Swinburne*, ed. E. Gosse and T. J. Wise (2 vols., London, 1918), II.253–4, 265–6.

To EDMUND GOSSE

MAX GATE, | DORCHESTER. | 27: 1: 1915

My dear Gosse:

Yes, certainly put me down on the memorial to Robert Ross: I thought I had signed to that effect.

I'll be careful about the journalists & S's letters. Nobody had ever seen them except myself till I sent them to you.

Always truly yrs
T. Hy

Text MS. (correspondence card) Leeds.
to Robert Ross: Robert Baldwin Ross (1869–1918), author, Oscar Wilde's literary executor; TH was one of approximately 300 writers who signed the *Address and Presentation to Mr. Robert Ross,* pub. by the Chiswick Press in 1915. *S's*: Swinburne's; see letter of 22 Jan 15.

To EDMUND GOSSE

MAX GATE, | DORCHESTER. [27 January 1915]

(2d card)

Did I ever tell you this story of S?—One day I arrived at The Pines & found him in great glee. He said he had just read in some paper that had been sent him with a marked article on literature or some subject of the sort: "Swinbne planted, Hardy watered, & Satan giveth the increase".

T.H.

Text MS. (postcard) BL. *Date* From postmark.
story of S?: TH seems first to have told this Swinburne story in 1905; see III.175. *The Pines*: the house in Putney where Swinburne lived with Theodore Watts-Dunton (see II.216) for the last 30 years of his life.

To A. E. DRINKWATER

MAX GATE, | DORCHESTER. | 28th. January 1915

Dear Mr Drinkwater:

Though you have to end the career of "The Dynasts," seventy performances will be really a very respectable run.

It will be interesting if you can do anything with it in the country, but I can quite see the difficulties. Probably you would get full houses, owing to the great discussion of the London performances.

I have roughly shaped a gorgeous play (also from "The Dynasts") of the fall of Prussia and Austria—But I only did it for amusement, and shall not go on with it.

Yours sincerely,
T. Hardy.

Text MS. (typewritten) Adams.
in the country: Granville Barker's production of *The Dynasts* does not appear to have been staged outside London. *gorgeous play*: presumably a wry joke on TH's part; no trace of any such scheme has survived.

To CALEB SALEEBY

MAX GATE, | DORCHESTER. | Feb 2: 1915

Dear Dr Saleeby:

Your activities are unlimited. I should like to hear your address on "Our War for International Law".

Personally I feel rather disheartened when I think it probable that the War will end by the sheer exhaustion of the combatants, & that things will be left much as they were before. But I hope not.

I have been now & then dipping into your Bergson, & shall be returning the volume soon. I suppose I may assume that you are more or less a disciple, or fellow-philosopher, of his. Therefore you may be rather shocked by some views I hold about his teachings—if I may say I hold any views about anything whatever, which I hardly do.

His theories are certainly much more delightful than those they contest, & I for one would gladly believe them, but I cannot help feeling all the time that he is rather an imaginative & poetical writer than a reasoner, & that for his attractive assertions he does not adduce any proofs whatever. His use of the word "Creation" seems loose to me. Then, as to "conduct". I fail to see how, if it is not mechanism, it can be other than caprice, though he denies it (p.50). And he says that Mechanism & Finalism (I agree with him as to Finalism)—are only external views of our conduct. "Our conduct extends between them, & slips much further". Well, I hope it may, but he nowhere shows that it does. And again: "a mechanistic conception . . . treats the living as the inert . . . Let us on the contrary, trace a line of demarcation between the inert & the living", (208). Well, let us, to our great pleasure, if we can see why we should introduce an inconsistent rupture of order into uniform & consistent laws of the same.

You will see how much I want to be a Bergsonian (indeed I have for many years). But I fear that his philosophy is, in the bulk, only our old friend Dualism in a new suit of clothes—an ingenious fancy without real foundation, & more complicated, & therefore less likely, than the determinist fancy & others that he endeavours to overthrow.

You must not think me a hard-headed rationalist for all this. Half my time (particularly when I write verse) I believe—in the modern use of the word—not only in things that Bergson does, but in spectres, mysterious voices, intuitions, omens, dreams, haunted places, &c., &c. But then, I do not believe in these in the old sense of belief any more for that; & in arguing against Bergonism I have of course, meant belief in its old sense when I aver myself incredulous.

By the way, as a kindred matter can you explain the meaning of the paragraph I enclose? To me it seems nonsense. Please return it when writing, in case I should want to ask the author when I am at Cambridge.

Sincerely yours
Thomas Hardy.

Text MS. (with envelope) Adams.
your address: evidently described by Saleeby in a letter to TH no longer extant. *your Bergson*: Bergson's *Creative Evolution*; see letter of 21 Dec 14. Saleeby had sent the translation by Arthur Mitchell (London, 1911). *much further*": TH misquotes; the passage in fact reads, 'Mechanism and finalism are therefore, here, only external views of our conduct. They extract its intellectuality. But our conduct slips between them and extends much further.' *the living*", (*208*): this quotation has been extracted, and slightly adapted, from three separate paragraphs on pp. 207 and 208. *paragraph I enclose*: two versions of this letter appear in *LY*, one (270–2) a substantially accurate transcription of this MS., based on a copy supplied by Saleeby after TH's death, the other (167–8) extensively revised by TH from a draft in DCM. The latter incorporates in its (entirely rewritten) final paragraphs an extract from a notice in the *Cambridge Review*, 30 Jan 1915, of Alfred W. Tillett, *Spencer's Synthetic Philosophy: What It Is All About* (London, 1914). *the author*: the notice is signed 'T.L.'

To MACMILLAN & CO.

Max Gate | Dorchester. | Feb 5: 1915

Dear Sirs:

(Reprint: Satires of Circumstance.)

As I had already marked the few errors that I had noticed or had been pointed out, I send the list herewith. No shifting of type will be necessitated, as you will see.

Very truly yours
T. Hardy.

Text MS. (pre-addressed Macmillan postcard used as correspondence card) BL.
list herewith: this no longer accompanies the card; as TH says, however, the changes in the second printing of *Satires of Circumstance* were all minor.

To CLEMENT SHORTER

Sunday [Early February 1915]

Dear Shorter.

Many thanks, I am sorry to hear about Symons: I fear he will not recover. Certainly Robertson Nicoll might have called.

I don't know what to make of the war. We reckon men in terms of millions now, yet Blenheim was won with 52,000 and Waterloo with 70,000. I hope [*word omitted*] is well. Our days are all rain here.

Always sincerely
T.H.

I have never dreamt of giving a book to an Editor! By the way, the 1st edn of "Satires of S" has sold out, and they are reprinting: I mention this in case you want a 1st edn. T.H.

Text Typed transcript (by Howard Bliss) Purdy. *Date* From internal evidence.
Symons: Arthur Symons had perhaps suffered a recurrence of his mental illness of 1908 (see III.352–3); see, however, letter of 31 May 15 to Symons. *Nicoll*: William Robertson Nicoll, Scottish man of letters, editor of the *Bookman*; see I.244. He was knighted in 1909. *Blenheim . . . Waterloo*: TH's figures are substantially correct. omitted]: the transcript has a blank space at this point; TH had presumably made a direct or indirect reference to Shorter's wife. *to an Editor*: Shorter had evidently hoped to receive a presentation copy of *Satires of Circumstance*. *reprinting*: see letter of 5 Feb 15.

To EDWARD CLODD

Max Gate | 11: 2: 1915

My dear Clodd:

As what you don't know about money is not monetary knowledge will you be so kind as to say (quite an off hand opinion, for which I shall not bring you to book whatever happens) if you think it right to buy just now,

Consols, or
Liverpool Corpn 3½%, or
Bath Corpn 3%, or
New South Wales 4% inscribed, or
Adelaide Electric Supply Co. debents.

My publishers, by paying up promptly, as they always do, have put me in this dilemma of not knowing what to do with a few superfluous pounds.

I myself thought, if Europe is going scat, why not invest in America? But the brokers turn a cold shoulder to this idea apparently.

We have not heard a sound of you lately (though I read an article of yours in the D.C. a few days ago,) & hope you are both well. We are quite dormant at present, but mean to wake up in the spring; when, or in early summer, we hope to see you here & Mrs Clodd.

Sincerely yours
Thomas Hardy.

To this I add affectionate greetings to you & your wife & hope that very soon, as soon as this dismal wintery weather is over, we may have the great pleasure of seeing you both at Max Gate. T. is like a dormouse & loves to be curled up in his study waiting for the spring. We have been married a year & a day, & *really & truly* (I am not joking now) it has been a year of *great* happiness.

F.H.

Text MS. (with supplementary note by FEH) Leeds.
know about money: an allusion to Clodd's position as Secretary of the London Joint Stock Bank. *in the D.C.*: Clodd's review of J. T. Mers, *A History of European Thought in the Nineteenth Century, Daily Chronicle,* 6 Feb 1915. *mean to wake up*: TH first wrote 'hope to wake up'. *Mrs Clodd*: Clodd's estranged first wife died 13 May 1911—'Relieved to find myself a widower', he wrote in his diary (Alan Clodd)—and in December 1914 he married Phyllis Rope, who had been his secretary. really & truly: it appears from Clodd's diary that FEH had previously written to him about her marriage in more negative terms.

To THE REVD. J. H. DICKINSON

MAX GATE, | DORCHESTER. | Feb 23: 1915

Dear Mr Dickinson:

In turning over some papers lately I came upon two little sketches I made of details in old St. Juliot Church that are, I believe, now swept away. As I thought they might be of more interest to the parish than elsewhere I have put them into a frame, & send them by parcel post herewith, for hanging up, if you think fit, in the Vestry as a trifling record of the Church's history.

You are happily remoter than we are from probable raids by the enemy, & can afford to contemplate the war with some philosophy.

With kind regards to Miss Dickinson.

Yours sincerely
Thomas Hardy.

I wonder if old Mr Jose is still living, & if he remembers my late wife as Miss Gifford. T.H.

Text MS. (with envelope) Berg.
in the Vestry: TH's sketches hung just inside the church door for many years but have now been replaced by photographic copies. *raids by the enemy*: the first German air raids on England (by Zeppelin airships) occurred 19–20 Jan 1915. *old Mr Jose*: probably John Jose, farmer, churchwarden of St. Juliot at the time of its restoration in 1870–3; his age was given as 38 in the 1871 census.

To J. S. FURLEY

MAX GATE, | DORCHESTER. | Feb 24: 1915

My dear Sir:

It would have given me the greatest pleasure to be associated with the City of Winchester in the way your Library Committee proposes, for it is a spot in which I have always taken a deep interest. But reasons, mainly physical, render it so difficult for me to do anything of the sort that I am compelled to renounce all thought of such at this time of my life.

It was by the merest chance that I did not settle at Winchester instead of Dorsetshire many years ago when I was obliged to leave London on account of health, & it has often been a matter of regret with me that I decided not to do so.

Some day I should like to present a book or small MS. to the library, if acceptable.

Please thank the Committee for the honour offered, & believe me

Very truly yours
Thomas Hardy.

J. S. Furley Esq.

Text MS. Hampshire County Library.
Furley: J. S. Furley, a Winchester councillor and former mayor, currently chairman of the city's Museums and Library Committee; he had invited TH to re-open the city's re-organized Public Library. *if acceptable*: TH seems not to have followed up this suggestion.

To HAMO THORNYCROFT

MAX GATE, | DORCHESTER. | 24 Feb 1915

My dear Thornycroft:

It would give me the greatest pleasure to have my name associated with yours in the way you propose, & to feel that, whatever the short-comings of the sitter, the sculptor's art will be sufficient to hand on his name to posterity, (I have, as you may know, always been an admirer of your virile style of presentation).

No image of me more than a little terra cotta bust a few inches high has been produced as yet, though painters have done their best, & worst, with me from time to time.

We go to London at indefinite dates, & I think the best way would be for you to propose a time that is convenient.

When the war is over you will have your hands full enough of military & naval heroes, so I must slip in before that time comes!

Always sincerely
Thomas Hardy.

Text MS. DCM.
terra cotta bust: presumably the one manufactured and sold by J. T. Godwin, the Dorchester

china merchant. *the sculptor's art*: a white marble bust of TH by Thornycroft is in DCM, a bronze in the National Portrait Gallery.

To HERMANN LEA

MAX GATE, | DORCHESTER. | Saturday. [6 March 1915]

Many thanks. Excellent. Quite unexpected.

T.H.

Text MS. (postcard) DCM. *Date* From postmark.
Lea: Hermann Lea, Dorset photographer; see II.232. *Many thanks*: TH was perhaps acknowledging the 'enlarged photograph' of FEH mentioned in the letter of 31 May 15 to FEH.

To WILLIAM WATSON

MAX GATE, | DORCHESTER. | 12: 3: 1915

Dear Mr Watson:

I have just read the sonnet to America, reprinted in *The Times*, (which I had never read before) & I think it one of the finest things—if not the very finest—you have ever written, & possibly any poet, both in craftsmanship & feeling. I hope you are well, & am

Sincerely yours
Thomas Hardy.

Text MS. (correspondence card, with envelope) Texas.
Watson: William Watson, poet; see I.241. *in* The Times: Watson's sonnet, 'To America, Concerning England', first pub. in the *Evening News*, 8 Dec 1914, reprinted in *The Times*, 12 Mar 1915 together with a letter from Watson protesting against what he considered its misrepresentation by Colonel George Harvey, editor of the *North American Review* (see letter of Sept 14) in *The Times* of 10 Mar 1914. Watson, thanking TH (17 Mar 15, DCM), confessed that his pride in TH's letter had impelled him to show it to the editor of the *Evening News*.

To SIR FREDERICK MACMILLAN

MAX GATE, | DORCHESTER. | March 16: 1915

My dear Macmillan:

Miss Alice Kauser, a well-known dramatists' agent of New York, wants to consult about "the moving picture rights" of some of my novels. I enclose the introduction she brings, so she seems to be all right, Mr Fiske being a man of probity.

I do not know what you may have done about "The Trumpet-Major" with those other people, so I have asked her to call on you.

Of course if anything is to be made out of such exhibitions it is just as well to make it in these hard times: & please (if anything comes of it) charge whatever percentage on results that you think proportionate.

Very truly yours
Thomas Hardy.

P.S. When the reprint of "Satires of Circumstance" comes out, I should like to have a copy. T.H.

Text MS. BL.
Kauser: Alice Kauser (d. 1945), American dramatic agent. *Mr Fiske*: still accompanying this letter is a letter to TH, 2 Mar 15, from Harrison Grey Fiske (see II.110), husband of Minnie Maddern Fiske, the impersonator of Tess (see II.111). *call on you*: Macmillan (17 Mar 15, Macmillan letterbooks, BL) made no reference to any projected film of *The Trumpet-Major* but said that he would see Miss Kauser and make the best arrangements he could, charging TH a 10% commission on net receipts. *reprint*: see letter of 5 Feb 15.

To CALEB SALEEBY

MAX GATE, | DORCHESTER. | 16: 3: 1915

Dear Dr Saleeby:

My thanks for the revised form of "The Longest Price of War", which I am reading.

I do not know if you mean to accept the invitation to speak at the Temperance meeting in Dorchester; but if you do I shall hope to see you. We live a mile from the Town, & I am not sure if our house would be convenient for staying at, on account of the distance at night, &c, & our not keeping a car. But we could put you up here with pleasure if that would be no objection.

I am returning, or shall be in a day or two, your volume of Bergson. It is most interesting reading, & one likes to give way to its views & assurances without criticizing them. If however we ask for reasons & proofs (which I don't care to do) I am afraid we do not get them. An *élan vital*—by which I understand him to mean a sort of additional & spiritual force, beyond the merely unconscious push of life—the "will" of other philosophers that propels growth & development—seems much less probable than single & simple determinism, or what he calls mechanism, because it is more complex; & where proof is impossible probability must be our guide. His partly mechanistic & partly creative theory seems to me clumsy & confused.

He speaks of "the enormous gap that separates even the lowest form of life from the inorganic world". Here again it is more probable that organic & inorganic modulate into each other, one nature & law operating throughout.

But the most fatal objection to his view of creation *plus* propulsion seems to me to lie in the existence of pain. If nature were creative she would have created painlessness, or be in process of creating it—pain being the first thing we instinctively fly from. If on the other hand we cannot introduce into life what is not already there, & are bound to mere recombination of old materials, the persistence of pain is intelligible.

Sincerely yours
Thomas Hardy.

Text MS. Adams.
revised form: Saleeby had apparently adapted his original lecture (see letter of 21 Dec 14) to the

purposes of a temperance campaign, arguing that the use of alcohol shortened life and hence constituted 'the enemy within our gates'. *Temperance meeting*: the mass meeting of local branches of the Church of England Temperance Society held in the Corn Exchange, Dorchester, 29 Apr 1915. *no objection*: Saleeby accepted TH's invitation 17 Mar 15 (DCM); this entire paragraph, from 'I do not know' to 'no objection', is omitted from the text of this letter pub. in *LY*, 272–3. *volume of Bergson*: see letter of 2 Feb 15. *inorganic world*": this is actually a quotation, on p. 38 of *Creative Evolution*, from E. B. Wilson, *The Cell in Development and Inheritance* (New York, 1897); TH's 'form of life' should read 'forms of life'.

To SIR EVELYN WOOD

Max Gate. | Dorchester. | 19. March, 1915.

Dear Sir Evelyn Wood,

A young barrister in whom I am interested, Mr F. W. George, enlisted at the beginning of the war from a sense of duty, and is now applying for a commission in the Dorset Regiment. I can say from personal knowledge that he is a most deserving man, who worked his way into the law by his own exertions; cool in judgment; while abandoning a promising position to defend his country shows his character. I think he would make a good officer.

He is I may add a distant cousin of mine.

His nomination paper is just being forwarded to Colonel Hannay, Dorset Regiment. Knowing your willingness to do anything for those who are worth it it has occurred to me to ask if you could support his application by a line to Colonel Hannay on the strength of my information, if the request be regular, not trespassing on your kindness, and if you think it would be of service. If you do not think so, please disregard this letter.

Yours sincerely,
Thomas Hardy.

P.S. In case Mr George's address should be necessary, I give it:

No 56, Private F. W. George,
"C." Platoon.
South Midland Div: Cyclist's Corp.

(He has temporarily volunteered from the Gloucestershire, into the Cyclist's.) T.H.

Text Typed transcript DCM.
Wood: Sir Evelyn Wood (see II.258), professional soldier, created Field Marshal in 1903. *George*: Frank William George (1880–1915), TH's second cousin once removed; he had worked in banks before being called to the bar in 1913. He wrote to TH 4 Apr 15 (DCM) to say that he had been attached to the Dorsetshire Regiment; for his subsequent fate see letter of 1 Sept 15 to Cockerell. *Hannay*: Cathcart Christian Hannay (1872–1942), currently commanding the 5th battalion, Dorsetshire Regiment; Wood (20 Mar 15, DCM) responded by sending TH a letter to forward to Hannay, since he didn't himself know where the battalion was currently stationed. *request be regular*: an editorial correction of the transcript's reading 'request be not regular'; the entire transcript is careless, and a few other minor corrections have been made silently.

To WINIFRED THOMSON

MAX GATE, | DORCHESTER. | 21: 3: 1915

Dear Miss Thomson:

Certainly send it, if you think it will fetch anything! The war-allusions are a curious coincidence.

A day or two ago we were talking about you considerably, & indeed your name is often mentioned here, so many people preferring your picture of me to Herkomer's. I should like you to see it, after all these years, & perhaps we may be able to get you down here some day. It would be a great pleasure.

Believe me always

Yours sincerely
Thomas Hardy.

Text MS. DCM; envelope Colby.
Thomson: Winifred Hope Thomson (d. 1944), painter; see II.79. *send it*: TH's letter to Miss Thomson of 26 Dec 99 (II.242) was sold at the Red Cross Sale at Christie's on 26 Apr 1915. *your picture of me*: the portrait, painted 1895–6, is now in the Dorchester Grammar School. *Herkomer's*: this portrait, painted by Sir Hubert von Herkomer (see I.255) in 1908 (see III.323), is now in DCM.

To FLORENCE HENNIKER

MAX GATE, | DORCHESTER. | 23: 3: 1915

My dear friend:

In your last letter you asked me, I remember, what I thought about the duration of the war, which question I did not answer, to my shame, though my reason was my perplexity on the point. I can only make guesses, & the one I think the most probable is that it will last till one of the combatants is exhausted & sues for peace without being beaten, or till one or more country is bankrupt, or starved, or till there is a revolution in Germany; a rupture between the dual monarchies of Austria might, too, help on peace. I hardly think it will end by the sheer victory of one side or the other in the field—unless Italy joins the allies, in which case it might.

I, too, like you, think the Germans happy & contented as a people: but the group of oligarchs & munition-makers whose interest is war, have stirred them up to their purposes—at least so it seems. I have expressed the thought in a sonnet that is coming out in the Fortnightly. I enclose a proof of it, which, as I have no other copy, you can return at your leisure.

As you say, & as it also has struck me, how can we consistently crush German militarism without reducing armaments & armies all round: & diminishing our navy?

You have no doubt read in the papers today Sir E. Grey's synopsis of the beginning of the war. England has been so often the arrogant aggressor in past wars that it would have been quite in keeping with her history if she had been in this: but really, when you honestly look at the facts marshalled by Sir E. G. England is innocent for once. They show that the war began because the Germans wanted to fight.

In this connection I am much puzzled as to the attitude of Lord Morley & John Burns in resigning office—particularly the former. When I saw him last he had aged much, & was getting deaf, so at first I thought he had given up on those accounts. But if so, it would have been stated, to strengthen his colleagues' position: on the other hand, how can he hold that we ought not to have fought? Perhaps you can solve this conundrum?

I am so glad you liked the play, which though not "The Dynasts" as I wrote it, was interesting to me also. Florence sends best love. I am sorry to say she has been confined to her bed with *sciatica*—left by some chill she caught. She is better, & would much like to see you again—as should I also.

Your affectte friend
Tho. H.

Text MS. DCM.
Italy joins the allies: see letter to Mrs. Henniker of 25 May 15. *in the Fortnightly*: TH's 'The Pity of It', *Fortnightly Review*, April 1915. *at your leisure*: Mrs. Henniker returned the proof with her letter of 31 Mar 15 (transcript, DCM). *Grey's synopsis*: Sir Edward Grey, Bt. (1862–1933; *D.N.B.*), British Foreign Secretary 1905–16; on 22 Mar 1915 he had introduced a lecture by John Buchan (see letter of 20 June 17) on the early battles of the War by reviewing the origin and causes of the War itself. *resigning office*: Viscount Morley (see I.119), Lord President of the Council, and John Elliot Burns (1858–1943; *D.N.B.*), President of the Board of Trade, had resigned from the Asquith government at the outbreak of war on the grounds that the conflict could and should have been averted. *the play*: the Granville Barker production of *The Dynasts*.

To EDWARD THOMAS

MAX GATE, | DORCHESTER. | 23: 3: 1915

My dear Sir:

Pray choose whichever you like best for your purpose. I am unable to criticize your selection, as I do not know the principle you are following. If your book is to represent a *mood* throughout—that mood being a buoyant one—they are well-chosen probably: if to illustrate the idiosyncrasy of each writer, I am not sure that they are so good as would be, say, "When I set out for Lyonnesse" (Satires of Circumstance), or "To meet or otherwise" (same volume), or "The Ballad Singer" (Time's Laughingstocks).

By the way, there are two Sergeants' songs—"When Lawyers Strive" (written nearly 40 years ago!), and "Budmouth Dears" (from The Dynasts Part III, Act II. Sc. II)—better suited to present times, perhaps than the other.

Yours very truly
Thomas Hardy.

Text MS. Texas.
Thomas: Philip Edward Thomas (1878–1917), critic and poet; *D.N.B.* Writing to TH 18 Mar 15 (DCM) he expressed the hope that TH had forgotten his (Thomas's) article about him in *Poetry and Drama* two years previously; see IV.307. *your selection*: as reported in

Thomas's letter of 21 Mar 15 (DCM); for his *This England: An Anthology from Her Writers* (London, 1915) he had chosen TH's 'The Sergeant's Song' (from *Wessex Poems*) and 'The Spring Call'.

To CLEMENT SHORTER

FROM THO. HARDY, | MAX GATE, | DORCHESTER. | 26: 3: 1915

Many thanks for copy of The Herald containing verses on "The Dynasts". I had not seen the periodical before. How blind the workmen are!

Text MS. (postcard) T. Trafton.
on "The Dynasts": W. N. Ewer's poem 'On Reading *The Dynasts*', *Herald*, 20 Mar 1915; it argued that although the current war was supposed to be in defence of freedom the tyrants would re-assert themselves once the war was over, as they had done at Peterloo in the aftermath of the war against Napoleon. *the workmen*: the *Herald*, edited by George Lansbury (1859–1940; *D.N.B.*), supported the Labour Party; in 1923 it became the Party's official organ.

To HAMO THORNYCROFT

MAX GATE, | DORCHESTER. | 29: 3: 1915

My dear Thornycroft:

I am sending an old straw hat by the next post, because it exactly fits me, & is the only stiff hat I have except a silk hat, which I will send if you prefer it: I thought however that as the straw shows the rise of the head as well as the horizontal outline it would be more useful.

Overleaf you will find a highly scientific representation of the same.

Ever sincerely
Thomas Hardy

I enclose a little print which may give a rough hint for the clay block. T.H.

Text MS. DCM.
old straw hat: Thornycroft, writing (n.d., DCM) to arrange a date for TH's first sitting (see letter to him of 24 Feb 15), had asked TH to send one of his old hats as a guide to preparing the block of clay in advance of his arrival. *Overleaf*: TH's drawing (see opposite page) is on the inside fold of the MS. *little print*: it no longer accompanies the letter and cannot be identified.

To SIR GEORGE DOUGLAS

MAX GATE, | DORCHESTER. | April 5: 1915

My dear Douglas:

I have not heard from you for a very long time, the shock of arms around us seeming to drown all sound of friends. So I make use of a question that has been put to me to-day to send this line to you.

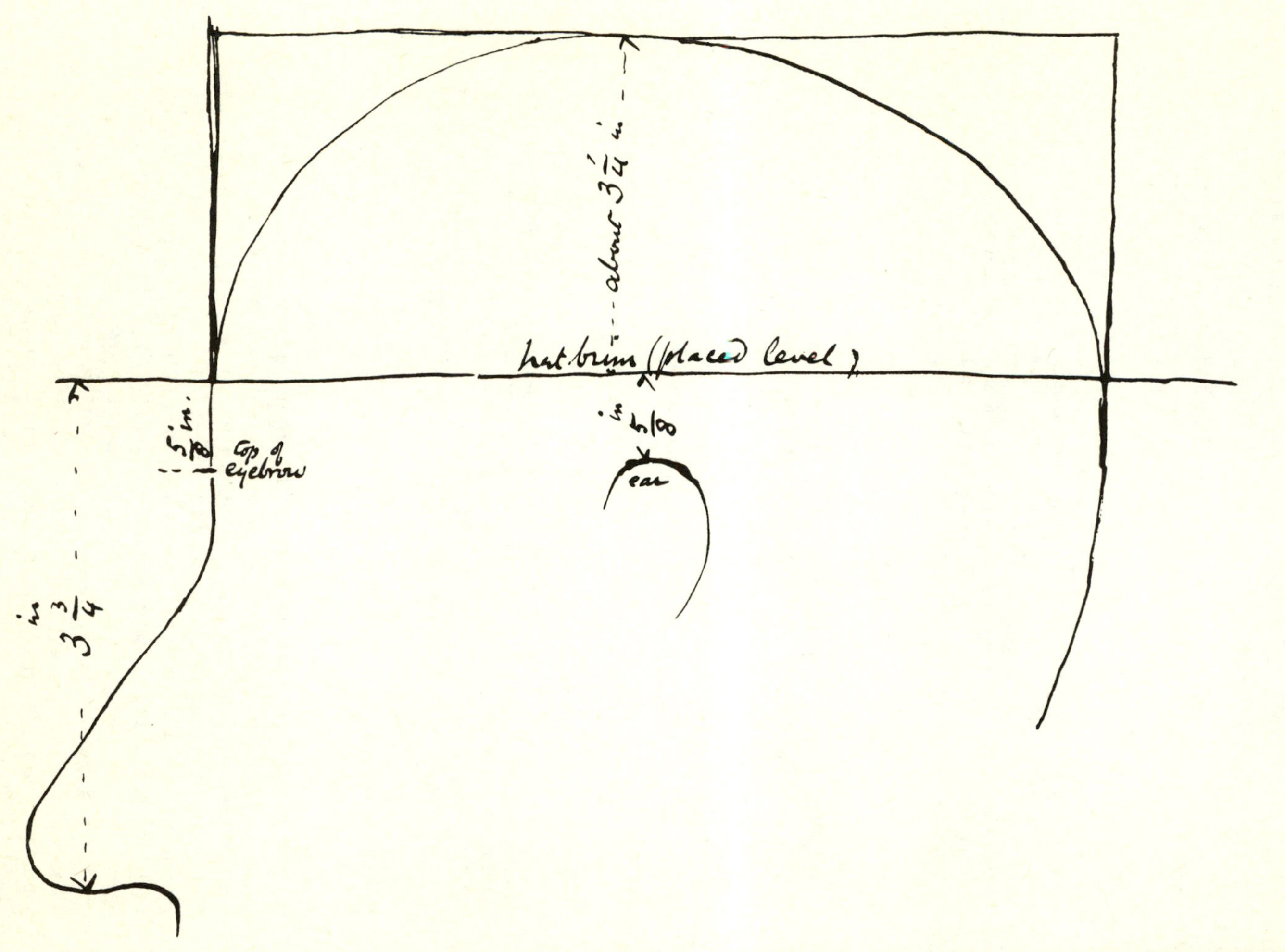

about 3 1/4 in
hat brim (placed level)
5/8 in.
top of eyebrow
in 5/8
ear
in 3 3/4

The Kings Own Scottish Borderers are quartered here, & one of them we know has asked me if I can tell him where to get the song "As I came down through Cannobie" which he much wants to have, Cannobie being his native place. He thought I should be sure to know all about it, as I make Farfrae sing it in "The Mayor of Casterbridge." But I have not the slightest idea where I saw or heard the song, or how it got into the novel. As I should like to oblige him—Lieut. Maxwell—if possible, I ask you on the chance of your knowing it. All I could tell him was that it was a real old song, though further than that my memory does not serve me.

I hope you keep well, & wonder what you think about this ghastly war, & of its probable results.

Always sincerely yours
Thomas Hardy.

Text MS. NLS.
Cannobie": i.e., Canonbie, just on the Scottish side of the border N. of Carlisle. *of Casterbridge."*: at the end of chap. 14 (Wessex edn., 108); the line is apparently a variant line of Robert Burns's 'Bonnie Peg', the song Farfrae had sung when he first met Elizabeth-Jane (63). *Lieut. Maxwell*: either Lt. B. B. Maxwell or 2nd Lt. R. Maxwell, both serving with the King's Own Scottish Borderers at this date.

To SIR SIDNEY COLVIN

FROM THO. HARDY, | MAX GATE, | DORCHESTER. | 8: 4: 1915

I just remember this trifle, & send it on for what it may be worth in your *Life*.

Swinburne told me that Mrs Proctor, (Barry Cornwall's widow) told him that one day when Leigh Hunt called on her father he brought with him an unknown youth who was casually mentioned as being a Mr John Keats.

Sincerely yrs
T.H.

Text MS. (postcard) Berg.
your Life: of Keats; see first letter to Colvin of 14 June 14. *Cornwall's widow*): Anne Procter (see I.114), wife of the poet Bryan Waller Procter (1787–1874; *D.N.B.*); TH often visited her in the 1870s and 1880s and this anecdote is itself told in *EL*, 177. See *The Keats Circle: Letters and Papers 1816–1878*, ed. Hyder E. Rollins (Cambridge, Mass., 1948), II.157–8. *Leigh Hunt*: James Henry Leigh Hunt (1784–1859), essayist and poet; *D.N.B.* *her father*: i.e., her step-father, Basil Montagu (1770–1851; *D.N.B.*), lawyer, miscellaneous writer, and friend of Wordsworth, Coleridge, and many other writers of his day.

To HAMO THORNYCROFT

Max Gate | 14: 4: 1915

My dear Thornycroft:

We propose to be in London next Monday, & I shall aim to appear at 2A Melbury Road at 10.45. Have you any idea how many sittings you will require? It is not important that you answer this question, which I put merely that we may give the servants here some directions.

Owing to the war & other circumstances I am not going to have a "season" in London as in old times. Kindest regards to Mrs Thornycroft, & believe me

Sincerely yrs
T.H.

Text MS. DCM.
2A Melbury Road: Thornycroft's studio; his home was in Hampstead.

To WILLIAM ROTHENSTEIN

MAX GATE, | DORCHESTER. | 15: 4: 1915

Dear Mr Rothenstein:

We are here till Monday morning next, when we purpose leaving. Shall be at home after 4 on Saturday, or if that shd be inconvenient for you, on Sunday the same time. I am glad you like Dorset.

Sincerely yrs
T. Hardy.

We shall both have much pleasure in seeing you.

Text MS. (correspondence card) Harvard.
Rothenstein: William Rothenstein, painter; see II.149. *like Dorset*: Rothenstein was not coming to draw TH but to see some Dorset buildings and scenery.

To SIR GEORGE DOUGLAS

MAX GATE, | DORCHESTER. | April 17: 1915

Dear Douglas:

Lieut. Maxwell ought to be greatly obliged to you for trying to unearth the song about his native place, which he tells me, & as you will know, has nowadays modernized its name from "Cannobie" to "Canonbie".

I am as deep in darkness as ever as to where I got the line, & it is amusing that Farfrae was made to whistle it because it was, as I supposed, a song known to every Scotchman!

Another of the K.O.S.B. is coming here to tea this afternoon—Lieut. Gillon—a well-read & most intelligent man.

We have also between 2000 & 3000 German prisoners here.

We propose to pay a visit to London on Monday next for a few days: not for pleasure, but to see to household matters, &c. I dislike going very much, & shall be glad to come away.

Don't forget to let me know if you ever think of coming south: we can accommodate you, & should much like to do so, if you don't mind "the simple life."

I am glad to hear that Lady Douglas keeps up her strength so well. My mother lived till near 91. By this time I hope Miss Douglas is better.

Always yrs sincerely
Thomas Hardy.

Text MS. NLS.
Lieut. Maxwell . . . "Canonbie": see letter of 5 Apr 15. *K.O.S.B.*: King's Own Scottish Borderers. *Lieut. Gillon*: Stair Agnew Gillon (1877–1954), in civilian life an Edinburgh lawyer, subsequently solicitor in Scotland to the Board of Inland Revenue. Several letters of his from the period 1915–25 are in DCM but TH's side of the correspondence has not been traced. *Lady Douglas*: Douglas's mother. *Miss Douglas*: his sister.

To CALEB SALEEBY

FROM THO. HARDY, | MAX GATE, | DORCHESTER. | 19: 4: 1915

Dear Dr Saleeby:

We were much pleased to hear that you can come here for the lecture on the 29th (I think?) We are just now leaving for London, but expect to return in a few days. Please let me know in the course of a week day & hour for receiving you.

Sincerely yours
T. Hardy.

Text MS. (correspondence card) Adams.
on the 29th: see letter to Saleeby of 16 Mar 15.

To CLEMENT SHORTER

Hôtel Russell | Russell Sq. | 20: 4: 1915

Dear Shorter:

We are up here till the latter part of the week, & I—& I think my wife—shall have much pleasure in joining you at dinner to-morrow—Wedny at 8. We will come in morning clothes as you suggest.

Sincerely yours
T.H.

Text MS. (correspondence card, Athenaeum stationery, with envelope) Berg.
at 8: on the back of the envelope TH has written 'Arrive 7.45 not 8.0'.

To LADY ST. HELIER

THE ATHENAEUM, | PALL MALL. S.W. | 22: 4: 1915

My dear friend:

Just to tell you that we are in London till some time next week, & don't like to come & go without letting you know. I, or Florence, can call any afternoon—or morning—that you may be at home. Till Saturday we shall be at the Hotel Russell, Russell Sq. if you should be passing.

Ever affectly
Thomas Hardy.

Text MS. (correspondence card) Purdy.
St. Helier: Mary, widow of Lord St. Helier, formerly Sir Francis Jeune; see I.144 and III.167. Well known for many years as a hostess, she had more recently been active in social work and (since 1910) as an alderman of the London County Council.

To HAMO THORNYCROFT

MAX GATE, | DORCHESTER. | Tuesday April 27, '15.

My dear Thornycroft:

You will have received my telegram saying I was leaving yesterday. The fact was that I seemed quite unable to get rid of that troublesome attack of diarrhoea in London. It is already going off, & I propose to be at your studio next Tuesday or any day after that you like to name. Don't trouble to answer this if Tuesday morning suits you.

Always sincerely
T.H.

Text MS. (correspondence card) DCM.

To EDMUND GOSSE

MAX GATE, | DORCHESTER. | 30: 4: 1915

My dear Gosse:

I have just received your letter on the results from the sale, which are very satisfactory, & quite beyond my expectations.

We had intended to stay in London a few days longer, but I was rather unwell on Monday, so we came straight back. It was so pleasant that we found you & Mrs Gosse indoors when we called. We duly paid our respects to the publisher afterwards. I hope to see you again at no very distant date.

Sincerely yrs
Thomas Hardy.

Text MS. (with envelope) Leeds.
the sale: at Christie's, in aid of the Red Cross; see *LY*, 168, and letter of 21 Mar 15. *when we called*: on Sunday, 25 Apr 1915 ('Book of Gosse', Cambridge Univ. Library). *the publisher*: presumably one of the members of the Macmillan family.

To LADY ST. HELIER

Max Gate, | Dorchester. | 30 April 1915

My dear friend:

Alas—I have only just received your letter. I felt so unaccountably unwell last week in London that I decided to come back, and go up again to finish the few little matters I had at hand. So our present plan is to be there from next Monday for a few days onwards, when I will take my chance of finding you at home one day. Thanks for your very kind invitation, which we should so much have liked to accept. Believe me ever

Yours affectionately
T. Hardy.

Text Typed transcript DCM.
your letter: in response to TH's own letter of 22 Apr 15.

To HAROLD CHILD

THE ATHENAEUM, | PALL MALL. S.W. | 7: 5: 1915

Dear Mr Child:

If you would like to come & call on me in Dorset I should have much pleasure in seeing you; but I do not think I can give any information that would be of service, as all details of any value in writing the estimate or guide book you propose can be gained from the volumes themselves, it seems to me. Dates, which are the greatest help I suppose, are freely given in Macmillan's 20 vol. "Wessex Edn" of T.H.'s collected works "in prose & verse", & that is the edn I advise you to use, the prefaces having all been supplemented in it. The poems entitled "Satires of Circumstance" are not included, but you can get that volume separately: they will be ultimately included.

The most accurate *guide* book is Hermann Lea's "Thomas Hardy's Wessex"—also pubd by Macmillan's—which you ought to refer to.

As to your questions:—

I was living in London continuously from 1862 to 1867 (inclusively or almost) & wrote verse only while there, except a little architectural sketch in Chambers's Journal. I have of course lived there many years since, in fragments.

No new matter was written for the stage production of The Dynasts, except the Prologue & Epilogue, at Granville Barker's request. He was entirely responsible for the scenes selected. I should have made 3 plays of it. But then, it was not intended to be a play at all!

If I may give you a hint, I wd say that you wd introduce an element of novelty into a worn subject if you were to treat my verse (including the D.) as my *essential* writings, & my prose as my *accidental*, rather than the reverse: the fact being that I wrote prose only because I was obliged to. This is the view which I notice the keenest critics to be gradually coming to.

You will find all the early poems dated in the edition I refer to.

However, do not let me influence you to write in a way contrary to your own judgment.

Yours very truly
Thomas Hardy.

P.S. I return to Max Gate, Dorchester, to-morrow. T.H.

Text MS. Adams.
Child: Harold Hannyngton Child, literary critic; see III.333. He wrote 2 May 15 (DCM) to seek information for a book he was writing on TH. *ultimately included*: the vol. containing *Satires of Circumstance* and *Moments of Vision* was added to the Wessex edn. in 1919. *pubd by Macmillan's*: in 1913. *Chambers's Journal*: TH's 'How I Built Myself a House', *Chambers's Journal*, 18 Mar 1865. *& Epilogue*: see Purdy, 173; TH did in fact do a good deal of rewriting and even added a few lines here and there (see letter of 28 Oct 14 to Barker). *my* essential *writings*: Child (8 May 15, DCM) expressed particular appreciation of this suggestion.

To HAMO THORNYCROFT

MAX GATE, | DORCHESTER. | Sunday. [9 May 1915]

Back here again. Many thanks for Milton's house. Yes, I agree about Lincoln, & want to see it again. Kind regards.

T.H.

Text MS. (postcard) DCM. *Date* From postmark.
Milton's house: presumably a drawing or photograph of Milton's cottage at Chalfont St. Giles, Bucks. *Lincoln*: Lincoln Cathedral, visited by TH in 1906; see *LY*, 120.

To HAROLD CHILD

Max Gate | 10: 5: 1915

Dear Mr Child:

I leave it to you entirely whether you will run down here for a night or not. It will be no sort of inconvenience to us, if of any use to you, so pray don't hesitate to come, if you care to.

Lea's book, though not literary, is the only one that includes the poems in its survey, & is very accurate. It is also correct on points in "A Pair of Blue Eyes", which have a melancholy interest for me now.

Always sincerely
T. Hardy.

If you do come, you will find Great Western trains from Paddington—there is one at 12.22—safer than South Western in keeping time during the war. T.H.

Text MS. Adams.
Lea's book: see letter of 7 May 15. *melancholy interest*: because of their connection with ELH.

To CALEB SALEEBY

Max Gate | 10: 5: 1915

Dear Dr Saleeby:

I find the books here on returning from London (rather fagged) & will read the parts to which you draw my attention. My wife is deeply interested in the surgical one, which I have not yet looked at. I have however perused the article in the Statesman which is striking. She sends the Dorset paper.

Sincerely yrs
T. Hardy.

Text MS. (with envelope) Adams.
surgical one: Saleeby's *Modern Surgery and Its Making* (London, 1911); Saleeby's *The Progress of Eugenics* (London, 1914) was also in TH's library and is presumably the other book referred to here. *in the Statesman*: evidently 'The Fraternal Biology', by 'Lens' (a pseudonym of Saleeby's?), *New Statesman*, 24 Apr 1915; it has a reference in a footnote to 'the vision of all the human life in Europe as composing one body, in Mr. Hardy's *Dynasts*'. *the Dorset paper*: the *Dorset County Chronicle*, 6 May 1915, containing a report of the temperance meeting Saleeby had addressed; see letter to Saleeby of 16 Mar 15.

To JOHN DRINKWATER

Max Gate | May 11: 1915

Dear Mr Drinkwater:

I find the kind gifts of your book & play here on my return, & I shall read them I know, with much pleasure.

We had some interesting hours with your father during the run of "The Dynasts," & I am very glad to have made his acquaintance. Theatre management must provide him with some odd experiences, as the little we saw of it did ourselves, indeed. When you see him please convey our kind remembrances.

Sincerely yours
Thomas Hardy.

Text MS. Yale.
Drinkwater: John Drinkwater, poet and playwright; see IV.34. *book & play*: evidently Drinkwater's *Swords and Ploughshares* (London, 1915) and *Rebellion: A Play in Three Acts* (London, 1914). *them*: TH in fact wrote 'item', adding 'em' to the original 'it'. *your father*: A. E. Drinkwater; see letter of 10 Nov 14 to him.

To ARTHUR COMPTON RICKETT

MAX GATE, | DORCHESTER. | May 18: 1915

Dear Mr Ricketts:

I was away when your letter came, & it was not sent on to me.

As far as I remember, there is no information that I could give which would help you in your proposed biography of Mr Watts-Dunton. I used to see him, as others did, when I called on Swinburne, but that was all. If I should find any letter or letters from him I will let you have them, but I am not sure that I possess any.

I will bear in mind that you wish the project to be treated as confidential.

Yours very truly
T. Hardy.

I recall now that he came to see us on one or two occasions at our flat in London; but, alas, am blank as to what took place. T.H

Text MS. Texas.
Rickett: Arthur Compton Rickett (misspelled by TH), teacher and author; see III.234. *Mr Watts-Dunton*: see letter to him of 13 Feb 14; the biography was pub. as Thomas Hake and Arthur Compton-Rickett, *The Life and Letters of Theodore Watts-Dunton* (2 vols., London, 1916). *on Swinburne*: see second letter of 27 Jan 15 to Gosse. *possess any*: seven letters from Watts-Dunton to TH are in DCM, however.

To AGATHA THORNYCROFT

MAX GATE, | DORCHESTER. | 18 May 1915

Dear Mrs Thornycroft:

I entirely approve of the scheme for a scientific alphabet, which will I hope be pushed on when the war is over, or has at any rate turned the corner. It seems to paralyse all such good movements just now, at least with me.

I should imagine that the system adopted in the Oxford Dictionary would form a basis to work on, though it might be improved in some respects.

We felt no worse for the drive your son was kind enough to treat us to. The lightning, rain, & lamplights were very striking. Our kindest regards.

Always yrs sincerely
Thomas Hardy.

Text MS. DCM.
Thornycroft: Agatha Thornycroft, *née* Cox, wife of Hamo Thornycroft; TH once said that her beauty had inspired his descriptions of Tess Durbeyfield (see Millgate, 298). *scientific alphabet*: Mrs. Thornycroft's letter has not survived and it is not clear which particular system she was advocating. *Oxford Dictionary*: i.e., Sir James Murray's *Oxford English Dictionary*. *your son*: Oliver Thornycroft (1885–1956), consulting engineer, the Thornycrofts' only son.

To SIR FREDERICK MACMILLAN

MAX GATE, | DORCHESTER. | May 19th. 1915.

Dear Sir Frederick:

As you suggest I will ask the Messrs Harper to waive any claim they may have on the film rights in the prose books (besides *Tess*) that have copyright in America, namely *Jude*, *The Well-Beloved*, *Noble Dames*, *Life's Little Ironies*, and *A Changed Man*.

I am, however, not sure that their rights extend to cinema representation. In the case of *Tess* they wrote telling me that they had received a proposal for the cinema rights and asked if they should go on with the matter, and divide the royalty with me; to which I agreed (though their share was excessive I think).

In the above copyright books the agreements with Messrs Harper for publication are in the following words:—

1. . . . The said T.H. hereby grants and assigns to the said H. & B. the exclusive right of publication and sale in the United States of America & Canada only, of a work entitled . . . the said T.H. guaranteeing that he has full power, (&c.)

2. . . . H. & B. agree to print and publish the said work at their own expense . . . & in consideration of the rights herein granted they agree to pay to the said T.H. or his representatives or assigns twenty per cent on the retail price of all copies, (&c).

3. (Style of production, &c.)

4. (H. & B. shall be at liberty to cease publication after ten years break up type, &c.)

The last clause seems to imply that they do not hold the copyright, or the stipulation would not be needed?

However, I will write and hear what they say about the film-rights, unless you think it unnecessary.

With many thanks for your attention to this business I am,

Yours very truly,
Thomas Hardy.

P.S. I can send the agreements themselves with Messrs Harper, if you would like to see them. T.H.

Text MS. (typewritten) BL.
As you suggest: Macmillan (18 May 15, Macmillan letterbooks, BL) had pointed out that dealings with Miss Kauser (see letter to Macmillan of 16 Mar 15) and others interested in making films of TH's novels were greatly complicated by Harper & Brothers' ownership of the American rights to several books. *divide the royalty*: see IV.265. *P.S.*: the postscript is in TH's hand.

To J. STANLEY LITTLE

MAX GATE, | DORCHESTER. | 22: 5: 1915

Dear Sir:

My sincere thanks for the reprint of your article on my novels from "East & West". I am just reading it, & though it is difficult for me to enter into an estimate of my writings based on the less personal of them, which ceased 20 years ago, & to disregard what critics think the more characteristic—those of the latter half of my period of authorship—I shall I feel sure be interested in the article.

Yours very truly
T. Hardy.

J. Stanley Little Esq.

Text MS. (with envelope) Princeton.
& West": Little's 'Thomas Hardy: Our Greatest Prose Poet', *East & West* (Bombay), March and April 1915.

To FLORENCE HENNIKER

Max Gate | Tuesday morning. [25 May 1915]

My dear friend:

I send off the enclosed in a hurry; otherwise you may not get it to-morrow morning. If the words are not quite what is required I will write another. Don't mind asking me to.

F. is going to London this week to see a surgeon about a little nasal catarrh that she has been suffering from. I am staying here. Thanks for your kind wish to see me at Shoreham, but I cannot very well leave just now. I have to be in London for one day a little later on; not for longer, thank Heaven, for I dislike being there more & more, especially with the incessant evidences of this ghastly war under ones eyes everywhere in the streets, & no power to do anything. However I hope that the entrance of Italy upon the stage will shorten hostilities.

I am still puzzled at the attitude of Ld My &c. Surely, even if they believe the govt wrong in the steps they took, they should stand by it now to help us out of our peril?

Ever affectly yours
Tho H.

Also, I have misgivings on the sending Mr Balfour to the Admiralty, which seems to be decided on. T.

Text MS. DCM. *Date* From internal evidence.
the enclosed: a testimonial to the character and loyalty of Mrs. Henniker's German maid Anna Hirschmann; Mrs. Henniker was applying to the Home Office for permission to keep Miss Hirschmann with her despite the outbreak of war and had asked TH (23 May 15, transcript DCM) for this supporting document. *a surgeon*: see letter of 25 May 15 to Yearsley. *at Shoreham*: see letter to Mrs. Henniker of 11 Feb 14. *entrance of Italy*: Italy entered the war on the Allied side on 23 May 1915. *Ld My &c.*: Lord Morley and John Burns; see letter to Mrs. Henniker of 23 Mar 15. *to the Admiralty*: in a new coalition administration announced in early June 1915 A. J. Balfour (see II.185) became First Lord of the Admiralty in succession to Winston Churchill.

To MACLEOD YEARSLEY

MAX GATE, | DORCHESTER. | May 25: 1915

Dear Mr Yearsley:

I write a line to say that I should have accompanied my wife to London to-morrow, but that, owing to my being so often unwell when I am there, my presence would be an anxiety to her. I shall be within call, as I shall not leave this house.

I understand that it is quite a necessary operation, & have implicit confidence in your opinion on that point, & in your skill.

One opportunity I lose by not going up, & that is of making your acquaintance. But I hope that is merely a delay.

Please wire if any reason makes it desirable.

Yours very truly
Thomas Hardy.

Text MS. Roger Lonsdale.
Yearsley: Percival Macleod Yearsley (d. 1951), aural surgeon and author; FEH subsequently became friendly with his wife, Louise. *Dear Mr Yearsley*: an attempt has been made to obliterate the word 'Yearsley' from the MS. *necessary operation*: see letter of 25 May 15 to Mrs. Henniker.

To DOROTHY ALLHUSEN

Max Gate | 26: 5: 1915

My dear Dorothy:

Alas, what I can send for your admirable cause is a mere nothing. Literature is so hard-hit by the war that it has to struggle on as best it can, & when it will recover I don't know. A new edition of my books from which I was expecting much, is cancelled, I fear—not merely postponed.

I have, however, been able to do something in other ways—£50 for the Red Cross by sale of MSS., & a good deal by other writings.

Affectly yours
T. Hardy.

Text MS. Purdy.
admirable cause: Mrs. Allhusen was active in many wartime causes, among them aid to Belgian refugees and, later, the provision of canteens for French soldiers. *new edition*: it did eventually appear, as the Mellstock edn., in 1919–20; see letter of 15 July 14. *sale of MSS.*: see letter of 30 Apr 15 to Gosse.

To CONSTANCE DUGDALE

Max Gate | Wednesday [26 May 1915]

My dear Connie:

Florence has just left for London, & I am anxious about the operation, but quite hopeful. They say it is necessary, & if it is it must be done. Please let me know by wire when it is over, & if she is *really* going on well. You will know this better than anybody.

She felt she would rather have me stay here than go up with her, since, as I had to come home last time, it would have caused her to fidget about me, & so have done more harm than my presence would have done good. And I shall not go away from here, so that it will be easy to communicate.

Kindest regards to all.

Yours affectly
T.H.

Text MS. (with envelope) Purdy. *Date* From postmark.

Dugdale: Constance Dugdale, the third of the Dugdale sisters, next in age to FEH herself; see IV.103.

To FLORENCE HARDY

Max Gate | Friday: 28th [May 1915]

My dearest Florrie:

I send on what has come, except one from the National Debt office "O.H.M.S." which you said I was not to send.

I was so relieved again this morning to get a card from Connie to say how you were, & so glad to get yours, not because it proved anything, but because it came from you. But if it is a strain you are not to write yourself, as I would rather put up with not getting one from you than make you over exert yourself. The only words on Connie's card that made me a little uneasy were that you had been sick, M. told her. Of course it may not mean anything, & I will think it does not till I hear to-morrow.

Do you *want* me to come up: if so say the word, & I start.

The war news to-day is not very pleasant. On the other hand there is a touch of grim humour in a paragraph that M. Tussaud is going to remove the Kaiser from the Royal group to the Chamber of Horrors.

I am closing this hastily, to have a few minutes to run out with Wessie.

Ever yours

T.

Text MS. Purdy. *Date* From internal evidence.
O.H.M.S.: On His Majesty's Service. *Connie*: Constance Dugdale. *M. told her*: Margaret Dugdale; see letter of 9 May 17. *not very pleasant*: the most important single item was the loss of a battleship at the Dardanelles. *M. Tussaud*: John Tussaud, director of Madame Tussaud's Waxwork Exhibition; see III.92. The paragraph itself has not been traced.

To ALFRED POPE

MAX GATE, | DORCHESTER. | 28: 5: 1915

Dear Mr Pope:

I would willingly distribute the Grammar School prizes if possible. But I doubt if I can be here this year at the date. My wife was advised the other day to undergo a slight external operation, which she has just done, & she is now in the London nursing home where it was performed. She is getting on quite satisfactorily I am assured, though her general health will naturally suffer, & I thought of taking her to the western coast when she has got over it, to pick up. So I am keeping out of all engagements for the next month or two, & if, therefore a substitute can be provided for the prize-giving it will be advisable.

I think that why I have not made the presentations before has been owing to absence from Dorchester.

I will endeavour to give myself the pleasure of calling on Mrs Pope & yourself next Sunday.

I don't seem to remember anything about "Slade's Way"—though I know "Barnsway".

I wish you could find out whereabouts in Dorchester "Twelve Men's Way" used to be (see Municipal Records). Such a fine old name, & it ought to be restored.

Yours very sincerely
Thomas Hardy.

P.S. Last, not least, I hope your patriotic sons are well & of good heart. T.H.

Text MS. Thomas Hardy Society.
Pope: Alfred Pope, brewer and leading Dorchester citizen; see I.100. He was Chairman of the Governors of Dorchester Grammar School. *"Slade's Way"*: later renamed Manor Road, Dorchester. *"Barnsway"*: a continuation of Slade's Way; the name (spelled Barnes Way) is still in use. *find out*: Pope was gathering material for his paper on 'Dorchester Walks', delivered 12 Dec 1916 and pub. in the 1916–17 vol. of the *Proceedings of the Dorset Natural History and Antiquarian Field Club*. *"Twelve Men's Way"*: it apparently ran into Shire-Hall Lane; see IV.136. *your patriotic sons*: all of Pope's ten surviving sons were engaged in some form of military service, a record later memorialized in *A Book of Remembrance* (privately printed, 1919), to which TH contributed a Foreword (see letter of 25 June 18).

To CONSTANCE DUGDALE

Max Gate | Saty morning [29 May 1915]

Many thanks for letting me know. Am expecting at mid-day your letter written last night. If necessary of course I will come up.

Ever affly
T.

Text MS. (postcard) Purdy. *Date* From postmark.
letting me know: about FEH, recovering in London from her operation.

To FLORENCE HARDY

Max Gate | Sunday. [30 May 1915]

My dearest F:

I am so glad to hear you are getting on so well. Your letter did not come that you said you were going to write, only the post card. I will write further to-morrow—about going up to fetch you &c—but to-day I am in a terrific press of things, about film-agreements, &c &c. that has necessitated a hunt through old business letters of years past, &c. And at 4 o'clock I promised to go to the Popes at South Court to tea. If I go to Talbothays I must go in the evening. (I wish I had never agreed to let the novels be used for cinema purposes; it is a perfect worry).

I send the OHMS envelope & wish I could write more, but must change my things &c.

Ever with love
T.

Text MS. (pencil) Purdy. *Date* From internal evidence.
film-agreements: see letter of 30 May 15 to Macmillan. *South Court*: the house occupied by Alfred Pope and his wife in South Walks Road, Dorchester; for TH's promise see letter of 28 May 15 to Pope. *Talbothays*: Talbothays Lodge, where TH's brother and two sisters were living; see letter of 23 Dec 14. *the OHMS envelope*: see letter to FEH of 28 May 15.

To SIR FREDERICK MACMILLAN

MAX GATE, | DORCHESTER. | May 30: 1915

Dear Sir Frederick:

You will remember our conveying the film-rights in "Far from the M. Crowd" to the Herkomer Co.

Sir H. Herkomer's son asked me in April if I would consent to his transferring his rights to another company through the agents Messrs Curtis Brown, & allow him a two months extension of time to do it in. From his words I gathered that he was in difficulties about it & other things, & that I could not refuse. I replied as follows:

"In the circumstances I have no objection to your disposing of your rights to produce 'Far from the Mg Crowd' to some satisfactory company through the agents Messrs Curtis Brown. I hope Messrs Brown may be successful", &c.

These agents now send me a new agreement, which I enclose herewith, as I judge that it is best for you to continue to act for me in the matter as previously, (though I had no idea that the transfer would involve another agreement.) I also attach the agent's letter, in which he, or they, seem to assume that *I* have employed them as agents, though I only wrote as above, & those words can hardly imply it, I think. As you have the Herkomer agreement you will be able to see if the new agreement accords with the old one, as they say.

Yours very truly
Thomas Hardy.

P.S. In Clause 1. should not the words "and in all foreign countries" be followed by "wherein the said work is copyright" or "wherein his power to grant such license exists"?—as the novel was published before there was copyright with the United States. But of course this particular film will be copyright everywhere. T.H.

P P.S. If there occur any very great difficulties, I am willing to let the whole thing drop, & return the £50 Herkomer paid as a deposit. T.H.

Text MS. BL.
the Herkomer Co.: formed by Sir Hubert von Herkomer (see letter of 21 Mar 15) and his son Siegfried; see IV.322. *Herkomer's son*: Herkomer himself died in 1914. *employed them as agents*: Macmillan replied (31 May 15, Macmillan letterbooks, BL) that Curtis Brown had no justification for assuming TH would engage him as agent, and that he would himself pursue the matter; see letter to Macmillan of 1 June 15.

To FLORENCE HARDY

Max Gate | Monday eveng. [31 May 1915]

My dearest F:

I was so glad to have your letter by the midday post & to know that your progress is all right. But I fear that you want to get about again too quickly, & think that you ought not to leave the home till the beginning of next week. I don't at all mind paying the extra days. The wind is still east, & a cold might cause the scarcely healed wound to burst out again, which, if you were down here out of the reach of Mr Yearsley, would be serious.

I am writing to Thornycroft to know when he wants me. If by about next Sunday I could go up Saty & bring you back on the following Tuesday or so. I will await his reply.

Sir H. & Lady Hoare wired this morning that they were going to motor over & call this afternoon, & they duly came, & had tea, staying nearly an hour. (He came to Dorchr to buy a horse) They are really very nice people; & we talked of you, & the war, & all sorts. She likes very much that enlarged photogh of you by Mr Lea—says it is the best. She could not resist telling me how much she liked the cretonnes, & asked if you chose them. I think she will get some like them.

I had tea with the Popes yesterday. Their prisoner son says he is well fed (but this he may be *made* to say) & asks if they can send him some currant bread, which as Mrs P. says, seems as if he were hungry. I went to Talbotys after tea, & as I forgot the asparagus, K brought it this morning—the first time anybody has come. She also admired the cretonne covers.

I got through my gale of correspondence yesterday. It has arisen through my kindness in letting Mr Herkomer transfer his cinema rights to a company, so that he might not lose the money he had spent on the preparations. I hope it will be settled up all right.

Please don't hurry to resume activities. H. says he could not sleep the night before the operation for thinking about it. I dare say when I have closed this up I shall think of something else. I have now quite recovered the strength I had before I went to London, & did not feel my double walk yesterday. With best love

Yours ever
T.

Shall be so glad to see you gardening here again. T.

Text MS. (with envelope) Purdy.
prisoner son: Lieut. Cyril Pope, the Popes' youngest son, was taken prisoner at Ypres in

November 1914. *hungry*: according to *A Book of Remembrance* (see letter of 28 May 15 to Pope), 125, Lieut. Pope was being well fed in his prison-camp at Mainz at this stage of the war. *K*: TH's sister Katharine. *his cinema rights*: see letter of 30 May 15 to Macmillan. *H.*: TH's brother Henry; see letter of 11 Feb 14 to Clodd. *double walk*: from Max Gate to Talbothays Lodge and back, a distance of just under 5 miles.

To LADY ST. HELIER

MAX GATE, | DORCHESTER. | 31 May: 1915.

My dear friend:

I am sending a scarce reprint of "Men who march away"—of which the MS. sold for about £25 at Christie's Red Cross Sale in April. Please accept it for the soldiers' sake.

I am sorry to say that my wife has had to undergo an operation for nasal catarrh. She is, however, nearly well, & is in the nursing home established by Sir F. Treves (Welbeck House, 51 Welbeck Street).

If you should be passing, & were to look in upon her, she would be delighted I know. But if you are busy & find it difficult do not trouble.

Affectly yours
Thomas Hardy.

Text MS. Purdy.
reprint: there were several reprintings, in leaflet form, of this poem; see Purdy, 157–8, where the MS. is also described. *Treves*: Sir Frederick Treves, the distinguished surgeon (see III.53), was born in Dorchester and had known TH for many years.

To ARTHUR SYMONS

Max Gate | Dorchester | May 31: 1915

My dear Symons:

I have read with much interest the pages you sent, & return them herewith lest you should not have kept a fair copy.

I do not call the composition quite a story: it seems rather a study of a certain class of womankind, & mind.

As you ask me for advice I daresay you mean advice in a practical sense: i.e., as to the advisability of printing the MS.—without reference to the goodness or otherwise of the work. Also that you wish me to speak quite frankly, whether or no my view accords with your own wishes.

Candidly then, I should not, if I were you, publish the study. The present time is particularly unsympathetic with such phases of life, & your reputation might not be advanced by printing this.

The colossal war in which Europe is engaged must be very suggestive of many things to you, & I should not be surprised to hear that the lively imagination which prompted these pages you send has exercised itself in raising some nightmare-ish vision of the terrible events that are happening.

Sincerely yours
Thomas Hardy.

Text MS. Adams.
pages you sent: evidently a version of Symons' unpublished documentary novel 'The Life and Adventures of Lucy Newcome', perhaps (since TH twice refers to 'pages') bearing the title 'Pages from the Life of Lucy Newcome'; see Alan P. Johnson, 'Arthur Symons' "Novel à la Goncourt"', *Journal of Modern Literature* (1981–2). *class of womankind*: Lucy Newcome becomes a prostitute; her career is closely based on that of her 'original', Muriel Broadbent, whom Symons had known in the early 1890s.

To SIR FREDERICK MACMILLAN

MAX GATE, | DORCHESTER. | June 1: 1915

Dear Sir Frederick:

Many thanks for seeing to the matter. I send for your guidance the correspondence with Mr Herkomer.

My supposition, in assenting to the transfer of his film-rights, was that the Herkomer Film Co. would convey these directly to the new company without my being obliged to re-enter the business & sign a contract with the new people. If this is correct, & you see no objection, will you please reply to Mr Curtis Brown that, as it is unnecessary, I decline to enter into a new contract, the transfer to which I agreed being from the Herkomer Co. to the new Co.

If however, you hold that a new contract with me is indispensable, or advisable, will you see that it is in the terms of the old one? My impression is that the form sent by Mr Curtis Brown is different, binding me to guarantee copyright in all countries, which I do not think the old one did.

Mr Curtis Brown is a stranger to me, but it seems from the wording of the contract he has submitted, & from his letter to me, that he must without my knowledge have been acting as my agent in treating with the new company.

Yours very truly
T. Hardy.

Text MS. BL.
Mr Herkomer: Siegfried Herkomer; see letter to Macmillan of 30 May 15. *stranger to me*: TH had, however, corresponded with Albert Curtis Brown, journalist and literary agent, on at least one occasion in 1904; see III.101. *new company*: see letter to Macmillan of 9 June 15.

To HAMO THORNYCROFT

Max Gate | 1: 6: 1915

My dear Thornycroft:

I think I may have to go to London between next Saturday & the middle of the following week, to fetch my wife back from a nursing home, where she has been staying for the purpose of undergoing a slight operation from which she is now recovering. Would this time suit you for giving the finishing touches to my image? Of course the exact day of my arrival would depend upon when she is quite fit to travel, but I should go up two or three days before her return.

Should these dates be too early for you please dont mind telling me, & I will come up later on, as I do not wish to hurry you.

Kindest regards to the household.

Ever sincerely
Thomas Hardy.

Text MS. DCM.
my image: i.e., Thornycroft's bust of TH.

To CONSTANCE DUGDALE

Wednesday 2: 6: 1915

Many thanks: Same wishes to you when yours comes. I hope to fetch F. early next week, if the raiders will let me.

I hope there will be no more of these, or no serious ones.

Kind regards to the household.

Yrs affectly
T.

Text MS. (postcard) Purdy.
Many thanks: for her wishes on TH's 75th birthday, 2 June 1915. *the raiders*: i.e., the German Zeppelin attacks, of which the most recent (on the outskirts of London) had occurred during the night of 31 May-1 June. *the household*: that of FEH's parents and sisters at Enfield, Middlesex.

To CALEB SALEEBY

MAX GATE, | DORCHESTER. | 2: 6: 1915

Dear Dr Saleeby:

Many thanks for your good wishes for my birthday.

I have sent on to Mrs Hardy your kind offer to call: if she does not write you will know she is not quite up to the mark for seeing friends. But I think she is out of bed. I was going to read your books: at least one of them, the other day; but I fancy she took them to London with her. However she will bring them back.

Yrs very truly,
T. Hardy.

Text MS. (correspondence card, with envelope) Adams.
your books: see letter to Saleeby of 10 May 15.

To EDWARD CLODD

June 3: 1915

My dear Clodd:

It is so very good of you to remember my birthday, as your own has not yet come along to remind you that another lurks near it. Many thanks, in which my wife would join if she were here.

You put the war in a nutshell in defining it an atavistic outburst of the ape & tiger in man.

I imagine Mrs Clodd & you journeying down to Aldeburgh to-morrow afternoon. Kind regards to her.

Sincerely yours,
T. Hardy.

Text MS. BL.
lurks near it: Clodd's birthday fell on 1 July; see letter of 30 June 15.

To ELLEN GOSSE

MAX GATE, | DORCHESTER. | 3: 6: 1915

My dear Mrs Gosse:

Warm thanks for birthday wishes from your household. I wish you all the same thing when your birthdays come!

Always sincerely
Thomas Hardy.

Text MS. (correspondence card, with envelope) Huntington Library.
Gosse: Edmund Gosse's wife Ellen ('Nellie'); see IV.239.

To FLORENCE HARDY

Thursday eveng. [3 June 1915]

My dearest F:

Glad to get your dear letter this morning as usual. A letter came by midday from Lady St H. confirming what you said about our going there Saturday. As I have not heard yet from Thornycroft, & felt uncertain what to do, I wired to her (as I told you in my telegram which I hope you got) that *you* wd go to her Saty & that I would join you unless prevented. I know her well enough to say that I am sure she wd as soon have you alone as have me also (if I find it difficult to go). She does it out of pure hospitality, & expects us to suit our own convenience. So, to make sure that *you* can go, whether I come up or not, I sent off by parcel post today the two frocks you asked for in your letter. You will laugh at my packing (unless you cry at its effect upon the frocks!)

You see, unless I hear otherwise from Thornyft before Saturday, if I go up now I shall have the weariness of going up again when he is ready. Please go to her yourself, there's a dear, in any case, & send her a line to say you are coming, with or without me. Perhaps I shall feel brisker Saty than I have felt to-day, & may start after all. If you *will not* go to Portland Place without me, I will appear, & go up again for Thft, as I don't want to disappoint you. I shall be so glad when this rush of things is over.

I delivered your messages to Jane. Lady Ilchester has sent the rest of the diary, wh. we are to keep till the end of June when she means to see us again. She writes from Holland H. & is going to Melbury the end of this week.

The "old friend" was—Curzon. I have had other letters & telegrams from Mr Page (the American Ambassador) Mr Courtney, (Ed. of Fortnightly), the "Chevalier St George" (the mad poet), Mrs Sheridan, the Gosses, Judge Udal &c.

I must answer some at least of these—& I will cut short this letter, there being so many to do.

Ever your affecte husbd
T.

Yearsley says you will be able to join me & return to Dorchester "if nothing unforeseen happens"—so it will be well for you to be near him for a few days more. T.

Text MS. (with envelope) Purdy. *Date* From postmark.
Portland Place: Lady St. Helier lived at 52 Portland Place. *Jane*: presumably Jane Riggs, the Max Gate cook. *Ilchester*: the Dowager Lady Ilchester, widow of the 5th Earl. *the diary*: of Lady Susan Sarah Louisa Fox-Strangways (1744–1827), in whose romantic marriage to William O'Brien, the Irish actor and dramatist (d. 1815; *D.N.B.*), TH had always been interested; see *EL*, 11–12. *Holland H.*: Holland House, Kensington, the Ilchesters' London house, formerly the property of Henry Fox, 1st Lord Holland. *Melbury*: Melbury House, in NW Dorset, the Ilchesters' country seat. *Curzon*: TH had known Lord Curzon, the former Viceroy of India, since the early 1890s; see I.273. *Mr Page*: see letter of 3 June 15 to him. *Mr Courtney*: William Leonard Courtney (1850–1928), philosopher and journalist, editor of *Fortnightly Review* 1894–1928; *D.N.B.* *St George"*: unidentified. *Mrs Sheridan*: see letter of 7 Dec 15 to her. *Judge Udal*: see letter of 9 June 15 to him.

To WALTER HINES PAGE

MAX GATE, | DORCHESTER. | 3: 6: 1915

Dear Mr Page:

Just a line of thanks for your kind wishes for my birthday. The same good wishes to you when yours comes!

Sincerely yours
Thomas Hardy.

Text MS. (correspondence card) Harvard.
Page: Walter Hines Page (1855–1918), American journalist and diplomat, U.S. ambassador to England 1913–18.

To ANNIE WATSON

MAX GATE, | DORCHESTER. | June 5: 1915

Dear Miss Watson:

My best thanks for good wishes & birthday card. My wife would also send hers if she were here, but she is in London till next week.

I am glad to hear that the grave is well kept. It was very kind of your sister to go & see.

One puzzling point I should like to settle is whereabouts in that churchyard Emma's grandmother (& your great grandmother) Helen (née Davie) is buried: also your grandmother Helen Charlotte Watson, your great-aunt, great uncle, &c. From my late wife's papers I find they lie all together in a vault there somewhere; but that when the church was restored in 1889—26 years ago—the vault was cut into, or built up, or interfered with in some way, to improve the approach to the church on that side, or make new steps, so that Emma's father could not be put into it. The Gifford gravestones were then placed where they now stand, just inside the gates of the north enclosure. By unlocking the gates, which the pew-opener will do, you can go inside & read them.

If you are interested, you & your sister might like to ascertain from any old people living close to the church if they remember what was done to the entrance that side. Possibly that street running along the north side of the church was made then, or widened.

Perhaps the incumbent has a record showing what was done, how the Gifford vault was affected, &c.

Please do not take this trouble unless you are interested yourselves in finding out where your ancestors are lying, or if their vault was much injured. No doubt there is a plan of the churchyard, with graves, vaults, &c, as they were before the alterations.

Believe me, with kind regards to your mother & sister,

Sincerely yours
T. Hardy.

Text MS. Berg.
the grave: of ELH's parents, in Charles Churchyard, Plymouth; see letter to Miss Watson of 15 June 14. *your sister*: presumably Helena, the youngest of the three Watson sisters; TH's 'pedigree' of the Gifford family (DCM) does not give the middle sister's name. *your mother*: see letter to Miss Watson of 15 June 14.

To FLORENCE HARDY

Sunday [6 June 1915]

My dearest F:

As you will be leaving when you get this I will only write a line. How glad I shall be to see you again. Do not trouble about the fly: I have already written the postcard to Hammond, & will be there myself to meet you. It is, by the way a slow train, arriving here at 4.38.

Also note: it leaves Paddington 12.25—not 12.30. (unless altered for June).

I send on two letters.

I wonder if Mr Warner Jones ought to be operating on you so soon after the other operation. Are you really well enough to come alone?

Ever
T.

You might stay till Tuesday if weak.

Text MS. (with envelope) Purdy. *Date* From postmark.
Hammond: William Hammond, jobmaster at the Antelope and King's Arms livery stables, Dorchester. *Mr Warner Jones*: Frederick Warner Jones, dental surgeon; he had an appointment at the Royal Dental Hospital, London, and a practice in Enfield, where FEH had lived before her marriage. *operating on you*: FEH, writing on this date to Rebekah Owen (Colby), said that her dentist was injecting something into her gums between every tooth.

To SIR FREDERICK MACMILLAN

MAX GATE, | DORCHESTER. | 9th. June 1915.

Dear Sir Frederick Macmillan:

I have signed the form of agreement with the Turner Film Company and return it herewith. On the first page where the written insertion occurs I have added the word "yearly", which seems to be meant, and if so will you ink it over? If not meant please take it out.

Yours very truly,
T. Hardy.

Text MS. (typewritten) BL.
form of agreement: see letter to Macmillan of 1 June 15. *Turner Film Company*: their film of *Far from the Madding Crowd*, directed by Larry Trimble and starring Florence Turner, was released in February 1916; TH wrote a synopsis of the story for the souvenir programme of the trade showing in November 1915 (see Purdy, 318). *ink it over?*: Macmillan (10 June 15, Macmillan letterbooks, BL) confirmed that TH's insertion was in order.

To J.S. UDAL

MAX GATE, | DORCHESTER. | June 9: 1915

Dear Udal:

My warm thanks for your kind wishes on my birthday. I have reached an age at which I do not exactly jump at birthdays as one does in childhood, but letters from friends make them tolerable anyhow. You probably are getting on to share my views of such anniversaries.

I quite remember the pilgrimage to Pilsdon Hill with the Dorset Field Club, & I can hardly forgive you for deserting that beautiful district, though where you are is not a bad spot if you must live in London. We took a house in Hamilton Terrace one London Season, & another in Abercorn Place, so I know the neighbourhood. We have been in Town off & on since the spring, but are always glad to get back here.

I wish your "Dorset Folklore" all success, though I suppose you will have to keep it by you till after the war. There are a good many scraps of folklore in my old books, but I never studied it systematically, which a well-known folklorist tells me makes the items I mention the more valuable. They have nearly disappeared, however, from Wessex life.

When your birthday comes round accept from me the same congratulations, & with kind regards believe me

Sincerely yours
Thomas Hardy.

Text MS. Eton College.
Udal: John Symonds Udal, colonial judge and Dorsetshire folklorist; see I.136. *to Pilsdon Hill*: in SW Dorset; this was the occasion of TH's first meeting with Udal in 1885 (see I.136). *the neighbourhood*: Maida Vale. *after the war*: Udal's *Dorsetshire Folklore* eventually appeared in 1922. *valuable. They have*: TH first wrote 'valuable, as they have'.

To A.E. DRINKWATER

MAX GATE, | DORCHESTER. | 12th. June 1915.

Dear Mr Drinkwater:

I acknowledge the receipt of schedules of performances at the Kingsway Theatre, and of cheque, for the latter of which I enclose a formal receipt. In doing this I bow to the decision of Miss McCarthy and Mr Granville Barker that they will pay the amount, without feeling that they ought to.

Please convey my thanks to them when you write, and let them know how very conscious I am of their scrupulousness in carrying out to the end an agreement which I did not wish them to regard as being at all binding upon them in the extraordinary times and circumstances under which the play was produced.

We often talk of them, and earnestly hope that they will get back safely to England.

I hope also that you keep quite well, and are not worse hit by the war than the average of us—

Yours sincerely,
T. Hardy.

Text MS. (typewritten) Colby.
McCarthy: see letter of 27 Sept 14. *an agreement*: i.e., for the production of *The Dynasts*. *to England*: they had been in the United States, returning to England in late June 1915.

To CLEMENT SHORTER

M. G. | 13: 6: 1915

Parcel received. Best thanks. Quite sufficient.

T.H.

Text MS. (postcard) Berg.
Parcel received: its contents remain unknown.

To MAURICE MACMILLAN

MAX GATE, | DORCHESTER. | 16 June: 1915

Dear Mr Macmillan:

Herewith the agreement signed.

I take this opportunity of saying that last month we were in London for a week or ten days, & intended to call on you & Mrs Macmillan among other friends, but I was unwell (from eating something or other), & we had to get back here.

If the necessity of taking your holiday in England brings you west, or anywhere near, please let us know. I fancy you have never been here. It would be a great pleasure to see you. With kind regards,

Sincerely yours
Thomas Hardy.

Text MS. BL.
Macmillan: Maurice Crawford Macmillan, publisher (see III.261); he was Sir Frederick Macmillan's brother. *the agreement*: Maurice Macmillan had asked TH (15 June 15, Macmillan letterbooks, BL) to sign a second copy of the Turner Film Company agreement (see letter of 9 June 15 to Sir F. Macmillan); it was important to exchange agreements as soon as possible but TH's original was unobtainable as a consequence of the illness of one of the agents involved.

To EDWARD CLODD

Max Gate | 30: 6: 15

My dear Clodd:

I remember that your birthday comes along to-morrow, & send this line to wish you many more happy anniversaries of the day in the dignified leisure which will soon fall, or has already fallen, to your lot.

I wish I could have congratulated you on the general outlook. But whether you & I are going to wind up our earthly career under a cloud or not is at present a matter of conjecture. I hope Mrs Clodd is well, & send her best regards.

Sincerely yrs
Thomas Hardy.

Text MS. Purdy.
your birthday: Clodd was born in 1840 and thus only a month younger than TH himself.

To MAURICE MACMILLAN

MAX GATE, | DORCHESTER. | 2: 7: 1915

My dear Macmillan:

Could you send me, *in sheets*, the 3 vols of verse in the Wessex Edition, & the Satires of Circumstance? I would then pick out & fasten together the short pieces suitable for the little volume of selections we discussed publishing after the War—whenever that may be.

Sincerely yrs
T. Hardy.

Text MS. (correspondence card) BL.
volume of selections: *Selected Poems of Thomas Hardy* was, in the event, pub. in 1916, well before the end of the First World War.

To MAURICE MACMILLAN

Max Gate | Dorchester | 6: 7: '15

Verses in sheets received. Best thanks for same.

T.H.

Text MS. (postcard) BL.

To D. S. MacCOLL

FROM THO. HARDY, | MAX GATE, | DORCHESTER. | July 8: 1915

Many thanks. Am reading it with interest.

T.H.

Text MS. (postcard) Glasgow Univ.
MacColl: Dugald Sutherland MacColl (1859–1948), art critic, keeper of the Wallace Collection 1911–24. *reading it*: MacColl had perhaps sent TH his *Catalogue of Cartoons, Paintings, and Drawings by Alfred Stevens* (London, 1915), knowing of TH's interest in the Dorset-born artist (see IV.289).

To HAMO THORNYCROFT

Max Gate | 9: 7: 1915

My dear Thornycroft:

We have planned to be in London about the middle of next week; so that please expect me to put in an appearance at Melbury Road on Wednesday morning between 10 & 11. I hope you have had more summer weather in the country, & am

Sincerely yours
Thomas Hardy.

Text MS. DCM.

To FLORENCE HENNIKER

Max Gate | Saturday [10 July 1915]

My dear friend:

Here is a letter from America, & I hope it contains good news.

We expect to be staying at Lady St. Helier's from Tuesday to Thursday next week—merely lodging there while we attend to prosy London matters which will leave no time for running down to see you, pleasant as it would be. Why not meet us there at lunch or tea: she said last time that she would be so glad if you would; &, as you know, I can invite anybody there at any time.

We almost wish you were not in Kent, as you may be in the track of some Zeppelin on its way to London. Still, you are not so badly off as some. A friend of ours—Colonel Inglis, stationed here—has his house but 2 miles from Dover. My cousin Frank George—Lieut. 5th Dorset Battalion—sailed for the Dardanelles or Egypt this week.

Your affectionate friend
Th. H.

Text MS. DCM. *Date* From internal evidence.
good news: TH was still receiving letters addressed to 'G. Worlingworth', the pseudonym Mrs. Henniker used for her work as a playwright; see IV.177 and letter of 4 Sept 16. *next week*: evidently 13–15 July 1915; see letter of 9 July 15 and *LY*, 168. *in Kent*: she was still living at Shoreham. *Inglis*: Henry Alves Inglis (1859–1924), commander of the Royal Artillery barracks at Weymouth 1914–18; his wife, Ethel, became a close friend of FEH's. *George*: he had called at Max Gate in April 1915 before his departure; see *LY*, 168.

To HAMO THORNYCROFT

Max Gate: Saturday. [17 July 1915]

Back here again. Will do my best to reappear in autumn or winter if necessary. The shortness of the sitting was really more convenient for me than a longer one wd have been, as I had to call at some places before leaving.

Ever yrs
T.H.

Text MS. (postcard) DCM. *Date* From postmark.
if necessary: Thornycroft (16 July 15, DCM) had said that he would need to see TH again once he had started work on the marble bust itself.

To HABBERTON LULHAM

FROM THO. HARDY, | MAX GATE, | DORCHESTER. | 18: 7: 1915

Dear Sir:

I come back from London to find "The Other Side of Silence" awaiting me, & the distinction of a poem in it bearing my name. I shall be reading the volume with great pleasure this week, & am, with many thanks for the gift

Yours very truly
Thomas Hardy.

P. H. Lulham Esq.

Text MS. (correspondence card) Hove Central Library.
Lulham: Edwin Percy Habberton Lulham, Sussex doctor and poet; see III.191. *of Silence*": Lulham's *The Other Side of Silence* (London, 1915). *bearing my name*: 'To Thomas Hardy', a poem of 6 quatrains.

To CLEMENT SHORTER

Max Gate | July 18. [1915]

Letter just received here. Thanks. Alas: while you were smoking we were rushing to Paddington Station. Another time perhaps.

Th. H.

Text MS. (postcard) Berg. *Date* From postmark.
smoking: Shorter had presumably invited TH to meet him in the smoking-room of his club.

To MARY HARDY

Seaton | Thursday. [29 July 1915]

Mr Lea has motored us down here today. Just returning.

T.H.

Text MS. (pencil, picture postcard of Seaton) DCM. *Date* From postmark.
Hardy: Mary Hardy, the elder of TH's sisters; see I.1. *Seaton*: a small Devon seaside resort just W. of Lyme Regis; see letter of 29 July 15 to Mrs. Henniker. *Mr Lea*: Hermann Lea; according to Lea's notes in *Thomas Hardy Through the Camera's Eye* (Beaminster, Dorset, 1964), 36, TH made thirty-six excursions in Lea's car during 1915.

To FLORENCE HENNIKER

Max Gate | Thursday. [29 July 1915]

My dear friend:

I think you must mean "The Society of Architects." It is not absolutely new, but since my time. Its address a year or two ago was 28 Bedford Square, & the secy C.M. Butler. I know nothing about its standing.

There is, of course, The "Royal Institute of British Architects"—a dignified & venerable body, & the chief architecl society in England. The President is a well-known architect. I cannot for the moment remember his name—the secy is Ian MacAlister, B.A. & its address 9 Conduit Street.

There is also a junior society called "The Architectural Association"—18 Tufton St. Westminster: Sec. F.R. Yerbury.

We have just come back from a motor ride to Seaton, & Beer, a little beyond. The views along the route have been beautiful.

I was so sorry to let you go in the rain from Lady St. Helier's. I wish, if you get rid of your house, you would take or buy one down this way: I think the air would suit you.

We have a huge cavalry camp here, & hear the reveillé sounded at 5 in the morning. We have also foot: so that the town sometimes is a surging mass of soldiers. F. sends love—

Affectly yours
Th. H.

The post goes in a few minutes, wh. is why I am so brief. T.H.

Text MS. DCM. *Date* From internal evidence.
of Architects.": founded in 1884 with the object of establishing statutory registration of architects; in 1925 the Society was amalgamated with the R.I.B.A. (see below). *Butler*: Charles McArthur Butler (d. 1936), secretary to the Society of Architects 1898–1925. *of British Architects*": TH won the R.I.B.A.'s Silver Medal in 1863 and was elected an Honorary Fellow in 1920 (see *LY*, 210). *well-known architect*: Ernest Newton (1856–1922; *D.N.B.*). *MacAlister*: George Ian MacAlister (1878–1957), architect; *D.N.B.* *Architectural Association*": of which TH was a member in the 1860s; see I.2–3. *Yerbury*: Francis Rowland Yerbury (1885–1970), architect; *D.N.B.* *Seaton, & Beer*: see letter of 29 July 15 to M. Hardy; Beer is also on the coast. *from Lady St. Helier's*: Mrs. Henniker had evidently taken up TH's suggestion in his letter of 10 July 15.

To CHARLES WATTS

MAX GATE, | DORCHESTER. | 1st. August 1915.

Dear Sir:

I should much like to contribute something to the 1916 edition of your Annual, especially as some of my friends are doing so: but I fear it is beyond my power. My writing days are almost past; moreover I am compelled by the exigencies of the war to give every scrap I do contrive to write to aid some charitable object that this brutal European massacre has rendered necessary. I hope nevertheless that you will get together a good list from more productive pens than mine, and am

Yours very truly,
Thomas Hardy.

Charles A. Watts Esq.

Text MS. (typewritten) Rationalist Press Association.
your Annual: i.e., the annual of the Rationalist Press Association, called at this date *The R.P.A. Annual and Ethical Review.* *some of my friends*: the contributors to the 1916 vol. included William Archer, Professor J. B. Bury, and Mrs. W. K. Clifford.

To HENRY JAMES

MAX GATE, | DORCHESTER. | 8: 8: 1915.

My dear Henry James:

I send the enclosed page, for what it may be worth, as not quite the right thing. I am sorry to think that being in verse it is awkward for one of the conditions—that of translation. However perhaps a prose rendering would be better than nothing.

Anyhow I hope it may help, though infinitesimally, in the good cause, & am,

Always yours sincerely
Thomas Hardy.

Any more fit title may be given to the verses. T. H.

Text MS. Yale.
James: Henry James, novelist and critic; see III.90. *enclosed page*: the MS. of TH's poem 'Cry of the Homeless', sent in response to James's requests of 21 and 28 July 15 (DCM) for a contribution to *The Book of the Homeless*, ed. Edith Wharton (New York, 1916); see Purdy, 192. *hope it may help*: James sent a letter of thanks 10 Aug 15 (DCM); see also letter of 14 Aug 15.

To NELSON RICHARDSON

Max Gate | 9 Aug: 1915

Dear Mr Richardson:

I don't personally take enough interest in my ancestry to get the letter you write of from the bookseller. I daresay its author was collaterally a connection of my people more or less remote, as all the Hardys of Dorset seem to have sprung from one stock—the de Hardys who came across here from Jersey in the 15th Century.

Thank you & Mrs Richardson for your kind invitation. But as we have been spending odd week ends in London during the summer, & taking trips into Devon & Somerset, I fear we must drop further outings at present. The war rather takes away from me all enterprise, for visiting as for other things.

Yours sincerely
T. Hardy.

Text MS. (with envelope) T. Trafton.
de Hardys: correctly, le Hardys; see *EL*, 5. *invitation*: the Richardsons lived in Weymouth.

To EDITH WHARTON

MAX GATE, | DORCHESTER. | Aug 14: 1915

Dear Mrs Wharton:

I am glad to hear that the verses may help the book, though I could wish to have done better for it.

I am also glad that they have brought me letters from you. I remember, of course, our pleasant meetings at Lady St Helier's. My wife & I have been staying with her lately; though our sojourn in London this year has not been a long one. The war casts such a shade over everything.

I hope your admirable labours will be well rewarded & am,

Sincerely yrs
Thomas Hardy.

Text MS. (with envelope) Yale.
Wharton: Edith Newbold Jones Wharton (1862–1937), American novelist. *to hear*: from her letter of 12 Aug 15 (DCM). *help the book*: see letter of 8 Aug 15. *at Lady St Helier's*: these occasions are evoked by Mrs. Wharton in her *A Backward Glance* (New York, 1934), 215–16.

To G. HERBERT THRING

MAX GATE, | DORCHESTER. | 19th. August 1915.

Dear Mr Thring,

I am in receipt of your note and the letter you enclose from the British Academy to the Society of Authors respecting the Library of Louvain.

While my immediate feeling is that it will be soon enough to start the movement for reconstituting the Library when the Germans are driven out of Belgium, I agree that an early expression of sympathy with the University of Louvain in its deplorable loss, such as is proposed by the Institute of France, would be eminently genuine and proper, and that English representative men might be asked to join in it.

How this should be carried out is a question that will be better left to the Committee of Management, if they are of the same opinion.

I return Lord Bryce's letter herewith, and am

Yours very truly,
Thomas Hardy.

The Secretary, | Society of Authors.

Text MS. (typewritten) BL.
Library of Louvain: it had been destroyed during the German invasion of Belgium in 1914. *out of Belgium*: the rebuilding and restocking of the library took place in 1921–8, although it was again destroyed in May 1940. *Committee of Management*: of the Incorporated Society of Authors; Thring, as Secretary, was consulting TH in his capacity as President. *Lord Bryce's letter*: Bryce (see letter of 26 June 14) was President of the British Academy 1913–17; his circular letter, of 21 July 15, still accompanies this letter of TH's.

To JOHN GALSWORTHY

Max Gate | Dorchester. | 25: 8: 1915

Dear Mr Galsworthy:

I have received your new book, & value it much, both as a gift from you, & for its intrinsic worth. I have not got on far with it yet, as my wife reads it aloud to me in the evening, which is pleasanter than reading it separately.

I believe you are meaning to call here on your way to London this autumn. I hope this is true.

The look of things in Europe is not cheering, so far as I can see, to an impartial eye.—At least to mine Germany seems slowly attaining her object of mastering the rest of us. But in England one must not look things in the face: yet my experience has been that nothing leads to success like doing so.

Sincerely yours
Thomas Hardy.

Text MS. Univ. of Birmingham.
Galsworthy: John Galsworthy, novelist and playwright; see III.202. *your new book*: Galsworthy's novel *The Freelands* (London, 1915), sent to TH with an admiring inscription on 19 Aug 1915, the day after its publication.

To SYDNEY COCKERELL

Max Gate | Sept 1: 1915

My dear Cockerell:

I have been going to write to you for weeks, to ask how you and yours are getting on in this trying time, but events distract me from all my plans.

The bound MSS. arrived to-day uninjured, & I really owe you a lot for getting them done, beyond actual expense. I must talk to you about that when I see you.

We were much distressed two days ago by a telegram which had come through from the War Office, telling us that the most promising young relative I had in the world had been killed in action on Aug 22, in Gallipoli. His mother is a widow, & how she is going to bear it I don't know. She has two other sons, but they are both in the trenches in France, & may, of course, not get through safely. However, it is not such absolute massacre there, so far as I can judge, as it is in the Dardanelles. He was 2d Lieut. F.W. George, Dorset Regt & you may see perhaps a biographical note about him in the Times. Heaven only knows where & how his body lies, & the particulars of his death.

It is indeed time that we should hear of something better than we have heard lately. I am not at all sure that we are not going to be beaten (though one dares not say so). I try to take an unbiassed view, & that seems to show that now that the Germans have crippled Russia for a time, they are going to come westward & cripple us. Absit omen! however, & certainly Napoleon, who carried all before him at first, was not the ultimate Conqueror.

Ever sincerely yours
Thomas Hardy.

My wife is out this afternoon, or she would send her best regards.

I don't at all mind the pages being bound facing each other. Indeed I rather like it. T. H.

Text MS. (mourning stationery) Adams.
bound MSS.: these included the two fragments of the first draft of *Far from the Madding Crowd* which are now in DCM. *young relative*: Frank George; see letter of 19 Mar 15. *His mother*: TH's second cousin Angelina, *née* Hardy (1851–1918); she married William George, a Bere Regis publican, in 1878. *two other sons*: Charles and Cecil, both of whom survived the war. *in the Times*: the paragraph, written by TH himself, appeared in *The Times*, 3 Sept 1915.

To CONSTANCE DUGDALE

Max Gate | Wedny 1: 9: '15

My dear Connie:

It is so kind of you to write me a line about my cousin Frank George. It was a very great pity that he was doomed to mere brutal fighting, when he was, as you know, capable of so much better things. We have heard from his sister this morning, who says that her mother is bearing up as well as she can, but as she has two more sons, now in the ranks in Flanders, where soon there is to be very hot work we are told, we dread lest anything should happen to them too, or either of them; I fear such an event would kill her.

You will see the obituary notice of poor Frank in to-morrow's Times, or next day's.

Affectly yours
T. Hardy.

Kind regards to all, & thanks for their messages.

Text MS. (mourning stationery, with envelope) Texas.
his sister: Frank George had two sisters, Bertha (the elder) and Kathleen.

To FLORENCE HENNIKER

Max Gate | Sept 2: 1915

My dear friend:

I am sorry not to have acknowledged your letter & the enclosure sooner. As to the enclosure, upon the whole I would rather not take part in any movement of a spiritual or even ethical nature: it would in fact not quite accord with my feelings—at any rate just at present—to do so. My "faith in the good there is in humankind"—except in isolated individuals, of whom happily there are many—has been rudely shaken of late. I mention this parenthetically—not as my reason for abstention—which is purely owing to circumstances of a personal nature—

We were much distressed on Monday morning by this brief telegram:—

"Frank was killed on the 22nd."

This referred to a very dear cousin of mine, Frank George, 2d Lieut. in the 5th Dorsets, who has fallen in action in the Gallipoli peninsula—almost the only, if not the only, blood relative of the next generation in whom I have taken any interest. The death of a "cousin" does not seem a very harrowing matter as a rule, but he was such an intimate friend here, & Florence & I both were so attached to him, that his loss will affect our lives largely. His mother (who was a Hardy) is a widow, & we don't know how she is going to get over it.

We shall be glad to know when you move into your new Kensington House, though I fear we shall not be much in London for some time. I have many requests for war poetry, but what good comes of writing & publishing it I don't know, though the different charities ask for it.

We are just going to take a walk entirely for the sake of our dog "Wessie"—who *lives* for these little rambles. F. sends her love, & I am

Your affectte friend
Tho H.

Text MS. (mourning stationery) DCM.
"faith . . . humankind": evidently a quotation either from Mrs. Henniker's letter or from the

document (no longer extant) which she enclosed. *Kensington House*: her house at 15 Kensington Gore, London, S.W.

To EDEN PHILLPOTTS

Max Gate | Sept 4: 1915

Dear Mr Phillpotts:

My best thanks for your note, & your kind sympathy & Mrs Phillpotts's. He was so much more to us than a cousin, & the most promising member of my family. I wish he were not lying mangled in that shambles of the Gallipoli Peninsula, where we ought never to have gone. However, nothing can touch him further.

Sincerely yours
Thomas Hardy.

Text MS. (mourning stationery) NYU.

To CLEMENT SHORTER

Max Gate | 7 Sept 1915

Dear Shorter:

Just a line to thank you for your letter. Please do not trouble about putting in that portrait till quite convenient. It is really for the sake of his poor mother. When he told us he was going to that shambles Gallipoli we thought he was doomed.

Very truly yours
T. Hardy.

You probably saw his biography in the Times notices of fallen officers.

Text MS. (mourning stationery, with envelope) T. Trafton.
that portrait: a photograph of Frank George appeared on a page headed 'The Roll of Honour', *Sphere*, 25 Sept 1915; Shorter also mentioned him—as 'a young kinsman, who stood well-nigh in the relationship of a son, of Mr. Thomas Hardy'—in his 'A Literary Letter' in the same issue.

To SIR EVELYN WOOD

Max Gate | Dorchester | Sept 12. 1915

Dear Sir Evelyn Wood:

You may be interested in hearing of the end of my cousin young Frank George, whom you so kindly recommended for a commission in the 5th Dorsets. He was in that frightful night attack in Suvla Bay Aug 21–22, & was killed just as his company was leaving the trenches.

His colonel—(now Brig. General Hannay) tells me that he had done splendidly since they started fighting out there on the 7th August. On the 17th he distinguished himself particularly, & brought great credit to the

5th by rushing a Turkish trench with his platoon, for which his name was sent forward for reward. He bayonetted some 8 or 10 Turks & brought back 14 prisoners.

I called on his mother last week. Poor woman; she is a widow, but bears up as well as she can.

I hope you keep well, & ask you to believe me

Sincerely yours
Thomas Hardy.

Text MS. (mourning stationery) Adams.
recommended: see letter of 19 Mar 15. *Suvla Bay*: on the Gallipoli Peninsula; the British troops were attempting to move inland from a beachhead recently established. *Hannay*: see letter of 19 Mar 15; his letter to TH was dated 24 Aug 15 (copy in TH's hand, DCM).

To SYDNEY COCKERELL

Max Gate | 17 Sept. 1915

My dear Cockerell:

I am sending the "Far from the Madding Crowd" that I promised, which is a copy from the classified edition, containing both prose & verse, & has less misprints than any other. This "Wessex Edition", called in America the "Definitive Edition", will I suppose, be the last, as the Edition de luxe we intended to publish was stopped by the war. I say stopped, & not postponed, for I do not see much probability of any ventures of that sort being undertaken again for many a long year.

We went two days ago to see & bid goodbye to a brother of the boy who was killed at the Dardanelles last month. He had only 3 days leave after 11 months in France & Flanders. The third brother of the family is in the front line of trenches. All the soldiers one meets have a pathetic hope that "the war will soon be over": fortunately they do not realize the imbecility of our Ministers or the treachery of sections of the press which try to make political capital out of the country's needs.

I hope I am wrong, but at present it looks to me as if everything were tending to an indecisive issue of the war, Germany preponderating, & a huge indemnity to be paid by England to be let go in peace & quietness, as long as Germany chooses. The attitude of Labour is a very ugly one.

I read "The Daffodil Murderer"—Its fault is that it is not quite sufficiently burlesque to be understood.

Sincerely yours
Thomas Hardy.

Text MS. (mourning stationery) Adams.
I promised: following the visit TH and Cockerell had made together, on 27 June 1915, to the old tithe barn (still standing) at Cerne Abbas, Dorset; TH's inscription reads 'To / Sydney C. Cockerell, / (After a visit to a medieval barn typified / in the description at pp. 164–165.) / from / Thomas Hardy. / Sept: 1915.' (Adams). *stopped by the war*: see letter of 15 July 14. *Daffodil Murderer*": a parody of John Masefield's *The Everlasting Mercy* by Siegfried Sassoon (see letter of 4 Feb 17), pub. under the pseudonym of Saul Kain (London, 1913).

To SYDNEY COCKERELL

Max Gate | 2 Oct. 1915

My dear Cockerell:

A mere line to say that I have been overhauling some of my books, & find that I can, & will, with pleasure, give you the whole of the Wessex Edition, of which I sent the Far from the Madding Crowd volume lately. I want you to have it all, because of some new information given in additions to prefaces, that it may be well you should be aware of, & I could not think of letting you buy the edition.

I hope you are all well.

Ever yours,
Thomas Hardy.

Text MS. (mourning stationery) Adams.
the Wessex Edition: the set TH sent to Cockerell, with a presentation inscription dated 20 Feb 1916, is now in the Adams collection.

To CHARLES GIFFORD

Max Gate | Dorchester | Oct 4: 1915

Dear Mr Gifford:

I am writing to ask you what I have often been going to ask, & what Emma meant to inquire about years ago:—where the name of *Ireland*, that was her grandfather's second name, & of course your grandfather's also, came from. Did a family of that name ever marry into the Gifford family, & if so were they of Irish extraction? Anything about her people naturally interests me.

I also should like to know how you are, your health being but indifferent when I last wrote. If you are not up to much (which I hope is not the case) please let Miss Gifford write for you.

We should much like to see her again, & you too, & if you would put up here for a night or two in going to or coming from Launceston or come direct, we should be delighted. Or your son if he is this way.

I am sending this to Blackheath but I hope you are not there, as it lies rather in the line of the Zeppelins' track to London.

I trust you have lost no relative in this cruel war. I have lost a dear cousin, 2d Lieut. in the 5th Dorsets, killed in action in the Gallipoli peninsula—one whom Emma also was very fond of.

With kindest regards I am,

Sincerely yours
Thomas Hardy.

P.S. One other inquiry: when I was in Plymouth I tried to find the vault in Charles churchyard in which Emma's grandmother & other relatives lie. I found the gravestones, but they seemed to have been shifted & the vault swept away at the church restoration. Was that the case?

A connection of yours has bought the Kingston estate & mansion, about a mile from us, & we often see them. They are delightful friends. T.H.

Text MS. (mourning stationery) C. H. Gifford.
Gifford: Charles Edwin Gifford, ELH's first cousin; see II.17. *name of* Ireland: Mary Attersoll, the mother of ELH's grandfather Richard Ireland Gifford (1775–1825), was apparently brought up as the ward of Richard Ireland, owner of Reigate Priory; see Henry Gifford, 'Thomas Hardy and Emma', *Essays and Studies*, 1966. *Miss Gifford*: Gifford's daughter Léonie. *Launceston*: in Cornwall, where Gifford's parents had lived; see ELH, *Some Recollections*, ed. Evelyn Hardy and Robert Gittings (London, 1961), 29. *your son*: Walter Stanley Gifford (1884–1961), consulting engineer. *Blackheath*: in SE London, where Gifford was living. *Charles churchyard*: see letter of 5 June 15. *connection of yours*: see letter of 13 Oct 15.

To CHARLES RUMBOLD

Max Gate | Dorchester | Oct 4: 1915

Dear Capt. Rumbold:

Your letter has reached me, & I am glad to know—not from its contents but from its vague address—that you are among the worthy ones who are doing good work for us against the enemy. I, alas, have lost one dear friend & relative who was doing the same in the Dardanelles, till shrapnel put an end to him, to our grief.

I well remember your coming here with Lionel Fox-Pitt one November afternoon, & I happen to know the year—1912—for a very good reason: you & he were the last guests, I think, that my late wife entertained, & she died on the 27th of that month.

As to my writing another Wessex tale, as you so flatteringly suggest, I fear that will never be done. Of late years—indeed for more than 20 years—my attention & efforts have been given to that branch of literature which originally attracted me—before novel-writing did—poetry. You will find tales quite as good among "Wessex Poems", "Time's Laughingstocks", &c, as in the prose volumes, with the added advantage that they are short & condensed.

With best wishes for you in this Campaign, I am,

Yours very truly
Thomas Hardy.

Text MS. (mourning stationery) Adams.
Rumbold: Captain Charles E. A. L. Rumbold, of Marnhull, Dorset, currently serving in the Royal Engineers. *vague address*: Rumbold's letter of 1 Sept 15 (DCM) was addressed not from any specific place but from 'British Expeditionary Force'. *Fox-Pitt*: Lionel Charles Lane Fox-Pitt (1860–1937), Fellow of the Royal Geographical Society; he was the brother of TH's friend Lady Grove. *flatteringly suggest*: Rumbold had asked TH to 'give us another Wessex tale—even a short one if need be—of the present time on the lines of "The Trumpet Major"'.

To G. HERBERT THRING

Max Gate, | Dorchester. | 6th. October 1915.

Dear Mr Thring:

I gather from your letter of yesterday that our Committee of Management have decided to join the British Academy in the formation of a Committee to consider the question of the destroyed Library of Louvain.

I have much pleasure in agreeing to their proposal that my name should be placed on the list of such Committee.

Yours very truly,
Thomas Hardy.

Text MS. (typewritten) BL.
of Louvain: see letter of 19 Aug 15.

To G. HERBERT THRING

MAX GATE, | DORCHESTER. | 6th. October 1915.

Dear Mr Thring:

In reference to your inquiry if I will join in signing a congratulatory letter from the Society to Mr Henry James on the event of his becoming a naturalized British subject, I can say that nothing will please me better than to do so.

As to your suggestion that I should draft such a letter, I fear that, isolated here, I could not do it so appropriately and with so wide a survey of the circumstances as some members of the society acting in conjunction would be able to do. I therefore propose that they draw it up and send it down to me to sign.

Yours very truly,
Thomas Hardy.

Text MS. (typewritten) BL.
British subject: James's naturalization became effective on 28 July 1915. *to sign*: nothing seems to have been done, however, until early 1916, when a letter was written congratulating James both upon his naturalization and upon his appointment to the Order of Merit; see letter of 10 Jan 16.

To CHARLES GIFFORD

Max Gate | Dorchester | Oct 13: 1915

Dear Mr Gifford:

I am obliged to you for answering my inquiries so far as you can. I have always been interested in such subjects—often when the persons concerned have no sort of connection with me. Possibly it may be that in my youth I had a good deal to do with the examination and delineation of old churches and tombs.

The gentleman who has bought the Kingston estate, about a mile from here, is Mr Cecil Hanbury—son of the late Sir Thos Hanbury. Your Aunt Margaret Gifford is also Mrs Hanbury's aunt—she (Mrs H.) being the daughter of Mr Symons Jeune, brother of your aunt, who was of course Emma's aunt too by marriage.

I am glad to hear that your youngest daughter is so enterprizing in school management. May she prosper. And if your son should ever care to take the trouble to call on us here when he is in or near Dorchester we should be delighted to see him.

My wife sends her kindest regards to Léonie & yourself, as I do also.

Sincerely yours
Thomas Hardy.

Text MS. (mourning stationery) C. H. Gifford.
my inquiries: see letter to Gifford of 4 Oct 15. *Cecil Hanbury*: see letter of 28 June 14 to Gosse. *Thos Hanbury*: Sir Thomas Hanbury (1832–1907), merchant, owner of the famous gardens at La Mortola, Ventimiglia, Italy. *by marriage*: see letter of 28 June 14. *youngest daughter*: Helen Gifford; see letter of 25 Nov 19. *school management*: see letter of 25 Nov 19. *son . . . Léonie*: see letter to Gifford of 4 Oct 15.

To J. W. D. COLLINS

Oct 15. 1915.

(Ansr)
Dear Sir:

In reply to your inquiry received this morning I am able to inform you that I have known Miss Rebekah Owen for many years. She & her late sister were introduced to me by a publisher more than twenty years ago as American ladies who desired to make my acquaintance; and they came to live in Dorchester till twelve or fifteen years ago, when they went to the north of England. While here many local people became friendly with them in addition to myself & they were always known as amiable & interesting ladies.

I do not, of course, know anything of Miss Owen's business affairs, but I have always imagined them to be of ordinary stability.

Yours truly.
. . . .

Text MS. (pencil draft) DCM.
Collins: an agent at the London office of the American Express Company. *your inquiry*: Collins wrote (13 Oct 15) to say that Rebekah Owen, in seeking to open a bank account with the American Express Company, had given TH's name as a reference. *Owen*: an American Hardy enthusiast, currently living in England; see II.147.

To EDEN PHILLPOTTS

Max Gate | Oct 24: 1915

My dear Mr Phillpotts:

"Old Delabole" has arrived, for which much thanks. We began reading it last night from after dinner till bedtime.

It carries me back to the place, which I visited 45 years ago, before so much machinery was used. My experience was, I remember, not one which impressed me with the water-drinking & tea-indulging habits of the quarriers. The manager who took me round finished up by conducting me to his house & treating me to hot gin-&-water.

You have (so far as I have seen yet) resisted the temptation to conventional romanticism, & produced a record which is photographic of the quarriers as they really are. I should add that I like the description of the two men driving into Delabole at sunset as well as anything I have yet come to.

Always sincerely yours
Thomas Hardy.

P.S. Thanks too for "Old Plymouth," which I am returning. T. H.

Text MS. NYU.
Delabole": Phillpotts's novel *Old Delabole* (London, 1915) contains descriptions of the large slate quarries at Delabole, near Tintagel, Cornwall; the book is dedicated to TH. *45 years ago*: i.e., in 1870, when he first visited St. Juliot to arrange for restoration work on the church. *tea-indulging habits*: in chaps. 4 and 6 Phillpotts describes the quarriers as accompanying their meals with water or 'plenty of tea' (65). *at sunset*: the passage occurs on pp. 8–9. *"Old Plymouth,"*: unidentified.

To CLEMENT SHORTER

FROM THO. HARDY, | MAX GATE, | DORCHESTER. | 24 Oct 1915

Dear Shorter:

Many thanks for renewed request. I offer serial rights of the poem enclosed—if it will do?—It may be suitable either for Christmas, or any other time.

Very truly yours
T.H.

Text MS. (correspondence card) Yale.
poem enclosed: 'The Dead and the Living One', *Sphere*, 25 Dec 1915.

To ISRAEL GOLLANCZ

Max Gate | Dorchester. | Oct 29: 1915.

Dear Sir:

In respect of the Shakespeare Tercentenary Celebration of which you write, I do not like to promise any contribution to the proposed book, having, alas, arrived at an age at which energy is not a chief characteristic; & being too, like other people, obsessed by the war, which destroys spontaneity for ideas disconnected from it, especially in those who have lost friends or relatives. Nevertheless I will bear in mind the request you honour me with.

I had, in truth, assumed that the celebration would be postponed till peace-time, since Shakespeare could very well take care of himself for another year or two, & the European convulsion might possibly make it a meagre & absent-minded event if persisted in during the present suspense. However I do not wish to advance this opinion in the face of those of better judgment.

I am, dear Sir

Yours very truly
Thomas Hardy.

Text MS. (mourning stationery, with envelope) Rosenbach Foundation.
Gollancz: Israel Gollancz (see III.175) was now Professor of English Language and Literature, King's College, London. *you write*: on 22 Oct 15 (DCM); Gollancz was Hon. Secretary of the Executive Committee for the Shakespeare Tercentenary Celebration, 1916. *proposed book*: *A Book of Homage to Shakespeare*, ed. I. Gollancz (London, 1916), to which TH contributed his poem 'To Shakespeare After Three Hundred Years'.

To CLEMENT SHORTER

FROM THO. HARDY, | MAX GATE, | DORCHESTER. | 29: 10: 1915

Thanks for letter. What you say is quite satisfactory.

Text MS. (postcard) Berg.
What you say: about the pub. of 'The Dead and the Living One'; see letter to Shorter of 24 Oct 15.

To REYMOND ABBOTT

Max Gate | 5: 11: 1915

Dear Abbott:

Although I have not written for so long a time you must not suppose I have not thought of you. I am glad to hear, or to infer from your letter, that you keep well, & are cheerful under the shadow of this war—now reaching such a critical stage.

Really I hardly think it worth while for you to read "Ethelberta" & "The Trumpet Major" over again. However you must do as you will—

I have not heard "Cutler" for ages, but I think I will get my niece, who is here for a few days, to play it over this evening.

Whether you come to Weymouth soon or later you must let us know & give us a call at least. It is quiet now, but interesting. Convalescent men are to be seen on the front. At night the place is, of course, as dark as a hedge, as is Dorchester; & every place I suppose must be so.

I have not read "Notes on Novelists"—not caring much for those personages. Though I always can read H. J.

Believe me,

Always yrs sincerely
Thomas Hardy.

Text MS. (with envelope) Mrs. Michael MacCarthy.
"Cutler": a setting of Psalm 126 by the early 19th-century English composer William Henry Cutler; see III.88. *my niece*: i.e., ELH's niece, Lilian Gifford. *must be so*: to comply with war-time 'blackout' regulations. *on Novelists*": Henry James's *Notes on Novelists* (London, 1914).

To H. C. MACILWAINE

Max Gate | Dorchester. | 5 Nov. 1915

My dear Sir:

Looking over some letters to-day I came across yours of last May, requesting permission to arrange The Dynasts for cinema pictures.

As nothing came of it at that time I think it worthwhile to say that I could not now consent to it being done, which I mention in case you may be induced to take up the matter again.

Believe me

Yours very truly
T. Hardy

H. C. MacIlwaine Esq | Authors' Club.

Text MS. (pencil draft) DCM.
Macilwaine: Herbert Charles Macilwaine, novelist, author of *Dinkinbar* (1898), *Anthony Britten* (1906), etc. *for cinema pictures*: the only letter from Macilwaine in DCM is dated 5 June 15; it envisages *The Dynasts* as a 'patriotic film' that 'might appeal to the national imagination in a nobler strain than as yet has been attempted'. See letter of 6 Nov 15. *Authors' Club*: of which Macilwaine had been a member since 1910.

To A. E. DRINKWATER

(COPY.) MAX GATE, | DORCHESTER. | November 6th. '15.

Dear Mr Drinkwater:

I am much obliged for your information about your interview with the manager of a leading Cinema Company respecting The Dynasts.

I am sorry to say however that I have for some time been inclined to look upon the film production of the drama with any completeness or dignity, as impracticable. While to produce merely the scenes played at the Kingsway—which was what we talked about at the time—would I fear hardly be sufficient to make a success, lacking the speeches &c, that really form the substance of the Drama.

If it should happen that on reflection, or an improvement in the present state of affairs, I am led to think otherwise, I will write to my publishers the Messrs Macmillan (who act for me with the film-companies) and hear what they have to say.

Yours sincerely,
Thomas Hardy.

Text Typed transcript BL.
(*COPY*.): for Sir Frederick Macmillan; see letter of 7 Nov 15. *Cinema Company*: Drinkwater had apparently approached the Turner Film Company, producers of the film of *Far from the Madding Crowd*. *at the Kingsway*: i.e., in the Granville Barker production. *at the time*: see letter to Drinkwater of 22 Nov 14.

To SIR FREDERICK MACMILLAN

MAX GATE, | DORCHESTER. | Nov 7: 1915

My dear Macmillan:

I send on the enclosed. Do you think The Dynasts could really be done in films, & that it would be worth while to let Mr Drinkwater go on?

You probably know him as the manager who was entrusted with Mr Granville Barker's production, & who had the entire responsibility of it after Mr Barker had gone to America. I have proved him to be a man of integrity, & I should like him to have some little advantage from such production, if it were done.

If contrary to my late opinion you do think it practicable, I could put you in communication with him. My letter, as you will see, leaves the matter open.

Sincerely yours
Thomas Hardy.

Text MS. BL.
the enclosed: copy of letter of 6 Nov 15. *Drinkwater go on?*: see letter to Macmillan of 17 Nov 15.

To PAT À BECKETT

MAX GATE, | DORCHESTER. | 10th. November '15.

Dear Sir:

In reply to your letter I am sorry to say that I have nothing on hand which has not been printed, but I send on the enclosed from my drama called "The Dynasts", which seems to be the sort of thing you require. It is more important, I should think, that you should have something of the right sort than anything that is absolutely new. If this is not what you want perhaps you will let me know. The song being copyright is not yet common property.

I hope that your effort in aid of the hospital will meet with every success.

Yours very truly,
Thomas Hardy.

Captain Pat a Beckett. R.A.

Text MS. (typewritten) NYU.
à Beckett: Patrick Abbott Forbes Winslow à Beckett, currently an officer at the Royal Artillery barracks on Portland. *your letter*: of 6 Nov 15 (DCM); à Beckett had solicited a contribution of some sort to the souvenir programme of the Portland Garrison Gala Performance in Aid of the Royal Weymouth Hospital, 20 Dec 1915. *enclosed*: TH has annotated à Beckett's letter, '("Budmouth Dears" sent)'. *the hospital*: à Beckett told TH that the Garrison Football League, of which he was chairman, was 'making a gigantic effort to pay off the debt of £250 on the Royal Hospital before New Years Day'.

To EDMUND GOSSE

MAX GATE, | DORCHESTER. | Nov 11: 1915

My dear Gosse:

This is very very kind of you. But I don't feel that I can possibly be in London on Dec 9. If I should really have to be there I would let you know in good time. Between ourselves my dining-out days are nearly over. We had a week in June at Lady St Helier's (where you met us); since then I have been nowhere except motoring about the country here.

By a coincidence, in a letter to my wife just before yours came Mrs Henniker told her what a happy evening she had had at your house, & we said how much we should have liked to drop in upon you. I am so glad to hear that she is looking well.

How *do* you get about Town after dark nowadays. I banged myself against some railings in Dorchester High St. the other night—where it is as dark as a cave.

Always sincerely
Thomas Hardy.

Kindest regards to Mrs Gosse & the juniors. T. H.

Text MS. (with envelope) Adams.
on Dec 9: when Gosse entertained the Prime Minister (Asquith), John Drinkwater, and others to dinner at the National Club ('Book of Gosse', Cambridge Univ. Library). *Lady St Helier's*: i.e., at her London house; the visit was, however, made in July (see letter of 10 July 15). *at your house*: on 17 Oct 1915 ('Book of Gosse', Cambridge Univ. Library). *after dark nowadays*: i.e., during the 'blackout', which came into effect for the London area 1 Oct 1915. *the juniors*: the Gosses' daughters, Tessa (see I.167) and Sylvia (see II.287).

To SIR FREDERICK MACMILLAN

MAX GATE, | DORCHESTER. | November 17. 1915.

Dear Sir Frederick:

I should think A Changed Man might go into the 3s./6d. edition; and leave it to you.

I am hoping that some day you will bring the 3s./6d. edition into line with the Wessex Edition as to grouping the volumes, or what would be still better, a small cheap reprint of the Wessex Edition, to include everything. I fancy there might be a demand for it when we have settled down in our right minds after the war.

By the way, my idea, before the war broke out, was to ask you if you would include in your Golden Treasury Series at 2s./6d. a selection of my lyrical and other short poems, including some lyrics from "The Dynasts". I think these selections lead to the complete works being bought. I remember that was the effect Smith and Elder's selection from Browning had on me. The copy is lying ready, but I am in no hurry—and merely want you to be aware that there it is, whenever the times may be propitious, or the printers have nothing else to do.

I am glad to hear that Far from the Madding Crowd comes out so well. Herkomer, I know, took a lot of trouble about it before he fell ill.

"The Dynasts" is still more interesting as a possible film. The spoken parts will I think help it. Mr Drinkwater, with his experience of the acting version, will I think be very useful in this.

Sincerely yours,
Thomas Hardy.

Text MS. (typewritten) BL.
3s./6d. edition: Macmillan's 'Uniform' edn. of TH's works (in fact a re-issue of the Osgood McIlvaine edn. of 1895–6). *include everything*: neither of these possibilities was realized in TH's lifetime. *a selection*: *Selected Poems of Thomas Hardy* was pub. in Macmillan's 'Golden Treasury' series 3 Oct 1916; it contained 6 verse extracts from *The Dynasts*. *from Browning*: *Pocket Volume of Selections from the Poetical Works of Robert Browning*, pub. in London by Smith, Elder in 1890; TH's copy, dated 1893, was given to him by Mrs. Henniker in July 1894 (DCM). *comes out so well*: i.e., in the Turner Film Company's version; see letter to Macmillan of 9 June 15. *Herkomer*: see letter to Macmillan of 30 May 15. *useful in this*: see letter of 6 Nov 15; Macmillan, in his letters of 8 and 16 Nov 15 (Macmillan letterbooks, BL), had responded positively to the idea of filming *The Dynasts*.

To ALFRED POPE

Max Gate | Wednesday | 17: 11: 1915

Dear Mr Pope:

We learn to-day that you are not able to hear any hopeful news of your missing son, & sincerely sympathize with you & Mrs Pope in the extreme anxiety you must have suffered from. Unfortunately, while all these young lives are being risked & lost, there seems no prospect of the war approaching its end. I hope you keep well personally, & am

Very truly yours
Thomas Hardy.

We have lost a distant cousin, but nobody nearer as yet. He was a fine & promising young fellow. T. H.

Text MS. (mourning stationery) Thomas Hardy Society.
learn to-day: presumably through a mutual acquaintance. *missing son*: 2nd Lt. Percy Paris Pope (1882–1915), Pope's sixth son, was reported missing while serving with the 1st Welch Regiment at the battle of Loos, 1–2 Oct 1915; he was subsequently presumed to be dead (see letter of 27 Nov 16 to Jeune).

To SYDNEY COCKERELL

MELBURY, | DORCHESTER. | Nov 18: 1915

My dear Cockerell:

Yes, certainly. I shall like to read the letters, & will return them duly.

I was so glad to hear that Arthur Benson was to be the new master. It seemed to me the obvious thing, & I really think it will be good for the College.

We are staying here till Saturday. This is an old & interesting house, which you may know of either personally or from Hutchins's History of the County. It is the scene of that story of mine called "The First Countess of Wessex"—(for writing which the family have now quite forgiven me). Ld Ilchester is away at the Dardanelles, so we are very quiet. Kindest regards to Mrs Cockerell. I daresay you feel this raw atmosphere very much at Cambridge.

Believe me to be

Always yours
Thomas Hardy.

Text MS. Adams.
Melbury: Melbury House; see letter of 3 June 15 to FEH. *the letters*: FEH, writing to Lady Hoare 27 Nov 15 (Wiltshire Record Office), speaks of them as written to Philip Webb (1831–1915; *D.N.B.*), the architect, by 'a man dying of consumption, madly in love with a horrible wife who is unfaithful to him'; their author was apparently Alphonse Warington Taylor (1835–70), manager of the decorating firm in which Webb, William Morris, and others were partners. *Benson*: A. C. Benson had recently been elected master of Magdalene College, Cambridge, following the death of S. A. Donaldson. *Hutchins's History*: see Hutchins, *The History and Antiquities of the County of Dorset* (see letter of 13 Feb 14 to Lady Grove), II.672–4. *of Wessex*": included in *A Group of Noble Dames*; its plot was largely derived from the accounts of Elizabeth Horner, wife of the 1st Earl of Ilchester, in Hutchins, II.663, 667, 679. *at the Dardanelles*: as an officer in the Coldstream Guards.

To LADY ILCHESTER

26th Nov, 1915.

Dear Lady Ilchester,

As I promised, I am sending the MS of the poem written in Melbury Park years and years ago. Please do not trouble to acknowledge.

Sincerely yours,
Thomas Hardy.

Text Transcript (supplied by Lady Ilchester) Purdy.
the poem: a fair copy in TH's hand of 'Autumn in King's Hintock Park'; see Purdy, 140–1.

To EMMA DUGDALE

Max Gate | Dorchester. | Nov 30: 1915

Dear Mrs Dugdale:

Just a line or two of thanks for your kind letter on our loss of my sister Mary. We saw & talked to her the day before her death, & I did not think it would be so soon. The funeral yesterday was attended by many friends, though if it had not been a drizzling rain all day there would no doubt have been many more. The weather however did not inconvenience us much, her grave being under the yew tree close to where the rest of us lie.

You will remember that she painted an exceedingly pretty portrait of Florence—the last she did at the art painting-room in Dorchester. They were both much attached to each other.

We shall miss her greatly as you will imagine.

Kindest regards to Mr Dugdale & the others.

Ever sincerely yours
Thomas Hardy.

Text MS. (mourning stationery, with envelope) Purdy.
sister Mary: Mary Hardy died of emphysema on 24 Nov 1915, at the age of 73. *funeral*: at Stinsford Church; see *LY*, 170. *portrait of Florence*: it is now in DCM. *art painting-room*: a private art-school operated in Dorchester for many years in a building since absorbed into the galleries of the DCM.

To SYDNEY COCKERELL

Max Gate | Dec 5: 1915

My dear Cockerell:

I ought to have acknowledged receipt of the letters sooner. We have read them, & they shall be returned in a few days. What you say is quite true: they are a very human document.

I have lost my elder sister since I last wrote. I don't think you ever met her—though now I wish you had done so, as you & she had much in common, in respect of your interests in art. She was of rather an unusual type, but of late years had been such an invalid that it was difficult for her to talk to people. I send the short account of her which appeared in our local paper this week, that you may put it aside for reference if necessary. She was almost my only companion in childhood.

We send kindest remembrances. It is a gloomy time, in which the world, having like a spider climbed to a certain height, seems slipping back to where it was long ago.

Ever yours
Thomas Hardy.

Text MS. (mourning stationery) Victoria and Albert Museum.
the letters: see letter of 18 Nov 15. *talk to people*: evidently an allusion to Mary Hardy's respiratory difficulties, although Evangeline Smith (see I.46) told Harold Hoffman that Mary

became very deaf in her late years (Hoffman papers, Miami Univ. of Ohio). *local paper*: *Dorset County Chronicle*, 2 Dec 1915; the obituary of Mary Hardy, though not the accompanying report of her funeral, was written by TH himself.

To J. S. UDAL

Max Gate | Dorchester | 5 Dec. 1915

Dear Udal:

Many thanks for the Folk Lore number containing your article, which I am going to read—I am sure with interest.

I have never systematically studied Folk lore, nor collected dialect words. If I had done either I might have gained some valuable material in both kinds. I used in fiction such folklore as came into my mind casually, & the same with local words.

I don't know where first editions of my books can be obtained now. Besides the bookseller in Marylebone Lane, Spencer, New Oxford Street, used to have some.

I should fancy that "Under the Greenwood Tree" would have most dialect words in it. The *last* edn of this ("Wessex" Edn Macmillan) is the most correct in such words. There are also some that may never have been elsewhere printed in the rural scenes in "The Dynasts" (the 1 vol. edn is the most handy.)

I am sorry to answer you so briefly, but I have had much correspondence to attend to owing to my sister's death a fortnight ago.

Sincerely yours
Thomas Hardy.

Text MS. (mourning stationery) Colby.
your article: Udal's 'Obeah in the West Indies', *Folk-Lore*, September 1915. *Spencer*: Walter T. Spencer; see III.33. *"Wessex" Edn*: of 1912. *1 vol. edn*: of 1910.

To SIR GEORGE DOUGLAS

Max Gate | Dec 7: 1915

My dear Douglas:

I am grateful to you for your sympathy on the loss of my sister Mary, whom I regret very deeply. She was the only one of the three besides myself who had a keen appreciation of literature, & as a painter of portraits she had a real skill in catching the character of her sitter.

I am very sorry to hear that Miss Douglas is so indisposed. How long ago it seems since I met her! Also since I knew your brother Frank at Wimborne. That he has come to live near you is wise, in my opinion, which has always been that the way in which families scatter themselves with a light heart is a mistake.

The difficulty about the war for men at home is that what we feel about it we must not say, & what we must say about it we seldom think. However there is some little promise, perhaps, that things may take a turn for the better.

My reminiscences: no, never!

We have been reading Lord Redesdale's *Memories* lately: it is severely Old-Orderish, but amusing, particularly in the way in which he first makes a spotless wax figure of the contemporary he exhibits, & then disconcerts the trusting reader by putting in warts, moles & freckles incontinently.

I saw Robertson Nicoll in the summer at the Hôtel Russell, where he called & had tea with us. (My wife used to write children's & other books for his firm). He seemed active enough then.

Why don't you manage to see us? We should much like to see you, anyhow.

Always sincerely
Thomas Hardy.

Text MS. (mourning stationery) NLS.
your sympathy: in Douglas's letter of 28 Nov 15 (DCM). *so indisposed*: Douglas reported that his sister had suffered a nervous breakdown. *at Wimborne*: where Frank Douglas had been studying land-agency; see I.166 and Millgate, 222. *My reminiscences*: Douglas had asked when TH would begin writing his reminiscences. *Redesdale's* Memories: Algernon Bertram Freeman-Mitford, 1st Lord Redesdale (1837–1916), diplomat and author; *D.N.B.* His *Memories* were pub., in 2 vols., in 1915. *Nicoll*: see letter of early Feb 15 to Shorter. *his firm*: Hodder & Stoughton; one such book was *In Lucy's Garden*, pub. by Henry Frowde and Hodder & Stoughton (London, n.d.). *active enough then*: Douglas had heard that Nicoll lived 'mainly in bed', getting up only to fulfil public engagements.

To MARY SHERIDAN

Max Gate | Dec 7: 1915

My dear Mrs Sheridan:

My sincerest thanks for your sympathetic letter. I miss my sister very much. In childhood she was almost my only companion—the others being younger—& she had always been the one with the keenest literary tastes & instincts. She could paint a good likeness, too—particularly of women—& I have wished that she could have done you: she *always* pleased a sitter of her own sex. Her portrait of my mother went the round of nearly all the illustrated papers, you may remember, after my mother's death.

However it is no use thinking of this now. When you think of coming please let us know, that we may not be out.

What losses of loved ones all are suffering nowadays.

Yours always
Thomas Hardy.

Text MS. (mourning stationery) Rosenbach Foundation.
Sheridan: Mary Sheridan, American-born wife of Algernon Brinsley Sheridan, of Frampton Court, near Dorchester; TH had known her for many years (see I.184). *portrait of my mother*: see III.118–20, 123. *all are suffering*: Mrs. Sheridan had herself lost her son Wilfred in action on 15 Sept 1915.

To CLEMENT SHORTER

Max Gate | Dec 8: 1915

My dear Shorter:

It was well to send a proof. The "foreword" was written by my wife, so that you must put either her initials to it or none.

Sincere thanks to you & Mrs Shorter for your kind sympathy on the loss of my sister, whom I miss much.

Very truly yours
Th. Hardy.

I am so sorry the other poem wd not illustrate. I chose it because I thought it wd afford weird Xmas illustrations. T. H.

Text MS. (mourning stationery) Texas.
a proof: of Shorter's privately printed edn. of TH's 'Before Marching and After', a tribute to the memory of Frank George; see Purdy, 174. *or none*: the Foreword as printed is signed 'F. E. H.' *Mrs Shorter*: Dora Sigerson Shorter, poet; see IV.287. *other poem*: 'The Dead and the Living One'; see letter to Shorter of 24 Oct 15.

To SYDNEY COCKERELL

Max Gate | 13: 12: 1915

My dear Cockerell:

Warm thanks for your sympathetic letter about my poor sister Mary. I should have replied before this time & included in my reply an invitation from us both to come here whenever the train can bring you, as we should have been most glad to see you again. But I am disappointed to say that I have been suffering from dyspepsia, & am now from a cold, of which the cough is very troublesome, so that I am not fit to talk to anybody, & mope over the fire all day. Therefore it is advisable that you don't come till after Christmas, at what time then we will fix as soon as I know that I am out of this trouble.

I may mention that my brother is, to our anxiety, in such a precarious state of health as to necessitate much attention on him. His illness also began with a cold, & the state of his heart & chest is such that he cannot lie down. But it is *mainly* a severe chill after all, & I hope that a few days will enable him to get over it, though the doctor seems to do little good.

We will talk over the letters when we meet. We have been reading the "Memories" of Lord Redesdale.

Our greetings to all your house.

Every sincerely yours
Thomas Hardy.

Text MS. (mourning stationery) Adams.
sympathetic letter: of 7 Dec 15 (DCM). *get over it*: Kate Hardy's diary (Lock Collection, Dorset County Library) indicates that Henry's condition in fact worsened, showing no

improvement until Christmas Day. *the letters*: of Warington Taylor; see letter of 18 Nov 15. *of Lord Redesdale*: see letter of 7 Dec 15 to Douglas.

To EDWARD CLODD

Max Gate | Dec 31: 1915

My dear Clodd:

My best thanks for your good wishes for us at Christmas, which I reciprocate by wishing you mine for the New Year that is now imminent,—though the evolution of morals has taken a strange turn of late, & must puzzle you as a philosopher.

I have had rather a bad cold lately, but it appears to be going off. The temperature here is unusually high for the season—warmer than yours, I imagine. We have had no snow at all as yet, but of course there is time enough.

I remember reading *Panthera*—& that it had the usual result, of listening to opinions & acting upon one's own.

I hope you still find yourself not at all burdened by excess of leisure, but rather the reverse. I think you are well to be out of the City in these stressful & short-handed times. Indeed you could not have managed better if you had known a war was coming. Our kindest regards to both.

Yours very sincerely

[*signature excised*]

Text MS. (mourning stationery) Leeds.
reading Panthera: at Clodd's Aldeburgh house in August 1909; see IV.47. *excess of leisure*: Clodd was, like TH, in his 76th year but had not retired from the London Joint Stock Bank until earlier in 1915. *to both*: Clodd and his wife; see letter of 11 Feb 15.

1916

To EDMUND GOSSE

Max Gate | 2 Jan 1916

My dear Gosse:

I am grateful for your New Year's letter—& kind inquiries. I am glad to be able to say that I am intending to go downstairs tomorrow if all is well, after near a month up here, though I have not quite got rid of the troublesome cough.

I am really not particularly reluctant to be a prisoner in this dismal weather, & can sit over the fire for hours without any ambition to do otherwise.

I have never seen, so far as I remember, the elevated part of the country you have been visiting. We get the wind here too, of course, laden with marine qualities from the Channel & Atlantic.

Last night we read aloud your paper on the Wartons, whom I know only casually by T.W.'s History of Poetry—a book extraordinarily closely packed with matter. My wife sends her thanks for the pamphlet. I wish you would do one on Thomson, whose close observation of country detail has been rather neglected in the attention given to the later nature poets.

Philip's account of his adventures must have been worth listening to with his dry & racy manner of description. I hope he will get through safely.

I also was relieved to see that Henry James has (apparently) turned the corner in his illness. I thought he seemed rather weak when I accidentally met him for a minute last summer.

Our kindest regards to the household.

Always yrs sincerely
Thomas Hardy.

Text MS. (mourning stationery) Adams; envelope Leeds.
kind inquiries: Gosse (31 Dec 15, DCM) asked especially after TH's health, of which J.F. Symons Jeune (see letter of 7 June 16) had given him a 'poor account'. *been visiting*: Gosse wrote from Lyme Park, Disley, Cheshire, a house which he described as 'the highest of its size in England'. *paper on the Wartons*: Gosse's *Two Pioneers of Romanticism: Joseph and Thomas Warton* (London, 1915), delivered as a lecture before the British Academy. *of Poetry*: Thomas Warton's *The History of English Poetry from the Close of the Eleventh to the Commencement of the Eighteenth Century*, first pub. 1774–81. *Thomson*: James Thomson (1700–48), poet; *D.N.B.* TH's copy of his *Poetical Works*, purchased in 1865, is in DCM. *get through safely*: Gosse's son Philip was serving in France as a doctor with the 23rd Division. *in his illness*: James had suffered two strokes in early December 1915; his condition improved at the end of the month but he became seriously ill again in late February 1916 and died on the 28th.

To HENRY JAMES

THE | INCORPORATED SOCIETY OF AUTHORS, PLAYWRIGHTS & COMPOSERS. | 1, CENTRAL BUILDINGS, TOTHILL STREET, WESTMINSTER, S.W. | January 10th. 1916.

Dear Henry James,

I have been asked by the Committee of Management of the Society of Authors, Playwrights & Composers, to convey to you their sincere felicitations on your appointment to the Order of Merit. It is my pleasure, as well as my duty, at one and the same time to welcome a new citizen who elected to join our Commonwealth at a season when sympathy and support were eminently grateful, and to acclaim the great and appropriate Honour that has been bestowed upon him. The Society over which I preside is concerned with the prosaic interests of authors rather than with their intimate aspirations, but we are all members of a noble craft; and I venture to say that there is not one among the two thousand five hundred members of this Society who does not feel that he is honoured in yourself, an old and faithful Member of the Society, and an Englishman by choice.

Permit me to hope that your health which by recent reports has been seriously endangered is now restored. That it may be completely established will be the wish of all our Society.

I remain, with all good wishes,

Most truly Yours,
Thomas Hardy.

Henry James Esq., O.M.

Text MS. (typewritten, signed but not composed by TH) Harvard.
of Management: the letter was in fact composed by Stanley Leathes (see letter of mid-December 16), chairman of the Committee of Management of the Society, and forwarded to TH for signature (G. H. Thring to TH, 6 Jan 16, DCM); see second letter of 6 Oct 15. *Order of Merit*: as announced on 1 Jan 1916; the citation asserted that his genius had 'placed him with Mr. Thomas Hardy unquestionably at the head of living masters of English'. *now restored*: see, however, letter of 2 Jan 16.

To LADY HOARE

MAX GATE, | DORCHESTER. | Jan 14: 1916

Many & best thanks for letter, enclosure, kind message, & hopeful news. Please excuse card—I am sure you will.

T.H.

Text MS. (postcard) Wiltshire Record Office.
hopeful news: presumably of her son (see letter to Lady Hoare of 28 Oct 14), currently serving with the 1st Dorset Queen's Own Yeomanry.

To HAMO THORNYCROFT

Max Gate | Dorchester. | 19 Jan: 1916

My dear Thornycroft:

Strangely enough, I took particular notice of those verses by "S.S." in The Times of a few days ago—reading them over twice & wondering whose they were. I thought their craftsmanship promising, & more.

Our best thanks for your good wishes, which we heartily reciprocate. I have been confined to the house (until this week) for a month or more by a lingering cold & cough—apparently now gone off. I hope you & Mrs Thornycroft have not suffered from the general dampness.

How gloomy the times are. What will happen this year one who is outside the political world (as I am) quite fails to conjecture.

We will duly let you know if, & when, we come to town.

Always yrs sincerely
Thomas Hardy.

Text MS. (mourning stationery) DCM.
verses by "S.S.": Thornycroft (18 Jan 16, DCM) pointed out that the poem 'To Victory. (By a Private Soldier at the Front.)', *The Times*, 15 Jan 1916, was the work of his nephew (and ward) Siegfried Sassoon; on 31 Jan 16 (DCM) Sassoon himself wrote to ask if he might dedicate his next vol. to TH. See letter of 4 Feb 17.

To H. O. LOCK

Max Gate | Dorchester. | Jan 22: 1916

Dear Captain Lock:

It is very kind of you to write all the way from India & let me know that you sympathize with me in the loss of my elder sister. Many thanks for your letter. I remember when you underwent the same sad experience as I have lately gone through, & you will know very well that nobody else in the world can quite fill the same place in one's life as a sister about one's own age.

I hope you still find Ambala a fairly good part of the globe to be in during this convulsion that is tearing Europe to pieces. The best informed of the people I come in contact with have not the vaguest idea how long the war is going to last, though of course some of the less informed have a cut & dry theory thereupon. A few things make me uncomfortable as to its issue, though it seems that if staying power is to settle it the Allies have the best chance.

Best New Year's wishes (of a belated kind) from both my wife & myself. We see your mother occasionally, & she seems keeping up cheerfully.

Sincerely yours,
Thomas Hardy.

Text MS. (mourning stationery) Charles Lock.
from India: the 1st and 4th Dorsets, with whom Lock was serving, remained in India until

1918. *same sad experience*: Lock's only sister, Eveline Mary, married Ryle Swift in 1909 and died in 1913. *Ambala*: in the Punjab, N. of Delhi. *your mother*: Emma, widow of Arthur Lock; see letter to Lock of 16 Feb 14.

To HAROLD CHILD

Max Gate | Dorchester. | Feb 1. 1916

Dear Mr Child:

It is a pleasant surprise to me to find that you have launched the little book in spite of the times—I have not done justice to its contents as yet, but it seems, as far as I have seen, most penetrating, & I may say illuminating. Too generous also to the subject of it! as I feel dismally when thinking of the pot-boiling performances of years ago in fiction to which I had to school myself.

The one or two reviews I have read of your work seem also to indicate a high opinion of it. I am glad to hear that the subscribing is good.

However, this is not what I immediately write about, which is to remind you that you were in the mood some time back to come & see us here for a day or two. It so happens that a friend of ours, Sydney Cockerell, director of the Fitzwilliam Museum Cambridge, has just let us know that he is, D.V., going to run down & pay us a visit for the week-end Feb. 12 & 13. Now cannot you come at the same time? My wife (for whom I am asking this) desires me to say that she will be delighted if you can. It will be quite a bachelor thing, so that no preparation will be necessary.

Sincerely yours
Thomas Hardy.

By the way: there is a misprint at p. 144, where "Still be cancelled" should be "Shall be cancelled"—

Also p. 41, where "Beemy" should be "Beeny"—(I mention these unimportant items in case you should be reprinting.) T.H.

Text MS. (mourning stationery) Adams.
little book: Child's *Thomas Hardy* (London, 1916), sent by Child 29 Jan 16 (DCM). *at the same time?*: TH was unwell that weekend, however, and neither Cockerell nor Child came to Max Gate. *p. 144*: TH's reference is itself an error for p. 114.

To EDMUND GOSSE

MAX GATE, | DORCHESTER. | 1 Feb: 1916.

Thanks for letter. Am doing as desired with pleasure. Will write in a day or two.

T.H.

Text MS. (postcard, mourning stationery) Leeds.
doing as desired: Gosse wrote 31 Jan 16 (DCM) to solicit items for another Red Cross Sale.

To CLEMENT SHORTER

FROM THO. HARDY, | MAX GATE, | DORCHESTER. | Feb 2: 1916.

Anybody is at liberty to reprint poem.

Text MS. (postcard) Berg.
poem: the first appearance of TH's 'In Time of "The Breaking of Nations"', *Saturday Review*, 29 Jan 1916, was accompanied by the statement that copyright was not reserved; Shorter reprinted the poem in one of his privately printed pamphlets very shortly afterwards (see Purdy, 176).

To WILLIAM ROTHENSTEIN

Max Gate | Dorchester. | Feb 6: 1916.

Dear Mr Rothenstein:

I should have written a day or two sooner, but have been suffering from a cold in the head. I shall be pleased to sit to you for the portrait whenever you happen to be at Moreton House, & like to motor over here. If you let me know the time a day or two beforehand it would perhaps be safer, though I do not think it likely that I shall be going out much till the spring, having this winter become so susceptible to colds.

Believe me,

Sincerely yours
Thomas Hardy.

Text MS. (mourning stationery) Harvard.
the portrait: one of the drawings of TH made by Rothenstein on this occasion subsequently appeared in his *Twenty-four Portraits* (London, 1920). *Moreton House*: near Dorchester, the seat of the Fetherstonhaugh–Frampton family but apparently let at this period to Ernest Ridley Debenham (1865–1952), draper and agriculturalist. *motor over here*: Rothenstein (1 Feb 16, DCM) had suggested he might drive over to Max Gate when he was next visiting Debenham at Moreton House.

To EDMUND GOSSE

Max Gate, | 7 Feb: 1916

My dear Gosse:

As I did not think the previous puny MSS. worth sending, my wife sent them on her own responsibility, so please put them down in her name if you *do* accept them. I myself send by this post "A sheaf of Victorian Letters"—not important ones, I am sorry to say, but interesting—which I have found after rummaging. They are addressed to you at 48 Pall Mall. (my wife's parcel was addressed 83 Pall Mall).

I hope you are all well. My cold is "still running", like Charley's Aunt—though better.

Always sincerely
Thomas Hardy.

Text MS. (with envelope, mourning stationery) Leeds.
previous puny MSS.: manuscripts of TH's poems 'The Oxen' and 'In Time of "The Breaking of Nations"' and a 3-page fragment of the story 'What the Shepherd Saw'; see *LY*, 171. *accept them*: for the Red Cross Sale; see letter to Gosse of 1 Feb 16. *Victorian Letters"*: a group of letters (now in the Berg Collection) written to TH by William Black, R. D. Blackmore, George Du Maurier, Charles S. Keene, George Meredith, Leslie Stephen, Marion Terry, Anthony Trollope, and Thomas Woolner. *Charley's Aunt*: the immensely popular stage comedy by Brandon Thomas.

To ISRAEL GOLLANCZ

FROM THO. HARDY, | MAX GATE, | DORCHESTER. | 11 Feb: 1916.

Dear Professor Gollancz:

Many thanks for your letter. I have been suffering from a long cold, or I would have sent something, however short, before this time, for the Book of Homage. I can promise to forward some lines, that are partly written, in the course of a week or ten days, if that would be soon enough?

Very truly yours,
T. Hardy.

Text MS. (correspondence card) Rosenbach Foundation.
your letter: of 7 Feb 16 (DCM). *before this time*: see letter to Gollancz of 29 Oct 15.

To ISRAEL GOLLANCZ

FROM THO. HARDY, | MAX GATE, | DORCHESTER. | Feb 15: 1916

Contribution to Book of Homage is now ready. Please say when and where it is to be sent.

T.H.

Text MS. (postcard) Rosenbach Foundation.

To ISRAEL GOLLANCZ

FROM THO. HARDY, | MAX GATE, | DORCHESTER. | 17: 2: 1916.

Dear Dr Gollancz:

Many thanks for letting me know. Here is my small contribution, for what it may be worth.

T.H.

Text MS. (correspondence card) Rosenbach Foundation.
my small contribution: TH's poem 'To Shakespeare After Three Hundred Years', first pub. in *A Book of Homage to Shakespeare*, ed. Israel Gollancz (London, 1916).

To ISRAEL GOLLANCZ

MAX GATE, | DORCHESTER. | 19: 2: 1916

Dear Dr Gollancz:

The most interesting book you send has arrived. My sincerest thanks. I shall go into it soon.

I am glad you think my lines appropriate. I suppose you will send a proof, that I may remove a few cacophanies which I perpetrated in my haste.

Yrs v. truly
T. Hardy.

Text MS. (correspondence card, mourning stationery) Folger Shakespeare Library.
interesting book: Giovanni Boccaccio, *Olympia*, ed. with an English rendering by Israel Gollancz (London, 1913). *appropriate*: as Gollancz had assured him, 18 Feb 16 (DCM).

To WILLIAM ROTHENSTEIN

Max Gate: Dorchester. | Feb 23: 1916

Dear Mr Rothenstein:

It is most kind of you to give me this book of drawings, for I am sure the little I did for you in sitting does not deserve them. I fear I am a troublesome sitter, though I try to be as good as possible. Anyhow the deficiency, if any, will not be on the side of the artist.

The cold which was still a little upon me when you were here has gone off at last, I think, but I dare not go out in this north wind, which looks very like the vehicle of snow.

I have read Tagore's poem, & return it herewith. It is striking, & I can imagine what it must be in the original. It is to his great disadvantage with us that he does not *think* in English.

The Association of which you send the manifesto seems to promise to do excellent work. It is unhappily too true that our cities exhibit & encourage lamentable taste in the arts which attach to them. I hope the effort will make a mark. If I were only ten years younger I would join in it, but I have now reached an age when I am obliged to hold aloof & let "movements" be carried on by younger people. I have been compelled already to withdraw my name from societies in which I take much interest. But of course I will recommend the Association to others.

Sincerely yours
Thomas Hardy.

Text MS. Harvard.
book of drawings: Rothenstein's *Six Portraits of Sir Rabindranath Tagore*, with a prefatory note by Max Beerbohm (London, 1915), sent by Rothenstein 18 Feb 16 (DCM). *in sitting*: see letter of 6 Feb 16. *Tagore's poem*: Sir Rabindranath Tagore (1861–1941; *D.N.B.*), Indian writer, awarded the Nobel Prize for Literature in 1913. The 'poem' was presumably his *Gitanjali* (first pub. 1913), comprising his own English translations of some of his poems; Rothenstein had been largely instrumental in its publication. *The Association*: the recently

founded Civic Arts Association, devoted to promoting the use of arts and crafts for civic purposes and especially to enhancing the quality of future war memorials.

To SYDNEY COCKERELL

Max Gate Feb 24. 1916.

My dear Cockerell:

It is fortunate that you got home before this snow came.

I am struck with the thoroughness of this Mr Danielson, whoever he may be, if all he announces is true. As to the MS. of "A Pair of Blue Eyes", there is no doubt that its history is this. When I wrote it in 1872–73 for Tinsley's Magazine the MS. of each number was not returned with the proof, & its earlier chapters being (as I remember) thought little of by Tinsley, the MS. of them was probably destroyed. But about the middle the story began to excite attention, & so Tinsley must have thought it worth while to preserve the MS. of it on the chance of it being worth something. His business was sold later on, & I suppose Matthews & Lane bought the MS., letters, &c. at the sale.

I do not know the law with regard to MSS, but I know that an architect's drawings belong to the architect, & that he can demand their return when the building has been erected.

Private. Since you were here I have thought that it would be as well to get those little matters of the Literary Executorship settled. Do you think that my wife & yourself would be a sufficient number to act, or would you like a third?

Also: what do you think of this: a sum of £200 to Exors to cover the first 3 years of their labours; afterwards a percentage per year on the author's royalties from the publishers. This would then automatically continue to any new Executor who might have to be brought in in the event of the death or what not of the first. It is entirely my own idea, & seems fair.

Please be quite frank on this.

Sincerely yours
Thomas Hardy.

I pay agents 10 per cent for acting for me—& this would I suppose suit the case of Executors. T.H.

Text MS. Victoria and Albert Museum; envelope Adams.
got home: from his delayed visit to Max Gate; see letter of 1 Feb 16 to Child. *Mr Danielson*: see letter to him of 27 July 16 *all he announces*: Cockerell (23 Feb 16, DCM) reported receipt of the proof-sheets of Danielson's *The First Editions of the Writings of Thomas Hardy and Their Values: A Bibliographical Handbook for Collectors, Booksellers, Librarians and Others* (London, 1916); he also transcribed (from the proofs) and sent to TH a prospectus of *A Bibliography of the Works of Thomas Hardy 1865–1916* announced by Danielson as being 'In preparation'. *probably destroyed*: TH's speculation was based upon Cockerell's report that the sale of the stock of the publishing house of Elkin Mathews and John Lane, 16 May 1895, had included the original MS. of 'most' of *A Pair of Blue Eyes*; in fact chaps. 1–8 and 15–18, now in the Berg collection, are the only portions of the MS. known to have survived (see Purdy, 11). Private: inserted by TH as an afterthought. *like a third?*: Cockerell and

FEH remained TH's only literary executors, although his will, executed in 1922, specified that should Cockerell 'die in my lifetime or be unable or unwilling to act', he would be succeeded first by Edmund Gosse and then by Charles Harry St. John Hornby (1867–1946; *D.N.B.*), printer and connoisseur. *seems fair*: this provision for a 10% royalty was incorporated into TH's will.

To SIR FREDERICK MACMILLAN

MAX GATE, | DORCHESTER. | 24th. February 1916.

Dear Sir Frederick Macmillan:

As things still look so bad in England for issuing books, particularly 'pure literature', I have been thinking what can be done in America. The Americans, I find, are unexpectedly getting interested in all my verse, including The Dynasts, but so far as I know none of it is accessible to them in any brief and handy form.

So I fancy it might be possible to publish over there that little book of selections from the poems which I mentioned to you, and which I am assuming you do not think it advisable to issue here just at present.

As the selections are from all the poetical volumes, I have to consider what position we are in with the Harpers about the verse. Do they now hold the publishing rights of all the verse, or did they only acquire the right from your New York branch to print in the Wessex Edition (which they call the Autograph Edition) what was published by your branch? As I cannot remember, I do not know whether to propose to the Harpers, or to the Macmillan Co of New York, the publication of the selections.

Yours very truly,
Thomas Hardy.

Text MS. (typewritten) BL.
mentioned to you: see letter to Macmillan of 17 Nov 15. (*which ... Edition*): inserted in TH's hand. *publication of the selections*: Macmillan proposed (25 Feb 16, Macmillan letterbooks, BL) that his firm should pub. the vol. first in its Golden Treasury Series, as TH had earlier suggested (see letter to Macmillan of 17 Nov 15), and then supply sheets to the American market.

To SIR FREDERICK MACMILLAN

MAX GATE, | DORCHESTER. | 28: 2: 1916

My dear Macmillan:

It will of course be better to publish them in England first, in your Golden Treasury. So I will send up the copy in a few days, when I have gone through it again to save as much correction as possible in proofs.

Sincerely yours
Thomas Hardy.

Text MS. (correspondence card, mourning stationery) BL.

To SIR FREDERICK MACMILLAN

MAX GATE, | DORCHESTER. | March 14: 1916

Dear Sir Frederick:

I am sending up the copy to you for the Selection—that you may at least have it in your custody. It has been chosen with a view to general circulation, & contains nothing controversial, so far as I see.

I daresay there would be some demand for it in America, if you send sheets over there, & I suppose there would be no difficulty in arranging with the Harpers for including the few in the book that they published.

Sincerely yours
Thomas Hardy.

Text MS. BL.
nothing controversial: FEH told Cockerell (25 July 16, Purdy) that TH wanted it to be 'a little volume that one can give to a school girl, or the most particular person'.

To EDMUND GOSSE

Max Gate; | 15 March '16

My dear Chairman:

I am glad to find that you are still actively engaged in your gratuitous work. It is rather barefaced of me, I confess, to be a Committee man, & never go near the scene of my supposed labours. However it is your fault, which is a comforting reflection, so that I picture the unpacking of those 2400 packages by other hands than my own with comparative calm.

I am *much* interested to hear about Philip. If poverty makes strange bedfellows, war makes strange yokefellows.—I mean, how it mixes us all up. We here get men in Khaki from the camp to tea, & discover under their uniform men of every profession: lawyers, artists, bankers, &c, &c. all painted one colour for the nonce.

I hope you are economizing? We put on our coals as it were with sugartongs, drink cider only, in wineglasses, & send our ancient shoes to be mended instead of buying new ones—So you see we are getting on.

What is going to happen to English literature I don't know—if the war goes on long. I have many misgivings.

Just now I am making up a patchwork of some scenes from The Dynasts for our local actors to perform in aid of the Anglo-Russian hospital,—tedious, ephemeral labour—but what can one do else?

I wish we *could* drop in! Those Sunday evenings were indeed pleasant. But like the man in the Toccata of Galuppi's: "I feel chilly & grown old."

Always sincerely
Thomas Hardy.

Text MS. BL.
your gratuitous work: as chairman of the committee organizing the Red Cross Sale of books and manuscripts. *Philip*: Philip Gosse's wartime adventures were later described in his

Memoirs of a Camp-Follower (London, 1934). *from The Dynasts*: *Wessex Scenes from The Dynasts*, first performed in Weymouth 22 June 1916. *of Galuppi's*: the allusion is to stanza 15 of Browning's 'A Toccata of Galuppi's'.

To CLEMENT SHORTER

Max Gate: 15: 3: 1916

My dear Shorter:

My wife was leaving home for two or three days when your letter & parcel came, & she asked me to acknowledge the receipt of them, which I gladly do; & also of the book you enclosed for me to read.

The verses you speak of are published in America also; & being hastily written & subject to annihilation, I don't care to have them reprinted in your pet limited edition. Of course, if what you say is true—that anybody may print such an edition of anybody's writings without permission, you must do your worst.

I don't think much will come of voluntary abstemiousness—do you? As to leaving off meat for a day or two, that I believe in, for it really is beneficial, war or no war, as I have proved.

By the way we drink cider—in wine glasses to make it seem precious—& find it just as good for us as wine & better than spirits. If you want to get up with a clear head in the morning, try cider for dinner.

Other matters shall stand over till my wife returns, & with thanks for kindnesses, I am

Yours very truly
Thomas Hardy.

Text MS. Leeds.
leaving home: for a visit to her parents at Enfield. *parcel*: presumably containing books for her to review for Shorter's *Sphere*. *the book*: unidentified. *pet limited edition*: Shorter was perhaps contemplating a privately printed pamphlet of TH's 'The Dead and the Living One', pub. in the *Sphere*, 25 Dec 1915, and in the *World* (New York), 2 Jan 1916; Cockerell (23 Feb 16, DCM) had recently urged TH not to give his consent to such publications in the future. See Purdy, 349–50.

To SIR ARTHUR QUILLER-COUCH

Max Gate. | March 19: 1916

My dear Q:

We are reading aloud in the evenings, with great pleasure, I need not say, the handsome book you have been so kind as to send. (My wife has gone ahead privately with it, & says that now at last she thinks she may become a great writer in spite of me)

It is a charm to turn to its pages between one & another hour of the drudgery in which I am just now involved—the preparation of a play for our local actors (merely patchwork from some scenes in The Dynasts) by which money is to be raised for the Red Cross Society—a job I could not, however, refuse to do with any sort of conscience.

A man must have a good deal of magnanimity in him, I have been thinking, to tell the rising youth with such hearty unreserve the principles of a trade—I ought to say art as you do, of course—which so many of us have to find out laboriously for ourselves. I am sure I can assert truly, like the old gentleman in Longfellow's poem (was it?)—"I learn"—after reading many of your remarks. You will allow me nevertheless to be sceptical on some points: e.g: that the sequence of vowels in Mr Yeats's poem has much to do with its beauty, or whether any great poet ever thought much about such sequences—except perhaps Gray & Tennyson.

I believe I said to you when I was at Cambridge that we shd be delighted if you would—preferably in summer—break your journey here in coming from or going into Cornwall—that county which was the scene of the greatest romance of my life.

I hope you are not too depressed by the position in Europe, & am always

Sincerely yours,
Thomas Hardy.

Text MS. (mourning stationery) Miss F. F. Quiller-Couch.
Quiller-Couch: Arthur Thomas Quiller-Couch (see II.277), man of letters; he was knighted in 1910. *handsome book*: Quiller-Couch's *On the Art of Writing* (Cambridge, 1916). *in The Dynasts*: see letter of 15 Mar 16 to Gosse. *Longfellow's poem*: an apparent allusion to the last two stanzas of Longfellow's 'Travels by the Fireside'. *in Mr Yeats's poem*: 'The Lake Isle of Innisfree'; Quiller-Couch (141) comments upon the way in which its 'vowels play and ring and chime and toll'. *at Cambridge*: see *LY*, 159. *into Cornwall*: Quiller-Couch's house was at Fowey, Cornwall.

To ALBERT HARDY

Max Gate | Dorchester | March 20. 1916

Dear Mr Hardy,

I have just received your letter telling me of the death of your father, which I am much grieved to hear, as I knew him, of course, earlier in life than any other person now living, though later on we became divided, practically, for the rest of our existence. Yet I am glad to think now that I did see him very occasionally. When the last time was I have no means of ascertaining, but it was an immense number of years ago.

If I had been in London—as formerly I used to be in the spring very often—I should certainly have gone down to his funeral. But of late years I have not been able to go to town so frequently, & during this past winter I have been almost entirely confined to the house by a lingering cold.

With much sympathy, & best wishes for all, believe me

Sincerely yours
T. Hardy.

Text MS. (mourning stationery, with envelope) DCM.
Hardy: Albert Augustus Hardy (1862–1930), the son of TH's cousin Augustus; the family was living at Twickenham. *your father*: Augustus Hardy (1839–1916), the third son of TH's uncle James; they had been children at Higher Bockhampton together.

To SIR FREDERICK MACMILLAN

MAX GATE, | DORCHESTER. | March 22: 1916

My dear Macmillan:

We are delighted with the appearance of the specimen pages, which seem likely to make a charming volume.

I leave the terms entirely to you, & think those you mention are quite fair, which therefore I accept—viz., one-sixth the published price (2s/6d) on all copies sold except those sold in America—on which ten per cent.

Yours very truly
Thomas Hardy.

Text MS. BL.
specimen pages: of *Selected Poems of Thomas Hardy*, to be pub. in Macmillan's Golden Treasury series; see letter to Macmillan of 24 Feb 16. *you mention*: in Macmillan's letter of 21 Mar 16 (Macmillan letterbooks, BL) which accompanied the specimen pages.

To EDWARD CLODD

Max Gate | March 25: '16

My dear Clodd:

I have just finished the reading of your memorial lecture on Gibbon that you have been so mindful as to send me. Apart from the essential subject, what strikes me first is your undiminished power of dispatch in these offhand achievements. I have no doubt that the inhaling of more Aldeburgh air than you used to get in busier days will keep this up indefinitely.

You have, of course, limited, or mainly limited, your discourse to the renowned 15th & 16th chapters. My suspicion is that when people say they have been "reading Gibbon" they have not gone much further than those chapters, though there are so many equally interesting.

I wonder if I ever told you that I once found myself in Gibbon's old garden at Lausanne on the very anniversary of the night on which he finished his work.

Gibbon's style, alluded to by your Chairman, does not oppress everybody as it does certainly some of the historian's modern readers. I have always rather delighted in it.

I am sending this to Strafford House, though I gather that you are a good deal in London. We hope Mrs Clodd is now well, after her experiences in the nursing home. With many thanks I am

Yours sincerely
Thomas Hardy.

Text MS. (mourning stationery) BL.
lecture on Gibbon: Clodd's Moncure Conway Memorial lecture, *Gibbon and Christianity* (London, 1916). *chapters*: of Edward Gibbon's *Decline and Fall of the Roman Empire*. *at Lausanne*: see *LY*, 67–9. *your Chairman*: Sir Sydney Olivier (1859–1943; *D.N.B.*), currently Permanent Secretary of the Board of Agriculture and Fisheries; he had compared the experience of reading Gibbon to that of 'wading through a bog in a nightmare'. *Strafford House*: Clodd's Aldeburgh address. *Mrs Clodd*: see letter of 11 Feb 15.

To JOHN GALSWORTHY

Max Gate. | March 31, 1916.

Dear Mr. Galsworthy,

I am sorry about the influenza, though it has certainly done me an indirect service by bringing this letter from you. It has been flirting with us off and on for the last three months. The conclusion I have come to about it is that people who live away from crowds get extraordinarily susceptible to the complaint—to infection, I mean; which would explain the story that the inhabitants of St. Kilda catch cold on the landing of strangers, of which we are told somewhere in Boswell's *Johnson*. One day in London is enough to give it to me at this time of the year.

I much appreciate your tackling *The Dynasts*. Well, I suppose it would never have been finished if war had broken out when I was in the middle of it.

I am not a philosopher any more than you are, though from your letter I think I can hardly let you off the charge of at least having associated with Philosophy. The question you open up—of Free Will *versus* Determinism—is perennially absorbing, though less so when we find how much depends, in arguments on the subject, on the definition of the terms. Your own ingenious view of Free Will as a man's privileged ignorance of how he is going to act until he has acted would hardly suit the veterans who constitute the Old Guard of Free Will, but it suits me well enough.

If we could get outside the Universe and look back at it, Free Will as commonly understood would appear impossible; while by going inside one's individual self and looking at it, its difficulties appear less formidable, though I do not fancy they quite vanish.

That there seems no ultimate reason for existence, if not a staggering idea, does make most of us feel that, if there could be a reason, life would be far more interesting than it is. The mystery of consciousness having appeared in the world when apparently it would have done much better by keeping away is one of the many involved in the whole business.

Your likening Pity to the pearl in the oyster is a very beautiful idea, and, I think, a very close parallel.

As to visiting the West, I don't know, though I was full of the notion some time ago. We would, of course, let you see us, somehow.

Kindest regards to both from us.

Always sincerely,
Thomas Hardy.

Text H. V. Marrot, *The Life and Letters of John Galsworthy* (London, 1935), 751–2. *letter from you*: of 27 Mar 16 (DCM; pub. in Marrot, 749–51). *in Boswell's* Johnson: see *Life of Johnson*, ed. G. Birkbeck Hill, rev. L. F. Powell (4 vols., Oxford, 1934), II. 51. *tackling* The Dynasts: Galsworthy reported having just read the three parts straight through. *any more than you are*: Galsworthy confessed himself 'miserably read in Philosophy'. *privileged . . . has acted*: taken verbatim from Galsworthy's letter. *in the oyster*: Galsworthy suggested that Pity, defined as man's anguished search for a meaning in the universe, was 'a kind of excrescence, a pearl as it were on the oyster of Life', adding that while the oyster itself had become diseased 'the pearls thereof are the most beautiful things we know; and have become more precious than the oyster'. *the West*: Galsworthy was accustomed to spend his summers at Manaton, Devon.

To HENRY W. NEVINSON

Max Gate | Dorchester. | 31: 3: 1916

Dear Mr Nevinson:

I cannot possibly sign the paper, holding the opinions I do hold, & with the experiences I have had since the war began. It is not worth while to give my reasons, as it would be a useless labour.

We were talking about you quite lately, & I said that I guessed you were far away somewhere as a war-correspondent. You may have been in or near the Gallipoli Peninsula when the most promising relative I had was killed there last year.

We hope you are none the worse for your absence, & my wife sends her kind regards.

Sincerely yours
Thomas Hardy.

Text MS. (mourning stationery) Yale.
Nevinson: Henry Woodd Nevinson, journalist and essayist; see III.223. *the paper*: unidentified; TH distressed Nevinson later in 1916 by his refusal to sign a petition for the reprieve of Sir Roger Casement, but at this date the arrest of Casement and the Dublin rising of Easter 1916 were still in the future. *Gallipoli Peninsula*: Nevinson had indeed just returned from service as a war correspondent in the Dardanelles and in Greece. *killed there last year*: Frank George (see letter of 1 Sept 15 to Cockerell); TH's use of mourning stationery, however, relates primarily to Mary Hardy's death in November 1915.

To SYDNEY COCKERELL

MAX GATE, | DORCHESTER. | Saturday: 8: 4: 1916

My dear Cockerell:

I was glad to see your handwriting again. The fresh cold did not come to much, & I am quite right now. The weather you talk of did not reach here, where the dust flies mountains high.

As the moon is full on or about the 18th (Tuesday week), why not come here for the next week end,—viz: Saturday next? I don't like to press you, as you know how dull it is here; but here we are, & perhaps we could invent some business matter to discuss? In fact I can think already of two or three.

I hardly think the Germans will ever be able to hit Cambridge: still I quite see your reason for liking best to be away on light nights. The police are getting stricter here about illuminated windows, &c, but I fancy we are not worth their attention down Wessex way.

What a curious thing—that of this Mr Danielson's interest in my scraps of writing.

I sent some old letters—(not mine; addressed to me)—to the Red Cross Sale, & am interested in knowing if they will fetch anything next week.

I will, I think, send the reference to "upping-stock" to the O.E.D.

Always yours
Thomas Hardy.

P.S. We regret so much to hear that Mrs Cockerell is not yet quite well. My wife is not so strong as she ought to be in this good air, & I can't think why. She, of course, joins me in feeling how pleasant it wd be for you to come next Saty. T.H.

Text MS. Princeton.
moon is full: as the next paragraph makes clear, Cockerell was worried about the possibility of Zeppelin raids. *down Wessex way*: TH first wrote 'down here'. *Mr Danielson's interest*: see letter to Cockerell of 24 Feb 16. *some old letters*: see letter of 7 Feb 16. *"upping-stock"*: defined in the O.E.D. as 'a horse-block, a mounting-stone'; since the relevant section of the Dictionary was not pub. until 1926 it is possible that one of the three illustrative quotations was supplied by TH. *next Saty*: Cockerell seems in fact to have stayed at Max Gate from Monday 17 April to Wednesday 19 April.

To G. HERBERT THRING

MAX GATE, | DORCHESTER. | April 15. 1916.

Dear Mr Thring,

As I have arrived at a time of life when one has to think of such things, I enclose a list of questions on which you and the Society's advisers may perhaps not object to give your views.

It may be possible to answer them easily off-hand from rules already drawn up; but if they are troublesome and require consultation I shall be happy to pay a proper fee.

I would not have cumbered you with the enquiries at all, were it not that I think them of a kind which the society may have already handled, or should be prepared to handle in the future,

Yours very truly,
Thomas Hardy.

G. Herbert Thring. Esq.

Questions on the copyrights of deceased authors.

1. Has not the new fifty-years-copyright from an author's death created a necessity of appointing a successor or successors to the first literary executor or executors, seeing that, unlike when the old law of a short copyright ruled, an executor can hardly be expected to act for the whole term?
2. If so, who usually appoints such a successor or successors?
3. Does the Society see any objection to remunerating a literary executor by a yearly per-centage of the author's royalties for as long as his work requires attention, instead of, as is usual, by a lump sum at the beginning—or in addition to it? Would it be any temptation to the executor to go on longer than necessary, to meddle too much, etc.
4. Does the Society ever act as literary executor to authors?

Text MS. (typewritten) BL.
give your views: Thring replied 6 June 16 (DCM); see letter of 9 June 16. *yearly percentage*: see letter of 24 Feb 16 to Cockerell.

To JOHN GALSWORTHY

Max Gate. | April 16, 1916.

Mr dear Galsworthy,

I have been conning your diagram, and I see what you mean. I once made some such sketch to illustrate Will, Circumstance, etc., but I cannot find it.

Your view of existence "swelling and shrinking" is not altogether unlike Spencer's, in his *First Principles*, though I fancy not quite the same.

The only thing which puzzles me rather is your use of the word "reason" in the phrase "the reason of existence is but a gradual ceasing to exist." It seems to me that the word "good" instead of "reason" would be more accurate. But I am a miserable reasoner.

I hope you have entirely got rid of the "flu." We both want to go West still—mainly (did I tell you?) to see if a tablet to my first wife, who was also a great friend of my present wife's, has been put up properly in St. Juliot Church, near Boscastle. But we find a trouble in leaving the house, and, too, have to go to London for two or three days.

Always sincerely,
Thomas Hardy.

Text H. V. Marrot, *The Life and Letters of John Galsworthy* (London, 1935), 753.
your diagram: in Galsworthy's apparently undated letter to TH pub. in Marrot, 752–3; the diagram, reproduced on p. 752, is intended to illustrate Galsworthy's notion of existence as 'a limitless circle—swelling and shrinking, rising and falling, in an endless band of curves'. First Principles: see II.24–5. *a tablet*: designed by TH himself; see *LY*, 156, 172.

To H. C. DUFFIN

MAX GATE, | DORCHESTER. | 17th. April 1916.

Dear Sir:

I write to acknowledge the receipt of your book on the Wessex Novels, and must thank you for the generous opinions you express on them, and for feeling that they deserved such ingenious analyses.

To go beyond the novels, some of your pages seem to me to show that you possess a discriminating insight into English literature in general.

You may be amused when I add that we are puzzled why an elaborate critical work, which frequently assumes to treat of "The Art of Hardy", "Hardy's Message", "Hardy's view of life" etc, as a whole, should ignore that part of his art and message to which half his writing life has been devoted, and almost the only part in which self-expression has been quite unfettered. Yet I am not at all sure on second thoughts that you have not done wisely in leaving it alone.

With renewed thanks believe me,

Yours very truly,
Thomas Hardy.

H.C. Duffin Esq. M.A.

Text MS. (typewritten) Taylor.
Duffin: Henry Charles Duffin, schoolmaster and author. *your book*: Duffin's *Thomas Hardy: A Study of the Wessex Novels* (Manchester, 1916). *leaving it alone*: later editions of Duffin's book were, however, expanded to include discussion of TH's poems and of *The Dynasts*.

To SYDNEY COCKERELL

MAX GATE, | DORCHESTER. | April 26: 1916

My dear Cockerell:

I did not act upon your good suggestion that I should write to The Times to the effect that the democratic principle must be suspended in conducting a war, from the very nature of things. I saw after you had left that the principle was so clearly recognized by so many other people in the press that to reiterate it was unnecessary.

My more particular object in writing at this moment is to tell you of a bright idea which has come to me since my wife received your letter this morning. I have a Bath chair of the very best make & appearance, which I bought for my late wife, & which she used a little though not much. It is at the furniture dealer's here, & I am paying for its storage, &, of course, the cushions, &c, are getting injured by neglect. If you will accept this chair as a gift from me for the use of Mrs Cockerell I shall be delighted. The thought of selling it has always gone rather against my feeling, so my compunctions would be removed by your having it. It is a big thing to send so far, but it can be done, as it goes into a great case, which locks up, & therefore would not injure by railway transit. Let me know if you would *rather* hire one, but if not, I will pack it off to you. If inconvenient to keep, you could sell it when done with.

My wife will answer the rest of your letter: I am trying to catch the morning post with this. She probably did not tell you clearly what I meant about Lucas's account of his interview & dinner with Watts Dunton & Swinburne. It was his making a ridiculous picture of Swinburne that I most objected to. However, apart from that, to go to a man's house & eat his dinner, & *after his death* to belittle him from facts observed while you were enjoying his hospitality, is in my opinion contemptible. Believe me,

Yours always
Thomas Hardy.

P.S. Of course, if you do not want the chair just yet you cd let it stay till you come again, & cd look at it. T.H.

Text MS. Adams.
in the press: TH appears to have been making a general observation rather than commenting upon an ongoing correspondence. *for the use of Mrs Cockerell*: who was suffering from multiple sclerosis; see letter of 21 Jan 17. *most objected to*: FEH, writing to Cockerell 22 Apr 16 (Purdy), had in fact given a vivid impression of TH's indignant response to *At the Pines*, reprinted in pamphlet form by Clement Shorter from E. V. Lucas's article, 'At "The Pines"', *New Statesman*, 25 Mar 1916.

To SYDNEY COCKERELL

Max Gate | Sunday. [30 April 1916]

My dear Cockerell:

My wife has just returned from London, & we have considered about the Chair. What I think is, & she agrees with me, that, instead of sending off such a heavy article to Cambridge on the chance of it suiting, it will be better to let it stay till you have seen it, & the case that was made for it (with wheels &c), so that you may decide for yourself if it is too heavy. It is of course much heavier than a wicker chair, & well padded with cushions. Our man used to drag my late wife to church in it every Sunday. I suppose Whitsuntide would be a date for running down that would suit you, but any time would suit us—you might just come for one night & back, if your spare time is limited. The chief trouble is, the stowage. Perhaps your new house has a sort of coach house attached. It should be a lock-up place.

I could not on any account let you pay anything for it.

Florence saw the bronze head of me done by Thornycroft, at the Private View, & likes it immensely. She says the general show is not very striking this year. She was present at the sale of the MSS. & letters we sent to the Red Cross—They fetched £72..10..0—the little MS. of 12 lines called "The Breaking of the Nations", which was printed in the Saturday R. reaching £17. (I thought £5 at the outside.)

Mr & Mrs G.B. Shaw are staying at Weymouth, & they came here Friday afternoon—accidentally meeting the Burys, who also dropped in to tea. My wife is sorry to have missed G.B.S. Mrs Bury & Mrs Shaw went arguing about the Irish rising, of course.

Always sincerely
Thomas Hardy.

Will send back the flying man's letter next time.

Text MS. (with envelope) Adams. *Date* Supplied on letter in Cockerell's hand.
from London: where she had consulted Macleod Yearsley, the surgeon, about a problem with the bone behind her left ear. *the Chair*: see letter of 26 Apr 16. *by Thornycroft*: see letter of 30 Apr 16 to Thornycroft. *to the Red Cross*: see letter of 7 Feb 16 and *LY*, 171. *Saturday R.*: *Saturday Review*; see letter of 2 Feb 16. *Shaw*: George Bernard Shaw (1856-1950), Irish-born playwright; *D.N.B.* His wife Charlotte (*née* Payne-Townsend) was Anglo-Irish. *the Burys*: both John Bagnell Bury, the historian (see IV.155), and his wife Jane were of Irish birth. *the Irish rising*: which began in Dublin on 24 Apr 1916. *the flying man's letter*: unidentified, but presumably written to Cockerell by a former Cambridge undergraduate.

To HAMO THORNYCROFT

MAX GATE, | DORCHESTER. | 30: 4: 1916

My dear Thornycroft:

We are much struck with the photographs. That of my head shows what a good & forcible likeness the bronze is. I must try to live up to such a reproduction of life: but I feel a feeble person beside it.

My wife says that your marble "Kiss" is the most beautiful thing in the Exhibition, with all the distinction of Greek art at its best. I wish I had gone up, as the lady had not got entirely outside the block of stone when I beheld her in your studio. I am very glad that it will be at the Tate gallery.

We hear that the 3 scraps of MS. & letters we sent to the Red Cross Sale fetched £72..10.0. I expected £15 or £20.

Please remain at your zenith as long as you conveniently can, & don't think of sloping towards the West. I fancy you will find your hands pretty full after the war.

Always sincerely
Thomas Hardy.

Text MS. DCM.
the photographs: of Thornycroft's recent sculptures, including his bust of TH (see letter to Thornycroft of 24 Feb 15), sent 28 Apr 16 (DCM). *the Exhibition*: the Summer Exhibition of the Royal Academy. *at the Tate gallery*: where it has since remained, although it is not now on exhibition.

To CLEMENT SHORTER

Max Gate | May 6: 1916

My dear Shorter:

As you are likely to go to Devonshire, & as we lie on the way to Devonshire, my wife desires me to say (& I join in her wish) that instead of just calling here she will be pleased if you stay over one night, which will take up very little of your time: this either going or coming back, & on whatever day suits you best.

When I see you I will tell you why I cannot very well agree to a reprint of the Shakespeare poem. Apart from that, I fancy you are getting off the track in these private printings. Surely they are meant to be curiosities which for some reason have been or can be printed in no other form—not productions that the authors issue to the public in the ordinary way, as I shall probably do with this one if I bring out another volume of verses.

I hope nothing will happen to cause Mrs Shorter any trouble in her pilgrimage. Poor Ireland: we are very sorry for her; but I fear this event shows indubitably that her people are too imaginative to be able to govern themselves, always seeing snakes where there are none.

Yours sincerely
Thomas Hardy.

Text MS. BL.
Shakespeare poem: 'To Shakespeare After Three Hundred Years'; see letter of 17 Feb 16. *these private printings*: the poem was, however, printed by FEH later in 1916; see Purdy, 178. *her pilgrimage*: she was evidently planning to visit her native Ireland. *this event*: the Easter Rising; see letter of 30 Apr 16 to Cockerell.

To BENJAMIN DE CASSERES

MAX GATE, | DORCHESTER. | 17th. May 1916.

Dear Sir:

I acknowledge with thanks your gift of the volume entitled "The Shadow-Eater" which reached me a few days ago, and in which I have read some of the poems with much interest.

Yours truly,
Thomas Hardy.

B. de Casseres Esq.

Text MS. (typewritten, with envelope in hand of FEH) Brooklyn Public Library.
Shadow-Eater": De Casseres's *The Shadow-Eater* (New York, 1915).

To CLEMENT SHORTER

MAX GATE, | DORCHESTER. | 18th. May 1916.

My dear Shorter:

Six guineas for English serial right of the two poems quite satisfies me—in fact I was going to ask you five, with some tremulousness. I am glad you are going to bring them out soon. The poems are quite new (what I mean is they have never been out of my drawer till now—though when they were actually written I don't remember) and they have been seen by no eyes but my own and those of the lady who shall be nameless.

My wife asks me to say that you do not enclose the letter from Stevens and Brown about Lady Harcourt's letter. We are delighted with Mrs Shorter's poem.

As to Ireland, time will tell whose ideas are "wrong"—or perhaps will never tell. I cannot myself see that she has a "right to preserve her own soul" by murdering her fellow creatures. But I won't argue. If I did I should say that the Irish must be either senseless, and therefore deserving of pity, or normal and malignantly ungrateful for 30 or 40 years of kindness, and therefore deserving no further consideration. However I don't say so.

I will see about the MS.

Yours very truly,
Thomas Hardy.

P.S. I almost forgot to say that the Shakespeare poem is coming out in the Fortnightly for June. You will know better than I when this appears, and be able to avoid publishing your poems that week. I think any week in June will anticipate the book. T.H.

Text MS. (typewritten, with envelope in TH's hand) Berg.
the two poems: 'The Wound' and 'A Merrymaking in Question', both pub. in the *Sphere*, 27 May 1916. *nameless*: she remains unidentified, unless FEH is intended. *Lady Harcourt's letter*: Messrs B. F. Stevens & Brown were the London booksellers who had participated in the publication of the special printing of TH's 'The Convergence of the Twain' (see IV.223), of which Lady Harcourt, niece of TH's friend Mary Sheridan, was perhaps seeking a copy. *Mrs Shorter's poem*: unidentified; for Dora Sigerson Shorter, see letter of 8 Dec 15. *"right . . . soul"*: evidently a quotation from Shorter's letter, which has not survived. *the MS.*: Shorter had perhaps requested one of TH's MSS., either for himself or to be sold for charity. *Shakespeare poem*: 'To Shakespeare After Three Hundred Years' was reprinted in the *Fortnightly Review*, June 1916; see letter of 6 May 16. *the book*: TH's *Selected Poems*, including both of the *Sphere* poems, was pub. 3 Oct 1916.

To WALTER HOUNSELL

FROM THO. HARDY, | MAX GATE, | DORCHESTER. | 21: 5: 1916

Please cut the inscription deep, so that when the rain splashes up from the ledger it will not wash out.

I hope the drawing of the Tomb itself, with full size mouldings &c. reached you. It was sent 2 or 3 weeks ago.—

Text MS. (postcard) Adams.
Hounsell: Walter Hounsell, local stonemason; see IV.262. *the ledger*: sloping stone just above the base of the tomb; see IV.263. *the Tomb*: for TH's sister Mary; TH's drawing is now in the Adams collection.

To SIR FREDERICK MACMILLAN

Max Gate | 22: 5: 1916

Dear Sir Frederick:

I notice that some of the G.T. series have a vignette, & some a portrait; & I send up the enclosed, not from any *wish* that you should put it into our little volume, but in case you should have nothing with which to fill up the blank page. It has never been published.

If you have any other plan for it, or think it does not want any vignette, please retain the photograph for any future purpose. There is no copyright in it.

Yours sincerely
Thomas Hardy

P.S. If you shd ever take a western trip, please let us know. Reginald & Mrs Smith dropped in last week. T.H.

Text MS. (mourning stationery) BL.
G.T.: Golden Treasury. *the enclosed*: a photograph of himself as a young man; for its consideration and then rejection as a title-page vignette for *Selected Poems of Thomas Hardy*

see letter of 22 July 16 and letter of 27 July 16 to M. Macmillan. *Reginald & Mrs Smith*: Reginald John Smith, publisher (see II.249), and his wife Isabel, youngest daughter of George Smith (see I.35).

To T. H. TILLEY

FROM THO. HARDY, | MAX GATE, | DORCHESTER. | May 23. 1916

Copy for programme enclosed, as Mr Martin requested.

Please fill in names of Cast, if these are to appear on the programme. If not, strike out those that are written down.

There are particular reasons why the reader of the Prologue & Epilogue should be a woman. Therefore I hope you will be able to get one.

T. H

Text MS. (correspondence card) DCM.
programme: for the Weymouth production, 22 June 1916, of *Wessex Scenes from The Dynasts*; TH had apparently supplied the list of *dramatis personae* and the descriptions of the settings of each of the five scenes. *Mr Martin*: H. A. Martin, Hon. Secretary of the Dorchester Debating and Dramatic Society; see III.357. *Prologue & Epilogue*: these (originally written for the Granville Barker production of November 1914) were also printed in the programme. *a woman*: they were spoken at the Weymouth performance by Miss Ethel Hawker.

To J. L. RAYNER

[Late May 1916]

Dear Sir:

In reply to your inquiry respecting "The Dynasts" I write for Mr Hardy to say that the performance to be given by the Dorchester Dramatic Society on June 22 at the Weymouth Pavilion will not be a complete self-contained play, but only a selection of the Wessex scenes of the Drama as printed. Being for a temporary purpose (in aid of Red Cross funds) there is no copy of the selection available. But if you read through the above-mentioned scenes in the order in which they occur in the book you will have the gist of the presentation, many of the pages having not a word altered, though some unimportant detail is necessarily added to give coherence to the scenes.

Yours truly

P.S. Please do not print this letter.

Text MS. (pencil draft) DCM.
Rayner: John L. Rayner, journalist, currently literary editor of the *Weekly Dispatch*, a London Sunday newspaper. He had requested (28 May 16, DCM) a copy of the condensed version of *The Dynasts* that was to be performed at Weymouth, explaining that he wished to write about it in his column of book notes; after receiving this letter he apparently changed his mind.

To CONSTANCE DUGDALE

MAX GATE, | DORCHESTER. | 2: 6: 1916

Many thanks. *Opened yours first.*

Affly
T.

Cornwall postponed till later.

Text MS. (correspondence card, mourning stationery, with envelope) Purdy.
Opened yours first: i.e., first among the day's many messages of congratulation on his 76th birthday. *postponed till later*: TH and FEH went to Cornwall, including St. Juliot, in September 1916; see *LY*, 172–3.

To EDWARD CLODD

MAX GATE, | DORCHESTER. | 3: 6: 1916.

My dear Clodd:

This will, I fear, be a meagre & inadequate reply to your kind letter of congratulation on the arrival of my birthday, for among other things the news has just reached us here (though known in Dorchester last night) of the naval battle on Wednesday, & we are anxious about the fate of friends. I fancy we may have got the hardest hits, but as I am starting for the town I may hear a better & later account there—as I certainly hope to do.

The particulars in decimals that you give from Whitaker of the Expectation of human Life, though interesting to you as a man of science, do not help me much as to the quality of the life expressed by the decimals, which is all I really care for.

The war is, as you say truly, an accursed thing. It affects us all down to the smallest detail of existence, & its shadow will be upon us for half a century after its end—if it ever ends.

With renewed thanks & kindest regards I am

Always sincerely yrs
Thomas Hardy

Text MS. BL.
naval battle: the battle of Jutland, 31 May 1916. *Whitaker*: *Whitaker's Almanack* for 1916; the table, 'Expectation of Life', appears on p. 446.

To ALBERT MORDELL

MAX GATE, | DORCHESTER. | 3rd. June 1916.

Dear Sir:

I have to thank you sincerely for your book on "Dante and other waning classics", which I have just finished reading. I may say that I like the essays on the theologians who do not write as poets better on the whole than those on the writers who aimed at being poets first and theologians afterwards,

Yours truly,
Thomas Hardy.

Mr Albert Mordell.

Text MS. (typewritten, with envelope partly in TH's hand and partly in FEH's) Univ. of Pennsylvania.
Mordell: Albert Mordell (1885–1965), Philadelphia lawyer and writer. *your book*: Mordell's *Dante and Other Waning Classics* (Philadelphia, 1915) discusses Dante, Milton, Bunyan, Thomas à Kempis, St. Augustine, and Pascal. *Mr Albert Mordell*: added in TH's hand.

To JOHN SYMONS JEUNE

MAX GATE, | DORCHESTER. | June 7: 1916

My dear Mr Symons-Jeune:

Nobody has written a birthday letter to me which I value more than yours. My warmest thanks for the same. In spite of friends' kindnesses, however, I feel that such a puny matter as the date of my personal appearance here scarcely bears mention in the presence of the stunning events that are almost hourly happening.

Also thanks for E.G.'s essays. We are going to read them out in the evenings—I mean my wife will read them to me. She sends kind regards, & hopes soon to see you again—as do I.

Always sincerely
Thomas Hardy.

Text MS. Eton College.
Jeune: John Frederic Symons Jeune (1849–1925), Examiner of Standing Orders for the Houses of Lords and Commons; he was the father of Dorothy Hanbury of Kingston Maurward and related by marriage to TH's friend Lady St. Helier and to ELH's uncle E. H. Gifford (see letter of 28 June 14 to Gosse). *more than yours*: of 5 June 16 (DCM). *stunning events*: notably the Battle of Jutland, 31 May, and the drowning of Lord Kitchener and his staff off the Orkneys, 5 June 1916. *E.G.'s essays*: Edmund Gosse, *Inter Arma: Being Essays Written in Time of War* (London, 1916); Jeune's presentation inscription was dated 2 June 1916.

To G. HERBERT THRING

MAX GATE, | DORCHESTER. | 9th. June 1916.

Dear Sir:

I am pleased to hear of the Committee's attention to the suggestions I made—which were brought to my mind, as I may have told you, by some provisions I felt compelled to make in my own case, and I have now, at least temporarily, carried out.

Due consideration will, of course, have to be given by the committee to the various arguments that will occur to them, for and against their taking

Literary Executorships upon themselves, which would, as you rightly say, involve a good deal of responsibility.

Yours truly,
Thomas Hardy.

G. Herbert Thring, Esq. | Sec. Society of Authors.

Text MS. (typewritten) BL.
to hear: from Thring's letter of 6 June 16 (DCM), replying to TH's inquiry of 15 Apr 16.

To T. H. TILLEY

FROM THO. HARDY, | MAX GATE, | DORCHESTER. | Thursday. [15 June 1916]

May possibly not be able to attend to-morrow evening, but will come Monday, or whenever you let me know that all the Company will be present.

Text MS. (postcard) DCM. *Date* From postmark.
to attend: a rehearsal of *Wessex Scenes from The Dynasts*.

To WALTER HINES PAGE

MAX GATE, | DORCHESTER. | June 18: 1916

Dear Dr Page:

Very many thanks for your letter & the one from the Secretary giving directions. I am letting Judge Lock know, & he will be most grateful for your attention, whatever may come of it.

We are so sorry to hear of Mrs Page's illness, which I did not see mentioned in the papers till the day after I had written to her. Our best wishes for her speedy recovery.

Sincerely yours
Thomas Hardy.

Text MS. Harvard.
Judge Lock: Benjamin Fossett Lock (1847–1922), jurist and Positivist, younger brother of the late Arthur Lock of Dorchester (see I.73), formerly TH's solicitor. *whatever may come of it*: Lock was seeking information about his youngest son, Arthur Cuthbert Lock, who was captured at Kut-el-Amara (see letter of 20 July 16 to à Beckett) and died on or about 1 Aug 1916 while still a prisoner-of-war. *Mrs Page's illness*: the Court Circular in *The Times*, 14 June 1916, announced that Mrs. Page would not be 'At Home' at the American Embassy 'for the present'.

To FLORENCE HENNIKER

Max Gate | 28: 6: 1916

My dear Friend:

Florence has written to ask for Sir F. Wedmore's book for review, but she does not know whether it may have been sent out to anybody else. She has just finished & posted off six reviews of other books. I cannot think how she gets through them so fast. It would take me a week to do one I am quite sure. A few days ago she told the editor that he need not send any more, but he would not let her off, saying that hers are more trustworthy than any he can get elsewhere.

We had a mild excitement last week—the Wessex Scenes from the Dynasts having been performed by the Dorchester players at the Weymouth theatre. The house was crammed—many wounded men & officers being present—& the money raised for the Red Cross & Russian wounded—was a substantial sum. Of course the interest to us lay not in the artistic effect of the play—which was really rather a patchwork affair, for the occasion—but in the humours of the characters whom we knew in private life as matter-of-fact shopkeepers & clerks. However, the Times thought it worth while to send down a critic.

We were at Melbury on Monday. Lady Ilchester had her sister-in-law young Lady Londonderry staying with her. Ld Ilchester comes home for a day or two now & then, & disappears again (he is King's Messenger). She has shut up the large rooms & covered up the furniture with ghostly white cloths, & lives in the smaller ones. At the next performance of The Dynasts, which is to be in Dorchester, she is going to make a speech before the curtain rises. She asked very warmly for you, & if we had heard from you lately.

I daresay you get rumours of war news which don't reach us here. People seem to think we shall do something decisive soon, but I don't know. Mr Jeune comes often to see us (he is the father of Mrs Hanbury our neighbour at Kingston House—) & as he comes from the House of Lords he brings us all sorts of reports. I have been invited to visit & address the wounded soldiers at Netley Hospital, where they also want us to perform the play: perhaps the latter may be done; but I cannot go—

Always affectly
Th. H.

F. sends love: she will write. Th.

Text MS. (mourning stationery) DCM.
Wedmore's book: Sir Frederick Wedmore's novel *Brenda Walks On* (London, 1916). *other books*: she was evidently responsible for the anonymous reviews of two novels in the *Sphere*, 1 July 1916, and of four more novels, 8 July 1916. *the editor*: Clement Shorter. *patch-work affair*: it had, however, been put together by TH himself. *send down a critic*: the performance was reviewed in *The Times*, 23 June 1916; see *LY*, 172. TH was not present himself and seems to have based this paragraph largely on *The Times* report. *Melbury*: see letter of 3 June 15 to FEH. *Lady Ilchester*: see letter of 2 Nov 16. *young Lady Londonderry*: Edith, wife of Lady Ilchester's brother the 7th Marquis of Londonderry; the Dowager Lady Londonderry, widow of the 6th Marquis, was still alive. *King's Messenger*: i.e., a carrier of dispatches to or from the King. *in Dorchester*: on 6 Dec 1916, though originally planned for a somewhat earlier date; see letter of 15 Oct 16. *make a speech*: her daughter in fact acted in her stead; see letters of 2 and 14 Nov 16. *from the House of Lords*: see letter of 7 June 16. *Netley Hospital*: a large military hospital on Southampton Water; *Wessex Scenes* seems not to have been performed there, however.

To SYDNEY COCKERELL

MAX GATE, | DORCHESTER. | 6: 7: 1916.

Glad you got back safely, & to hear of *Its* adventures, which I feared might be more disconcerting. We read them with great interest. Please thank Mrs C. for her letter.

T.H.

Text MS. (postcard) Taylor.
Its: the bathchair TH had given Mrs. Cockerell; see letter of 26 Apr 16. As Cockerell's note on the letter indicates, he had reported to TH the difficulties experienced in getting it from Dorchester to Cambridge.

To CLEMENT SHORTER

MAX GATE, | DORCHESTER. | July 7: 1916

Dear Shorter:

I am sorry to say that, having no special knowledge, I cannot attempt to interfere with the Government by signing the paper.

If it had been simply a question of mercy to one man, which would end there, the case would be different. But it is, alas, much more than that.

Yours very truly
T. Hardy.

Text MS. Berg.
the paper: Shorter (3 July 16, DCM) had asked TH to sign a petition, initiated by Sir Arthur Conan Doyle (1859–1930; *D.N.B.*), for the reprieve of Sir Roger Casement (1864–1916; *D.N.B.*), sentenced to death for treason after being intercepted in an attempt to supply arms to those involved in the Dublin uprising of Easter 1916. TH's draft of this letter (DCM) is accompanied by his transcription of one of the petition's principal clauses.

To J. S. UDAL

MAX GATE, | DORCHESTER. | July 19: 1916

My dear Udal:

I find among my pile of unanswered letters, which unhappily increases every year, one from you enclosing 2 numbers of the Somerset & Dorset Notes & queries, with your Dialect Glossary (in which, by the way I do not see that old word "Ingledog" or "Inkledog", for "earthworm".). Many thanks for the same, which I am sorry not to have acknowledged before.

I quite remember the occasion when the Field Club went to Pilsdon. Why don't you hail from that way now, instead of from prosy Marlborough Hill? I motored past there a few months back, but did not go to the top. The point of interest to me this time was the farm-house of Racedown, where Wordsworth lived awhile. You probably know it well.

As to the first editions of my books, if you will call, when you are next in Dorchester, & bring under your arm the copies you wish me to sign, I will sign them, & you can take them back again with you. This will save me a good deal of trouble, so many people being in the habit of sending me my own books for the purpose, & (as I regret to find) selling them afterwards for double the price they paid for them. Perhaps you can answer for me a question that has been put to me by another collector respecting these first editions. Was the original binding of "A Pair of Blue Eyes" blue or green? I fancy green, but I am assured that it was blue, & I have never set eyes on a first edition of it since it came out in 1873.

Our simple pleasures down here are beginning to be much curtailed by the petrol restrictions. I hope yours are not, & am

Yours sincerely
Thomas Hardy.

His Hon. J. S. Udal.
P.S. I hope it may not be long before you appear. T.H.

Text MS. Adams.
your Dialect Glossary: Udal's two-part article 'Dorset Dialect Words Unrecorded in Dictionary or Glossary', *Somerset and Dorset Notes & Queries*, March and June 1916; TH inserted the second part (only) into his copy of William Barnes's *Grammar and Glossary of the Dorset Dialect* (Purdy). *"Inkledog"*: for an earlier reference to this word see II.299. *lived awhile*: William Wordsworth and his sister Dorothy lived at Racedown Lodge, Dorset, from September 1795 to June 1797. *blue or green?*: the original binding was green, but two of the secondary bindings were blue; see Purdy, 9–10.

To PAT À BECKETT

MAX GATE, | DORCHESTER. | July 20: 1916

Dear Major à Beckett:

I find that I am quite unable to write anything special on the subject of the Dorset men in Kut—having in fact, become squeezed dry by this time by the many demands upon my pen for such contributions,—at a date, too, when I have not the productive power I had formerly.

Of course, anything that I have already published is at your service—if you can find such in my volumes. The only piece I have been able to light on in a cursory examination is one in "The Dynasts", Part Second, Act IV, Scene VIII (page 251 in the 1 vol. edn). It is a chorus concerning Walcheren, where the situation was not unlike that of our regt in the swamps of Mesopotamia. Some of the verses bear closely on it, & the metre wd go well in a recitation.

Anyhow, I hope to be present at the Dorchester show, & that it will be a great success.

We are at home here almost any afternoon, & should of course be pleased to see you & Lady Norah à Beckett.

Sincerely yours
Thomas Hardy.

Text MS. (with envelope) Princeton.
in Kut: 370 members of the Dorset Regiment were among the British forces that surrendered

to the Turkish army at Kut-el-Amara, in what is now Iraq, on 29 April 1916. *at your service*: à Beckett, as chairman of the Weymouth Garrison League, was gathering material for a souvenir programme to be sold at the League's concerts and other fund-raising events in Dorchester on 'Kut-Fund Day', 26 July 1916; the proceeds were to be devoted to sending food and comforts to the Dorset men who were now prisoners-of-war. *in a recitation*: this suggestion seems not to have been adopted. *Lady Norah à Beckett*: à Beckett's wife.

To G. HERBERT THRING

MAX GATE, | DORCHESTER. | 20th. July 1916.

Dear Mr Thring:

Literary Executorships.

I think the Committee act wisely in proceeding cautiously with the above question, considering the seriousness of the responsibilities involved. Future years, however, will probably see such a step taken, which would be in keeping with the general movement in favour of public Trusteeships and suchlike.

My personal Literary Executorship will, I believe, be a very simple matter, and will be in the hands of a friend and my wife, so far as I see at present. I may mention that I have requested them, in case of any difficulty in the matter, to ask the advice of the Society. This will not commit the Society to anything beyond an opinion, to which I think the Committee will see no objection. In furtherance of this my wife intends (on the strength of her own numerous fugitive publications) to apply for membership of the Society at the beginning of next year.

Yours very truly,
Thomas Hardy.

Secretary Society of Authors.

Text MS. (typewritten) BL.
act wisely: Thring (17 July 16, DCM) reported the conclusion of the Committee of Management of the Incorporated Society of Authors that a change in the Memorandum of Association of the Society would be needed before it could act in the capacity of literary executor. *a friend*: Sydney Cockerell; see letter of 24 Feb 16 to Cockerell.

To MACMILLAN & CO.

MAX GATE, | DORCHESTER. | July 22nd. 1916.

Dear Sirs:

I return the proof of the vignette, which is quite satisfactory.

I have pencilled

AN. ÆT. SUÆ XXI

under it, by way of explanation, for though it seems to myself that such personal detail is better reserved till an author is dead, so that my feeling is against it, Mrs Hardy and others think, on the contrary, that it would make the book more valued by people who care for such things. This, of course, is a practical consideration which I suppose should overrule others. Please make the lettering quite faint if you agree that it ought to be put.

Yours very truly,
Thomas Hardy.

Text MS. (typewritten) BL.
the vignette: see letter of 22 May 16 and letter of 27 July 16 to M. Macmillan. *AN. . . XXI*: inserted in TH's hand.

To HENRY DANIELSON

MAX GATE, DORCHESTER. | July 27: 1916

Dear Sir:

I am greatly obliged to you for sending me this beautifully bound & printed copy of the bibliography you have compiled.

Yours very truly
Thomas Hardy.

Henry Danielson Esq.

Text MS. (with envelope) DCM.
Danielson: Henry Danielson, bookseller and bibliographer. *the bibliography*: Danielson's *The First Editions of the Writings of Thomas Hardy and Their Values* (see letter of 24 Feb 16 to Cockerell); TH's copy, extensively annotated, is in DCM.

To MAURICE MACMILLAN

MAX GATE, | DORCHESTER. | 27 July 1916

Dear Mr Macmillan:

I am glad to get your opinion on the vignette. My only reason for suggesting that particular one was that it seemed to fit the space. What do you say to the one I send (under a separate cover). I feel sure that Mr Hamo Thornycroft would not mind our using it, but it would have to be reduced to about two inches in total height, to look well.

Should this be done, his name as sculptor, would be too small as written on the photograph, & would therefore have to be put under, in italics (as is done in the Wordsworth volume of the series for instance). I don't think my name need appear at all—simply: "From the bust by Hamo Thornycroft, R.A."

Please consider this, & decide between the two. Either the first, or the one I send will satisfy me.

A friend writes to me to say he is going to buy 100 copies to give away!

Sincerely yours
Thomas Hardy.

Text MS. BL.
the vignette: see letter of 22 July 16. *Thornycroft, R.A.*": these suggestions of TH's for the title-page of *Selected Poems of Thomas Hardy* were adopted almost in their entirety; see, however, the letter to M. Macmillan of 2 Aug 16.

To HAMO THORNYCROFT

MAX GATE, | DORCHESTER. | July 29: 1916

My dear Thornycroft:

Would you have any objection to a small vignette of the photograph of the bust that you kindly sent me being put on the titlepage of a volume of my poems that my publishers are going to bring out, in their "Golden Treasury" series? If you don't mind, I shall be delighted to have your name associated with mine at the front of such a popular series.

I wonder if you & Mrs Thornycroft still hold on to London in this heat. Are you going east west north or south for air? If S.W., we will put you up with pleasure.

My wife sends best regards & I am sincerely yours

Thomas Hardy.

P.S. I have not been to London all the year! T.H.
P.P.S. A strange coincidence! Since writing the above, I hear that the promising young poet your nephew has won the Military Cross. My congratulations to him. T.H.

Text MS. DCM.
kindly sent me: see letter of 27 July 16 to M. Macmillan. *your nephew*: Siegfried Sassoon; see letter of 4 Feb 17. An announcement of the award appeared in *The Times*, 28 July 1916.

To THE REVD. J. H. DICKINSON

MAX GATE, | DORCHESTER. | July 30: 1916

Dear Mr Dickinson:

You were, I believe, interested in learning that S. Juliot Church, before alteration, had a transept. I find I have a sketch showing the outside of the transept, &c, and I should be much pleased to send it to you as a record of the church's history, if you think it worth preserving in the building?

With kind regards I am

Yours very truly
Thomas Hardy.

Text MS. (with envelope) Berg.
a sketch: by ELH.

To REYMOND ABBOTT

MAX GATE, | DORCHESTER. [2 August 1916]

Many thanks. An excellent review I agree. To omit all mention of the *key* to the books—i.e. the verse—was odd.

T.H.

Text MS. (postcard) Mrs. Michael MacCarthy. *Date* From postmark.
excellent review: unidentified, but probably of H. C. Duffin's study of the novels; see letter of 17 Apr 16.

To MAURICE MACMILLAN

MAX GATE, | DORCHESTER. | Aug 2. 1916.

Dear Mr Macmillan:

I have today heard from Mr Thornycroft, who says he shall be delighted to see the photo of his bronze on the titlepage.

With regard to the inscription in italics under it, perhaps the words, "By Hamo Thornycroft R.A." would be enough, without the words "from a bust",—"bust" strictly meaning head and shoulders, and this is only a head. While "From a head" is, I fancy, ambiguous.

Yours sincerely,
Thomas Hardy.

Text MS. (typewritten) BL.
today heard: Thornycroft wrote 31 July 16 (DCM). *"By . . . R.A."*: this was the phrasing used.

To J. S. UDAL

MAX GATE, | DORCHESTER. | 5: 8: '16

Yes. Will sign *two* for you when you bring them. Am compelled to limit number to this. Shall be glad to see you—

Text MS. (postcard) Texas.
bring them: i.e., the copies of TH's books; see letter of 19 July 16.

To MAURICE MACMILLAN

MAX GATE, | DORCHESTER. | August 10th. 1916.

Dear Mr Macmillan:

I have received the enclosed letter, and know of no objection to the Book Company's use of the two short stories the editor mentions, if they pay (say, a guinea each?) for the permission to print them in the work described.

Should you be of the same opinion it will save sending two answers if you will reply for me to the above effect as well as for yourselves.

Believe me,

Yours very truly,
Thomas Hardy.

Text MS. (typewritten) BL.
Book Company's: the Educational Book Company, of 17 New Bridge Street, London, E.C. *two short stories*: 'The Melancholy Hussar' and 'Absent-Mindedness in a Parish Choir'; the anthology itself, apparently a selection of stories from several countries, has not been identified. *a guinea each?*: see letter of 12 Aug 16.

To SIR FREDERICK MACMILLIAN

MAX GATE, | DORCHESTER. | August 12th. 1916.

Dear Sir Frederick Macmillan:

I am quite willing to adopt your suggestion that the Book Company should be asked to pay one guinea per printed page of their book for the two stories they propose to use in it, and I leave you to reply to that effect.

So far as my experience has gone, no harm is done by allowing short pieces to be included in such collections.

Yours very truly,
Thomas Hardy.

Text MS. (typewritten) BL.
your suggestion: in his letter of 11 Aug 16 (Macmillan letterbooks, BL), replying to TH's letter of 10 Aug 16 to Maurice Macmillan. *no harm is done*: apparently a response to Macmillan's remark that Kipling had refused permission for two of his stories to be included in the projected volume.

To J. W. MACKAIL

MAX GATE, | DORCHESTER. | Aug 13: 1916

My dear Mackail:

I have been looking into your lecture on Shakespeare (which it is very kind of you to send) & it suggests all sorts of ideas about him. That Shakespeare was like putty is "a thought to look at"—as the natives say about here—& it does explain matters enormously. *That* is, in fact, the artist-nature without any other ingredient whatever—for good or for ill.

As to W.S.'s characters, he can quite stand our finding fault with some of them. It is amusing to see that he blandly exhibits to us the impossible in humanity at times—e.g. makes his villains say things that such villains never could have said; & indeed, speaking generally, puts into his ordinary folk's mouths sentiments that they would have expressed if they could, but never could have in this world. Yet when we see what the realistic writing of to-day is coming to, how blest we are that he did so.

I am glad to come across your remark that Iago is not quite a real person. I have got into hot water times & times by saying that I thought Iago the greatest failure in S.'s characters (Perhaps that shocks even you.) & it has always been a mystery to me why S. didn't blue-pencil that worthy pretty extensively. But I shouldn't wonder if he (Iago) didn't "slip idly from" S. just as a matter of potboiling.

Though you seem not to, I think the knocking scene in Macbeth *is* S.'s. But then, the only staging of it that remains with me is that of the old Drury days of Phelps. I was impressionable at that time, so may be wrong.

Alas—how one wastes one's life, even with the best intentions. I read S. more closely from 23 to 26 than I have ever done since, or probably ever shall again.

But this will never do, as Jeffrey said about The Excursion—I mean my inflicting upon you Shakespeare-criticism & water. I wish you would go more into that curious question of dates that you mention in your letter. But it would be a ticklish job—the "idolaters" are so touchy, or to use the more genteel term, sensitive.

I have not finished reading your paper yet. This weather has brought me a weak eye (as it mostly does, & will probably do more & more) & I am dependent upon my wife a good deal for reading to me.

We could not go to Tonerspuddle after all, but I believe she has written about that. I am so pleased that you & your household like Dorset—a poor neglected county formerly. The weather has changed here, & it is just possible that your daughter, & the damsels who leave with her, will be off in time to escape dampness. I hope the harvesting won't be interfered with.

Sincerely yours
Thomas Hardy.

Text MS. (with envelope) Yale.
Mackail: John William Mackail (1859–1945), scholar, critic, poet, and civil servant; *D.N.B.* *lecture on Shakespeare*: Mackail's *Shakespeare After Three Hundred Years* (London, 1916), the Annual Shakespeare Lecture of the British Academy. *to send*: with his letter of 10 Aug 16 (DCM). *"slip idly from"*: from *Timon of Athens*, I.i.20; the passage was quoted by Mackail in his lecture. *Phelps*: Samuel Phelps (1804–78), actor; *D.N.B.* See Millgate, 99. *about The Excursion*: Francis Jeffrey (1773–1850; *D.N.B.*), Scottish judge and critic, opened his review of Wordsworth's *The Excursion* with the sentence, 'This will never do' (*Edinburgh Review*, November 1814). *question of dates*: Mackail had suggested that there was something odd, in terms of Shakespeare's biography, about the dates of his daughter Susannah's marriage and of the birth of *her* daughter. *Tonerspuddle*: an alternative name for the hamlet of Turnerspuddle, SW of Bere Regis, Dorset. *your daughter*: Clare Mackail, younger sister of Angela Thirkell, the novelist; she had apparently been staying or working on a Dorset farm.

To JOHN ACLAND

MAX GATE, | DORCHESTER. | Aug 14: 1916

Dear Captain Acland:

I delayed answering by letter your interesting intelligence, thinking to call & discuss it with you. This however I must postpone, on account of having my hands rather full just now.

Your most valuable acquisition is, I think, the MS. of the "Rural Poems in Common English", which were for some reason, or none, undervalued by the critics when published.

I *wish* you could get some MS. of the dialect Poems—or even of *one* of them. I fear however they all may have perished.

More anon, when I see you.

Sincerely yours
Thomas Hardy.

Text MS. Manchester Central Library.
Acland: John Edward Acland, Curator of the DCM; see III.262. *acquisition*: there seems to have been some confusion either on Acland's part or on TH's; as subsequently reported in vol. 28 of the *Proceedings of the Dorset Natural History and Antiquarian Field Club*, the William Barnes MSS. deposited at the museum included the original MS. of *Poems of Rural Life in the Dorset Dialect* but *not* that of the vol., correctly entitled *Poems of Rural Life in Common English*, mentioned in this letter.

To F. W. SLATER

Aug 30. 1916

Dear Mr Slater:

The reference in "The Sphere" to a Bibliography which Mrs Hardy is said to be compiling & of which you inquire particulars, seems to be based on a remark of hers concerning some erroneous bibliographies recently published, to the effect that she hopes, or would like, to make a correct bibliography of my works some day.

In respect of the volume of selections from my poems, they will of course be poems already published in past years. The war makes it uncertain when they will appear. I am not much interested in its publication in America, for though I have a great many American readers of my verse, I am much puzzled by the fact that I can hardly get a poem into an American newspaper.

Yours very truly

Text MS. (pencil draft) DCM.
Slater: Frederick William Slater, London representative of the American publishing house of Harper & Brothers for many years. *said to be compiling*: Clement Shorter's 'A Literary Letter', *Sphere*, 29 July 1916, reports FEH as 'engaged upon a bibliography of her husband's writings, which may be long in coming but is certain to be interesting'. *inquire particulars*: Slater (28 Aug 16, DCM) said that Harper & Brothers were eager to handle both the bibliography and the poems (see below) in the United States. *erroneous bibliographies*: i.e., Danielson's book (see letter of 27 July 16 to Danielson) and A. P. Webb's *A Bibliography of the Works of Thomas Hardy* (London, 1916). *its publication in America*: TH seems to be avoiding any direct acknowledgment of his having agreed that sheets of *Selected Poems* should be sent to, and sold in, the United States by Macmillan.

To HAMO THORNYCROFT

MAX GATE, | DORCHESTER. | Sept 1. 1916

My dear Thornycroft:

Our enterprise is not, alas, equal to a descent upon you at The Bull, even though helped by your kind invitation, & by our own wish to see you there. I have, I think, to go to Cornwall next week, but only for a few days. I wish I had a little of your energy: if I had, I should fly round to you & then on to Cornwall.

We had—my wife had—a note from Gosse this morning. He is still enjoying London in his usual blithe spirits.

Always sincerely
Thomas Hardy.

It is rather amusing to see that the public are cautioned against putting up extravagant memorials to departed soldiers & others (if anything can be amusing at this time). Sculptors please copy. T.H.

Text MS. Adams.
The Bull: the inn at Burford, W. of Oxford, where Thornycroft and his family were staying.

To FLORENCE HENNIKER

MAX GATE, | DORCHESTER. | 4 Sept. 1916

My dear friend:

Herewith I send "Worlingworth" results so far. The post-card is a mystery, as I did not mention the Christian name of Mr. W. to Sir G. Alexander, & it came at the same time as his letter this morning.

We propose, D.V., to go to Cornwall for 3 or 4 days this week, starting I believe Thursday. The memories it will revive will of course be rather sad ones for me, but I want to see the tablet that has been erected in St Juliot Church, near Boscastle, to Emma, recording that she lived there, played in church, laid the foundation stone of the new part, &c. & Florence wants to see the place & the cliff scenery, never having been there. We mean to stay at Tintagel 2 or 3 days, & a day or two at Boscastle. But perhaps she has already told you of this.

The Macmillans are going to include a selection from my poems in their Golden Treasury series; but when it will come out I do not know. We have been to Melbury since I last wrote—& we met Lady I. last week at a bazaar. She is going to preside at a performance of the Wessex Scenes from The Dynasts at Dorchester some time this autumn—that is, she will, as I understand, make a little speech at the beginning, stating the objects of the performance, &c. She makes those little speeches very well. The people here are getting much attached to her—as, indeed, they ought to be.

The morning papers have this moment arrived, telling us that a Zeppelin was brought down near London on Saturday. The war news is exciting almost every day: but I think our papers rather too sanguine. We have not beaten the Germans by any means yet.

F. is not here this moment, or she would send her love with mine.

Always yours
Th. H.

Text MS. DCM.
"Worlingworth" results: see letter of 10 July 15. Mrs. Henniker, writing to TH on this same date (transcript, DCM), described her new play as 'quite a simple little comedy, with perhaps a more serious touch, here and there, than belongs to *comedy proper*'. *post-card*: evidently one of the items TH was forwarding. *Alexander*: Sir George Alexander (1858–1918), actor-manager; *D.N.B.* TH had written 1 Sept 16 (present whereabouts unknown) on 'Worlingworth's' behalf. *to Cornwall*: see letter of 2 June 16. *at a bazaar*: Lady Ilchester had opened a garden fête held (in aid of the Dorchester Red Cross Depot) at Kingston Maurward House, 31 Aug 1916; newspaper reports also mention the presence of TH and FEH. *make a little speech*: see, however, letters of 2 and 14 Nov 16. *brought down*: it was said to be one of a force of 13, representing the most serious attack on Britain to date. *war news*: the main headline in *The Times* of 4 Sept 1916 announced 'Great Allied Advance' on the Somme.

To THE REVD. J. H. DICKINSON

MAX GATE, | DORCHESTER. | 6: 9: 1916

Dear Mr Dickinson:

I am glad to hear that the sketch reached you safely. I write at this moment to tell you what I did not know when I wrote last, that my wife & I are going if all's well to Tintagel this week for a couple of days, & also to Launceston to see a relative of my late wife's. We propose to call on you & Miss Dickinson either on Friday afternoon, or Saturday morning, (as we can fit it in) & it will be a pleasure to find you at home. But please do not inconvenience yourself to stay in if you happen to have an engagement. My wife was a friend of the first Mrs Hardy, & is naturally interested in seeing where she lived.

I hope to be able to explain to you where the old church foundations extended.

Believe me

Sincerely yours
Thomas Hardy.

Text MS. (with envelope) Berg.
the sketch: see letter of 30 July 16. *of my late wife's*: presumably Kate Gifford; see letter of 12 Feb 14 to her.

To FLORENCE HENNIKER

Saturday 9: 9: '16

Thanks for 2d letter, which was forwarded here. Hope Worlingworth will achieve his attempt.

We have been to St Juliot—& return to D. Monday.

Text MS. (picture postcard of Tintagel) DCM.
Worlingworth: see letter of 4 Sept 16.

To JOHN MASEFIELD

MAX GATE, | DORCHESTER. | Sept 15: 1916

Dear Mr Masefield:

I have received your kind gift of "Sonnets & Poems" & my wife has read some of them to me. I like very much the one beginning "Night is on the downland" the scenery being like that so familiar to me. But I have not studied many of the verses yet, having but just come back from Cornwall where we have been for a short change. I shall read them all at an early date.

Sincerely yours
Thomas Hardy.

Text MS. Bodleian Library.
Masefield: John Masefield, poet; see IV.189. *& Poems*": Masefield's *Sonnets and Poems* (Cholsey, Berks., 1916). *on the downland*": the poem numbered XXXVI.

To JEAN JULLIEN

(Ansr) Max Gate | Dorchester | September 16. 1916

Dear Sir;

I acknowledge the receipt of your letter informing me that the Committee of the Société des Gens de Lettres has nominated me a corresponding member of the Society; & also the receipt of the Diploma.

I much value the honour done me by the Committee in their unanimous resolution, & accept with pleasure the honorary membership offered.

I commend the efforts of the Society to develope the mental union of the writers of France & England, which, I feel convinced, will tend to further the concord already existing between the peoples of the two countries.

Believe me to be, dear Sir,

Yours very truly
T.H.

To M. Jean Jullien | Société des Gens de Lettres.

Text MS. (pencil draft) DCM.
Jullien: Jean Jullien (1854–1919), French playwright, currently le Delégué Général of the Société des Gens de Lettres, Paris. *Société*: TH seems to have written 'Societé'.

To SYDNEY COCKERELL

MAX GATE, | DORCHESTER. | Sept 20: 1916

My dear Cockerell:

We shall be much pleased to see you again: I had hoped it would be this week. We went to Cornwall—& saw the tablet at St. Juliot, Boscastle; &

thence to Tintagel. Alas, I fear your hopes of a poem on Iseult—the English, or British, Helen—will be disappointed: I visited the place 44 years ago with an Iseult of my own, & of course she was mixed in the vision of the other. The hotel-crowd rather jarred: but the situation of the hotel is unrivalled.

Yours ever
Thomas Hardy.

Text MS. Berg; envelope Adams.
disappointed: TH did, however, publish *The Famous History of the Queen of Cornwall* seven years later; see Purdy, 228–9.

To GORDON GIFFORD

MAX GATE, | DORCHESTER. | Sept 20: 1916

Dear Gordon:

I am glad to hear that you think of attempting to pass a technical examination. I think Mr Riley suggested that of the Surveyor's Institute, but you will know.

When you see Lilian will you tell her that we went to look at the tablet I have put up to your aunt in St. Juliot Church, Boscastle. It is quite satisfactory, & if I should ever get a photograph of it I will send her one as she wished.

Your affectionate uncle
T. Hardy

Text MS. Mrs. Ethel Skinner.
Mr Riley: William Edward Riley, architect to the London County Council at this date.
Lilian: Gifford's sister, ELH's niece.

To ARTHUR MAQUARIE

MAX GATE, | DORCHESTER. | Sept. 22. 1916.

Dear Sir:

In conformity with your letter and enclosure I am quite willing that my name should stand on the Provisional Committee List for the furtherance of an intellectual entente among friendly nations.

I fear it will not be possible for me to be present at the conference on October 3.

Yours very truly,
Thomas Hardy.

Arthur Maquarie Esq.

Text MS. (typewritten) Royal Society of Literature.
Maquarie: Arthur Maquarie, author and artist, currently Hon. Foreign Secretary of the Royal Society of Literature. *Committee List*: i.e., the list of members of the Provisional Committee (see below). *the conference*: it was held on 3 Oct 1916 and recommended 'the appointment of a Committee to act in drawing closer the intellectual ties between the United

Kingdom and Allied Countries'; although TH was appointed to the committee he seems not to have attended any of its meetings (see letter of 8 Feb 17).

To WALTER HOUNSELL

MAX GATE, | DORCHESTER. | 27th. September '16

Dear Sir:

If I should not be able to meet you at Stinsford, will you see whether, by placing the tomb exactly over the grave, the space between that and the next will be the same as the other space. I fancy it may be 4 inches wider, but on second thoughts I do not think this will matter, as I believe the middle tomb was kept two or three inches south of the actual centre of the grave. This could either now or some day be shifted to the centre, so as to bring the spaces equal.

However, I will try to meet you, when we can settle the point.

Yours truly,
T. Hardy.

Text MS. (typewritten, with envelope) Adams.
the tomb: of TH's sister Mary.

To THE REVD. H. G. B. COWLEY

MAX GATE, | DORCHESTER. | 3 Oct. 1916

Dear Mr Cowley:

I have a deep sense of your kindly feeling in learning that your regard for my dear sister prompts you to forego the fee for the tomb—in which my brother & sister Katharine will I am sure join with me when they know.

As we have often said, we all feel ourselves your parishioners still—I suppose from our family's 100 years association with the parish & church-music. Please treat us as such if any contribution for repairs, &c., should be required.

Sincerely yours
Thomas Hardy.

Text MS. Canon Cowley.
my dear sister: Mary Hardy. *the tomb*: at Stinsford; see letter of 27 Sept 16. *your parishioners still*: TH's Higher Bockhampton birthplace was in Cowley's parish of Stinsford; Max Gate was in the parish of Fordington St. George.

To J. J. FOSTER

FROM THO. HARDY, | MAX GATE, | DORCHESTER. | 3: 10: '16

Many thanks for press notices of Miniature Painters, & The Athenaeum. Am reading both.

T.H.

Text MS. (correspondence card, with envelope) Eton College.
Foster: Joshua James Foster, art historian and antiquary; see I.160. *Miniature Painters*: Foster's ***Samuel Cooper and the English Miniature Painters of the XVII. Century*** (2 vols., London, 1914–16). *The Athenaeum*: for September 1916, containing Foster's article, 'Some Notes on the Exhibition of the Buccleuch Miniatures' (422–4).

To THOMAS HUMPHRY WARD

MAX GATE, | DORCHESTER. | Oct 11: 1916

Dear Mr Ward:

Since receiving your letter I have been looking into Barnes, & I think I can undertake to do the selection you require, & the short introduction, by the end of the year.

I fear that what I should have to say would not be much more than a paraphrase of what I have said about him elsewhere in past years. This is almost inevitable.

I am honoured by being asked to join the noble army of critics who figure in your previous volumes—which I have possessed for a long time.

I notice that each essay has a brief chronological summary at the beginning. I will prefix to mine about a dozen lines of this sort, unless you say otherwise.

My kindest regards to Mrs Ward who I hope is well.

Yours very truly
Thomas Hardy.

Text MS. (with envelope) Texas.
Ward: Thomas Humphry Ward, journalist and author; see III.90. *your letter*: of 5 Oct 16 (DCM). *selection . . . introduction*: TH selected and introduced the short section devoted to William Barnes in *The English Poets*, Vol. V, ed. Thomas Humphry Ward (London, 1918). *in past years*: notably in his preface to *Select Poems of William Barnes* (London, 1908). *Mrs Ward*: Ward's wife, Mary Augusta Ward, the novelist; see I.263.

To HAMO THORNYCROFT

MAX GATE, | DORCHESTER. | 13: 10: '16

Photograph received. Best thanks. Have put it up in study, where it looks very striking.

Always
T.H.

Text MS. (postcard) DCM. *Date* The postmark is dated 15 Oct 16.
Photograph: Thornycroft's letter of 6 Oct 16 (DCM) refers to a photograph of his 'marble group' at the Tate Gallery, evidently 'The Kiss'; see letter to Thornycroft of 30 Apr 16.

To JOHN GALSWORTHY

MAX GATE, | DORCHESTER. | Oct 15: 1916

My dear Galsworthy:

My best thanks for the book, which I am reading. I need not say that I agree with every word of it. I confess I had never thought of the gold fish in those glass globes.

I dont feel very hopeful about such things, & as I get older fall back upon the reflection that there is but one life for each individual & that happily it will soon be over.

Sincerely yours
Thomas Hardy.

P.S. We are getting up a Red-Cross performance here for November which nails me to the spot. So we cannot get away to London. I hope your labours at the Hospital will be appreciated. I am too feeble now to do anything physical, unfortunately. T.H.

Text MS. Univ. of Birmingham.
the book: Galsworthy's *A Sheaf* (London, 1916). *in those glass globes*: the first piece in the book, 'For Love of Beasts', opens with a reference to goldfish being 'kept in misery' in a bowl 'about twice the length of their own tails' (4). *for November*: the Dorchester performance of *Wessex Scenes from The Dynasts*, later postponed to December. *at the Hospital*: Galsworthy and his wife were preparing to go to France to work—as, respectively, masseur and linen superintendent—in Dorothy Allhusen's Convalescent Hospital for French soldiers; see H. V. Marrot, *The Life and Letters of John Galsworthy* (London, 1935), 422–7.

To THE REVD. S. E. V. FILLEUL

MAX GATE, | DORCHESTER. | Oct 17: 1916

Dear Mr Filleul:

Just a line to thank you for your letter. Your practical co-operation will I hope be imitated by many, but people are as a rule more willing to give their names than of their substance. There is, of course, an excuse in these times of heavy demands. With kind regards,

Yours sincerely,
T. Hardy.

Text MS. (correspondence card, with envelope) Eton College.
Filleul: the Revd. Samuel Edward Valpy Filleul, rector of All Saints' Church, Dorchester; see III.35. *practical co-operation*: Filleul had perhaps made a financial contribution to the Red Cross fund to which the proceeds of the *Wessex Scenes* performance were to be devoted; see letter of 15 Oct 16.

To SIR ARTHUR QUILLER-COUCH

MAX GATE, | DORCHESTER. | Oct 22: 1916

My dear Q:

(Certainly I like to call you that much better) I am delighted that you are pleased to have the selection. There was not any particular rule followed in picking them out. They are just specimens.

If I do go to Cambridge I will not fail to let you know. But I am beginning to feel chilly & grown old, as the man did who listened to the Toccata of Galuppi's, & I doubt if I shall get there.

I cannot remember now what criticism of yours it was that I thought wrong—something you wrote in your salad days when you were more dogmatic than you probably are now. It was when I was interested in novels, which I have not been for the last 20 years & more. However, whatever it was it did not much hurt my feelings. I simply said to myself, "He be d——d: I know better." (at least I feel sure I said that, just because that's what the victim always says).

And as to any other kind of writing interesting me (than novels) I sometimes wonder if it is not beneath the dignity of literature to attempt to please longer a world which is capable of such atrocities as these days have brought, & think that it ought to hold its peace for ever.

But they bring out heroism, though at what an expense! I am really glad to hear that your son is showing himself such a fine fellow. My wife sends kindest regards & says she so much enjoyed that short visit to you.

Sincerely yours
Thomas Hardy.

Text MS. Miss F.F. Quiller-Couch.
much better: since TH had already addressed him as 'Q' (see letter of 19 Mar 16) the allusion is unclear. *the selection*: *Selected Poems of Thomas Hardy*, pub. 3 Oct 16. *of Galuppi's*: another allusion to Browning's poem; see letter of 15 Mar 16 to Gosse. *criticism of yours*: probably Quiller-Couch's expressed preference—e.g., in the *Speaker*, 31 Mar 1894, and *Adventures in Criticism* (London, 1896)—for George Moore's *Esther Waters* over TH's *Tess of the d'Urbervilles*. *a fine fellow*: Quiller-Couch's son Bevil had been awarded a Military Cross for bravery in April 1916; he survived the war but died of pneumonia in Germany in 1919 while serving with the army of occupation.

To ARTHUR CLAYTON

Max Gate | Oct 25. 1916

Dear Sir,

Your letter reminds me of what I had forgotten—that I wrote to the Mayor of Weymouth on the advisability of marking in some way the residence of King George the Third when he came to the town, & the names of some of the notabilities who visited him there, with the view of adding to its interest in the eyes of residents & others.

It occurred to me that if the Corporation were to erect such a record it would hardly be within their province to affix it to a building which did not belong to them, & I therefore suggested a stone on the Esplanade. But of course if the Directors of the Hotel Company like to take the matter into their own hands they can with great advantage affix it to their own property without consulting anybody.

I think a plain slab of Portland Stone would be sufficient—say 2 feet 6 inches high by 3 feet 6 inches long. For convenience of reading it might perhaps be affixed to the wall on which the iron railing stands, close to the pavement. But I cannot remember if there is wall-space enough for this.

If it were put on the building itself the lettering might not be easily read from the pavement. However, all this could be settled by marking the inscription on a sheet of paper, or board, full size, & trying it up in different places.

I enclose a rough idea of the form I think the inscription should take. Many more names might be added, but these I send *certainly* came to Gloucester Lodge (as it was then called). Any other opinion I can give is at your service.

Yours faithfully

Arthur E. Clayton Esq. | Sec. Gloucester Hotel, Weymouth.

Text MS. (pencil draft) DCM.
Clayton: Arthur Essex Clayton, Dorchester accountant; he was secretary of the firm which owned the Gloucester Hotel, Weymouth. The hotel, built in the late 18th century as a house for the Duke of Gloucester, was used by King George III as a summer retreat during some of the most critical years of the wars against Napoleon; see TH's pencil drawing of the proposed plaque (opposite page) and the various references in *The Trumpet-Major* and *The Dynasts*, Part First. *Mayor of Weymouth*: TH may be thinking of his letter to the Town Clerk of Weymouth, 9 Aug 1913 (IV. 294). *at your service*: nothing had been done, however, by October 1923, when TH's interest in a plaque and his willingness to come and unveil it were mentioned at a dinner given by the hotel's directors (*Dorset County Chronicle*, 27 Oct 1923); for the wording of the plaque as finally installed see IV.295.

To LADY ILCHESTER

Max Gate, | Dorchester. | November 2: 1916

Dear Lady Ilchester:

How sorry I am that you have to go to Bath for such a reason. Surely you must have been getting damp somewhere, & have not been quite careful enough. Bath is really a good place for a cure, & I hope the best things for you.

As to the play, you will probably have heard by this time that it has had to be postponed. The Secretary has written to say that both the Corn Exchange & Town Hall are requisitioned for soldiers, & by no contrivance can the performance be fitted in while they are there. The date to which it is deferred is vague, but it may be January or February, when I hope we may have you after all, as you are such an important asset. Though really it would have been most interesting to have your sweet daughter trying her prentice hand at the job. However, her time will come.

HERE LIVED AT VARIOUS TIMES

KING GEORGE THE THIRD, QUEEN CHARLOTTE (MISS BURNEY IN ATTENDANCE) & THE ROYAL PRINCESSES AND HERE THE KING WAS VISITED BY THE FOLLOWING HISTORIC PERSONAGES AMONG MANY OTHERS

WILLIAM PITT
LORD ELDON
LORD NELSON
CAPTAIN HARDY
LORD MULGRAVE
COUNT MUNSTER
LORD CHESTERFIELD

DUKE OF GLOUCESTER
DUKE OF YORK
DUKE OF CUMBERLAND
DUKE OF CAMBRIDGE
DUKE OF SUSSEX
GEORGE PRINCE OF WALES
AND MANY OTHERS

or

LORD CHESTERFIELD
LORD DUNDAS
LORD CHATHAM (?)
THE ROYAL DUKES
GEORGE PRINCE OF WALES
AND MANY OTHERS

(In Miss Burney's time) Ld. Chatham, Dk of Richmond Mr Villiers, Sir W. Clerke
In attendance were Dr Gisburne, Genl. Garth. Col. Fitzroy.

With renewed hopes that that little ache will soon disappear I am

Sincerely yours

Thomas Hardy.

P.S. My wife has just heard from Mrs Henniker, who is busy getting up a book stall which she is going to hold at a Bazaar. T.H.

Text Transcript (by Henry Reed) Purdy.
Ilchester: Lady Helen Mary Theresa Fox-Strangways, wife of the 6th Earl of Ilchester; see III.235. *for such a reason*: in her letter of 1 Nov 16 (DCM) she spoke of seeking a cure for her lumbago. *postponed*: *Wessex Scenes from The Dynasts* was to have been performed in Dorchester in November 1916. *or February*: the performances were, however, arranged for 6 and 7 Dec 1916; see letter of 14 Nov 16. *as you are*: TH wrote 'are you are'. *your sweet daughter*: Lady Mary Theresa Fox-Strangways (1903-48), later the wife of John Arthur Herbert. *at the job*: i.e., the job of making a speech (written by TH) prior to one of the performances; Lady Ilchester's letter of 24 Oct 16 (DCM) indicates that TH had already sent her the text of the speech.

To EVELYN SHARP

Nov 7. 1916

Dear Miss Sharp:

I am sorry to have to tell you in reply to your letter on Adult Suffrage that I am not able to be a member of the Council for advocating it.

I may say that, apart from the question itself, I have never taken any practical part in controversial politics; & if I had it would now, alas, be time to give up—

Yours very truly

Text MS. (pencil draft) DCM.
Sharp: Evelyn Sharp, journalist and social activist; see III.210. *letter on Adult Suffrage*: she wrote 6 Nov 16 (DCM) inviting TH to become a member of the National Council for Adult Suffrage, dedicated to securing votes for women before the end of the war.

To LADY ILCHESTER

Max Gate, | Dorchester. | Nov 14: 1916

Dear Lady Ilchester:

The dates Dec. 6 (Wedny) for the evening performance, & the next day, the 7th. for the matinée, have been provisionally fixed by the Dramatic Society as most convenient for the company, & I have informed Mr Martin the secretary in reply to his inquiry that the time quite suited me, & that he had better ask if it also suited you & Mrs Hanbury. So he probably wrote to her to consult you.

Unless I hear again from him I shall conclude that those are the days.

Everybody will, of course, hope to see you, but if necessity compels I am sure that all the audience will be pleased with your substitute.

It was thought best to allot the afternoon performance to you, as you would have so much further to go home than Mrs Hanbury. We hope that the postponement will have no ill effect on the receipts!

I trust that the cure is progressing satisfactorily, & am

Always yrs sincerely,
Thomas Hardy.

Text Transcript (by Henry Reed) Purdy.
Mr Martin: Henry Austin Martin, Hon. Secretary of the Dorchester Debating and Dramatic Society; see IV.57. *you & Mrs Hanbury*: who had been asked to give speeches prior to the Dorchester performances of *Wessex Scenes from The Dynasts*; for Mrs. Hanbury see letter to her of 27 Nov 16. *your substitute*: Lady Ilchester's daughter (see letter of 2 Nov 16) did deliver the speech on her mother's behalf; see Purdy, 319. *the cure*: see letter of 2 Nov 16.

To J. H. MORGAN

Max Gate | Dorchester | 21: 11: '16

Dear Captain Morgan:

Many thanks for the copy of Land & Water containing your article that gives such graphic descriptions of the Front—the dead man peering into the distance is particularly striking.

If you are ever in the neighbourhood of Dorchester we shall be delighted to see you again. My wife sends kind regards.

Yours very truly
Thomas Hardy.

Text MS. Berg.
Morgan: John Hartman Morgan (1876–1955), lawyer, author, and authority on constitutional law; *D.N.B.* *your article*: 'A Day on the Somme' by 'Centurion' (i.e., Morgan), *Land & Water*, 16 Nov 1916.

To THOMAS HUMPHRY WARD

MAX GATE, | DORCHESTER. | 24 Nov: 1916

Dear Mr Ward:

I am sending in a separate cover my paper on Barnes, such as it is. You must not be alarmed at the formidable size of the parcel: it is because it will not bend, owing to my having used scissors & paste for the extracts—the copying of dialect being so difficult, & leading to endless printers' errors. I do not think it is much longer than you stipulated, if any. If it should be please cut it down.

I hope you & Mrs Ward are not getting much depressed by the apparent remoteness of peace. I must admit that we are, though I suppose one must not say so openly. With kind regards I am

Sincerely yours
Thomas Hardy.

Text MS. (with envelope) Texas.
paper on Barnes: see letter of 11 Oct 16.

To DOROTHY HANBURY

Max Gate | 27: 11: 16

Dear Mrs Hanbury:

Would you be so kind as to send on the enclosed, as I don't know where Mr Jeune may be at the present moment. You will see what it concerns before you fasten it.

Mr Martin is rather anxious about the bookings for the play, & says he hopes the Patronesses will send for seats, which not many have done yet.

Sincerely yrs
Thomas Hardy.

Text MS. NYU.
Hanbury: Effield Dorothy Hanbury (1871–1937), wife of Cecil Hanbury (see letter of 28 June 14 to Gosse), owner of Kingston Maurward House. *the enclosed*: TH's letter of 27 Nov 16 to J. F. Symons Jeune, Mrs. Hanbury's father. *the Patronesses*: of whom Mrs. Hanbury was one.

To JOHN SYMONS JEUNE

MAX GATE, | DORCHESTER. | Nov. 27: 1916

Dear Mr Jeune:

I have been asked on behalf of the mother of the soldier of whom I enclose particulars if I can do anything to help on inquiries about him. I fear he must have been killed, but it struck me that as you were in the way of making such inquiries it would do no harm to send on the particulars to you. The case is a sad one, as his mother is suffering from a painful illness which her constant anxiety about the boy aggravates, & may, the doctor says, be the cause of its ending fatally. At any rate you will not mind my asking if anything can be done.

We shall hope to see you soon. The arrangements for producing the play are proceeding, though they are outside my department which ends with the words.

Always yrs sincerely
Thomas Hardy.

Text MS. Eton College.
the soldier: probably Percy Paris Pope (see letter of 17 Nov 15 to Pope); his body was never found but his family did not abandon hope until March 1917, when his will was proved (*A Book of Remembrance*, 77). *such inquiries*: Symons Jeune was working with the Red Cross in France.

To EVELYN GIFFORD

MAX GATE, | DORCHESTER. | 29: 11: 1916

Dear Miss Gifford:

I hope you will accept this little book of selections from my poems—some of them written before you were born!

I am sorry I did not quite recognize who you were when we met at Mrs Hanbury's, until after you had gone. We often see them, & next week she is going to make a speech from the stage in Dorchester, before the curtain rises for the performance of my play called "Scenes from the Dynasts", in aid of the Red Cross funds. My wife's kind regards.

Sincerely yours
Thomas Hardy.

Text MS. (with envelope) UCLA.
Gifford: Evelyn Hamilton Gifford (1876–1920), daughter of Edwin Hamilton Gifford and cousin of ELH. *from my poems*: the copy of *Selected Poems* which TH inscribed and sent to Miss Gifford is now at UCLA. *Mrs Hanbury's*: whose first cousin she also was.

To SIR HENRY NEWBOLT

MAX GATE, | DORCHESTER. | Dec 3: 1916

My dear Newbolt:

We have read the book, & enjoyed it much—particularly the retreat from Mons—without any consciousness of having gone back to boyishness in relishing it. If the war were *over*, how much less of misgiving & sadness those pages would convey with the literary pleasure they give.

I fear there is going to be no end to this strife—by no end I mean no settlement. We shall simply go on till we leave off from exhaustion—Germany unconquered, the Allies unassured, & both sides sullenly picking up the pieces & mending them as well as they can for another smash some day. But I may be all wrong, & most likely am, for I really have no clear facts to go upon.

Our kindest regards to you both, & with thanks for the book I am

Ever sincerely
Thomas Hardy.

Text MS. Colby.
Newbolt: Henry Newbolt, poet and man of letters; see III.21. He was knighted in 1915. *the book*: Newbolt's *Tales of the Great War* (London, 1916); the retreat from Mons is described on pp.159–64. *back to boyishness*: Newbolt, sending the book (4 Nov 16, Texas), had said that it was intended for boys, though a few of its pages might interest TH.

To G. HERBERT THRING

(Ansr) Max Gate, | December 10. 1916

Dear Mr Thring:

I am sorry that I did not reply to your letter of Novbr concerning Charity Books (as they have been called). But I understood from its wording that unless I could support the Resolutions of the Comee of Managt no answer wd be required. That I cd not subscribe as requested I felt immediately.

The question is, indeed, purely a Trades-Union one, & the framers of the Resolutions appear to be entirely engrossed by the commercial aspect of word-selling.

On the other hand the difficulty of my objecting to the Resolution lies in the fact that the S. of Authors, strange as it may sound when baldly expressed, is merely a word-selling society, & has nothing whatever to do with literature as an art, or a passion, or a dream. It was founded as a trades-union & as such must remain. Moreover I have no doubt that the matter is serious for straitened authors—at least for those who cannot temporarily turn their hands to Munition-making, like some I know, & commend. So that in retaining the Presidency of a body so constituted I am at least bound not to obstruct its views, however often I may privately feel that the society should sometimes give a little consideration to that side of the literary pursuit on which money-returns are not the sole thought of the writer.

It is, of course, open to question whether one whose personal instinct is entirely against doing anything to hinder spontaneous gifts to Charity Funds by any literary man of his writings, or lending his name to such—particularly to War Charities in these exceptional times, & who has himself contributed to many Charity books & Bazaars during the war—has any right to hold the Presidency of a body of writers opposed to such doings, or at any rate wd wish them to be suspended from this moment. But as I think you & the Council know, I have always been willing to give place to any member who more truly represents the purposes of the society.

I regret that owing to my having been confined to bed by a chill for the last few days I am only able to dictate this brief & imperfect reply, & if I do not appear to give sufficient consideration to authors who are much affected by the results of the war it is not that I do not feel the hardness of their case.

I am,

Yours very truly

. . . .

The Secretary. | Incorporated Society of Authors.

Text MS. (pencil draft) DCM.
letter of Novbr: this letter seems not to have survived; TH was now replying to Thring's letter of 8 Dec 16, soliciting his support (as President) of a resolution passed by the Committee of Management of the Incorporated Society of Authors respecting the need to protect the rights of authors, especially those suffering financial hardship, from the importunities of those seeking gratuitous contributions to books sold for charitable purposes. *willing to give place*: TH had been reluctant to assume the presidency at all; see IV.27–9.

To EDMUND GOSSE

MAX GATE, | DORCHESTER. | Dec 13: 1916

My dear Gosse:

Of course, if the slightest good is likely to be done by putting down my name as before, please do so, though my working powers will be nil. You will quite understand why it is that I shall be such a dead-head, for I am getting on in years, & far away. I have not been in London *this year*—an unprecedented thing for one who was once half a Londoner.

However, if people should grumble at my figuring in your excellent work without working at it, I may be excused saying that I have been doing things down here for the same Cause. You may have seen in the papers about our dramatic efforts: & at the rehearsals for last week's production I caught such a chill that to-day is the first morning I have got up to breakfast for a week & more. So I feel in the Red Cross business as it were, like the rest of you.

I am sorry you lost your friend Ld Redesdale, though I did not know him. Barrie, by the way, came to our performance, & Granville Barker was coming, but prevented by his military duties. Barrie has I think mellowed into a very nice fellow. You don't say a word about Philip, & I conclude from that that he is well. I am not in the best of spirits about the issue of the war; & a book my wife has been reading to me does not help me—Sir Oliver Lodge's Raymond. Poor dear amiable man.

I suppose you are never coming into Dorset any more, but if you do "after the war" you will know where to find us. I hope Mrs Gosse is well, & we send her best Christmas wishes—if it is not too dangerously near satire to send such messages in these ferocious times.

Always yrs sincerely
Thomas Hardy.

Text MS. Adams.
putting down my name: as a member of the committee responsible for organizing the annual Red Cross sales of books and manuscripts. *the same Cause*: the proceeds from the performances of *Wessex Scenes from The Dynasts* went to the Red Cross. *Ld Redesdale*: see letter of 7 Dec 15 to Douglas; Gosse had formed a close friendship with Redesdale during his last years. *Lodge's Raymond*: Sir Oliver Joseph Lodge (1851–1940), scientist, first Principal of the Univ. of Birmingham; *D.N.B.* His spiritualist views found expression in *Raymond; or, Life and Death. With Examples of the Evidence for Survival of Memory and Affection After Death* (London, 1916).

To STANLEY LEATHES

[Mid-December 1916]

Dear Mr Leathes:

I am much obliged for yr letter on the very troublesome question of Charity Books, & I feel that the Commee may possibly be right in looking into it, at least: it being obvious that, as you say, the Society does quite legitimately, & must, deal with the material interests of Authors; & though I have sometimes wished it had more to do with their higher aims I frankly own that I don't see how it can.

I am quite in doubt whether or not action in this practical matter is necessary or desirable. Hence I have thought my proper course to be to remain neutral, voting neither for nor against any Resolns that may be adopted by the Comttee of Mant.

In view of yr letter I may add that as long as the Society wishes me to retain the honour of being its nominal head I am happy to remain so; since this does not, I imagine mean that in details of procedure I am always acting with the managers.

V. truly yrs
T.H.

Text MS. (pencil draft) DCM. *Date* Replies to letter of 13 Dec 16.
Leathes: Stanley Mordaunt Leathes (1861–1938), Civil Service Commissioner and author, currently chairman of the Committee of Management of the Incorporated Society of Authors; *D.N.B.* *yr letter*: Leathes (13 Dec 16, DCM), responding to TH's letter of 10 Dec 16 to Thring, observed that charity books were 'a most wasteful device for getting money' and did 'great damage to authors'; he also deplored TH's hint that he might resign his presidency and promised not to press him further on this particular matter.

To THOMAS J. WISE

MAX GATE, | DORCHESTER. | December 20: 1916

Dear Mr Wise:

The Wordsworth bibliography has arrived, & I am truly obliged to you for such a gift, for I consider myself a Faithful Wordsworthian, though not to the extent of those who follow him into the years when he became parochial & commonplace.

I suppose you will be doing Shelley or Byron next. With many thanks I am

Sincerely yours
Thomas Hardy.

Text MS. (with envelope) BL.
Wise: Thomas James Wise (1859–1937), book-collector, bibliographer, and forger; *D.N.B.* *Wordsworth bibliography*: Wise's privately printed *A Bibliography of the Writings in Prose and Verse of William Wordsworth* (London, 1916). *Shelley or Byron next*: Wise did in fact pub. *A Shelley Library* in 1924 and *A Bibliography of the Writings in Verse and Prose of George Gordon Noel, Baron Byron* in 1932.

To FLORENCE HENNIKER

MAX GATE, | DORCHESTER. | 22 Dec: '16

My dear friend:

I am writing a line to reach you at Christmas, though I don't know that it will, our post-office having behaved eccentrically of late. I am rejoiced to find that you liked the Golden Treasury Selection. Of course friends say—almost every one—that they miss so & so, but they could not all be got in.

I agree with Watson about the writers of *vers libre*, &c. I suppose it is only a passing fashion, the original sinner being Walt Whitman, who, I always think, wrote as he did, formlessly, because he could do no better.

Our blackbirds & thrushes have had a hard time on account of the frost & snow, but they are recovering now. We, like you, have plenty of Tits. Florence knows their varieties better than I do.

We have been reading Sir Oliver Lodge's "Raymond"—which you also probably have read. We found it unconvincing, particularly the "medium" business, all of which I remember going on 40 or 50 years ago, when they were treated as impostors. There will be one in every street after this. I daresay Lodge is sincere enough, but he is vilely victimized I think.

In the Sphere for Jan 6. there will be, I believe, a poem of mine called "A New Year's Eve in War Time". It is concerning an incident that happened here on a New Year's Eve not so long ago. I am glad to hear of Gerrie. F. Harrison told me that he tried to talk old Greek to the inhabitants when he was over there, but could not get on. We have had a performance of "Wessex Scenes from the Dynasts" here, for Red Cross purposes, & Lady Ilchester was to have made an introductory speech; but as she could not get here her daughter Mary delivered it faultlessly, it being her first appearance as a public orator.

Wessie is well, but has the defects of his qualities. F. has just come back from Weymouth, where she has a nice friend, a Mrs Inglis, wife of Col. Inglis.

With all best wishes, & F's love, I am

Yrs ever
Th. H.

Text MS. DCM.
with Watson: William Watson, the poet; see letter of 12 Mar 15. The specific reference is unclear, although Watson's just-published *Retrogression and Other Poems* (London,1917) was strongly hostile to recent poetic fashions. *Walt Whitman*: the American poet (1819–92); TH seems, however, to have been among his earliest English readers (see *EL*, 78, and Millgate, 112n). *have plenty of Tits*: TH wrote 'have, plenty of Tits'. *"Raymond"*: see letter of 13 Dec 16. *not so long ago*: see letter of 15 Jan 17. *Gerrie*: Mrs. Henniker's nephew Gerald Fitzgerald, son of Sir Gerald and Lady Fitzgerald (see II.21); he was serving with the army in Greece. *her daughter Mary*: see letter of 2 Nov 16. *Wessie*: see letter of 29 Jan 14. *Mrs Inglis . . . Col. Inglis*: see letter of 10 July 15.

To SIR ARTHUR QUILLER-COUCH

Max Gate, | Dorchester: | Dec 22: 1916

My dear Q:

We have read with much pleasure "The Sacred Way"—aloud; & it seems as if you must have been over there, & pondered on the scene. I thought the fourth verse a little obscure, but all the rest as lucid & limpid as could be wished.

I am sending this at a venture to Fowey, hardly supposing you will stay up at Jesus over Christmas in the east-coast air when you can breathe the zephyrs of Cornwall for the asking.

Cockerell came down here to see the "Scenes from the Dynasts" that our amateurs did a fortnight ago. He caught a bad cold in consequence, from me, I think, for I happened to be in the middle of one. Also J. M. Barrie (who came) was in the same predicament. However, they are better now they say.

To hark back to your poem, & poetry generally: I have been looking at reviews sent by the publishers of that little selection I sent you. What a pity that there is no school or science of criticism—especially in respect of verse. I cannot find a single idea in any one of them that is not obvious, but I suppose the verses that come to hand in newspaper offices are put into the hands of the youngest girl on the staff.

You might deliver an excellent series of lectures on the Vicissitudes of Poetry, as exhibited in the history of English literature—instancing such a queer phenomenon as that of Vaughan, for example, who for two centuries dropped into oblivion, & was then duly ressurected.

I hope it will not seem too obvious a satire to wish you & yours the best that Christmas can bring. I fear it will not be much that is cheering.

Always sincerely
Thomas Hardy.

Text MS. Miss F. F. Quiller-Couch.
Sacred Way": Quiller-Couch's war-poem 'The Sacred Way', first pub. *Cambridge Magazine*, 10 June 1916, later reprinted by Heffer's of Cambridge as no. 3 in a series of 'Reprints from *The Cambridge Magazine*'. *been over there*: i.e., at Verdun, under fierce German attack from February to September 1916; the French supply road to the fort was called the 'Sacred Way'. *all the rest*: there were eleven stanzas in all. *at Jesus*: Quiller-Couch's Cambridge college. *in the middle of one*: TH's cold kept him away from the performances of *Wessex Scenes*. *little selection*: *Selected Poems of Thomas Hardy*. *Vaughan*: Henry Vaughan (1622–95; *D.N.B.*); TH's copy of Vaughan's *Sacred Poems and Pious Ejaculations* (London, 1897), in DCM, bears numerous markings and annotations. *ressurected*: one of TH's rare spelling errors.

To J. S. UDAL

MAX GATE, | DORCHESTER. | Christmas Day 1916

Dear Udal:

I think it better to send you a brief letter immediately than intend to send you a long one later on, & forget to do it. Many thanks for the volume of Stone's poems just arrived. You should not have taken the trouble to get them bound.

I knew about him, but never met him, though I knew & liked his brother Walter. I was not aware that he was your cousin. His father was Giles Symonds's partner, & they had offices at the top of the town here, when I was a boy. The verses are pleasing, as far as I have got, but I have come to nothing very strong as yet.

We wrote to Mr Shorter to call on you, & he said he would when his wife got better: she has been very ill, but I think is improving. I am sure he will be glad to know you.

The book-dealer bought the copies of the programme on condition that I signed no more, but I can sign the volume of play-bills you propose to collect, though I should like you to send me a guinea to forward to the "Blue Cross" (horses) fund, if you can see your way to it: if not, let be.

I will, as promised, sign "The Dynasts" whenever you like to bring it.

I have got over the chill which prevented my going to the performance: I daresay the Dorset men in London will wish to have it done there, but the cast is a large one, & travelling expenses will be formidable. Our kind regards & best wishes for the New Year.

Sincerely yours
Thomas Hardy.

Text MS. Texas.
Stone's poems: the Revd. Edward Daniel Stone, Eton master, minister, and classical scholar, son of a Dorchester solicitor; his book of verse, *Dorica*, was pub. (London, 1888) over his initials only. *his brother Walter*: Walter George Boswell Stone, antiquarian; see IV.120. *your cousin*: Udal's maternal grandmother was the sister of Joseph Stone, father of Edward and Walter Stone. *Symonds's partner*: Giles Symonds (1812–92), Dorchester solicitor, was junior partner to Joseph Stone, whom he succeeded as Town Clerk of Dorchester upon his death in 1853; see also III.157. Though TH seems not to have realized it, Giles Symonds was Joseph Stone's nephew and uncle to Udal himself. *improving*: see letter of 26 Dec 16. *signed no more*: TH signed 12 copies of a special issue of the programme for the Dorchester performances of *Wessex Scenes from The Dynasts*. *"Blue Cross"*: a charitable organization, an off-shoot of Our Dumb Friends' League, devoted to the care of horses wounded in wartime. *done there*: *Wessex Scenes* was not in fact performed in London.

To CLEMENT SHORTER

Max Gate, | Dorchester | December 26: 1916

Dear Shorter:

Herewith I send the proofs corrected. What you propose about Collier's Weekly suits very well. Thanks for the trouble you are taking, & if it doesn't suit the Editor to have it, let the noble neutrals do their worst & pirate it. I hope Mrs. Shorter will soon be getting about again. I am

Sincerely yours
Thomas Hardy

Best new year's wishes.

Text Typed transcript J. S. Sample.
the proofs: of TH's poem 'A New Year's Eve in War Time', *Sphere*, 6 Jan 1917. *Collier's Weekly*: TH's poem seems not to have appeared there, however. *the noble neutrals*: i.e., the Americans. *getting about again*: Dora Sigerson Shorter's health remained poor, however, and she died in January 1918.

To J. W. MACKAIL

MAX GATE, | DORCHESTER. | Dec 30: 1916

My dear Mackail:

Best thanks for your kind New Year's wishes. I send mine: also the little book within, which I hope you will accept.

Mine was only a common cold, & it went away in due time. I am afraid Cockerell got it from me through coming here. If so I am sorry.

As for Iago: it *may* have been that I have always seen him badly presented: I should so much like to see the convincing one you speak of. Did I ever tell you that I went to the theatre long enough ago to see Phelps as Othello?

I shall be so glad to see Clare again. How much less regardful of self women are than men. She must not go knocking herself up again by too assiduous nursing.

It has just occurred to me that I am not wise in sending you poetry at the Education office, for the "Journal of Education" had but a poor opinion of the volume, which is ominous. And your mind must be full of more practical matters just now.

Sincerely yrs
Th. Hardy.

Text MS. Yale.
little book: the inscribed copy of *Selected Poems* is now at Yale. *Iago*: see letter of 13 Aug 16. *Phelps as Othello*: Samuel Phelps played Othello in London in 1864. *Clare*: Mackail's younger daughter; see letter of 13 Aug 16. *at the Education office*: Mackail was assistant secretary to the Education Department (later the Board of Education) 1903–19. *of the volume*: a brief unsigned notice of *Selected Poems, Journal of Education,* November 1916, declared that 'Poetry was not with Mr. Hardy a second nature'.

To LADY ST. HELIER

Max Gate. | Dorchester. | Dec. 30. 1916.

Best wishes for the new Year, my dear friend, and sustained vigour for your splendid activities, from both.

Always yours
Thomas Hardy.

Text Typed transcript DCM.
your splendid activities: as an alderman of the London County Council and a promoter of many charities.

1917

To ARTHUR SYMONS

MAX GATE, | DORCHESTER. | January 3: 1917

Dear Symons:

I have now read almost all of "Figures of Several Centuries" that you were good enough to send, & it has given me much pleasure. The essays are so terse, & the thoughts so undiluted, that they suggest a distillation remaining from a bulk of opinion which if fully expressed would have extended to ten times the space that you have allotted to them.

I don't quite know which of the articles I like best—perhaps the Ibsen, Donne, Meredith & Swinburne ones. As for the "note" on my own writings, I must not allow myself to say anything about it beyond the expression of a hope that I may not much disappoint readers who come to me after reading the essay!

With many thanks for the book, I am

Sincerely yours
T. Hardy.

Text MS. Hisazumi Tagiri.
of Several Centuries": Symons's *Figures of Several Centuries* (London, 1916). *the "note"*: the essay on TH was entitled 'A Note on the Genius of Thomas Hardy'.

To ISRAEL GOLLANCZ

FROM THO. HARDY, | MAX GATE, | DORCHESTER. | 8: 1: '17

Dear Dr Gollancz:

The receipt of your kind words on the book suddenly leads me to fear that I *may* not have acknowledged your Xmas gift of the Icelandic poem you have translated, which I read when it came, & thought most quaintly interesting. If I did not I do so now. My correspondence gets so confused that I forget my duties in it sometimes!

Sincerely yours
T.H.

Text MS. (correspondence card) Rosenbach Foundation.
the book: TH had presumably sent Gollancz a copy of *Selected Poems of Thomas Hardy*. *Icelandic poem*: Matthias Jochumsson, *1616-1916. On the Tercentenary Commemoration of Shakespeare Ultima Thule Sendeth Greetings: An Icelandic Poem*, trans. I. Gollancz (London, 1916).

To ALFRED POPE

MAX GATE, | DORCHESTER. | Jan. 10: 1917

Dear Mr Pope:

Thank you much for your paper on the Dorchester Walks in pamphlet form. I read it in the Chronicle with great interest, & it is desirable to have it in a more permanent shape.

I hope your ancle is getting right. I did not know till a day or two ago that it was more than a sprain, or I should have inquired.

Very truly yrs
Th. Hardy.

Text MS. Thomas Hardy Society.
pamphlet form: Pope's *The Walks and Avenues of Dorchester* (Dorchester, 1917). *in the Chronicle*: the paper, read at a meeting of the Dorset Natural History and Antiquarian Field Club on 12 Dec 1916, was first pub. in the *Dorset County Chronicle*, 14 Dec 1916.

To ALFRED DE LAFONTAINE

MAX GATE, | DORCHESTER. | January 11. 1917

Dear Mr de Lafontaine:

I am sorry to say that I have been unable, so far, to recall the name of the builder of Athelhampton Church in 1861 or 1862. Certainly it was not the Mr. Wellspring who has just died. He did not succeed to his father's business till after that date. Whether the builder was his father, or Hammett of Tolpuddle, I am not sure, but I think it was one of them.

Yet who ought to know better than I, for though you are wrong in supposing that I *designed* the church, I made many of the drawings for it under Hicks, (with whom I was a pupil) & I helped him to mark out the church & the churchyard; & I represented Hicks at the consecration, he being unable to attend. At least I believe I did so. At any rate I was there.

I remember the stonemason perfectly well—having had frequently to explain my drawings to him. He was Hounsell of Broadway—the father of the present one who is carrying on the business.

I think you may meet with some old native who will be able to tell you. I incline strongly to the belief that it was Hammett; but if I can tell you later on I will do so.

Yours sincerely,
Ths Hardy.

Text MS. (with envelope) R. Greenland.
de Lafontaine: Alfred C. de Lafontaine, owner and restorer of Athelhampton Hall, just E. of Puddletown; see II.305. *just died*: i.e., John Wellspring (1840–1916), Dorchester builder. *his father*: John Wellspring (1800?–75), Dorchester builder, with whom TH worked on several occasions during his career as an architect; see *EL*, 164–5. *Hammett*: William Hammett, builder, of Tolpuddle, Dorset; he was in fact the builder of Athelhampton Church. *Hicks*: John Hicks (1815–69), Dorchester architect; see *EL*, 35–6, etc. *I was there*: if so, he did not play any official role; the report of the Consecration service, 31 Dec 1861, names Hicks himself

as among those present (*Dorset County Chronicle*, 2 Jan 1862). *carrying on the business*: see letter of 21 May 16; the business continues still.

To SYDNEY COCKERELL

MAX GATE, | DORCHESTER. | January 15. 1917

My dear Cockerell:

I ought to have answered your very interesting letter ages ago, but I didn't.

I am rather surprised at people liking the *Sphere* poem, yourself the most trustworthy among them, for I thought it was of a middling sort. The incident of the horse galloping past precisely at the stroke of midnight between the old & new year is, by the way, true; it happened here, & we never learnt what horse it was. It is strange that you should have lighted on the Blake picture which in some respects almost matches the verses.

I am sorry to hear that Masefield has been aged by his war-experiences. Yet a man of deep feeling like him could not avoid it after coming in contact with the tragic scenes in France. It is grievous to think too that his writing of verse will probably be hindered for a time. I wish he would write more in his early style.

What a trouble you are taking with the Selected Poems. Please don't be too generous with them. I really don't deserve it.

Now as to the great nightcap question. If I begin to indulge in that apparel I shall most likely go on with it because of its comfort, whilst if I had never tried it I should have taken the colds in the head, &c., I might have got through lacking it, quite philosophically. Seriously it is too good of Mrs Cockerell to occupy herself with making it. We hope sincerely that she is mending in health.

A curious thing, in a small way, has come to my knowledge. You know I have no high opinion of American literary criticism, yet I learn from their newspapers that the verses I copied out for you—"When I set out for Lyonnesse"—because I fancied they showed something of the song-ecstasy that a lyric should have (other than an elegiac lyric) have become quite well known in the U. States & much quoted. Isn't it heaping coals of fire on my head! Not a soul in England—neither bishops, clerks, nor people of the critical hierarchy—has thought anything of them, so far as I know. Perhaps they are right, alas.

Tell Q. when you see him that I feel for him under the depression of influenza. Yes: of course you will come again & see us here later on. Last night was I think the coldest we have had in these parts this winter.

Ever yours
Thomas Hardy.

Text MS. Adams.
Sphere *poem*: 'A New Year's Eve in War Time'; see letter of 26 Dec 16. *the Blake picture*: the colour-print entitled 'Pity'; see *Friends of a Lifetime* (see letter to Cockerell of 9 Aug 14), 284. *scenes in France*: see John Masefield, *The Old Front Line: or, The Beginning of the Battle of the Somme* (London, 1917). *Selected Poems*: Cockerell was apparently giving the

vol. his customary close reading; TH had inscribed a copy to him in October 1916 (Adams). *nightcap . . . Mrs Cockerell*: see letter of 21 Jan 17. *from their newspapers*: TH's precise source has not been identified. *Q.*: Sir Arthur Quiller-Couch.

To EDMUND GOSSE

MAX GATE, | DORCHESTER. | January 18th. 1917.

My dear Gosse:

I should much like to be present at the meeting of the Red-Cross Books' Committee, but I am sorry to say that I find it increasingly difficult to go to London in the winter at all, and have lately been laid up with a cold.

I wish you and your colleagues every success in your unceasing efforts in furthering the humane and beneficent work of the Red Cross. It is a marvel to me that you, personally, should have had the courage to devote so much of your time to this work during the past two years when there is such a call for your labours in literary directions.

I have been trying to think what new plan there may be for tapping the immense stores of saleable objects that lie buried in English houses great and small, that would be of particular value in this sale, but I fear I can suggest nothing that you have not already considered. Unfortunately I have never been a collector and possess none of these objects.

However there are hundreds who are not so situated, and I earnestly hope you may have as good a haul this year as in previous years.

With kind regards to you and your house from both of us I am

Always sincerely yours,
Thomas Hardy.

P.S. This is typewritten as you may want to read it quickly. T.H.
Edmund Gosse Esq. C.B. Red Cross Books, MSS., and Autographs Committee.

Text MS. (typewritten) Leeds.
Books' Committee: see letter of 13 Dec 16.

To KATE COCKERELL

MAX GATE, | DORCHESTER. | Sunday night. [21 January 1917]

Dear Mrs Cockerell:

It was most kind of you to trouble yourself to make this quite becoming (as I am told) article of head-gear. It came at breakfast-time this morning, & I wore it all through the meal—very appropriately, for the morning was so dark that we were obliged to breakfast by candlelight, although it was ¼ past nine when we began. So that you see I *have* worn it already.

We have had a day of rime & sleet, with slippery roads. Nevertheless we have walked to Froom Hill this evening, just to exercise our dog, on whom we go humbly in attendance.

With many thanks I am,

Sincerely yours
Thomas Hardy.

Text MS. Taylor. *Date* From internal evidence.
Cockerell: Florence Kate Cockerell, *née* Kingsford (d. 1949), artist and illuminator; she married Sydney Cockerell in 1907 but developed multiple sclerosis and became increasingly incapacitated thereafter. See Wilfred Blunt, *Cockerell* (London, 1964), 165-8. *article of head-gear*: the nightcap Mrs. Cockerell had made was, FEH reported to Cockerell (26 Jan 17, Purdy), 'so pretty and most becoming to T.H.'; Cockerell sent it with his letter of 18 Jan 17 (DCM).

To SIEGFRIED SASSOON

MAX GATE, | DORCHESTER. | February 4: 1917

Dear Mr Sassoon:

I am pleased that you should care to inscribe your coming book of poems to me, which of course you have my permission to do—if you think it worth while!

Many thanks for enclosing the proof of the little one about Corbie Ridge (I don't know where that is.)

I hope the weather will be milder before you go back to France, & that you may have good luck over there.

Sincerely yours
Thomas Hardy.

Text MS. Eton College.
Sassoon: Siegfried Loraine Sassoon (1886–1967), poet and prose-writer; *D.N.B.* He was the nephew and ward of TH's friend Hamo Thornycroft. *book of poems*: Sassoon's *The Old Huntsman and Other Poems* (London, 1917), dedicated 'To / Thomas Hardy, O.M.' *about Corbie Ridge*: Sassoon's poem 'Two Hundred Years After' begins 'Trudging by Corbie Ridge one winter's night'. Corbie, a town on the River Somme east of Amiens, was the scene of heavy fighting in 1916; the allusion in Sassoon's title is to the battles fought in the region (though not at Corbie itself) by British troops under Marlborough in the early years of the 18th century.

To AN UNIDENTIFIED CORRESPONDENT

MAX GATE, | DORCHESTER. | February 5: 1917

Dear Madam:

My thanks for your volume of poems, which I mean to read—or some of them—even though I may not be able to find your solution of Life's problems.

Yours truly
Th. Hardy.

Text MS. David Holmes.
volume of poems: it remains, like its author, unidentified.

To PERCY AMES

MAX GATE, | DORCHESTER. | February 8th. 1917.

Dear Sir:

I regret that as I live in a remote part of the country I cannot attend the meeting of the Entente Committee.

In respect of the Memorandum proposing certain basic principles of International education for promoting ethical ideals that shall conduce to a League of Peace, I am in hearty agreement with the proposition. I would say in considering a *modus operandi*:

That nothing effectual will be done in the cause of peace till the sentiment of *Patriotism* be freed from the narrow meaning attaching to it in the past (and still upheld by Junkers and Jingoists)—and be extended to the whole globe.

On the other hand, that the sentiment of *Foreignness*—if the sense of contrast be necessary—attach only to other planets and their inhabitants if any.

I may add that I have written in advocacy of these views for the last twenty years.

Yours truly,
Thomas Hardy.

Percy W. Ames Esq. | Sec. R.S.L.

Text MS. (typewritten) Royal Society of Literature.
Ames: Percy W. Ames, Secretary of the Royal Society of Literature; see IV.215. *Entente Committee*: a committee, composed of distinguished Fellows of the Society, 'for promoting an intellectual entente among the allied and friendly countries'; see letter of 22 Sept 16. *the Memorandum*: incorporated in the report of the Society's Educational Sub-Committee, sent to TH together with an undated form-letter from Ames (DCM). *be necessary*: the slightly revised text in *LY*, 174, reads 'be really rhetorically necessary'.

To NEWMAN FLOWER

FROM THO. HARDY, | MAX GATE, | DORCHESTER. | Feb 12. 1917

Many thanks for the book. I am glad it is doing so well.

Th. H.

Text MS. (postcard) Texas.
the book: presumably Flower's novel *Crucifixion* (London, 1916), although the sixth vol. of *The History of the Great War*, ed. by Flower, appeared early in 1917.

To THOMAS J. WISE

FROM THO. HARDY, | MAX GATE, | DORCHESTER. | Feb 13: 1917

Many thanks for the reprint, which, as you say, might have been suggested by Coleridge's Fears in Solitude.

Text MS. (postcard) BL.
the reprint: Walter Savage Landor, *An Address to the Fellows of Trinity College, Oxford on the Alarm of Invasion* (London: privately printed, 1917); it was first written in 1798. *in Solitude*: Coleridge's poem is sub-titled 'Written in April 1798, During the Alarm of an Invasion'.

To SYDNEY COCKERELL

MAX GATE, | DORCHESTER. | Feb 23: 1917

My dear Cockerell:

I am answering your inquiries & sending back the proof of the "Trampwoman", as my wife went off to Enfield this morning to be present at her sister's wedding—if it comes off. It has been postponed two or three times, owing to the extreme difficulty of a flying man's getting leave. He has now only 10 days, for coming, returning, & the whole programme. We think them a pair of rather thoughtless young people, but they are having their own way.

I have inserted Roman figures in the proof. I don't remember why figures were put at all; however there they are. You can take them out if you incline to.

As to the notes, do you think they are of any service? Please do as you like about them. If you do insert them will you give them as in the definitive Wessex edition, in which my respected grandfather appears.

I forgot to ask my wife how many she wanted. What do you say to 20 or 25? I am a child in these matters of private printing's, & my idea in respect of such always is that they should be limited to what is never to be published. But this rule is not followed, I know.

We have nearly finished the Life of William Morris that you were so kind to send, & enjoy it much. He was fortunate in having such a sympathetic biographer. What a strenuous character Morris's was. *My* feeling is (though probably not yours) that he wasted on weaving what was meant for mankind at large. He may, however, have been helpless in the force of his tendencies.

We are having some trees rooted, so as to enlarge the kitchen garden for more potatoes, & the Commandant of the prison camp here has sent me out some prisoners for the job, with guards, rifles, interpreter, & all complete. Nothing has made me feel more sad about the war than the sight of these amiable young Germans in such a position through the machinations of some vile war-gang or other. Nevertheless they seem perfectly happy, (though they get only 1d an hour each of the 6d each that I pay). I am told that thousands of these prisoners are craving agricultural work instead of idleness, but cannot get it.

Always yours,
Thomas Hardy.

Text MS. Buffalo.
the "Trampwoman": i.e., FEH's privately printed pamphlet of TH's poem 'A Trampwoman's Tragedy'; see Purdy, 190–1. *sister's wedding*: Margaret Dugdale (see letter of 9 May 17)

married Reginald Henry Soundy (then serving with the Royal Flying Corps), 24 Feb 1917; they spent most of their honeymoon at Max Gate. *incline to*: the Roman numerals at the head of each stanza were retained. *the notes*: these were included in the pamphlet, following the wording of the Wessex edn. *my respected grandfather*: the note on 'Blue Jimmy' the horsethief (stanza x) mentions his having stolen a horse 'belonging to a neighbour of the writer's grandfather' (i.e., TH's father's father). A note in TH's 'Facts' notebook (DCM) identifies the neighbour as William Keats's father, of Bockhampton. *20 or 25?*: twenty-five copies of the pamphlet were in fact printed. *sympathetic biographer*: the Hardys were reading J. W. Mackail's *The Life of William Morris*, first pub., in 2 vols., in 1899. TH never met Morris (1834–96; *D.N.B.*) but Cockerell had been secretary to the Kelmscott Press during Morris's last years. *wasted on weaving*: FEH told Cockerell, 26 Feb 17 (Purdy), that TH could not understand how a man such as Morris, capable of 'real poetry', could 'care about tapestries and carpets'.

To J. S. UDAL

FROM THO. HARDY, | MAX GATE, | DORCHESTER. | March 2: 1917

Letter, P.O., & parcel received. Will reply in a few days.

T.H.

Text MS. (postcard) Adams.
P.O., & parcel: the parcel contained a collection of theatre programmes (of productions of TH's works) which TH had promised to sign; the postal order was the charitable donation of one guinea TH had requested in return (see letters of 25 Dec 16 and 4 Mar 17).

To FLORENCE HENNIKER

MAX GATE, | DORCHESTER. | March 4: 1917

My dear friend:

I have earned by the sale of an autograph the enclosed 1/1/- for the Blue Cross, & Florence suggests I should send it to the Fund through you, as you collect for the Society, so I do so, making it the excuse for a letter, though a poor one, as all my letters get to be somehow. We are living uneventful lives here (if the news of war events are not reckoned) feeling no enterprize for going about & seeing people while the issue of the great conflict is in the balance—& I fear that by the time the issue is reached I shall be too far on to old age to care to do so. The actual reminder in this house that the struggle is going on is that I have some German prisoners at work in the garden, cutting down some trees, & clearing the ground for more potato-room. They are amiable young fellows, & it does fill one with indignation that thousands of such are led to slaughter by the ambitions of Courts & Dynasties. If only there were no monarchies in the world, what a chance for its amelioration!

I am so glad you like some of the poems in the Golden Treasury selection. They were not, inclusively or exclusively, those I should have put there had I chosen them *entirely* for myself: but many of those I like best were included, my favourite lyric being the one called "When I set out for Lyonnesse", I think, as it has the qualities one should find in a lyric.

Florence's youngest sister Marjorie was married about a week ago to a young Lieutenant in the Royal Flying Corps, on duty every day in the air above the fighting line in France. We think it a hazardous marriage, not on account of the young people's characters, for they are much attached to each other, nor for possible lack of income, for his father is well-off, & he is an only son, but because of his dangerous post. He has only had ten days' leave for the whole business of getting home & back, marriage, & honeymoon, & it will be rather a sad parting for them next Wednesday.

Did I tell you that Sir J. Barrie came & stayed here for the play of The Dynasts. Believe me

Your affectionate friend
Th: H.

Text MS. DCM.
sale of an autograph: see letter of 2 Mar 17. *Blue Cross*: see letter of 25 Dec 16. *for Lyonnesse"*: see letter of 15 Jan 17. *Marjorie*: i.e., Margaret Dugdale; see letter of 23 Feb 17. *dangerous post*: he did survive the war, however. *Barrie*: see letter of 23 June 17 and *LY*, 174; in her reply (5 Mar 17, transcript, DCM) Mrs. Henniker expressed the view that Barrie's reputation had become somewhat inflated.

To J.S. UDAL

MAX GATE, | DORCHESTER. | 6th. March 1917.

My dear Udal:

(Please excuse my being compelled nowadays to send a machine-written letter) I acknowledge with many thanks the information you send about the first edition of Desperate Remedies. Why did you not tell me six months after it appeared—when I could have got you a copy for half-a-crown—to keep you one! I suddenly remember however that you did not know me then. Few people did.

I am sorry to hear that your arthritis is no better. Dorset air would probably make an enormous difference—but as to finding an old cottage near Dorchester, I fear it is quite beyond me. There is an airy house at Monkton—recently built—that is all I know of.

Very truly yours,
Th: Hardy.

P.S. Many thanks but I already have the Barnes volume you mention.

Text MS. (typewritten) Yale.
for half-a-crown: i.e., at its remaindered price; see *EL*, 112. *house at Monkton*: probably 'Penwithen', Winterborne Monkton, or one of the smaller 'lodges' in its grounds; the property is now owned by the Dorset County Council. *Barnes volume*: unidentified.

To FREDERICK HIGGINBOTTOM

MAX GATE, | DORCHESTER. | 7th. March 1917.

Dear Sir:

I am sending you herewith a Sonnet which I have written as an appeal for National Service, in response to your request.

It occurred to me that a brief and condensed appeal in verse would be more effectual for the purpose than an article in prose, especially as I am more at home nowadays with verse and feel somewhat awkward with prose, not having printed any for so many years.

I would ask that, in the event of your circulating it, misprints may be especially guarded against, as such are more disastrous to poetry than to prose.

I should like *The Times* to have an early copy, amongst the other papers you may send it to, as they are very courteous in printing my contributions.

I am perhaps rashly assuming that you and Mr Neville Chamberlain will think the effusion appropriate for your purpose. But of course it may not be, and in that case I should be obliged if you would return it to me.

Yours very truly,
Thomas Hardy.

P.S. I send the poem in duplicate.
Fredk. J. Higginbottom Esq.

Text MS. (typewritten) Adams.
Higginbottom: Frederick James Higginbottom (1859–1943), journalist, currently director of Press Intelligence, Ministry of National Service. *a Sonnet*: TH's 'A Call to National Service', first pub. 12 Mar 1917 in *The Times* and other newspapers; a typescript of the poem still accompanies this letter. See Purdy, 191. *Chamberlain*: Arthur Neville Chamberlain (1869–1940; *D.N.B.*), prime minister 1937–40, currently Director-General of National Service.

To LEON LITWINSKI

(Ans) March 7. 1917

Dear Sir,

I feel much honoured by your request that I should be a member of the Committee for commemorating two such writers of distinction as Verhaeren & Sienkiewich.

But for reasons of increasing age & my living so far from London I have latterly been compelled to give up membership with several associations; & I am sorry therefore to say that I must refrain from joining any new committee in which I am unable actively to support the cause, even when it is so worthy as the present one.

With my thanks I am,

Yours truly

To Dr L. Litwinski.

Text MS. (pencil draft) DCM.
Litwinski: Dr. Leon Litwinski, writer on Polish affairs, honorary literary secretary of the Polish Information Committee, London. *your request*: of 6 Mar 17 (DCM); Litwinski explained that the names of the two writers had been linked because their native lands, Belgium and Poland, were both 'in hostile occupation'. *Verhaeren*: Émile Verhaeren (1855–1916), Belgian poet. *Sienkiewich*: Henryk Sienkiewicz (1846–1916), Polish novelist, author of *Quo Vadis?*, winner of the 1905 Nobel Prize for Literature; the name is correctly spelled in the version of this letter pub. in *LY*, 175.

To CLEMENT SHORTER

FROM THO. HARDY, | MAX GATE, | DORCHESTER. | March 8: 1917.

Best thanks for letter & parcel, not yet fully investigated. Will do so, & reply in a few days—
(Received them only this morning, though dated March 5.)

Text MS. (postcard) Univ. of Kentucky.

To EDWARD CLODD

MAX GATE, | DORCHESTER. | 11 March 1917

My dear Clodd:

We shall be pleased to welcome the young lieutenant whenever he appears, & have written to him to that effect.

Best thanks for inquiries. We have been fairly free from colds (except for a small one I caught). We go nowhere, however, except in the immediate neighbourhood, the war cloud & the railway difficulties keeping us at home.

I think I saw in some paper that you had another book in hand. If so, it shows that you have not lost literary energy.

I hope you found your grandson in good spirits, & that he will help keep the enemy off Aldburgh.

With kind regards to Mrs Clodd in which my wife joins I am

Sincerely yours
Thomas Hardy.

Text MS. (correspondence card) Leeds.
young lieutenant: unidentified, but evidently a friend of Clodd's currently stationed near Dorchester. *book in hand*: Clodd's *The Question*; see letter of 1 Feb 18. *your grandson . . . off Aldburgh*: Derrick Graham, the eldest son of Clodd's daughter Edith, was currently serving in the Royal Navy; TH mispells Aldeburgh.

To C. K. OGDEN

FROM THO. HARDY, | MAX GATE, | DORCHESTER. | 14 March 1917

Dear Mr Ogden:

I have signed the declaration after changing a word or two (without doing which I could not sign) that would I think be regarded as an attack on all the rest of the English press, & would have the effect of setting it all against you, which I am sure you do not wish to do, & would certainly be bad policy. The other signatories will no doubt see this point & acquiesce.

Yours truly
T.H.

Text MS. (correspondence card) R. Greenland.
Ogden: Charles Kay Ogden (1889–1957; *D.N.B.*), psychologist and originator of Basic English, founder and editor (1912–22) of the *Cambridge Magazine*. *the declaration*: of support for the *Cambridge Magazine*, which had been attacked (especially by Sir Frederick Pollock and other members of the Fight for Right movement) for its policy of publishing a regular survey of the foreign press—which was not necessarily supportive of the British and Allied cause. Drafted by Gilbert Murray—as Ogden told TH, 12 Mar 17 (DCM)—the statement was pub. in the *Morning Post*, 17 Mar 1917, and in the *Cambridge Magazine*, 24 Mar 1917, TH's signature appearing along with those of Murray, Quiller-Couch, Jane Harrison, Arnold Bennett, and several others. *changing a word or two*: the copy signed by TH (still accompanying this letter) shows an alteration of 'the one-sided character of the extracts published in other British papers' to 'any one-sided views that may be engendered by the extracts published in other English papers'; the published text incorporates this revision.

To E. A. FFOOKS

[Mid-March 1917]

Dear Sir:

I write to thank the Magistrates at the Epiphany Adjourned Sessions for the honour of being re-appointed a representative Governor of the Dorchester Grammar School.

I fear that by the time the three years have run out I shall be compelled to withdraw from the office of representing them in favour of a younger & more active man.

Yours truly
(Signed) T.H

E. A. Ffooks Esq.

Text MS. (pencil draft) DCM. *Date* Replies to letter of 14 Mar 17.
Ffooks: Edward Archdall Ffooks, Clerk of the Peace for the County of Dorset; see III.18. He wrote to TH 14 Mar 17 (DCM). *representative Governor*: he served on the school's Board of Governors as a representative of the magistrates of the county. *withdraw from the office*: TH in fact remained a Governor until the end of 1925; see *LY*, 134.

To SIR FREDERICK MACMILLAN

MAX GATE, | DORCHESTER. | 18: 3: 1917

Dear Sir Frederick:

I enclose the authorization signed—as a formality—for I suppose the date is passed in which I had any power over the rights of translation. I hope Señor Gili will be as good as his word.

Yours truly
Th: Hardy.

Text MS. (correspondence card) BL.
authorization: for the translation of *A Pair of Blue Eyes* into Spanish; Macmillan had explained (16 Mar 17, Macmillan letterbooks, BL) that such an authorization was required by Spanish law. *Gili*: Gustavo Gili appears to have been the publisher involved; the translator of *Unos ojos azules* (Barcelona, 1919) was Emilio Martínez-Amador.

To J. S. UDAL

MAX GATE, | DORCHESTER. | March 19: 1917

My dear Udal:

I am sending off the Programmes at last. They have been waiting about solely to get packed up & carried to Dorchester. I do not know where you can get the others to complete the set; & the parcel being now tied up I cannot remember which are the missing ones.

I will return Mrs Boswell Stone's "Memories" as soon as we have looked at them. Thanks for lending them.

I find that the verses you enclosed, & I send back, are by the poet Coleridge. They were published anonymously in the Morning Post in 1798. I thought first—you can imagine with what feelings—that they were the original MS., but though the writing is a little like Coleridge's I conjecture the copy to have been made by some contemporary who saw it in the paper. However, you had better make sure, as there are some differences in the second one & as published.

I am sorry that the arthritis was strengthened by the cold weather; but it was to be expected, & I trust it may not at any rate get worse. I will mention you to Mr Shorter, as his wife is, I think slowly improving.

Sincerely yours
Th: Hardy.

P.S. I see the watermark to be "1805"—so that it cannot be the *original* MS. T.H.

Text MS. Adams.
the Programmes: see letter of 2 Mar 17. *"Memories"*: Lucia Catherine Boswell Stone, *Memories and Traditions* (privately printed, 1895); she was the mother of Walter and Edward Stone (see letter of 25 Dec 16). *Morning Post in 1798*: several poems by Samuel Taylor Coleridge appeared in the *Morning Post* during the course of 1798. *Mr Shorter*: who had apparently not yet introduced himself to Udal; see letter of 25 Dec 16.

To ARTHUR MAQUARIE

MAX GATE, | DORCHESTER. | 25th. March 1917.

My dear Mr Maquarie:

The idea of advancing the Intellectual Entente among the Allied Countries by establishing an Imperial Oriental Press seems to be a sound one. Upon the practical methods for achieving this I am not able to speak with knowledge, but the steps mentioned in the suggestions you send recommend themselves, and I assume that experts have been or will be consulted on their feasibility as a means for regaining and developing the business of Oriental printing in England.

Yours truly,
Th: Hardy.

Text MS. (typewritten) Royal Society of Literature.
a sound one: Maquarie (22 Mar 17, DCM) had reported that the topic would be discussed at the next meeting of the Entente Committee of the R.S.L.; see letter of 8 Feb 17.

To CHARLES LACEY

MAX GATE, | DORCHESTER. | 11th. April 1917.

Dear Sir:

In turning out the contents of a cupboard where old papers had been kept for many years I came across the numbers of the Dorset Chronicle which are returned in the accompanying parcel. They must have been borrowed I think from a former editor for reference to something or other connected with the first Reform Bill, and should of course have been returned long before this, but were somehow overlooked. However, better late than never, and, as you will see, they have been well taken care of.

With many thanks to the proprietors for this long loan I am,

Yours truly,
Th: Hardy.

The Editor, | Dorset County Chronicle.

Text MS. (typewritten) J. Stevens Cox.
Lacey: Charles Lacey, proprietor of the *Dorset County Chronicle*; see II.237. *turning out*: TH had embarked upon the process of setting his affairs in order which led, among other things, to the destruction of the majority of the letters he had thus far preserved and to the writing, in secret, of *EL* and *LY*. *first Reform Bill*: of 1832. At the time of the composition of *The Mayor of Casterbridge*, 1883–5, TH began reading systematically through back issues of the *Dorset County Chronicle* from January 1826 onwards; the last record of such reading in his 'Facts' notebook (DCM) relates to the issue of 9 Dec 1830, but it appears from this letter that he had intended to continue such reading at least into 1831–2—and that he may have kept the relevant copies in his possession since some time in the 1880s.

To MAURICE MACMILLAN

MAX GATE, | DORCHESTER. | April 15: 1917

Dear Mr Macmillan:

Certainly let them print it—from the volume copy, not from the newspaper, as I think a word or two may have been changed.

I hope you have been well through the late cold weather, & am,

Yrs sincerely
Th: Hardy.

Text MS. (correspondence card) BL.
let them print it: Macmillan (14 Apr 17, Macmillan letterbooks, BL) reported that an

organization for the presentation of the Allies' cause in other countries had requested TH's 'Men Who March Away' for inclusion in an anthology of war poetry to be pub. in the United States. *volume copy*: i.e., the text as pub. in *Satires of Circumstance*.

To EDMUND GOSSE

MAX GATE, | DORCHESTER. | April 26: 1917

My dear Gosse:

We have just been reading your Life of Swinburne with great pleasure & interest, & have now finished it. He was unhappy in many things, but in his biographer at least he was as fortunate as could be, & his shade is no doubt grateful to you, (if shades can be grateful) for what you have done.

It must have cost you much time & labour, & came out none too soon, his being the kind of life whose details wd soon have passed out of knowledge, till the world would have known not much more about him than about Shakespeare. It is sad to think that I was living quite near him (& quite near Browning) in the 'sixties, yet never knew either till long after.

Ever sincerely
Thomas Hardy

P.S. When are you coming Wessex way? T.H.

Text MS. Adams.
Life of Swinburne: Gosse's *The Life of Algernon Charles Swinburne* (London, 1917). *quite near him*: it was, however, approximately 1½ miles from TH's 1863–7 lodgings at 16 Westbourne Park Villas to Swinburne's lodgings at 22A Dorset Street. *near Browning*: his home at 19 Warwick Crescent was within half a mile of 16 Westbourne Park Villas.

To SIR HENRY AND LADY HOARE

MAX GATE, | DORCHESTER. | May 5: 1917

Dear Sir Henry & Lady Hoare:

I am glad to receive your very kind letters in response to what really gave me very little trouble. I too hope that your son may come back safe & sound. What an experience he will have had altogether.

My wife has just come back from London, where she has gathered all sorts of opinions on the progress of the war; but I don't find that the people who profess to have exclusive information on particular points know much more than others. Please excuse this brief note, & believe me

Sincerely yours
Th: Hardy.

Text MS. Wiltshire Record Office.
very little trouble: TH had apparently written a letter or letters on some matter relating to the Hoares' only son—who did not, however, survive the war; see letter of 26 Dec 17.

To MARGARET SOUNDY

MAX GATE, | DORCHESTER. | May 9: 1917

My dear Margaret:

I am glad to hear that the present suited. It was rather belated! I will not forget to visit Enfield when I next go to London.

Florence has been feeling rather tired since her return. London always takes so much out of her when she fags about shopping, &c. I hope your husband will get home safely, & that he will stay a long time.

Yours affectionately
Th: Hardy.

Text MS. Purdy.
Soundy: Margaret Alicia Soundy, *née* Dugdale (1893–1979), the youngest of FEH's sisters. *the present*: on the occasion of her wedding (see letter of 23 Feb 17); it was a leather-bound copy of *Far from the Madding Crowd* with an affectionate inscription from TH (Purdy). *her return*: not from the wedding but from a more recent visit to London, where she was receiving a series of bacteriological inoculations.

To LEWIS CHASE

MAX GATE, | DORCHESTER. | 15th. May 1917.

Dear Mr Chase:

(I am compelled to write by machinery nowadays, which declension I hope you will pardon).

As to your inquiry which are my favourites among my poems; I am quite unable to answer this, and if I could, my opinion would not be worth much, as I am in the position of a scene-painter standing close to the canvas. I may say, however, that a critic in whom I have great confidence thinks that "When I set out for Lyonnesse", "A Trampwoman's Tragedy", "The Ghost of the Past", "To meet or otherwise", & "The Phantom Horsewoman" as good as any of the short ones. All of these, except the "Trampwoman", are to be found in the Volume of "Selections"—Golden Treasury Series, (Macmillan)—a handy little book for reference. The first one named is the favourite I am told in America, and was first hailed by a still small voice in the far West.

The above mentioned do not, of course, show the variety of scope that you ask for. To get what there is of that you would have to include extracts showing the theory on which "The Dynasts" is based, and philosophic poems like "New Years Eve", "The Sleep Walker", etc.

As to the other queries—the circumstances under which certain poems were composed and personal details connected with them, I fear I am unable to give any information.

Believe me,

Yours very truly,
Th: Hardy.

Text MS. (typewritten, with envelope in FEH's hand) LC.
great confidence: TH probably meant FEH, or even himself. *& "The Phantom Horsewoman"*: inserted in TH's hand. *in America*: see letter of 15 Jan 17. *still small voice*: an allusion to I Kings 19: 12. *in the far West*: TH's (presumably Californian) reviewer or correspondent has not been identified. *include extracts*: Chase was apparently putting together a list of poems by contemporary poets to be used in teaching a course at the University of Wisconsin.

To SIEGFRIED SASSOON

MAX GATE, | DORCHESTER. | March [May] 18: 1917

Dear Mr Sassoon:

I write to thank you much for the gift of "The Old Huntsman" which came to me duly from the publishers. Also for the honour of the dedication.

I was going to wait till I could send an elaborate letter of commentary, after a thorough reading of the poems, but I then felt that you would prefer, as I do myself, just this simple line to tell you how much I like to have them. I should say that I am not reading them rapidly. I never do read rapidly anything I care about, so I have not as yet got further than about the middle.

I would not, even if I could, enter into a cold-blooded criticism. It occurs to me to tell you however that I appreciate thoroughly, "When I'm among a blaze of lights", & "Blighters", & much like the grim humour of "The Tombstone Maker", & "They", the pathos of "The Hero", & the reticent poignancy of "The Working Party". How we realize that young man!

I wonder how you are getting on in Hospital. Improving surely, I hope, even if slowly. I don't know how I should stand the suspense of this evil time if it were not for the sustaining power of poetry. May the war be over soon.

Believe me, with renewed thanks, & best wishes for your good luck,

Sincerely yours
Thomas Hardy.

Text MS. Eton College. *Date* Correction on MS. by Sassoon confirmed by internal evidence.
the dedication: see letter of 4 Feb 17. *"The Working Party"*: correctly 'A Working Party'; Sassoon (20 May 17, DCM) expressed his pleasure at TH's choice of poems and looked forward to meeting him in person. *in Hospital*: Sassoon had been wounded in April 1917 but TH did not know his precise whereabouts (see letter of 18 May 17 to Thornycroft).

To JAMES SPARKS

MAX GATE, | DORCHESTER. | May 18: 1917

Dear Mr Sparks:

Many thanks for the sketch of the headstone of Nathaniel Gifford. He died without issue, a widower, &, I believe, intestate, with considerable property; & nobody knows what became of it. Had the late Mrs Hardy been living she would have been deeply interested.

I congratulate you on your pictures in this year's Academy, & am

Very truly yours
Th: Hardy.

Text MS. Mrs. Celia Barclay.
Sparks: James Sparks, art teacher, older son of TH's first cousin Nathaniel Sparks; see II.188. *Gifford*: ELH's great-uncle, buried at Littleham, near Exmouth; the sketch forms part of Sparks's letter to TH of 12 May 17 (DCM). *this year's Academy*: i.e., the Summer Exhibition of the Royal Academy; two of Sparks's pictures, both of Exeter scenes, were hung.

To HAMO THORNYCROFT

MAX GATE, | DORCHESTER. | May 18: 1917

My dear Thornycroft:

I am sending this letter to young Sassoon through you, if you will be so kind as to forward it. I thought it a safer route than through a publishers office, & I don't know where he is. As it is about his poems, I have left it open for you to read. Please fasten it up.

My wife saw you at the Academy, she says, but not for so long as she would have liked to do had time served. We hope you & the household are well, & shall be glad to see you again.

Always yrs
T.H.

Text MS. DCM.
this letter: i.e., the letter of 18 May 17 to Sassoon. *at the Academy*: i.e., at the Private View of the Royal Academy's Summer Exhibition, 5 May 1917.

To FLORENCE HENNIKER

Max Gate | May 20: 1917

My dear Friend:

I am so sorry to learn that you have not been at all well, & so is Florence, as you will know. Somehow you have seemed to be so much in the active world, owing to your living in London, & I to be so entirely out of it, that it never occurred to me you might be ill. I wonder if you ought not to get away from Town? We have at last discovered the ideal place for making recoveries in. It is *Dartmoor*, the air of which is really wonderful. You may remember that Louis Stevenson was on his way there, as a last hope, when he was taken ill on the road, & could not get there. Mr Eden Phillpotts, who lives near it, would find you a place if you think anything of it. Mr Galsworthy lives close to it, but he is now away in France.

The war has taken all enterprize out of me (I should add that it is partly because of the practical difficulties of getting about), & I have almost registered a vow that I will not see London till the butchery is over. Another of my cousins has been killed, & though his mother is but a distant cousin I sympathize deeply with her, as she is herself dying.

People are in strangely irritable moods I fancy. I said very harmlessly in a poem (sonnet) entitled "The Pity of It" that the Germans were a "kin folk, kin tongued" (which is indisputable) & letters attacking me appeared, denying it! The fact of their being our enemies does not alter their race.

Did I tell you that some time ago we had a visit from a cousin of Emma's, who is also a cousin of our neighbours the Hanburys here who bought the Kingston estate lately a mile from here—& is a niece of the late Ld St. Helier? She is much like Emma, & I felt so sorry that the Hanburys did not come here till after Emma's death, as it wd have been pleasant for her.

Gosse's Swinburne book has been a great success I believe, which I am glad of, as it must have cost him much labour.

The young poets you allude to—I imagine you mean the "Georgians" (an absurd name, as if the Georgians were not Shelley Scott, Byron, &c.)—are I think or some of them, on a wrong track. They seem to forget that poetry must have symmetry in its form, & meaning in its content.

I have read young Sassoon's book dedicated to me. I think the poems show much promise.

We have just heard that F's sister's husband, Commander (I think that's his title) in the Royal Flying Corps, came home from the Front at 1.30 a.m. two nights ago to her great surprise. He has been in a position of much danger over the German lines & rear, & has been shot at & nearly brought down several times, & most of his comrades have been killed.

Florence says I am to tell you that she is looking eagerly forward to the issue of your book. She is hoping to be in London after Whitsuntide, & to call & see you. She still keeps up her reviewing, but will soon drop it; not having quite sufficient spare time with the household to look after, & the garden also, which she has taken upon herself, much to my relief. She sends her love, & I am

Always yrs affectionately
Th: H.

Text MS. DCM.
could not get there: after visiting Max Gate in August 1885; see *EL*, 229. *lives near it*: at Torquay; see letter of 26 Feb 14. *close to it*: at Manaton; see letter of 31 Mar 16 to Galsworthy. *distant cousin*: probably Floretta Cheesewright (*née* Meech), who was seriously ill following the death from war wounds of her son John Francis Cheesewright in March 1917; Mrs. Cheesewright was herself accustomed to claim cousinship with TH, although she was in fact only indirectly related to him—as the first cousin of his second cousin Angelina George, the mother of Frank George (see letter of 1 Sept 15 to Cockerell). *denying it!*: 'The Pity of It', first pub. April 1915, was reprinted in the 1916–17 *Year-book* of the Society of Dorset Men in London and quoted thence, almost in its entirety, in the *Daily News* of 30 Jan 1917; two hostile letters from Sir James Yokall, M.P., appeared in the same newspaper, 31 Jan and 2 Feb 1917. *cousin of Emma's*: Evelyn Gifford; see letter of 29 Nov 16. *Swinburne book*: see letter of 26 Apr 17. *Sassoon's book*: *The Old Huntsman*; see letter of 4 Feb 17. *F's sister's husband*: Reginald Soundy; see letter of 23 Feb 17. *your book*: Mrs. Henniker mentioned her 'new story' in confident terms in her letter of 5 Mar 17 (transcript, DCM), but it seems never to have achieved publication. *her reviewing*: of new novels, for the *Sphere*.

To SYDNEY COCKERELL

MAX GATE, | DORCHESTER. | June 3: 1917

My dear Cockerell:

You send me such a kind letter that I almost think it worth while to have birthdays, though I have felt that the present state of what we are so unctuous as to call civilization makes them not a particularly desirable possession just now.

I don't like to ask you to send that book with Wordsworth's signature, as it might be valued by one of your children some day, but of course I should like to have it; so you must decide.

The only one of my family, so far as I remember, who was active at 77 was my mother. I find from a note that she walked here from Bockhampton in that year of her life, & in slippery winter weather. On our asking her with alarm why she had ventured out she said coolly: "To enjoy the beauties of Nature of course: why should n't I?"

We were glad to hear that Mrs Cockerell has improved lately. I don't see why she should not go on doing so, & certainly hope so.

I have lately had sent me by Dr Christopher Childs, a third cousin of mine, a photograph of an oil painting by Eastlake of my great-great uncle on my mother's side, & my wife says there is a strong likeness to me in it. The original was Childs's great-grandfather, my great grandmother's brother.

Well: this is enough of me & my family for one day!—even a birthday.

By the way, to judge from the photogh, Eastlake cd paint a good portrait when he was young (when this one was done). Do people think anything of his portraits now?

Always sincerely
Thomas Hardy.

Text MS. Adams.
birthdays: TH was 77 on 2 June 1917. *Wordsworth's signature*: evidently the copy of Francis North, 1st Lord Guildford, *A Narrative of Some Passages in or Relating to the Long Parliament* (London, 1670), with Wordsworth's signature on the title-page, included in the sale of TH's library following FEH's death. *improved lately*: see letter of 21 Jan 17. *Childs*: a Weymouth physician; see *EL*, 302. The painting apparently belonged to John F. Childs, of Looe, Cornwall, who explained to TH (25 May 17, DCM) that he needed to have it valued for insurance purposes. *Eastlake*: Sir Charles Lock Eastlake (1793–1865), painter, President of the Royal Academy; *D.N.B.* *my great-great uncle*: Christopher Childs, mining engineer (see *EL*, 8, 303), brother of the Maria Childs who married John Swetman of Melbury in 1764 and became TH's great-grandmother.

To LADY HOARE

MAX GATE, | DORCHESTER. | June 3: 1917

Dear Lady Hoare:

How can I thank you for this pretty piece of old French silver that you sent for my birthday. I have been saying to another friend that these things make one almost think birthdays worth having, though I have doubted their worth in the present state of what we are pleased to call civilization. My kind regards to the two Henrys.

Your sincere friend
Thomas Hardy.

Text MS. (with envelope) Wiltshire Record Office.
the two Henrys: Lady Hoare's husband, Sir Henry Hoare, and their son Harry.

To MARGARET SOUNDY

MAX GATE, | DORCHESTER. | 3: 6: 1917

My dear Margaret:

You have quite set me up in ties, & these happen to be the shade that I mostly wear. Many thanks for such a nice birthday present. I hope your husband's indisposition will not last long, & that it was a temporary result of his many ascents.

Believe me

Yours affectionately
Th: Hardy.

Text MS. (correspondence card, with envelope) Purdy.
birthday present: TH was 77 on 2 June 1917. *husband's indisposition*: FEH, writing to Rebekah Owen 24 June 17 (Colby), reports that Reginald Soundy's 'heart has been bad, & so he does no flying for a time'.

To SIR HAMO THORNYCROFT

MAX GATE, | DORCHESTER. | 5: 6: 1917

My dear Thornycroft:

Please add our congratulations to the many you will have received on your new prefix which is called an honour, though it is really the other way. I have sometimes wondered why it did not happen to you before, but it was probably owing to your backwardness in the matter. Remembrances to Lady Thornycroft.

Always sincerely yrs
Th: Hardy.

Text MS. (correspondence card) DCM.
an honour: Thornycroft's knighthood had just been announced in the Birthday Honours List.

To RICHARD BAGOT

MAX GATE, | DORCHESTER. | June 7: 1917

Dear Mr Bagot:

The proposal to set up a Shakespeare memorial in Rome, to which you draw my attention in your letter of this morning, is a worthy one, & I support it willingly, though whether I am justified in letting my name appear in the list of the Central Committee I doubt, being no longer young enough to run up to London to attend meetings, &c., as I used to do; so I should be a mere dead-head I fear.

You will not mind my saying frankly that I advise, in the interests of the movement, the omission of the word "Christian" from the Memorandum you enclose. Many thoughtful people might be deterred from joining by seeing it there, & I for one could not subscribe to a manifesto which did not keep silence on that point.

If therefore you think one with the above limitations could consistently do so I accept the honour of being on the Committee.

Yours very truly
Thomas Hardy.

Text MS. (with envelope) Purdy.
Bagot: Richard Bagot (1860–1921), novelist and writer on Italy. *of this morning*: Bagot, 6 June 17 (DCM), sent TH a 'Memorandum' of his proposal to erect a monument to Shakespeare in Rome once the war was over and invited him to join the central committee which would oversee the project. *keep silence on that point*: Bagot (9 June 17, DCM) agreed to omit the phrase 'Christian civilization', proposing to replace 'Christian' either by 'Western' or by 'common'. *on the Committee*: TH's name was included in the list of committee members pub. in *The Times*, 13 July 1917.

To SYDNEY COCKERELL

FROM THO. HARDY, | MAX GATE, | DORCHESTER. | June 7: 1917.

Safely received. Best thanks. Happy returns of the day to Xtopher.

Text MS. (postcard) Texas.
Safely received: i.e., the book with Wordsworth's signature; see letter to Cockerell of 3 June 17. *Xtopher*: Cockerell's son Christopher, inventor of the hovercraft, born 4 June 1910; he was knighted in 1969.

To CLEMENT SHORTER

MAX GATE, | DORCHESTER. | 16 June: 1917

My dear Shorter:

She was away only 3 days, & came back last night: nevertheless I write these few lines to show my independence.

I made a vow when I last got back from London that I would not go again till after the war, the sight of the old place in such circumstances having been so sad.

Abstractedly I am in accord with Russian views; but temporarily I am not. She makes things awkward for us. A curious luck attends the Germans, or Prussians, as I prefer to call them. This is the anniversary of Quatre Bras, but who thinks of it now!

I am tired of birthdays (death-days are more interesting); & I am glad you did not write.

I like Mrs Shorters poem. It is what you newspaper men would call "Strong". Her pen is more facile than it used to be. I hope she is drawing near health. Forgive this hurry-skurry note. (Mrs Hardy will answer the rest of your letter). Believe me

Yours very truly
Th: Hardy.

Text MS. Univ. of British Columbia; envelope Berg.
only 3 days: FEH had been to London, chiefly to see medical specialists. *awkward for us*: a Russian Provisional Government, under Kerensky, had been formed, and was under pressure to conclude a separate peace with Germany. *Quatre Bras*: an important engagement between Wellington's and Napoleon's forces just prior to the battle of Waterloo itself (see letter of 18 June 17). *Mrs Shorters poem*: unidentified. *rest of your letter*: FEH's letter (untraced) must have been written and posted separately.

To COULSON KERNAHAN

MAX GATE, | DORCHESTER. | 17th. June 1916 [1917].

Dear Mr Coulson Kernahan:

It is very good of you to send your pleasant book to me as a gift. I do not remember the occasion you allude to, but I remember quite well Mrs Chandler Moulton, and the courage with which she used to undertake hot afternoon parties, at which you, and sometimes I, were guests.

I have not entered far into your "Good Company" at present, but mean to go on. These beguiling works are quite a modern product, and have given birth to a strange class of readers, whom one discovers more and more—those who take a deep interest in the lives of men of whose works they have never read a line. With thanks believe me,

Yours truly,
Thomas Hardy.

Text MS. (typewritten) NYU. *Date* '1916' must be a typing error for '1917'; see notes below.
Kernahan: Coulson Kernahan (1858–1943), journalist and author. *your pleasant book*: Kernahan's *In Good Company: Some Personal Recollections of Swinburne, Lord Roberts, Watts-Dunton, Oscar Wilde, Edward Whymper, S.J. Stone, Stephen Phillips* (London, 1917); it is dedicated to Mrs. Henniker. The announced publication date for the book was March 1917 and it was reviewed in *The Times* 12 Apr 1917. *Moulton*: Louise Chandler Moulton, American author and London hostess; see I.194. Kernahan (139) mentions a party at Mrs. Moulton's in the 1890s at which one of the guests, an opera singer, suddenly burst into song.

To THOMAS HUMPHRY WARD

MAX GATE, | DORCHESTER. | 18 June 1917 | [Waterloo Day]

Dear Humphry Ward:

Here are the proofs back. I think I have got the dialect spelling right at last.

Kindest regards to Mrs Ward. I wish I had some of her energy. However, in spite of war & hot weather I manage to keep going.

Sincerely yours
Thomas Hardy.

Text MS. Texas.
[*Waterloo Day*]: TH's square brackets; the battle was fought 18 June 1815. *dialect spelling*: of William Barnes's poems; see letters of 11 Oct and 24 Nov 16. *Mrs Ward*: see letter of 11 Oct 16.

To JOHN BUCHAN

MAX GATE, | DORCHESTER. | June 20: 1917

Dear Colonel Buchan:

I appreciate your thought of me: & there are many things that would have led me to embrace eagerly the opportunity of visiting the fighting lines in France in such attractive company. But I remember that I am not so young as I was, & am compelled to give up almost all enterprises nowadays that comprise travelling more than a few miles, though I am as well as anybody of my age.

I am endeavouring to console myself by thinking that in the past I have studied a good many battlefields and battles of the flint-lock & touch-hole period, & that it is really not worth while for me to open up an investigation of modern scientific warfare, but to leave it for those who are young in these days, or unborn.

I must thank you for your consideration in sending the passport form, which shall be returned if required: otherwise I will keep it to show what I was on the brink of doing at 77.

Most sincerely yours
Thomas Hardy.

Text MS. NLS.
Buchan: John Buchan (1875–1940; *D.N.B.*), author, later—as Lord Tweedsmuir—Governor-General of Canada. *attractive company*: Buchan wrote from the Foreign Office 18 June 17 (DCM) to invite TH to join Sir James Barrie and Sir Owen Seaman (1861-1936; *D.N.B.*), editor of *Punch*, on an official visit to General Headquarters in France; see letter of 23 June 17.

To SIR JAMES BARRIE

MAX GATE, | DORCHESTER. | 23 June 1917

My dear Barrie:

It was so kind of you to concoct the scheme for my accompanying you to the Front—or Back—in France. I thought it over carefully, as it was an attractive idea. But I have had to come to the conclusion that old men cannot be young men, & that I must content myself with the past battles of our country if I want to feel military. If I had been ten years younger I would have gone.

I hope you will have a pleasant, or rather impressive, time, & the good company you will be in will be helpful all round. I am living in hope of seeing you on the date my wife has fixed, & of renewing acquaintance with my old friend Adelphi Terrace.

Always sincerely yrs
Thomas Hardy.

Text MS. Colby.
Barrie: James Matthew Barrie, dramatist and novelist; see I.200. He was created a baronet in 1913. *in France*: see letter of 20 June 17 and *LY*, 177. *impressive, time*: see Denis Mackail, *The Story of J.M.B.* (London, 1941), 508. *my wife has fixed*: in late July 1917; see Barrie's letter to her of 20 June 17 in *Letters of J.M. Barrie*, ed. Viola Meynell (London, 1942), 144. *Adelphi Terrace*: where TH had worked in the 1860s (see I.4) and Barrie was now living (see *LY*, 177–8).

To JOHN GALSWORTHY

MAX GATE, | DORCHESTER. | June 26: 1917

My dear Galsworthy:

Certainly I accept the dedication, & consider it handsome of you to think of such a thing. I do not want to see & criticize the proofs, as I can trust you on points of literary taste, & they are all that I could remark upon if on any, which I doubt—(though I could on other people's; literature is getting too slovenly for words, what with the vers-librists et hoc genus omne.)

We think of running up to London at the end of July, or earlier, for a day or two. I should not go, but my wife has to see her doctor on some slight ailment. I don't altogether regret for your sake that you will have left: London does not seem your true place, & I shall much prefer to see you on Dartmoor some day.

Our kindest wishes to Mrs Galsworthy.

Ever sincerely,
Thomas Hardy.

Text MS. Univ. of Birmingham.
the dedication: Galsworthy's novel *Beyond* (London, 1917) is dedicated 'To/Thomas Hardy'; Galsworthy wrote 24 June 17 (DCM).

To ARTHUR SYMONS

July 15: 1917—

Dear Symons:

I am sorry to tell you that some jobs other than literary that I have in hand prevent my writing anything about Jane Austen, even if I could add to the good things that have been said about her by so many. However you can do well enough without me.

I am pleased to hear that your portrait is being painted, & hope Augustus John will make a good thing of it—

Sincerely yours,
Ths Hardy.

Text MS. (with envelope) Adams.
about Jane Austen: the precise occasion of Symons's request has not been determined, although 1917 marked the 100th anniversary of Jane Austen's death. *Augustus John*: Augustus Edwin John (1878–1961), painter; *D.N.B.* His portrait of Symons is reproduced in John Rothenstein, *Augustus John* (Oxford, 1944), plate 43.

To LADY ST. HELIER

Max Gate, | Dorchester. | July 20: 1917.

My dear friend:

I wonder if you are in London? We have arranged to stay with J.M. Barrie next Wednesday the 25th. while passing through London (sleeping at his flat, Adelphi House Tuesday night and *Wednesday* night) and propose to ring you up on the telephone Wednesday morning to ask when we can call, so as to fit in the time with other engagements—supposing you have a few minutes to spare, and are still in London.

Ever affectionately
Thomas Hardy.

Text Typed transcript DCM.

To GEORGE MACMILLAN

MAX GATE, | DORCHESTER. | July 31: 1917

Dear Mr Macmillan:

I am sorry that my carelessness has caused you this trouble. As I was going on to a lunch-party I posted the roll, not noticing that it was not directed to Max Gate. Moral: always look at the address before posting.

The amusing feature in it is that I am not the author of the song. It is Edmund Gosse's, & is given in "The Woodlanders" as a quotation from "a contemporary poet." The lady should have noticed this.

Very truly yours
Thomas Hardy.

Text MS. BL.
posted the roll: Macmillan (30 July 17, Macmillan letterbooks, BL) reported that he was sending on to TH a roll of music, given to TH while he was in London, which had mysteriously found its way back to the composer, Mrs. Eugenie Parton, via the Dead Letter Office. *the song*: Gosse's 'Two Points of View', quoted in *The Woodlanders* (Wessex edn.), 213; see I.153. *noticed this*: Macmillan replied (2 Aug 17, Macmillan letterbooks, BL) that Mrs. Parton had in fact protected herself by saying merely that the song occurred in *The Woodlanders*.

To SIR WILLIAM WATSON

MAX GATE, | DORCHESTER. | 16 August 1917

Dear Sir William Watson:

This morning I received your letter & its enclosure, & immediately signed & sent on the latter as directed, entirely from a lively faith in the bona fides of the signatures already appended (for to tell the truth I had never heard of the unfortunate lady before) & your assurance that the case was so exceptional.

Many thanks for kind inquiries. We have been suffering from the wet weather, like the potatoes & corn, but are physically well, as I hope you & yours are also.

Yours sincerely
Thomas Hardy.

Text MS. NYU.
Watson: knighted in June 1917. *letter & its enclosure*: Watson wrote 14 Aug 17 (DCM), enclosing for TH's signature a petition to the Prime Minister in support of a Civil List pension for Miss S. Gertrude Ford. An invalid for many years, Miss Ford had apparently earned a minimal living by the sale of her verse and prose; see the *Bookman*, August 1913, 189-91. *as directed*: i.e., to J.A. Spender (see III.178), editor of the *Westminster Gazette*; no pension seems to have been awarded Miss Ford, however.

To MACMILLAN & CO

FROM THO. HARDY, | MAX GATE, | DORCHESTER. | 21 Aug. 1917

Parcel sent to-day, as promised.

Text MS. (postcard) BL.
Parcel: containing the MS. of *Moments of Vision*; see letter of 24 Aug 17.

To SIR FREDERICK MACMILLAN

MAX GATE, | DORCHESTER. | August 24: 1917.

Dear Sir Frederick Macmillan:

I quite think that the Poems may as well be brought out as soon as convenient—the end of October or early in November as you say. I don't think there will be much correcting.

An editor was good enough to inform me some time ago that, in the case of poetry, a quite small first impression was a good plan, so as to set collectors advertising for it as soon as a second impression is announced, and thus drawing attention to the book. I mention this for what it may be worth.

Yours very truly,
Thomas Hardy.

Sir F. Macmillan. D.L.

Text MS. (typewritten) BL.
as you say: in his letter of 23 Aug 17 (Macmillan letterbooks, BL), acknowledging receipt of the MS.; *Moments of Vision* was in fact pub. by Macmillan 30 Nov 1917. *much correcting*: i.e., at proof stage.

To SIEGFRIED SASSOON

MAX GATE, | DORCHESTER. | Aug. 27: 1917

Dear Mr Sassoon:

We were beforehand with you in respect of "To any Dead Officer", for we cut it out of the Cambridge Magazine—not knowing that it would be reprinted. Many thanks for sending it all the same, as I have now two copies, one for lending to people who never return things. I am not clear as to where you are, so send this line through my friend Thornycroft.

Sincerely yours
Th: Hardy.

P.S. I need not say how much I like the poem. T.H.

Text MS. Eton College.
Cambridge Magazine: where it first appeared, 14 July 1917. *reprinted*: by Heffer of Cambridge, in their series of 'Reprints from *The Cambridge Magazine*'. *Thornycroft*: see letter of 18 May 17 to Thornycroft.

To EDWARD BELL

MAX GATE, | DORCHESTER. | 31st. August 1917.

Dear Sir:

I am honoured by your selecting me among others to whom you are transmitting your managing editor's request for articles on literary subjects.

But I am sorry to say that I am at present, and have been for several years, so entirely outside the literary circles wherein such subjects are discussed that I am not able to estimate current trends in literature, which the war renders difficult to judge of even by persons better situated than myself. Poetry is said—I know not with what authority—to be resuming its old sway again, and I hope it may be true, my own attention having been given to that branch of literature for many years past.

I am, dear Sir,

Yours very truly,
Th: Hardy.

E.P. Bell, Esq.

Text MS. (typewritten) Newberry Library.
Bell: Edward Price Bell (1869–1943), American journalist and author, London correspondent of the *Chicago Daily News* 1900–22.

To JOHN GALSWORTHY

MAX GATE, | DORCHESTER. | Sept 5: 1917

My dear Galsworthy:

Your new book with its kind inscription crept unobtrusively into this house two afternoons ago, & we are now reading it a bit at a time every evening. We have not got far enough to form any opinion on its development as yet. So far as I remember, to begin with a wedding at a registry office is a new stroke. I see you are not afraid of the good old epic plan of retrospective survey after the opening.

We are hoping to go into Devon this autumn, but whether we shall get as far as to you is doubtful. I am allowed 10 gallons of petrol a month by the Government (if I like to pay for it) but I have no car! So I fall back on the old bicycle.

With kind regards I am

Sincerely yours
Thomas Hardy.

Text MS. Univ. of Birmingham.
new book: Galsworthy's *Beyond*; see letter of 26 June 17. *as far as to you*: at Manaton, Devon.

To JOHN SYMONS JEUNE

MAX GATE, | DORCHESTER. | Sept 5: 1917

My dear Mr Jeune:

This is rather a strange coincidence: at or about the very time at which you were marking "Kingston Maurward" in your letter I was marking it on the proof-sheet of a poem expressing emotions that Kingston Maurward is supposed to give rise to. You will see the verses some day, so no more about them, except that I fear they are rather commonplace.

The dust of the old Maurwards under Stinsford Church must grunt with satisfaction—if dust can grunt—at having their name restored. They were, of course, long before the Greys, & I still hold that to establish the name permanently was a wise thing to do, in a practical sense, as well as an antiquarian.

We are sure to be home on either Saturday or Sunday afternoon next, & will expect you as convenient. I thought Mrs Hanbury was looking much better last week than she has lately done.

Yours most sincerely
Thomas Hardy.

We are looking forward to your coming. Th. H.

Text MS. (with envelope) Eton College.
a poem: 'In Her Precincts', first pub. in *Moments of Vision*; see Purdy, 198. *old Maurwards*: the ancient lords of the manor of Kingston Maurward. *the Greys*: the Grey family built the Elizabethan manor-house at Kingston Maurward and retained the estate until it passed, through marriage, into the Pitt family, builders of the 18th-century house referred to in this letter. *establish the name*: TH is endorsing the use of the name Kingston Maurward House instead of simply Kingston House; Jeune was coming to stay there with his daughter, Dorothy Hanbury.

To LLEWELYN ROBERTS

MAX GATE, | DORCHESTER. | 8th. September 1917.

Dear Sir:

The enclosed letter has reached me, and I send it on to you in some doubt, as I have no means of ascertaining if the case is genuine—or even if genuine, one that calls for any attention from any literary fund.

I should say that the Society of Authors is not well enough off to help outsiders, and can only do a very little for its own broken-down members.

Yours truly,
Thomas Hardy.

Text MS. (typewritten) Royal Literary Fund.
Roberts: A. Llewelyn Roberts, Secretary of the Royal Literary Fund. *the case*: TH had been applied to by James Macdougall Hay (1880?–1919), Scottish minister and novelist, who was subsequently granted £100.

To J.H. MORGAN

Max Gate. | Sept 19.'17

Dear Capt. Morgan:

I have read your humorous sketch of Wessex life, with enjoyment, & must thank you for sending it. We shall be pleased if you give us a call when you are next down here.

Sincerely yours
Th: Hardy.

Text MS. Berg.
sketch of Wessex life: Morgan's 'The Husbandmen', pub. under the pseudonym 'Centurion', *Land & Water*, 13 Sept 1917; it describes soldiers helping farmers with the harvest.

To JOHN GALSWORTHY

Max Gate. | Sept. 21, 1917.

My dear Galsworthy,

I must write just one line to tell you that we have, to our great regret, got to the end of the book, and had great pleasure from it—an unnecessary piece of information, probably, as you will have guessed we should.

I think it carries on the reader with more momentum than any other of your novels I have read, and I confess I was quite baffled as to what was going to happen, and I honourably refrained from peeping. I have a shrewd suspicion that my wife did peep, though she does not own it. If she did not, she is the first woman who has resisted such temptation in such circumstances.

I was surprised (not disagreeably) to find that it was a story of modern artificial life that was covered by the rather misty title of a book whose author hailed from Dartmoor! and I had not known that you could handle that sort of life with such familiarity. As to your bringing on the catastrophe by cutting the knot and killing off the lover by an inconsequent accident—well, I will say I have two minds upon it.

I daresay it has struck you that you could go on and write another novel, and yet another, on Gyp's life and adventures. Perhaps you mean to.

I hope to have a little book to send you sometime this year as a return gift.

Sincerely yours,
Thomas Hardy.

Text H. V. Marrot, *The Life and Letters of John Galsworthy* (London, 1935), 458–9. *the book*: Galsworthy's *Beyond*; see letter to Galsworthy of 5 Sept 17. *Gyp's*: Ghita ('Gyp') Winton, the heroine of *Beyond*. *little book*: *Moments of Vision*.

To J. J. FOSTER

MAX GATE, | DORCHESTER. | 12th. October 1917.

Dear Mr Foster:

In reference to your inquiry for the name of the best Dorset publisher I must confess that I am unable to say. You know, of course, Ling and Longman here, and also the Dorset County Chronicle, at which office books of the pamphlet kind are published. The Dorchester Dramatic Society employs Ling for printing the so-called "Hardy plays"—(which are really not mine, but Mr Evans's adaptations of my novels) and Ling seems to do them very well, with photographic illustrations.

Mate, of Poole, is also a publisher. A good plan would be if you could see personally any of these, as you might thus be able to ascertain more about their capabilities than by letter.

As to the question of my writing a full-dress introduction of 2,500 words to the volume, neither my knowledge nor my time would allow me to do so, I regret to say. But I enclose for your acceptance I need hardly say gratuitously, a brief statement, which I have called an "Introductory Note", that I have written. I do not myself think a book gains much by these forewords from another writer, but if it should, the few lines I send will be as effective as a long Preface. If there is anything incorrect or inexpedient in my wording please alter it, or send it back.

I think I have seen some of your books in the Dorchester Museum, and had a good opinion of them.

By the way, if you go outside Dorset into other parts of Wessex for a publisher I believe the Wessex Press, Taunton, is of a good class.

With best wishes for the result of your labours I am,

Yours very truly,
Th: Hardy.

P.S. Mrs Hardy says that you may possibly mean by "A Dorset publisher" a London publisher of Dorset books. If so, I do not know of any one in especial. But the Managing Director of Cassells is a Dorset man out and out, (he comes from Blackmore Vale), so that would be a reason for going to that firm. I could give you an introduction to him. Th: H.

Text MS. (typewritten) Eton College.
Ling: Henry Ling, printer and bookseller, 23 High East Street, Dorchester. *Longman*: Frederick George Longman, printer, bookseller, and stationer, 4 Cornhill, Dorchester. "*Hardy plays*": TH presumably means the theatre programmes for these plays. *Mr Evans's*: see letter of 9 Jan 14. *Mate*: W. Mate & Sons, publishers, 35 High Street, Poole, Dorset. *the volume*: Foster's *Wessex Worthies* (London, 1920). "*Introductory Note*": included in the vol. when pub., with TH's signature in facsimile. *Wessex Press*: Barnacot & Pearce, Wessex Press, 44 Fore Street, Taunton, Somerset. *Dorset man*: Newman Flower; see letter of 2 Apr 14. *introduction to him*: see letters of 14 Oct 17.

To LLEWELYN ROBERTS

MAX GATE, | DORCHESTER. | 12th. October 1917.

Dear Sir:

I am much obliged for your Society's attention and aid to Mr J.M. Hay. No doubt you found his case on investigation to be a genuine one, and though he is a stranger to me I hope the result may benefit him.

Yours very truly,
Th: Hardy.

A. Llewelyn Roberts Esq.

Text MS. (typewritten) Royal Literary Fund.
Hay: see letter of 8 Sept 17.

To SIR WILLIAM WATSON

MAX GATE, | DORCHESTER. | 12 Oct 1917

Dear Sir William Watson:

Real thanks for the copy of the poem, which I need not say I read with interest. Your happy power of lighting upon the indispensable word is very noticeable in these lines, though I fear that & the rest of their appeal will be wasted on poor wrongheaded Ireland.

Sincerely yours
Th: Hardy.

Text MS. (correspondence card, with envelope) Texas.
the poem: Watson's 'The Unreconciled', dated September 1917, first collected in his *The Superhuman Antagonists and Other Poems* (London, 1919).

To NEWMAN FLOWER

MAX GATE, | DORCHESTER. | October 14th. 1917.

Dear Mr Flower:

Since you called here I have been in correspondence with Mr. J.J. Foster, the antiquary, and probably the highest authority in England on miniatures, portrait-engravings, &c., &c.; and author of volumes on the French Painters, the Stuarts, and The Miniature Painters. He has, after a labour of years, prepared a book entitled "Wessex Worthies"—with a view to publishing it in due course; and, as it struck me it was a matter you, as a Dorset man, would thoroughly understand, I have suggested to him to submit the work to your house in the first place.

Mr Foster's family may be known to you, if not he himself personally. He is Dorchester born, and was for many years the active member in the above departments of the Bond-Street firm of Dickenson and Foster, till he retired some little time ago.

Whether you come to business with him, or whether you do not, you will, I feel sure, be interested in his enterprise, and give him the benefit of your opinions in respect of it.

Yours very truly,
Thomas Hardy.

Text MS. (typewritten) Texas.
suggested to him: see letters of 12 and 14 Oct 17 to Foster. *Dickenson and Foster*: apparently a reference to the firm of F. Dickinson, fine art dealer, at 104 New Bond Street, London.

To J.J. FOSTER

MAX GATE, | DORCHESTER. | October 14th. 1917.

Dear Mr Foster

I send the required introduction to Mr Flower, one of the Cassell firm. Perhaps the best plan would be for you to enclose my letter with one from yourself to him, and arrange to see him and discuss the book. He edits the Annual of the Dorset men in London every year.

Publishers are, as you know, very shy of new books in these war-times, but there can be no harm in your talking your scheme over with him.

I now recall that Carlyle said practically the same thing as L. Stephen: though I cannot find the exact words: will you therefore insert after my remark about L.S. "There is also a passage in Carlyle to the same effect"—or quote the passage.

The sudden break in the second paragraph is accidental and was to have been filled in.

Yours very truly,
Th: Hardy.

I hope the letter of introduction is correct. T.H.

Text MS. (typewritten) Eton College.
to Mr Flower: see letter of 14 Oct 17 to Flower. *as L. Stephen*: TH's Introductory Note to Foster's *Wessex Worthies* (see letter to Foster of 12 Oct 17) mentions, but does not quote, a remark of Leslie Stephen's upon the importance for a biographer of obtaining 'from portraits and traditions' the sense of 'the look of a man as he walked and talked'. *or quote the passage*: in the Introductory Note as pub. the words given here within quotation marks are used to introduce a quotation from Carlyle's 'Project of a National Exhibition of Scottish Portraits', first pub. 1855, included in his *Critical and Miscellaneous Essays* (London, 1894), III.517. *I hope . . . correct*: added in TH's hand.

To THOMAS HUMPHRY WARD

MAX GATE, | DORCHESTER. | October 15: 1917

Dear Mr Ward:

I return the Barnes pages, which have been printed with great care, & needed hardly any corrections in the dialect.

I hope your book will not be unduly delayed by the war, so wearing as it is. We are so sorry to hear of the loss of your nephew, but almost everybody is hit somewhere. I have lost two cousins, one killed in Gallipoli, the other on the West front. To-day's news of the German advance in Russia is disheartening. Our kindest regards to Mrs Ward. I don't know how she feels, but to write cheerful books for people (which they seem to ask for, or are said to) is hard work for me.

Very truly yours
Thomas Hardy.

Text MS. (with envelope) Texas.
Barnes pages: see letter of 11 Oct 16; TH was returning the proofs. *of your nephew*: Lieut. Thomas Sorell Arnold, the elder son of Mrs. Ward's brother Francis Sorell Arnold, died of wounds at Passchendaele 11 Oct 1917. *in Gallipoli*: Frank George. *on the West front*: see letter of 20 May 17. *German advance*: the action, by land and sea, was on the Baltic coast N. of Riga.

To SIR HENRY NEWBOLT

THE ROYAL HOTEL, | PLYMOUTH. | Oct 21: 1917

My dear Newbolt:

I discover that you have lectured on a subject not uninteresting to me, & I am sure that you have very generously treated the writer you discuss. It is a lecture I hope to read verbatim some day. Meanwhile as it happens to coincide, or almost, with my stay within a stone's throw or two of Plymouth Hoe, where the sailor-lads were dancing heel & toe—a spot as dear to you as to me, I cannot refrain from sending a line to you—about nothing.

When I am down here I always wish I was a Devon man—as you are, I believe? I have many romantic & (now) sad reasons for my interest in the county, which I need not particularize. Dorset, however, touches Devon, & I suppose I must not complain.

On our way here we went to see Eden Phillpotts. What a gentle & amiable man he is. I fear he has worked out Dartmoor, & I don't know what he can take in hand next.

I wonder if you come this way often. It is an excellent direction to take in these bombing days: though of course you are all right in Wiltshire.

Always sincerely yrs
Thomas Hardy.

(We go back to Dorchester to-morrow.)

Text MS. Texas.
Plymouth: TH and FEH were taking a short holiday; see *LY*, 178. *writer you discuss*: Newbolt spoke on 'The Poetry of Thomas Hardy' to the Royal Society of Literature, 17 Oct 1917. *heel & toe*: an allusion to Newbolt's poem 'Drake's Drum'. *worked out Dartmoor*: in a series of novels set in the region. *in Wiltshire*: Newbolt was living at Netherhampton House, SW of Salisbury.

To J.J. FOSTER

MAX GATE, | DORCHESTER. | 25th. October 1917.

Dear Mr Foster:

It is really very kind of you to send me these beautiful volumes of your "Miniature Painters", which I shall always keep. I have already dipped into them, and find that they are delightful for opening at odd moments; sad, too, as one looks at the various representations of human beauty and thinks how evanescent it all is, and how much more than has here left a record behind has passed utterly away without a trace remaining.

I should have written sooner, but have been away in Devonshire. With renewed thanks I am,

Yours very truly,
Thomas Hardy.

Text MS. (typewritten) Eton College.
"*Miniature Painters*": see letter to Foster of 3 Oct 16. *in Devonshire*: see letter of 21 Oct 17.

To SIR HAMO THORNYCROFT

MAX GATE, | DORCHESTER. | Sunday: 11: 11: 17

My dear Thornycroft:

Many thanks to the shade of Ovid for jogging your elbow to write—for to tell the truth we have been so benumbed by the events of the times as to have almost given up writing letters—or rather I have, for my wife still manages to keep on—unless some friend gives me a lead. However we are quite well, though London seems to get further & further off. We were there two days in the summer, & there was not time to do much, or see anybody, as you will imagine.

Yes: I quite agree with you about Gosse's Life of Swinburne. His reticence is I think admirable, in face of the present fashion of putting dirty linen under a glass case. What he has left out is absolutely inessential: otherwise there might be reason for the complaint some people make.

Just fancy your knowing S. when his hair was still red. I had no idea that you remembered him then.

Do you think the raids will go on? They must cost our enemies an amount out of all proportion to the results. As to the war generally, it is not exhilarating to think that Germany is in a better position (or seems so, at the moment) than she was in three years ago, after all our struggles. Kindest regards to all.

Yrs always sincerely
Thomas Hardy.

Text MS. DCM.
shade of Ovid: Thornycroft began his letter of 9 Nov 17 (DCM), '"Fert anima" as I think Ovid says, to send a line to you . . .' *Life of Swinburne*: see letter of 26 Apr 17; Thornycroft referred to it as 'a first rate book'. *still red*: Thornycroft's letter spoke of Swinburne as 'the little redhaired electrified manikin as if suspended on an invisible thread'. *raids will go on?*: Thornycroft mentioned the air raids as one of the disagreeable features of living in London.

To SIR FREDERICK MACMILLAN

MAX GATE, | DORCHESTER. | Monday. 12: 11: '17

My dear Macmillan:

The book came this morning, & looks very well in spite of wars & tumults—or perhaps in consequence, as it is rather in keeping with them. I will send in a day or two the names of the people you kindly offer to forward a copy to—only a few—whenever it is ready. About five will be enough for me here.

My wife sends her best regards. By the way she tells me she has lost her copy of "A Changed Man"—*Wessex* edn, so that her set is broken; & she will feel obliged if (at any time) you can let her have another.

Always truly yrs
Thomas Hardy.

Text MS. BL.
The book: TH's *Moments of Vision and Miscellaneous Verses* (London, 1917).

To WILLIAM STEBBING

MAX GATE, | DORCHESTER. | Nov. 15: 1917

Dear Mr Stebbing:

Your kind thought of me in sending the book of Translations has already given me & will give me still more half-hours of pleasure in its reading. The two fine minds you have selected to work upon in this volume—such differing minds, too—happen to be those which arrested me in times past perhaps more than any others of "the Ancients"—Virgil affectionately, Lucretius deferentially. I am looking into your renderings of the latter just now, & simultaneously into my old quarto edition, "in usum Serenissimi Delphini", dated 1680—which I have not opened for the last 20 years till now. Believe me

With sincerest thanks,

Always yrs truly
Thomas Hardy.

Text MS. Texas.
Stebbing: William Stebbing, leader-writer for *The Times*; see IV.273. *book of Translations*: Stebbing's *Virgil & Lucretius* (London, 1917) contains verse translations of selected passages; TH's copy is now in the Purdy collection. *Delphini*": 'for the use of His Highness the Dauphin', i.e., one of the editions of Latin works commissioned by Louis XIV of France for his son's education; the edition of the *De Rerum Natura* of Lucretius was pub. in Paris 1680. TH's copy was sold along with other books from his library in 1938. *for the last 20 years*: see II.143.

To J.M. BULLOCH

MAX GATE, | DORCHESTER. | 25th. November 1917.

Dear Mr Bulloch:

I should like to write something about the War for The Graphic if I ever wrote anything in prose nowadays. But I have got out of the way of that sort of thing—I suppose because I have written nothing but verse for the last twenty years and more.

I sent off elsewhere the only two war poems I had. If I had known I should have been pleased to let you have one. Perhaps another will come into my mind; but I don't know. The machine-made horrors of the present war make one's blood run cold rather than warm as a rule.

Yes: the Aberdeen time has receded far into distance! And yet I often think of the charm it had for me. If you can ever get away from Saturday to Monday why not come and see us? My wife says she would be so glad to put you up.

Yours sincerely,
Thomas Hardy.

Text MS. (typewritten) Aberdeen Univ.
Bulloch: John Malcolm Bulloch, editor of the *Graphic* 1909–24; see III.160. *only two war poems*: i.e., 'Often When Warring' and 'In Time of War and Tumults', pub. in the *Sphere*, 10 and 24 Nov 1917 respectively. *the Aberdeen time*: of April 1905, when TH travelled to Aberdeen to receive his first honorary degree; see *LY*, 108–10.

To SIR FREDERICK MACMILLAN

MAX GATE, | DORCHESTER. | 10th. December 1917.

Dear Sir Frederick:

I am asked by M. Georges Bazile of Paris to notify to you that several years ago I gave him permission to publish a translation of the short story entitled "An Imaginative Woman" from "Life's Little Ironies", which he now hopes to carry out in a periodical he edits.

The story having been in print more than ten years has, I imagine, passed out of copyright in translation.

I take this opportunity of sending up a few corrections to "Moments of Vision"—in case any reprint should be required.

Many thanks for the copies,

Yours very truly,
Th: Hardy.

Text MS. (typewritten) BL.
Bazile: Cecil Georges-Bazile, translator; he wrote to TH 5 Dec 17 (DCM). *several years ago*: his letter, dated 13 Mar 11, is in DCM. *a periodical he edits*: the story, 'Une Femme Imaginative', appeared (Paris, 1918) in the series of 'Cahiers britanniques et américains' edited and pub. by Georges-Bazile; the translation had appeared five years earlier in the *Revue politique et littéraire*. *reprint . . . required*: *Moments of Vision* appears not to have been reprinted prior to its inclusion in the Wessex edn. in 1919.

To EDMUND GOSSE

MAX GATE, | DORCHESTER. | Dec. 11. 1917

My dear Gosse:

I intended to send this before, but I have been having rheumatism, & letters have got behindhand. I hope it is what you meant.

The book went to you through the publishers because I knew that by the roundabout route of first coming here you would not get it so soon by a week or two—things having a way of lingering about while waiting for a messenger, &c., &c.

Thanks for inquiries. Beyond the rheumatism—which was caused, my wife says, by my working with a pickaxe in the garden!—we have been well. I hope you & yours continue so, so as to be able to sustain the apparent reversal of our hopes in the war.

Always yours
Thomas Hardy.

Text MS. Texas.
what you meant: Gosse, having received *Moments of Vision* directly from the publisher, evidently sent it on to TH with a request for a personal inscription; TH responded, referring to the poems as 'these late notes of a worn-out lyre' (Purdy, 208).

To JOHN DRINKWATER

MAX GATE, | DORCHESTER. | Dec. 19: 1917

Dear Mr Drinkwater:

My thanks for the little book entitled "Tides", which I have not yet read, but only dipped into. "My Estate", & "Politics," attract me: also "A Man's Daughter", though I am not sure I understand the last.

Truly yours
Th: H.

Text MS. Yale.
"Tides": Drinkwater's *Tides* (London, 1917).

To SIR HENRY AND LADY HOARE

MAX GATE, | DORCHESTER. | December 26: 1917

My dear Sir Henry & Lady Hoare:

Though one should be prepared for anything in these days it never struck me what I was going to read when I opened your letter.

It is no use to offer consolation. And not even Time may be able to give that—I mean real consolation. Once a wound, always a scar left, it seems to me. Though Time can & does enlarge our vision to perceive that the one who has gone has the best of it—& that we who are left are made to look rather poor creatures by comparison with the one who has got safely to the other side—has achieved Death triumphantly & can say:

"Nor steel nor poison—foreign levy—nothing
Can touch me further".

You may remember what was said by Ld Clarendon in his History of the Rebellion, on the death of Ld Falkland in the Battle of Newbury:

"If there were no other brand upon this odious & accursed War than that single loss, it must be most infamous & execrable to all posterity."

I write the above in great haste, to answer your letter quickly. Florence has been crying over her remembrance of climbing the tower with Harry. It is a satisfaction, if one may say so, to feel now that we did go to see you when you were all at home together. With deepest sympathy for both

Yours always sincerely
Thomas Hardy.

P.S. A touch of his humane character shows in that thought of the horses sufferings in his letter. Th.H.

Text MS. (with mourning envelope addressed to Lady Hoare) Wiltshire Record Office. *consolation*: Henry, the Hoares' only child (see letter to Lady Hoare of 28 Oct 14), died in Alexandria 20 Dec 1917 of wounds received while serving as a captain in the 1st Dorset Queen's Own Yeomanry. *touch me further"*: adapted from *Macbeth*, III.ii.24-6. *to all posterity"*: TH's quotation is accurate apart from the (deliberate) omission of 'Civil' before 'War'. *climbing the tower*: i.e., Stourton Tower, on the Hoares' Stourhead estate; see letter of 29 Apr 14. *go to see you*: in July 1914; see *LY*, 160.

To S.M. ELLIS

MAX GATE, | DORCHESTER. | 27th. December 1917.

Dear Mr Ellis:

I am glad to give you permission to use the poem on Meredith in your book.

Many thanks for good wishes, which we reciprocate for the coming year, though at present the outlook is gloomy.

Yours very truly,
Th: Hardy.

Text MS. (typewritten) Purdy.
Ellis: Stewart Marsh Ellis, author; see IV.272. *your book*: Ellis's *George Meredith: His Life and Friends in Relation to His Work* (London, 1919); TH's poem 'G.M.' is reprinted on pp. 209-10.

To SIEGFRIED SASSOON

MAX GATE, | DORCHESTER. | 28 Dec: 1917.

Dear Siegfried Sassoon:

I write a line to wish you as good a New Year as is possible in our day, & to thank you for the volume of Georgian Poetry containing some of your work. I see one or two of yours that I like, though I have hardly looked at it yet, & my mind has strayed to a point on which I have before wondered—one that has nothing to do with your verses, as you did not invent it—I mean the title of the collection. What are we to call the original Georgians, now that the post-Victorians have adopted their name. Still, I don't suppose the shades of Shelley, Byron, Wordsworth, &c will mind much.

With renewed thanks I am

Sincerely yours
Thomas Hardy.

P.S. I hope you are quite recovered: I don't know where you are! Th: H.

Text MS. Eton College.
some of your work: *Georgian Poetry 1916–1917*, ed. E.M. [i.e., Edward Marsh] (London, 1917), includes 8 poems from Sassoon's *The Old Huntsman*. *where you are!*: Sassoon seems to have just left the convalescent home at Craiglockhart, near Edinburgh, to which he had been sent in the summer of 1917.

To SIR JAMES BARRIE

MAX GATE, | DORCHESTER. | Dec. 30: 1917

My dear Barrie:

We wish you as good a new year as can be hoped for, & a better one than the old. We often think of you up aloft in that old spot I know so well, & shall always be

Most sincerely yours
Th: & F. Hardy.

Text MS. (correspondence card) Yale.
that old spot: Adelphi Terrace; see letter of 23 June 17.

To EDMUND GOSSE

MAX GATE, | DORCHESTER. | December 30: 1917

My dear Gosse:

Just a word of Salutation to you & your house on this eve of the New Year, for which you have our best wishes as fellow passengers in this precious war-galley.

Well: the poems are of a very mixed sort. To arrange them was beyond me. Speaking generally the dates at the beginning are when the event or experience happened; at the end when the writing was done.

The cold you had must needs come along to me, & following your advice I stayed in bed a day. I hope yours is quite gone by this time, as mine is.

I well remember that illness at Upper Tooting which brought you to my bedside. What a time of it I had—six months! Yes: I did dictate "A Laodicean" through it. It was an awful job.

Any forecast for the coming year is I confess beyond me, & I don't find that people who are supposed to be at the centre of things know much more than I do. We saw Symons-Jeune a few days ago: he is down here on a visit to his daughter. My wife joins with me in best wishes for you all. Believe me always

Your sincere friend
Thomas Hardy.

Text MS. (with envelope) Leeds.
the writing was done: TH was responding to speculations about the date of composition of his poems in Gosse's letter of 16 Dec 17 (DCM; pub. in Evan Charteris, *The Life and Letters of Sir Edmund Gosse*, London, 1931, 420–1). *to my bedside*: Gosse had recalled the occasion in his letter. *his daughter*: Dorothy Hanbury of Kingston Maurward House.

To CALEB SALEEBY

MAX GATE, | DORCHESTER. | December 30th. 1917.

Dear Dr. Saleeby:

Many thanks for your letter, and I time my reply to reach you about the New Year, for which you have our best wishes.

The Minuet of Mozart's mentioned in the poems is the one you refer to. To make the verses fit the music you would of course have to repeat the words of the last line but one in each verse.

I am in doubt when I shall see London again. It cannot be attractive this weather.

Yours very truly,
Th: Hardy.

Text MS. (typewritten) Adams.
the poems: *Moments of Vision*; the specific allusion is to the title of the poem 'Lines to a Movement in Mozart's E-Flat Symphony', TH apparently having forgotten that he had substituted 'Movement' for the MS. reading 'Minuet' (Purdy, 196).

To J. S. UDAL

MAX GATE, | DORCHESTER. | 30th. December 1917.

My dear Udal:

(Please forgive my writing by machinery—I cannot get through my letters without some such means.)

We thank you much for your good Christmas wishes, and I send this at the eve of the New Year to convey ours to you for the coming months—over which a veil of mystery hangs at present.

As to the letter of mine you found in the Graingerized Hutchins's "Dorset" at the Broadley sale, I have no recollection of it or its contents. I suppose it was written in reply to some importunate person or other.

I see no objection to your using "Dorsetshire" instead of "Dorset" in the title of the Folklore book.

It is interesting to think you may come back to the county again. Whenever I see Bridport and its neighbourhood, and the Symondsbury Hill you know so well, I think I would rather live a year there than five in St. John's Wood. But of course circumstances rule in such cases.

My wife sends kind regards and I am

Sincerely yours,
Th: Hardy.

Text MS. (typewritten) NYU.
Graingerized: correctly, Grangerized, i.e., extra-illustrated. *Hutchins's "Dorset"*: see letter of 13 Feb 14 to Lady Grove. *Broadley sale*: A. M. Broadley (see letter of 28 June 14) died in 1916; a portion of his extensive library had been auctioned in London earlier in December 1917. *Folklore book*: see letter to Udal of 9 June 15. *St. John's Wood*: the London district in which Udal was currently living.

To SIR HENRY NEWBOLT

MAX GATE, | DORCHESTER. | Dec. 31: 1917

My dear Newbolt:

We have been reading your lectures aloud, & have just come to the end of them, which as it coincides with the end of 1917, I write to tell you of, to have an excuse for wishing you as happy a new year as one can hope for in these times. I don't know that I have ever parted from an old year with less reluctance than from this.

The book was most interesting, & we were both very sorry to get to the end. It is a pity there is no direct railway between us, or we could meet & talk over the many subjects you open up. Our united kindest regards to you & all your house.

Always sincerely
Thomas Hardy.

Text MS. Texas.
your lectures: a series of lectures given by Newbolt (as Professor of Poetry) at the Royal Society of Literature had been pub. as *A New Study of English Poetry* (London, 1917).

1918

To SIR FREDERICK MACMILLAN

MAX GATE, | DORCHESTER. | 3rd. January 1917 [1918].

Dear Sir Frederick Macmillan:

I remember Mr Bertram Lloyd (whom I do not know) asking permission last November on behalf of the Humanitarian League to publish in an anthology to be issued by them three short poems of mine, viz, "The Puzzled Game Birds", "The Caged Thrush", and "Wagtail and Baby", subject to your permission to use them. An answer was sent two or three days ago, allowing him to do it, i.e., subject to your consent also.

I have sent him another note to make this clear. I do not often reply to anthologists, but I thought that the objects of the League should be considered favourably, though of course I have no proof that he is authorized by the League to make the request.

Very truly yours,
Th: Hardy.

Text MS. (typewritten) BL. *Date* Given correctly on pencil draft (DCM).
Lloyd: Bertram Lloyd (1881–1944), an early member of the Humanitarian League and secretary for 12 years of the National Society for the Abolition of Cruel Sports. He wrote to TH 30 Nov 17 (DCM) on Humanitarian League stationery; Macmillan wrote 2 Jan 18 (DCM) to say that Lloyd was claiming to have permission to quote any of TH's poems without payment. *anthology*: *The Great Kinship: An Anthology of Humanitarian Poetry*, ed. B. Lloyd (London, 1921); it includes the 3 poems mentioned here. *another note*: a typed draft of this letter to Lloyd, dated 3 Jan 17 [i.e., 18], is in DCM.

To DOROTHY ALLHUSEN

MAX GATE, | DORCHESTER. | Jan 4: 1918

My dear Dorothy:

How very nice of you to send good wishes. We do the same, as you will know—even though, as the Kaiser declared, Heaven seems to be on the German side.

We are doing what little we can down here, among other things getting up a play for Jan. 31 on behalf of the Dorsets in Mesopotamia. It will be delightful if you really do come in the spring. I hardly go anywhere now—particularly at this chilling time of year. Your trees have grown enormously, I imagine, since I saw them! I hope your daughter, whom I knew when she was a baby, is getting round again. Florence sends love.

Ever affectionately
Thomas Hardy.

Text MS. R. V. Weight.
on the German side: Kaiser Wilhelm II was reported in *The Times*, 26 Dec 1917, as having declared, 'The year 1917, with its great battles, has proved that the German people has in the Lord of Creation above an unconditional and avowed Ally, on Whom it can absolutely rely.' *a play*: *The Mellstock Quire*, adapted by A. H. Evans from TH's *Under the Greenwood Tree*; it was first produced in 1910. *in Mesopotamia*: the performance was to be in aid of the Comforts Fund of those formations of the Dorset Regiment which were currently serving in Mesopotamia, after having been in India for most of the war. *Your trees*: around the Allhusens' house at Stoke Poges. *your daughter*: Dorothea Elizabeth Allhusen (1903–26), Mrs. Allhusen's younger daughter; she had recently been ill.

To JOHN GALSWORTHY

MAX GATE, | DORCHESTER. | Jan. 4th, 1918.

My dear Galsworthy,

Our sincere thanks for your good wishes. You and Mrs. Galsworthy have, as you know, the same from us.

I don't think that mistake about the knighthood a disaster for you exactly, and probably you don't by this time. A friend of mine who happened to be here said "He has scored both ways. He has had the honour of being knighted, and the honour of having refused a knighthood. Many men would envy him." I said I would tell you this.

The same post that brought your letter brought also a bundle of reviews of my poems from the publisher's. I suppose English critics will always work on the old lines, and try to get behind the book to quiz the author—regarding his book as a deep-laid scheme of his, analysing the possible motives, his reason for publishing it at this particular moment, etc., etc., instead of seeing that he is almost irresponsible, that it is the result of haphazard circumstances, and that the writer rubs his eyes and wonders how this and that got into his pages as much as the reviewer does.

We are frozen up here—I don't mean water-pipes, because we have hardly any, but I mean fingers and nerves.

Always yours,
Thomas Hardy.

I don't quite know where to send this.—T.H.

Text H. V. Marrot, *The Life and Letters of John Galsworthy* (London, 1935), 438.
good wishes: of 1 Jan 18 (DCM). *about the knighthood*: Galsworthy's letter to TH expressed embarrassment at the fact that his recent refusal of a knighthood had become public knowledge; see Marrot, 435–8. *where to send this*: the Galsworthys were staying temporarily in Littlehampton, Sussex, while looking for a new country house.

To CLEMENT SHORTER

MAX GATE, | DORCHESTER. | Monday: 7: 1:'18

My dear Shorter:

This comes as a great shock to us—not only of sorrow but of surprise, for (so dense are people) neither my wife nor I realized that there was any likelihood of the illness you alluded to being fatal. I feared there might possibly be long invalid years for Mrs Shorter, not that the end would come like this.

I write immediately on seeing the sad intelligence. I am very very sorry, & can say no more, little as that is. I offer no consolation; there may be some, but I do not know it. If one has much feeling—& you have that I know—such a blow is heavy to bear. Believe me to be with deep sympathy

Most sincerely yours
Thomas Hardy.

Text MS. Berg.
fatal: Shorter's wife, Dora Sigerson Shorter (see letter of 8 Dec 15), died on 6 Jan 1918. *the sad intelligence*: an announcement of Mrs. Shorter's death appeared in *The Times*, 7 Jan 1918.

To SIEGFRIED SASSOON

MAX GATE, | DORCHESTER. | Jan 8: 1918

Dear Siegfried Sassoon:

We have read out loud the poems you mention, & liked them. Perhaps R. Nichols brings off his intention best in "To —", & "Fulfilment." But it is impossible to select, after all.

That photograph!—We divined it to be you, but I was not certain, till a friend told us positively only a day before your letter came. It has been standing in my writing room calmly overlooking a hopeless chaos of scribbler's litter.

I shall be so glad to see you walk in some day.

Always sincerely
Thomas Hardy.

Text MS. Eton College.
poems you mention: the reference is apparently to the seven poems by Robert Nichols (see letter of early Aug 19 to him) included in *Georgian Poetry 1916–1917* (see letter of 28 Dec 17), although Nichols's letter to TH of early Aug 19 (DCM) speaks of a copy of his *Ardours and Endurances* (1917) as having been sent to TH through Sassoon. *That photograph!*: as Sassoon explains in *Siegfried's Journey 1916–1920* (London, 1945), 88, he had sent TH, without covering letter, a photograph of the portrait of himself by Glyn Philpot (later reproduced as the frontispiece to *Siegfried's Journey*).

To WALTER POUNCY

Jan. 15. 1918.

Dear Sir,

I write for Mr Hardy to say that he has no objection at all to your issuing the portrait in post-card form, & that he hopes that you may sell a good many for the Dorsets' Fund.

With respect to your imitating his signature under it by reproductive process, he is sorry to say that he is unable to give his consent, as he finds that these reproductions are taken as originals by many people, & much confusion caused thereby.

The name can, of course, be printed under in ordinary Roman capitals, as is done by the London photographers.

Yours faithfully

Mr Walter Pouncy | Photographer | Dorchester

Text MS. (pencil draft) DCM.
Pouncy: Walter Pouncy (1844–1918), Dorchester photographer, son of John Pouncy, a photographic pioneer; see David N. Baron, 'Hardy and the Dorchester Pouncys', *Somerset and Dorset Notes & Queries*, March 1981. *the portrait*: in his letter of 14 Jan 18 (DCM) Pouncy speaks of it as a photograph taken at a sitting in 1913. *Dorsets' Fund*: see letter of 4 Jan 18 to Mrs. Allhusen; Pouncy proposed to sell the card for the first time at the performance of *The Mellstock Quire*, giving the proceeds to the fund.

To ISABEL SMITH

MAX GATE, | DORCHESTER. | Jan 23: 1918

Dear Mrs Reginald Smith:

How surprising that you should have found the MS. of Far from the Madding Crowd! I thought it "pulped" ages ago. And what a good thought of yours—to send it to the Red Cross, if anybody will buy it.

What I should best like you to do in forwarding it [is] to send it as from *yourself* (which of course it wd be), &, if you like, to add that it is sent with my approval & that I wrote the missing page at your suggestion. Any other details you can add as to its being lost for so many years (more than 40), &c, &c, would add to whatever value it may possess.

I am sending separately the missing page.

I mention—what you may already have thought of, that if the sheets are at present loose they should be fastened together before you part with them. I suppose there is not time to have them bound? which makes people bid higher. (How shameless I am to try to puff my own MS! But an author's proper modesty is cast to the winds in these times & in this cause.)

As to the portion of the Hand of Ethelberta MS. I should like to have it back if you are quite willing to return it—not otherwise. Then I will try to find the remainder.

We were talking of Mr Smith's pleasant visit to us with you, quite lately.

I always feel so glad that he came. I lunched at the Athenaeum once last year, & I so missed him. We used often to meet there. My wife sends her kindest remembrances, & I am

Yrs always sincerely
Thomas Hardy.

I forgot to say that, as to the "Souls of the Slain", I wd not, if I were you, send it also to the Red +. We are sending, by request, two poems, & perhaps another may have a cheapening effect. It will be kind of you to return it. Th. H.

Text MS, Edwin Thorne.
Smith: Isabel Smith, widow of Reginald John Smith (see II.249), editor of the *Cornhill*, and daughter of George Smith, its founder (see I.35); she wrote 21 Jan 18 (DCM). *Madding Crowd!*: serialized in the *Cornhill*, January–December 1874. *it* [*is*] *to send*: TH wrote 'it to send'. *to the Red Cross*: the MS. was sold at the Red Cross Sale at Christie's, 22 Apr 1918 (see *LY*, 186), and is now in the collection of Mr. Edwin Thorne. *missing page*: folio 107, containing the final paragraphs of chap. 9. *have them bound?*: the MS. was bound in blue morocco before being sold. *Ethelberta MS.*: Mrs. Smith had also reported finding some chapters of the MS. of TH's *The Hand of Ethelberta*, serialized in the *Cornhill* July 1875–May 1876; TH subsequently destroyed them. *visit to us*: the date of this occasion is unknown. *missed him*: Smith died in 1916. *of the Slain*": the MS. of this poem, first pub. in the *Cornhill*, April 1900, had also been found by Mrs. Smith; it is now in the Adams collection. *two poems*: the MSS. of 'Moments of Vision' and the closing chorus of the After Scene to *The Dynasts*, Part Third.

To R. S. COMBEN

Jan 24. 1918

Dear Sir:

In reply to your letter on the suggestion I made long ago that a tablet might be erected to record the historic visitors to Gloucester Lodge, now an hotel, perhaps it will be advisable that I should inform you of all I know about it so far.

I first wrote many years ago to the Weymouth Town Council through their then Town Clerk Mr Huxtable. I cannot say whether he mentioned the matter to the Council, but some years passed & nothing was done, so that I thought the idea had not been welcomed. In some way afterwards the proprietors of the Gloucester Hotel were in communication with me about it, & they inquired what inscription I proposed. I sent them one that might suit, suggesting that they should put it either on the building itself, or on the wall of the railings dividing their forecourt from the pavement. Nothing seems to have come of that either, as a long time has passed since their inquiry.

What had better be done you will be able to decide. They *may* mean to put up such a tablet some day, or they may not. But in either alternative there is, of course nothing to prevent the Town erecting a stone on the Esplanade in front of the Gloucester, recording that in the house opposite Geo. III resided, & was there visited by Pitt, Eldon, Hardy, & other distinguished people. If you really decide to do anything I will send what I think might suffice, though possibly the archives of the Borough would enable you to compile a more complete list than I can give.

It seems to me undeniable that such a memorial would add to the attractiveness of the town at a very trifling expense. And I think that if it were fixed on the Esplanade it would be seen by more people, & be more arresting, than if on the wall [of] the quondam Gloucester Lodge.

I am, Dear Sir
Yours truly

To His Worship the Mayor of Weymouth.

Text MS. (pencil draft) DCM.
Comben: Robert Stone Comben (d. 1958), mayor of Weymouth 1915–18. *your letter*: of 23 Jan 18 (DCM). *Mr Huxtable*: see IV.42. *sent them one*: see letter of 25 Oct 16. *other distinguished people*: see letter of 25 Oct 16. *the wall* [*of*] *the*: TH wrote 'the wall the'.

To EDMUND GOSSE

Private. MAX GATE, | DORCHESTER. | 28 Jan: 1918

My dear Gosse:

I send answers to questions—rather vague ones, unfortunately—on another sheet. I am honoured by your idea of a review.

The copies you have of the different volumes are, I believe, first editions. There are errors & careless passages in these, which were, to some extent corrected in later editions. I should like you to read from these later ones, naturally. The best is the "Wessex" Edition of "Works in Prose & Verse"—in the first volume of which (Tess of the d'Urbervilles) is a "general Preface", referring a good deal to the verse, that perhaps you ought to see. If you cannot get a copy of this edition in any other convenient way I can lend you the necessary volumes from a set I keep here for reference. I am sorry I have no spare set to give you to keep. Perhaps, however, that edition is in the London Library.

At any rate I can send you the little Golden Treasury selection, which will arrive herewith. Please keep it. You will see that all poems likely to lead to controversy, & those of the franker kind, have been necessarily omitted—though they are some of the strongest. On the whole, however, it is a nice little choice.

I was interested last week by an Oxford man of letters, & sound critic, telling me that the cuckoo-cry of the Fleet Street young men about "rugged language" (in my verse) is all nonsense.

If I can think of any other facts that you ought to know for your article I will write again.

Always sincerely
Thomas Hardy.

By the way—have you noticed "Near Lanivet, 1872" in "Moments of Vision?" I mention it not for literary reasons, but private ones—because you knew my late wife, & the scene occurred between us before our marriage. One careful reader tells me he likes it best. Th.H.

Owing to lack of time, through the necessity of novel-writing for magazines, many of the poems were temporarily jotted down to the extent of a stanza or two when the ideas occurred, and put aside till time should serve for finishing them—often not till years after. This makes it difficult to date those not dated in the volumes.

Answer 1. Am not sure when "Leipzig" & "San Sebastian" were written. They were conceived and a few lines written probably as early as you infer, but for the above reason the bulk of the pieces much later.

2. "The Dance at the Phoenix" (one of those Swinburne liked) is based on fact. The verse beginning "Twas Christmas" was written first, and quite early—at the time the tradition seemed to suggest a ballad. The rest left till later. "Friends Beyond" is undateable, memory not serving, though the idea of it was quite an old one.

3. As to date of poems in volumes published after 1898. Some are as old as those in Wessex Poems: e.g. "At a Lunar Eclipse", "Her Reproach" &c. But *which* besides, is doubtful.

The first idea of "The Dynasts". This occurs in an old notebook, in the form of a brief entry of an idea of "An Iliad of Europe from 1789 to 1815". The date of the note is June 20. 1875.

Text MS. Adams; answers (typewritten) Leeds.
questions: as posed by Gosse in his letter of 26 Jan 18 (DCM). *your idea of a review*: Gosse's 'Mr. Hardy's Lyrical Poems', *Edinburgh Review*, April 1918; the idea seems to have originated with the editor of the *Edinburgh* rather than with Gosse himself. *Oxford man of letters*: Arthur McDowall, fellow of All Souls, Oxford; see letter of 2 Feb 18 to him. He and his wife lunched at Max Gate 23 Jan 1918 (FEH diary fragment, Purdy). *before our marriage*: Lanivet is in Cornwall, between St. Austell and Bodmin; see Millgate, 143. *as early as you infer*: Gosse, in his letter, had suggested 1877–8 as the date of their composition. *Swinburne liked*: see II.209. *to 1815"*: see *EL*, 140.

To HALL CAINE

Max Gate, Dorchester, Jan. 29, 1918.

Dear Mr. Hall Caine,

My thanks for the newspaper cutting. If the mean age for the best *literary* work is thirty-seven it must be owing to the conditions of modern life; for we are told that Homer sang when old and blind, while Æschylus wrote his best tragedies when over sixty, Sophocles some of his best when nearly ninety, and Euripides did not begin to write till forty, and went on to seventy; and in these you have the pick of the greatest poets who ever lived. The philosophers, too, were nearly always old.

Yours very truly,
Th. Hardy.

Text *The Observer* [London], 3 Feb 1918.
Caine: Thomas Henry Hall Caine (1853–1931), novelist; *D.N.B.* *newspaper cutting*: from the *Observer*, 27 Jan 1918, in which Caine had taken issue with the assertion by Sir Edward Clarke (1841–1931; *D.N.B.*), lawyer and politician (see III.39), that the age of 37 marked the highest point of human intellectual development. Caine wrote to TH 27 Jan 18 and again on 31 Jan 18 (both DCM) to seek permission for this letter to be published.

To EDWARD CLODD

MAX GATE, | DORCHESTER. | Feb 1. 1918.

My dear Clodd:

My best thanks for "The Question" which I shall read with interest, as I do everything of yours. But I fear it has been hooked for me by a trick of imagination—not my own—& that therefore I don't deserve it in these times, when I present hardly any of my own books. For I have never asked Shorter to lend me a copy, or communicated with him about it. He has plainly mixed me up with somebody else in telling you so.

Why I have not bought it—I would never have asked for a loan of it—is that life is so short—the remainder of mine at any rate—& "the undone" is so vast, that I could assume certainly that your arguments would be those of every man of sound deductive power, which I fairly well knew already, & so take the volume "as read".

What a set-back this revival of superstition is! It makes one despair of the human mind. Where's Willy Shakespeare's "So noble in reason" now! In another quarter of a century we shall be burying food & money with our deceased, as was done with the Romano-British skeletons I used to find in my garden.

Sincerely yours
Th: Hardy.

Text MS. Leeds.
"The Question": Clodd's *The Question: "If a Man Die, Shall He Live Again?" Job. XIV. 14. A Brief History and Examination of Modern Spiritualism* (London, 1917). *in telling you so*: Clodd has annotated the MS. with a quotation from FEH's letter to Shorter of 20 Dec 17: 'Mr Clodd has not sent my husband his book. He says he would like to see it later-on, when you have done with it.' *"the undone"*: an allusion to Browning's 'The Last Ride Together'. *in reason"*: *Hamlet*, II.ii.304. *in my garden*: the subject of TH's paper of 1884, 'Some Romano-British Relics Found at Max Gate, Dorchester'; see *EL*, 212–13.

To SIR GEORGE DOUGLAS

MAX GATE, | DORCHESTER. | Feb 2: 1918

My dear Douglas:

Yes: I suppose it must be a year or more since we hailed each other across the counties, & a great deal has happened during the sad enough interval. I don't know that I can claim to be hopeful about the War, unless on the grounds that peace is better at any price than the struggle that has been going on these three years & more, for I fancy fighting will stop, somehow, not long hence, by the sheer force of world-weariness. Whether it will be "a German peace" or not events only can show. I sincerely hope not, for that will only mean new wars in the not very distant future.

I am glad to hear of your mother. What a ripe age: my mother lived to be a few months short of 91, as intelligent as ever till quite near the end. I hope your brother Francis's boy will continue to do well.

We have had no snow here to speak of, & have kept quite well. We have finished Morley's "Recollections", & are now reading Colvin's Keats, which is a painstaking, interesting book.

A friend of ours who is in the Intelligence Department at the War Office is coming here this evening: I don't know if he will enlighten us on any points; I suppose not. I am, with very kind remembrances,

Sincerely yours
Thomas Hardy.

Text MS. NLS.
hailed each other: TH is replying to Douglas's letter of 24 Jan 18 (DCM). *a ripe age*: she was not quite ninety; see letter of 4 May 18. *Francis's boy*: George Francis Valentine Scott Douglas (1898–1930), currently an officer with the 15th Hussars; his father, Francis John Scott-Douglas, had been a neighbour of TH's in Wimborne in the early 1880s (see I.166). *Morley's "Recollections"*: John Morley, Viscount Morley, *Recollections* (2 vols., London, 1917). *Colvin's Keats*: see first letter of 14 June 14 to Colvin; FEH reported to Cockerell, 12 Feb 18 (Purdy), that TH was 'deeply absorbed' in the book and felt that Fanny Brawne did not deserve the scorn she generally received. *at the War Office*: John Hartman Morgan; TH's postcard of 12 Apr 18 is addressed to him at the War Office.

To ARTHUR McDOWALL

MAX GATE, | DORCHESTER. | 2 Feb: 1918

Dear Mr McDowall:

"The Mellstock Quire" ought to be grateful to you for the beautifully written account of them the *Times* honours them with to-day. I don't think they have ever had anything that could be called literature expended on them before. How you got it into to-day's issue is a mystery to me. Our kindest regards to Mrs McDowall—

Always yrs
Thomas Hardy.

Text MS. (correspondence card, with envelope) T. R. Creighton.
McDowall: Arthur Sydney McDowall (1877–1933), critic and author, on the staff of *The Times* for many years; his *Thomas Hardy: A Critical Study* appeared in 1931. McDowall and his wife had recently visited Max Gate: see letter of 28 Jan 18. *the* Times: McDowall's review of the Dorchester production of *The Mellstock Quire*, 31 Jan 1918, appeared in *The Times*, 2 Feb 1918. *Mrs McDowall*: Mary, daughter of Bishop Mandell Creighton (see II.280).

To EDMUND GOSSE

MAX GATE, | DORCHESTER. | Feb 4: 1918

My dear Gosse:

What you say is true enough, if you define by the word "revolutionary" my feeling that the jewelled line was what I meant to avoid in poetry, as being effeminate. Possibly I felt this as early as the date you mention, 1866, but probably not till I left London for the country in 1867, & had time to reflect a little. However, you can judge from internal evidence, & also whether this was a mere rebellious fancy that passed off, or something inherent which remained. I judge from what some sensible critics have said that a good deal of my verse is, after all, comely & finished enough. But of course this may be true, & yet the nature of the finish be bold rather than minute—like a drawing on paper with a rough surface.

As to the catalogue, "Wessex Poems, First complete edition 1898" can only mean "first edition". Only two or three had appeared before that date, not in a book but in periodicals.

We hear that submarines are round about the shore of Portland like sharks. It seems so strange that they should be so near.

Always sincerely
Thomas Hardy.

Text MS. Adams.
true enough: Gosse was still working on his article on TH's poetry; see letter of 28 Jan 18. *in periodicals*: specifically, 'The Fire at Tranter Sweatley's' and 'Lines' (see Purdy, 103–4). *of Portland*: there was a naval base at Weymouth.

To FLORENCE HENNIKER

MAX GATE, | DORCHESTER. | Feb 7: 1918

My dear friend:

I have a guilty feeling that I did not reply to your previous letter. If I did not it was, at any rate, not from disinclination. I write much less promptly than I used to do, & if a letter gets covered over I sometimes do not remember that it is unanswered.

I am glad to find that you have gone away from the London atmosphere for a time: also from the contingency of bombs & shrapnell, the latter protective seeming more endangering, though in a smaller way, than the enemy's attack. But the defence is getting far more expert & thorough than at first I think.

I did not myself attend the performance of "The Mellstock Quire", though I was at the rehearsal of the dances, which I remembered seeing footed in country places when I was a boy. Florence & some friends however were there; & she entertained the actors at a tea in the Town Hall between the two performances, & had a speech made in her honour on account of it. Strange to say the man who played the parish clerk of 80 years ago is the clerk there now. Twelve of the present "Mellstock" (Stinsford) quire attended, to see the ghosts of their predecessors.

I gave very few copies of the poems to friends, as I thought they might not like them. As you have bought the book I am not responsible if they trouble you. I begin to think I shall never present any more of my own poems to anybody. I myself (naturally I suppose) like those best which are literally true—such as "At Lanivet,"—"At the word Farewell",—"Why did I sketch" &c, &c, which perhaps are quite unattractive to readers, & may have little literary merit.

Did you see the super-precious review of the verses in the Westminster Gazette? It amused me much (having no weight or value as criticism) as it was obviously written by a woman. It condemned the poem entitled "The pink frock" because the frock described was old-fashioned & Victorian! The publishers have sent me some fifty reviews—all of them, save 5 or 6, deplorably inept, purblind, & of far less *value* than the opinion of one's grocer or draper, though they were friendly enough, I must say. I always fancy I could point out the best, & the worst, in a volume of poems, which none of these did. But perhaps that is my self-conceit, for I have had no experience as a reviewer.

If what you call sad poems do preponderate, it may be owing to the fact that they were selected from many more, & the rejected ones were of the less solid kind, & considered not worth printing. The "Lalage" one—"Sitting on the Bridge", "Lyonnesse", &c. were of that sort which *were* thought worth retaining.

All our blue-tits, & other tits, have disappeared. We used to have great numbers. Our 3 magpies have also disappeared. Wessex still has the defects of his qualities.

Ever affectionately
Th: H.

Text MS. DCM.
attend the performance: TH's statement is contradicted by the report in the *Dorset County Chronicle*, 7 Feb 1918, and he seems in fact to have been present at the afternoon performance on 31 January and to have made a brief speech to the players during the interval before the evening performance—which he did not attend. *speech made in her honour*: by H. A. Martin (see III.357), Hon. Secretary of the Dorchester Debating and Dramatic Society. *clerk there now*: the part of Elias Spinks was played by Archie K. Holland. *the poems*: *Moments of Vision*. *Westminster Gazette*: of 8 Dec 1917; the review is unsigned. *written by a woman*: one of TH's scornful holograph annotations of his scrapbook (DCM) copy of the review indicates that he drew this inference from the 'preoccupation with dress' demonstrated in the observations on 'The Pink Frock'. *The "Lalage" one*: 'Timing Her', which opens with the line 'Lalage's coming'.

To DAVID ROBERTSON

MAX GATE, | DORCHESTER. | Engd | 7th. February 1918.

Dear Sir:

In reply to your inquiry if I am likely to visit the United States after the war, I am sorry to say that such a contingency is highly improbable.

That "The Dynasts" has a hold on the imagination of your class shows that your pupils are mentally alert, and is of good omen for your methods of training.

The opinion you quote from Lord Bryce to the effect that Americans do not think internationally, leads one to ask, does any country think internationally? I should say, none. But there can be no doubt that some countries think thus more than others; and in my opinion the people of America far more than the people of England.

Yours very truly,
Th: Hardy.

Professor D. A. Robertson, | President's Office,
The University, | Chicago. U. S. A.

Text Typed transcript (by D. A. Robertson, Jr.) Purdy.
Robertson: David Allan Robertson (1880–1961), American educator, currently associate professor of English and secretary to the president, University of Chicago. He had written 26 Dec 17 (DCM) to ask TH if he would lecture in Chicago when the war was over. *from Lord Bryce*: for Bryce see letter of 26 June 14. *more than others*: the reading 'more nearly than others' given in *LY*, 186, appears neither in the letter as sent nor in TH's pencil draft in DCM; *LY* also reads 'an event' for 'a contingency' in the opening sentence.

To SAMUEL CHEW

MAX GATE, | DORCHESTER, | 9th. February 1918.

Dear Sir:

In reply to your request for permission to quote from the poem entitled "A Singer Asleep—Algernon Charles Swinburne" in a Study of that poet, I am happy to grant it as to the stanzas you mention, or to whatever extent you may deem desirable.

As to your question based on statements that Mr Swinburne's later life was "atrophied", I can only say that he corresponded with me about many of my poems, including "The Dynasts", in which he seemed to be much interested, writing about certain details in its scenes; also, as I was informed after his death, speaking about it to friends.

I am honoured by your remarks on "Moments of Vision", and remain Dear Sir,

Yours very truly,
Th: Hardy.

Professor S. C. Chew. Bryn Mawr College.

Text MS. (typewritten, with envelope in FEH's hand) Adams.
Chew: Samuel Claggett Chew (1888–1960), American critic and teacher; his *Thomas Hardy: Poet and Novelist* first appeared in 1921. *a Study*: Chew's *Swinburne* (Boston, 1929); the second stanza of TH's 'A Singer Asleep' is quoted on p. 72. *your remarks*: in Chew's letter of 24 Jan 18 (DCM).

To E. V. LUCAS

Feb 9. 1918

Dear Mr Lucas:

1. Letters to Miss Winifred Thomson.

They are returned herewith. I do not object to the one dated "31 Oct. 1897" being made public & sold, but those dated "June 12. 1897", & "21.3.1915" please return to her, as they contain names & references which the persons alluded to or their representatives would probably wish to be kept private.

2. MS. of Far from the Madding Crowd.

I have no objection to an article being written about it, though I do not know what could be said. As to comparing the written text with the text as printed, all I stipulate is that anything in the MS. omitted in the printed volume as published by Macmillan be not revived, such a perpetuation of errors being a bad practice; but the passages that are additions to the MS. may be pointed out if desired; & these will be matter enough, as one whole chapter was written on the proof sheets.

Yours very truly

Text MS. (pencil draft) DCM.
Lucas: Edward Verrall Lucas (1868–1938), journalist and author; *D.N.B.* He was Hon. Secretary of the Books and Manuscripts Sub-Committee for the Red Cross Sale at Christie's, 22 Apr 1918. *Thomson*: Winifred Hope Thomson; see letter of 21 Mar 15. She had herself written to TH, 7 Feb 18 (DCM), to say that she had sent the letters to the sale. *"31 Oct. 1897"*: see II.181. *"June 12. 1897"*: see II.165; the letter mentions Mrs. Henniker. *"21.3.1915"*: see p. 86; it disparages Herkomer's portrait of TH. *with the text as printed*: Lucas (7 Feb 18, DCM) had suggested that publication of an article making such a comparison might help to arouse interest in the MS. (see letter of 23 Jan 18) and in the sale generally. *on the proof sheets*: chap. 16, 'All Saints' and All Souls"; see Purdy, 15.

To JOHN ACLAND

MAX GATE, | DORCHESTER. | Feb 12: 1918

Dear Captain Acland:

I feel much honoured by the request entrusted to you to make on behalf of the County Museum that I accept the office of a Vice-President. I do so with pleasure, though with a fear that my very limited activities hardly entitle me to the position, notwithstanding that I take a great interest in the welfare of the Institution.

Sincerely yours
Thomas Hardy.

Text MS. DCM.
a great interest: TH had in fact served on the Council of the Dorset County Museum since 1889.

To THE REVD. LIONEL HARRISON

[Mid-February 1918]

Dear Sir:

I write for Mr Hardy who is suffering from a bad cold to say that he regrets he has no special knowledge of old Burton Bradstock & that your best source of information would be Hutchins's History of Dorset.

I may mention a trivial detail in the parish chronicle that as an architect's pupil he made the drawings for the restoration of the church in 1861 or 1862.

Yours truly
F. Hardy

Text MS. (pencil draft) DCM.
Harrison: the Revd. Lionel Gordon Harrison, curate of Burton Bradstock (SW of Dorchester) 1914–19; he had sought TH's help (13 Feb 18, DCM) in preparing a lecture on old Burton Bradstock for a meeting of the local Women's Institute. *History of Dorset*: see letter of 13 Feb 14 to Lady Grove. *1861 or 1862*: Burton Bradstock church was not restored at this date; TH presumably meant Shipton Gorge, a chapel of Burton Bradstock, which was largely rebuilt in 1861–2 to the designs of John Hicks, his then employer.

To EDMUND GOSSE

MAX GATE, | DORCHESTER. | Feb 18: 1918.

My dear Gosse:

I am puzzled about the date of "The Widow," (or as it is called in the Wessex Edn "The Widow Betrothed"). Anyhow, though I thought of it about 1867 when looking at the house described, which is near here, it must have been written after I had read Wordsworth's famous preface to Lyrical Ballads, which influenced me much, & influences the style of the poem, as you can see for yourself. I am afraid that is all I can recall.

"Moments of Vision" has run the gauntlet of the papers by now, & I feel in no bright spirits about it, though perhaps upon the whole it was just as well to print it. I don't mean that the book has not been kindly received—far from it—but the lack of grasp in the people who write "notices" is disconcerting. One wonders why they quiz the author rather than review the book. In their super-preciosity, I notice, they still think literary form of more importance to poetry than vision, & that it is more damning to show absence of "poetic diction" in a poem of which it can be said "This is Life", than to show "This is not Life" in a poem which can boast of poetic diction.

For the relief of my necessities, as the Prayer Book puts it, I began writing novels, & made a sort of trade of it; but last night I found that I had spent more years in verse-writing than at prose-writing! (prose 25½ yrs—verse 26 yrs) Yet my verses will always be considered a bye-product, I suppose, owing to this odd accident of the printing press.

We have been reading the Life of Keats, & found it very saddening. It seems to be an honest & thorough book, but Colvin has not the knack of lighting up his subject I fear. I hope you & your household are not caused shocks & shudders by the week end visits you get overhead.

Always yours
Thomas Hardy.

Text MS. (with envelope) BL.
near here: as first pub. in *Poems of the Past and the Present* (1902), the poem opened with the line 'By Mellstock Lodge and Avenue'—an apparent reference to Stinsford House which was omitted from later edns. *see for yourself*: Gosse replied 21 Feb 18 (DCM; pub. in Evan Charteris, *The Life and Letters of Sir Edmund Gosse*, London, 1931, 421–2) that he had himself 'spotted' the influence on TH 'of Wordsworth's first preface'. *as the Prayer Book puts it*: an adaptation of a passage ('relieve them, according to their several necessities') from 'A Collect or Prayer for all Conditions of Men, to be used at such times when the Litany is not appointed to be said'. *my verses*: TH wrote 'my my verses'. *Life of Keats*: see letter of 2 Feb 18 to Douglas; Gosse in his reply called it 'a Blue Book about Keats'. *week end visits*: i.e., German air raids.

To MAURICE MACMILLAN

MAX GATE, | DORCHESTER. | 19th. February 1918.

Dear Mr Macmillan:

I think in respect of the application of the British Actors' Film Company that it will be just as well to arrange with them for the cinema rights in Great Britain of "Jude the Obscure". Please therefore act as best you can.—It is certainly an advantage to have the film prepared in England instead of having American accessories, as in "Tess of the d'Urbervilles".

It is possible that your correspondent on behalf of the Company is the person who wrote asking me to tell him the real names of places, &c,—in that novel, and whom I informed that when an agreement had been entered into through yourselves it would be soon enough to go into details of that kind.

Yours sincerely,
Thomas Hardy.

Text MS. (typewritten) BL.
Film Company: founded in 1915 by a group of actors including A. E. Matthews, Owen Nares, and Godfrey Tearle; it used the studio at Bushey established by Hubert von Herkomer (see letter of 30 May 15 to Sir Frederick Macmillan). *the Obscure*": no such film appears to have been made. *d'Urbervilles*": made by the Famous Players Film Company; see IV.265. *your correspondent*: Simon Wimborne, whose visiting card (annotated 'British Actors' Film Company') still accompanies this letter; TH had written to him, in the terms here summarized, 18 Feb 18 (draft, DCM).

To EDMUND GOSSE

Max Gate | 23: 2: 1918

My dear Gosse:

To save you further trouble I am sending a bundle of proofs of the verse part of the Wessex Edition: also the General Preface, so that you need not try for the volumes. I don't quite understand their being out of print, & will inquire about that. (It is, of course Macmillan's edition, not the old Harper one)

Beyond these proofs there are only 2 volumes to make up the lot—"Satires of C." & "Moments of V."—both of which I think you have.

I am ashamed to ask you to return the proofs, if not too much trouble. Down here we are so far away from printers, &c, that I have to keep lumber of that sort.

The selections were made on no very distinct principle excepting that, as few could be printed, those which would be acceptable to the "General Reader" were preferred. One poem by the way—the "Lyonnesse" one—is improved in the Selection (q.v.)

Believe me always yrs
Thomas Hardy.

Text MS. Adams; envelope Leeds.
out of print: as Gosse had reported 21 Feb 18 (see letter of 18 Feb 18). *the old Harper one)*: i.e., the 'Wessex Novels' edn. first pub. 1895–6; see Purdy, 280–1. *The selections*: Gosse had said in his 21 Feb 18 letter that the *Selected Poems of Thomas Hardy*, sent by TH 28 Jan 18, omitted many of his favourite poems; he added that he did not understand its principle of selection. *improved in the Selection*: TH's 'When I Set Out for Lyonnesse', first pub. in *Satires of Circumstance* (1914), was included in *Selected Poems* with a heavily revised final stanza.

To SIR FREDERICK MACMILLAN

MAX GATE, | DORCHESTER. | 27th. February 1918.

Dear Sir Frederick Macmillan:

I have received the two letters I enclose, which seem to refer to the same American Company. I do not know whether it would be well to treat with either of the writers for one of the novels not already appropriated, or to wait till the Company itself writes, if it should. I have often heard of Miss Elizabeth Marbury, but have never had any business with her. Perhaps of the two hers is the more solid agency, and the lease of rights that she suggests would leave us more in control than an out and out sale of them. But you will probably know something of the agencies and be able to decide what, if anything, should be done.

Yours very truly,
Thomas Hardy.

Text MS. (typewritten) BL.
two letters I enclose: one of them still accompanies this letter; written 23 Feb 18 from the London office of Miss Elisabeth Marbury's agency (see III.273), it expresses the interest of 'a leading American cinema company' in acquiring film rights to all novels and stories by TH 'that have not already been adapted for the cinema'.

To THE ROYAL SOCIETY OF LITERATURE

Feb. 27: 1918.

Subscription for 1918 enclosed herewith, from

Mr Thomas Hardy
Max Gate
Dorchester.

Text MS. Royal Society of Literature.

To SYDNEY COCKERELL

Max Gate | Thursday [28 February 1918]

My dear Cockerell

I am sending you what is probably as small in value as it is in bulk, but which you may like to possess, as you have the MS. of the story. About half a dozen copies were printed in New York in 1893 for copyright purposes merely, & the one I enclose is probably the only one in existence except a similar copy my wife has.

I hope you are well. I saw a brief report of Q's lecture in the Cambridge Magazine.

Sincerely yours
Th: Hardy.

Text MS. (with envelope) Harvard. *Date* From postmark.
MS. of the story: TH had earlier given Cockerell the MS. of his story 'The Three Strangers' and was now sending a copy of the 1893 Harper & Brothers edn. of the dramatized version, *The Three Wayfarers*. *Q's lecture*: Sir Arthur Quiller-Couch's lecture, 'The Poetry of Thomas Hardy', summarized in the *Cambridge Magazine*, [23] Feb 1918.

To EDMUND GOSSE

Max Gate | Sunday [3 March 1918]

My dear Gosse:

Your letter is most interesting, & I don't pretend to be able to answer it right off. All I am doing now is sending you the enclosed, which has been forwarded from Cambridge.

Always yrs
Th: H.

Text MS. (with envelope) Leeds. *Date* From postmark.
Your letter: of 2 Mar 18 (DCM). *answer it right off*: TH was perhaps annoyed by Gosse's having taken him severely to task for so strenuously objecting to the label of 'pessimist'; see letter of 4 Mar 18. *from Cambridge*: presumably the report of the Quiller-Couch lecture; see letter of 28 Feb 18.

To ARTHUR MACHEN

March 3. 1918

Dear Mr Machen:

I am much obliged to you & your editor Mr Turner for thinking of me in respect of the scheme for publishing Reminiscences in so widely circulated & influential a paper as The Evening News.

But I am sorry to answer that I have considered the matter on previous occasions when the idea has been mooted to me, & have decided that I should not like to write any account of myself for publication. I need not trouble you with reasons, & am, with thanks for the opportunity

Yours truly

Text MS. (pencil draft) DCM.
Machen: Arthur Machen, journalist and author; see IV.194. *Mr Turner*: Alfred Turner (1874–1922), acting editor of the London *Evening News* 1911–21; Machen (26 Feb 18, DCM) said that Turner had asked him to invite TH to contribute his reminiscences to the paper.

To SIR FREDERICK MACMILLAN

MAX GATE, | DORCHESTER. | 3rd March 1918.

Dear Sir Frederick Macmillan:

I am obliged by your suggestion that you will see Miss Elizabeth Marbury's representative, and shall be glad if you will do so.

I could not remember which of the novels were still available. Of these the question is whether to try her with all of them in a lump or to experiment with, say three of them. Perhaps you will consider this, and do as you think best.

A royalty, with the prepayments you mention, is a good plan, if one can get honest returns. One of Cassell's firm, whose friends live near here, called here last summer and spoke to me on that very subject. He said that in respect of their books they had a great difficulty in knowing what the receipts by the cinema companies were, and were trying the plan of a round sum for any particular novel. This, however, may not be easy in our case, and I mention it for what it may be worth. Miss Marbury perhaps has a way of ascertaining receipts.

I suppose there would be no reason for saying anything to her representative about The Dynasts. It would be too big a thing, I fear, for any company to undertake. You will remember that Mr Drinkwater was full of a scheme for doing it, and came to you about it I believe, but went no further so far as I know.

If, then, you don't mind, I will leave you to proceed in the matter.

Yours very truly,
Thomas Hardy.

Text MS. (typewritten) BL.
Marbury's representative: see letter to Macmillan of 27 Feb 18. *One of Cassell's firm*:

Newman Flower; see letter of 2 Apr 14. *so far as I know*: TH had in fact discouraged A. E. Drinkwater from pursuing the idea; see letter of 6 Nov 15.

To EDMUND GOSSE

MAX GATE, | DORCHESTER. | 4: 4: 1918 [4 March 1918]

On looking at the sentence you referred to, the error seems to be that "characteristic" is used for "consideration" i.e.

—"there is a higher *consideration* in philosophy than whether it be pessm or meliorm" &c &c.

Careless writing—very. But the contents are after all of more importance than the preface.

Th: H.

Text MS. (postcard) Leeds. *Date* Corrected from postmark; another slip, '1908' for '1918', was corrected by TH himself.
the sentence: from TH's General Preface to the Wessex edn., *Tess of the d'Urbervilles* (London, 1912), xii; it reads, 'It must be obvious that there is a higher characteristic of philosophy than pessimism, or than meliorism, or even than the optimism of these critics—which is truth'. *referred to*: in his letter of 2 Mar 18 (see letter to Gosse of 3 Mar 18) Gosse had argued that TH's sentence confused 'two classes of ideas', one philosophical, the other merely temperamental or attitudinal. *Careless writing*: TH seems never to have revised the printed text of the General Preface, however.

To JOHN DRINKWATER

MAX GATE, | DORCHESTER. | 5th. March 1917 [1918].

Dear Mr Drinkwater:

(Please pardon my being compelled to dictate my letters nowadays). I am much obliged to you for writing and sending your very generous review of Moments of Vision in the Manchester Guardian—a newspaper I highly value. You make me feel that, after all, it was worth while to bring out the poems, a point on which I had considerable doubt this time last year.

As to their comparative value, i.e., the comparative value of those in this volume, it is one of those questions on which a writer's own opinion is worthless, and I think I have discovered the reason to be that he judges from his affection for the incident or feeling that gave rise to the poem, while the reviewer judges, as he cannot help doing, from the presentation of it to him in the pages of the book.

If you come to Dorchester and will let us know we will be indoors any afternoon, with pleasure.

Believe me

Yours sincerely,
Thomas Hardy.

Text MS. (typewritten) Yale. *Date* Corrected on basis of internal evidence.
Guardian: 'Mr. Hardy's New Poems', *Manchester Guardian*, 1 Mar 1918. *let us know*: Drinkwater wrote 14 Mar 18 (DCM) to say that he hoped to call on 24 March.

To JOHN SYMONS JEUNE

FROM THO. HARDY, | MAX GATE, | DORCHESTER. | Tuesday eveng.
[19 March 1918]

Hope I made it clear that I would sign any volumes of poetry, particularly "Moments of Vision", for the Fund; but prefer not to sign prose, wh. was written more than 20 years ago—

Text MS. (postcard) Eton College. *Date* From postmark.
the Fund: see letter to Jeune of 25 Apr 18.

To SAMUEL CHEW

(Ansr) March 21. 1918

Dear Sir

I reply for Mr Hardy to your inquiries, he being compelled to do much of his correspondence by deputy nowadays.

He has no objection to your quoting from his prose works such passages as may be reasonable for illustrating your criticisms & comments. And from his verse, for the same purpose, two or three short poems entire, such as those you name, with fragments if necessary from other poems. It is to be understood that the recent edition of his collected works in prose & verse, containing the General Preface to novels & poems, & published by Messrs Harper (about 1912–3) is to be used for quoting from (except for Satires of Circumstance & Moments of Vision which are not yet included in that edition).

You are also at liberty to quote scattered passages from his poetry in your proposed History of English Poetry from the time of Arnold. I am, Dear Sir,

Yours truly
for Th. Hardy
F.E.H.

Text MS. (pencil draft) DCM.
reply: to Chew's letter of 28 Feb 18 (DCM). *your criticisms*: see letter to Chew of 9 Feb 18. *those you name*: 'Let Me Enjoy', 'The Darkling Thrush', and 'To Meet, or Otherwise'. *the recent edition*: TH first wrote 'the definitive edition'. *of English Poetry*: Chew seems never to have completed this project.

To SIR FREDERICK MACMILLAN

MAX GATE, | DORCHESTER. | March 24. 1918.

Dear Sir Frederick Macmillan:

Certainly let M. Mourey translate "Moments of Vision" into French. I leave it to you to judge whether to charge him a royalty of ten per cent on all copies sold, remembering that our chief advantage from his publication would be that his readers might buy the original. But if you think this condition would not deter him I quite agree to what you suggest.

By the way, I do not know if you have had occasion to reprint the book as yet, but if not, I will add to that list of corrections I sent up two or three more words, which I overlooked,

Yours very truly,
Thomas Hardy.

Text MS. (typewritten) BL.
M. Mourey: Gabriel Mourey (1865–1943), French art critic and historian; he had rendered Swinburne's *Poems and Ballads* into French prose in 1891 but seems not, in fact, to have translated *Moments of Vision*. *what you suggest*: Macmillan (22 Mar 18, Macmillan letterbooks, BL) had proposed a royalty of 10% on all copies sold.

To J.H. MORGAN

FROM THO. HARDY, | MAX GATE, | DORCHESTER. | April 12. 1918

Book received. Will read same. Best thanks.

Text MS. (postcard) T. Trafton.
Book: presumably *Gentlemen at Arms* (London, 1918), a volume of military sketches pub. by Morgan under the pseudonym 'Centurion'.

To EDMUND GOSSE

MAX GATE, | DORCHESTER. | April 16: 1918

My dear Gosse:

What can I say about this you send me? I have been reading it as if it were concerning a writer altogether unknown to me, & forming an image of him. I won't say what the image is like!

You don't need my telling you that it is really kind of you to take the trouble to think out such an essay. Such a troublesome business as it must be to pull together into one perspective a scattered lot of productions that may be viewed in so many lights. How you have got to know some of the things I cannot divine.

As to your own style, if a person who is no critic may be allowed to make a remark upon it, it has of late years gained considerably in solidity & dignity. I have thought this for some time, & on reading the present article—so closely packed with thought & observation—I am confirmed in my opinion. I think it unusual in a person who calls himself "an old man", for we mostly get very hide-bound.

Not knowing at all what you were going to say (except in so far as I could gather from the few dates you asked me for) the article came upon me with much freshness. By the way, the little group of what you call "searchlight" satires, first published in 1911 in the Fortnightly, cost me much sadness in having to reprint them in the volume in 1915. The scales had not fallen from my eyes when I wrote them, & when I reprinted them they had. But they had been largely imitated in America, & in such cases one is almost bound to re-assert ones self not to be charged with plagiarism from one's own imitators. Unfortunately I forgot to attach to them their original date.

I am rather puzzled by "audible intricacy", though I guess what it must mean.

Believe me, most sincerely yrs
Thomas Hardy.

Text MS. Adams.
this you send me: Gosse's *Edinburgh Review* (April 1918) essay on TH's verse; see letter of 28 Jan 18. *"searchlight" satires*: 11 of the 15 'Satires of Circumstance' which gave their name to TH's vol. of 1914 (not 1915) had previously appeared in the *Fortnightly Review*, April 1911; Gosse referred to them in his essay as 'hard and cruel shafts of searchlight' and suggested that TH was 'passing through a mental crisis' at the time he wrote them. *"audible intricacy"*: according to Gosse, TH was 'negligent of that eternal ornament of English verse, audible intricacy, probably because of Swinburne's abuse of it'; he retained the phrase when collecting the essay in his *Some Diversions of a Man of Letters* (London, 1919).

To EDMUND GOSSE

FROM THO. HARDY, | MAX GATE, | DORCHESTER. | April 25. [1918]

Have just received copy of your Swne from J.F.J. How very good of you to give photograph. First I have ever had!

Text MS. (postcard) Leeds. *Date* From postmark.
your Swne: Gosse's *The Life of Algernon Charles Swinburne*; see letter of 26 Apr 17. *J.F.J.*: J. F. Symons Jeune. *photograph*: see letter of 25 Apr 18 to Jeune.

To JOHN SYMONS JEUNE

MAX GATE, | DORCHESTER. | 25: 4: 1918

My dear Mr Jeune:

The book has come this morning, with the photograph in it. How clever of you to get it out of Gosse. Really you ought not to have taken the trouble to have the book bound in these days.

The inscription from Catullus is happy. I shall certainly accept & read the "cogitationes", whether Poet Caecilius did or did not.

I am much obliged to that shopman at Sotheran's for his good opinion.

Always yours truly
Thomas Hardy.

Text MS. (with envelope) Eton College.
the book: see letter of 25 Apr 18 to Gosse. *out of Gosse*: Jeune (22 Apr 18, DCM) expressed confidence that the signed photograph he had obtained from Gosse would 'give value to the book' in TH's eyes; it was apparently bound in facing the title-page. *from Catullus*: Jeune, an authority on Catullus, had quoted from the opening of Carmen 35, which invites a fellow poet named Caecilius to come to Verona and includes the lines 'nam quasdam nolo cogitationes / amici accipiat sui meique'. *his good opinion*: Jeune, thanking TH for inscribing books 'for the War Workers sale', remarked that at Sotheran's, the London booksellers, he had been assured that their value would be considerably enhanced, especially

since '"There is very little of Thomas Hardy's stuff about—he's never made himself cheap, he don't advertise"'.

To SIR GEORGE DOUGLAS

MAX GATE, | DORCHESTER. | May 4: 1918

My dear Douglas:

I saw in the papers the announcement of the loss of your mother, for which I am very sorry.

Her age was just the age of my own mother at her death, & I can say from experience that, in spite of people of 90 belonging more to past times than to the present, you will miss her much. I had not seen her for a number of years, as you are aware. I think the last time was during that London season when you had a house in Thurloe Square.

I have not been to London lately, & am not going, so far as I know, till the tide of things turns a little, so that one may know better what to think & do.

I hope you keep well: also your brother & sister, to whom please remember me.

Sincerely yours
Thomas Hardy.

Text MS. NLS.
of your mother: Lady Scott-Douglas (*née* de Piña) died 26 Apr 1918, aged 90. *your brother*: see letter to Douglas of 2 Feb 18. *& sister*: Mary; see III.82.

To SIR FREDERICK MACMILLAN

MAX GATE, | DORCHESTER. | May 18. 1918.

Dear Sir Frederick Macmillan:

I have received from Mr Slater (the Messrs Harpers' London manager) the letter on "Tess" Cinema rights which I enclose. Our agreement with the Famous Players for English rights (dated about Sept. 4. 1913) has been running simultaneously I suppose with that of Messrs Harper with the same film company for America, though I do not know if ours also was for five years like theirs, having no copy of the agreement. As you will see the company wish to renew their American agreement (a sign that the film pays well), and also to include England; and I am puzzled as to why they seem to be unaware of how the English rights stand, since the contract was with themselves, and why they did not apply to you for renewal.

Having arranged the previous contract you will probably know all about this, and will perhaps as my agents be able to settle the whole matter with Messrs Harper—either through Mr Slater, or in any other way. As to what commission they should have I leave you to judge. And if you find the matter troublesome I beg that you will increase your own commission in this case.

Yours very truly,
Thomas Hardy.

P.S. The references to the Stoddard play have nothing to do with the cinema rights, and concern the acting rights only. T.H.

Text MS. (typewritten) BL.
Mr Slater: see letter of 30 Aug 16; his letter of 17 May 18 still accompanies this letter. *Our agreement*: see IV.302. *As you will see*: Slater's letter quoted a letter from Harper & Brothers' New York office describing the negotiations that had taken place. *(a sign . . . well)*: added in TH's hand. *what commission*: Harper & Brothers had asked, through Slater, for a 20% commission. *the Stoddard play*: the letter quoted by Slater mentioned that the Vitagraph Company claimed film rights in *Tess* on the basis of their purchase of the rights formerly held by the now-bankrupt Harrison Grey Fiske in the dramatic version prepared by Lorimer Stoddard; see II.110–12 and Purdy, 77–8.

To RENDEL HARRIS

(Copy) Max Gate, May 20. 1918

Dear Mr Harris,

Your letter on the proposals you are bringing forward, in conjunction with Lord Bryce & Professor Gilbert Murray, for an Anglo-American University at Plymouth is of much interest to me, both for general reasons & from having had a domestic connection with the town for many years.

It appears to me that if the scheme as outlined could be carried out, the results would be far-reaching & admirable. And as to situation, the large population of Plymouth, the close relation of that port with American history, & the beauty of the town & neighbourhood, point to it as an ideal site for such a University. Curiously enough I was quite lately standing on the stone at the Barbican that marks the spot whence the Pilgrim Fathers embarked.

I quite understand that it would offer no rivalry to the proposed English University at Exeter & the Southampton University College.

The idea being but in embryo, as I gather, I am unable to offer any criticisms as you suggest, which would depend largely on details. However If any remarks upon the proposal should occur to me I will send them. Meanwhile I can only express my hope that the idea may mature.

Very truly yours
(signed) Th—— H——

Rendel Harris Esq. | 54 Wood Road | Whalley Range | Manchester

Text MS. (pencil draft) DCM.
Harris: James Rendel Harris (1852–1941), biblical scholar and orientalist, recently appointed curator of eastern manuscripts in the John Rylands Library, Manchester; *D.N.B.* *Your letter*: of 15 May 18 (DCM). *Murray*: see letter of 14 Oct 19 to him. *at Plymouth*: where Harris was born and brought up. *quite lately*: the previous October; see letter of 21 Oct 17. *However If*: the sentence originally began with 'If'. *may mature*: it did not in fact materialize.

To HALL CAINE

May 21. 1918.

Dear Mr H.C.

The scheme of a Natl Ca Film that you have arranged & superintd has every aspect of being a highly worthy one, & wins my best wishes for its success in promoting the ideals that we are fighting for. I am glad to hear that it is in so advanced a state & that the scenario is finished. My first knowlge of such an undertaking is derived from the letter recd from you yesterday. As to my collaborating in the final arrangts I much regret to say that I am prevented by physical reasons from doing so—a matter of really very little importance at such a late moment in the production of the exhibition. Owing to my being practically unable to be in London I find that what little I can do—a very little!—towards keeping up the national spirit I can do better independently when my energies happen to serve. Believe me, with renewed hopes for the effectiveness of the scheme,

Yours truly
Th: H.

Text MS. (pencil draft) DCM.
Natl Ca Film: Caine wrote (18 May 18, DCM) to seek TH's collaboration in the production of 'a national cinema film' expressive of 'the ideals for which we are fighting'. *scenario is finished*: Caine himself wrote the scenario of *Victory and Peace*, a 1918 production of the National War Aims Committee; it was apparently completed but never shown publicly.

To HALL CAINE

May 23. 1918

Dear Mr Hall Caine,

I am flattered by your feeling that some poem of mine might help in the cause, & you have my permission to choose such a piece. I imagine that one of the series of War Poems is what you would desire.

To save you trouble in hunting them up I send copies of two—"Men who march away", and "Then & Now"—which you may think suitable; though I am not sure.

Yours very truly
T. . . H. . .

[Copies enclosed]

Text MS. (pencil draft) DCM.
help in the cause: in pursuance of the scheme mentioned in the letter of 21 May 18, Caine wrote to TH (22 May 18, DCM) to ask for a poem 'suitable for setting to music by one of our best composers'. [*Copies enclosed*]: TH's square brackets.

To SIR FREDERICK MACMILLAN

MAX GATE, | DORCHESTER. | May 25: 1918

Dear Sir Frederick Macmillan:

Your proposal in your letter of the 23rd. seems a good one, and I therefore authorize you to act for me in the matter of the cinema production of "Tess of the d'Urbervilles" for another five years; in doing which you will as you say (unless you change your opinion) confer with Mr Slater, the Harper's London manager, and tell him that if they will make the arrangements for the usual commission of ten per cent, they can have the agency for both England and America, twenty per cent seeming excessive.

If they refuse the terms I should not object to let them arrange for America as last time on a fifteen per cent commission in order to avoid the inconvenience of beginning with a new agent, the agency for England remaining in your hands as before.

However all the above are suggestions only, as I wish to leave you free to act as you deem best.

If the Harpers are unreasonable it would of course be open to you to be my agent in the business for the whole world, instead of introducing a fresh agent. But probably they will not be; though I do not forget that at the beginning of the film negociations their New York director, Mr Duneka, proposed to take a half of whatever they could get from the company.

Yours very truly,
Thomas Hardy.

Text MS. (typewritten) BL.
Your proposal: evidently as summarized by TH in this first paragraph; Macmillan's letter 'of the 23rd.' has not been found. *seeming excessive*: see letter of 18 May 18. *take a half*: see IV.265.

To EDWARD CLODD

MAX GATE, | DORCHESTER. | Sunday. [2 June 1918]

My dear Clodd:

Many warm thanks to you & Mrs Clodd for good wishes.

As matters look at present one may fear that the world will see many more war-anniversaries than I shall see birthdays. I ought to be able to prophesy that this year will see the end of the strife, but I confess I have no ground for venturing such a prophesy, so I won't.

Yrs sincerely
Th: Hardy.

Text MS. (correspondence card) Leeds. *Date* Supplied by Clodd.
good wishes: on TH's 78th birthday, 2 June 1918. *I won't*: TH seems to have written 'I'won't'.

To EDWARD AND EMMA DUGDALE

Max Gate. | Sunday. [2 June 1918]

My best thanks for good wishes.

Sincerely yrs
Th. H.

Text MS. (postcard) Purdy. *Date* From postmark.

To EDMUND GOSSE

MAX GATE, | DORCHESTER. | June 3: 1918

My dear Gosse:

Sincere thanks for your kind remembrances of me yesterday, which kept us mental company, though we were physically alone except for one visitor who came out from the hotel uninvited. Our flowing bowl was cider, which is as far as we go toward alcohol nowadays.

Kindest regards from us to Mrs Gosse.

Always yours
Thomas Hardy.

Text MS. (with envelope) Leeds.
one visitor: Clement Shorter, as FEH reported to Cockerell 11 June 18 (Purdy).

To FLORENCE HENNIKER

MAX GATE, | DORCHESTER. | June 5: 1918

My dear friend:

It was so sweet of you to let me know of your good wishes, & it affords me an excuse for writing. I don't know how you stand this weather in London, but it must be trying, as you probably don't get the breeze we get here, except when we sit in the shelter of our trees, & then the sun is scorching.

I was thinking of you Saturday for another reason than your telegram. We were dining in the large room of the King's Arms here, & I remembered that the last time I was in it was when you came to Dorchester to see one of the performances of the local society. I wonder if you will ever come again.

I had an interesting letter from Mrs John Fortescue. I wonder if you know her, or him—the Librarian at Windsor Castle. Theirs is an extraordinarily happy marriage, & my poor Emma's last garden-party was the means of bringing it about. They met at it for the first time, as total strangers, & she says we were those who helped her to realize her ideal & make all her dreams come true. I wish Emma could know it. She & her husband have been staying at Melbury. Lady Ilchester & her mother came here to tea last week, & Birdie said she would so much like to have you at Melbury if you would come. If you were to go there I could get them to show you the house from which the two sisters of my maternal ancestor ran by the back staircase when pursued up the front stairs by the Kings soldiery in the Monmouth Rebellion.

Mr Gosse was kind enough to review my poetry in the last number of the Edinburgh Review. If you cannot lay hands on it & would like to read it I can lend it to you at any time.

To-morrow I have the tedious duty to perform of adjudicating on food profiteers. How I come in for the job is owing to the difficulty of getting magistrates who are absolutely detached from & uninfluenced by local interests.

Always yrs affectly
Th: H.

Florence sends love, & will be so glad to hear from you. Th: H.

Text MS. DCM.
came to Dorchester: in November 1911; see *LY*, 150. *come again*: she stayed in Dorchester for a week in the summer of 1922. *Fortescue*: Winifred Fortescue (*née* Beech), in her 1 June 18 (DCM) congratulatory letter to TH on his birthday, recalled that she had first met her husband, John Fortescue, the military historian (see IV.108), at a Max Gate garden party; she recounts the incident in '*There's Rosemary .... There's Rue*' (London, 1939), 111–12. *Birdie*: Lady Ilchester's nickname. *the house*: Townsend, Melbury Osmond; see *EL*, 7, and Millgate, 9n. *on food profiteers*: TH, serving as a Justice of the Peace at a special sitting of the Dorchester Borough Magistrates on 6 June 1918, found a local licensee (and magistrate) guilty of selling whisky for more than the controlled price.

To ALFRED POPE

MAX GATE, | DORCHESTER. | June 5: 1918

Dear Mr Pope:

I send a brief line to thank you & Mrs Pope for good wishes, & to express a hope in response that you will continue to be as robust as you usually appear to be when I see you. I believe that this week you have the pleasure of removing from the rather hot atmosphere of the town to the cooler airs of Wrackleford.

Yours sincerely
Th: Hardy.

Text MS. (with envelope) Thomas Hardy Society.
Wrackleford: the home of the Pope family, about 2½ miles NW of Dorchester.

To W.M. STONE

June 10: 1918

Dear Sir,

You have my permission to print "The Woodlanders" & "The Return of the Native" in Braille type for the use of the Blind, & I hope the books may be of interest to them.

Yrs truly
T.H.

Text MS. (pencil draft) DCM.
Stone: headmaster of the Royal Blind School, Edinburgh, until he retired in 1933 upon reaching the age of 70; he wrote TH 3 June 18 (DCM). Though apparently trivial, this letter was at one time intended to appear in *LY*; see *The Personal Notebooks of Thomas Hardy*, ed. Richard H. Taylor (London, 1978), 269. *the Native*": both titles are listed in the 1919 report of the Royal Blind School and Asylum as having been printed during that year.

To LADY HOARE

MAX GATE, | DORCHESTER. | Tuesday: June 11. [1918]

My dear friend:

I must write & thank you for the quaint & attractive birthday presents. I remember candlesnuffing in my boyhood, & these snuffers recall those long-gone times.

Florence says she is going to fix the knocker on my study door. I am sure she will scorn to use it, but burst in as unceremoniously as usual. Best remembrances to Sir Henry, & believe me

Always yours,
Thomas Hardy.

Text MS. Wiltshire Record Office. *Date* Year supplied by Lady Hoare.

To J. S. UDAL

MAX GATE, | DORCHESTER. | June 16. 1918.

My dear Udal:

Forgive my not writing sooner to thank you for your kind wishes on my birthday. I do not remember for the moment how far you are on the same road, or when your own birthday occurs, so will make sure of giving you my best wishes thereon by expressing them now, and hopes for its frequent happy return.

I have never seen the MS. you speak of since it left my hands 45 years ago and am glad that it has turned out useful after lying hid for so long.

I certainly did not know that you were an "ardent Dorset Carolean"—

why don't you support some more worthy historic character connected with the county.

Yours sincerely,
Th: Hardy.

P.S. The poet Crowe for instance, who lived at or near Symondsbury, and wrote about Lewesdon and Pilsdon.

Text MS. (typewritten, with envelope in FEH's hand) Adams.
the MS.: of *Far from the Madding Crowd*; see letter of 23 Jan 18. *Dorset Carolean*": i.e., admirer of King Charles II, who was a fugitive in Dorset for three weeks following the battle of Worcester (1651). *the poet Crowe*: William Crowe (1745–1829), poet and divine; *D.N.B.*

To FREDERIC HARRISON

Max Gate | 20 June 1918

My dear Harrison:

I have been looking for evidence of hanging in chains since you wrote, & have almost concluded that your clerical friend is right in saying, as I understand he does, that it had disappeared by 1831—indeed I am inclined to think that it did not long survive the 18th Century. There were, of course, great cruelties down to 1831, but gibbets were gone: & these were not physical cruelty, as the bodies were placed on them after hanging, I believe. My grandmother told me that when she was a girl—1785 to 1790—she used to pass a gibbet in Berkshire with great terror: & the stump of a gibbet was standing near Wincanton down to 1840 or so.

Evidence of ordinary hanging(!) before 1831, too, is not wanting. My father in 1829 saw a soldier hanged over the gaol entrance here, & he was buried in the precincts where they are buried now.

Other cruelties, as I say, were still going on. Culprits were whipped in the market place continually: here it was done on Saturdays, in a farmer's waggon by the town-pump. My mother when a girl saw a child whipped at the cart-tail round Yeovil for stealing a book from a stall. Also:

"Alice C. who was tried & convicted for stealing money from her fellow-chambermaid at the King's Arms [Dorchester], & on whom judgment of death was recorded, was removed from our jail . . . on board the ——, her sentence having been commuted to transportation for life." *Dorset Chronicle* July 2. 1829.

"Burglars' execution. . . . After hanging the usual time the bodies were taken into Newgate, & will be delivered to their friends this evening." ib. Oct 22: 1829

"The gibbet . . . presents an extraordinary sight, upon which Thos Otter was hanged in chains for the murder of his wife 5 years ago . . . Under the jawbone of the skeleton a small bird has built her nest. . . ." Morning Chronicle June 4: 1811.

The last mentioned is the latest I can find of actual hanging in chains.

I must be getting rusty, I suppose, for I think we have *retrograded* in civilization since those times: such isolated cruelties were, after all, not so fiendish as the cold scientific slaughter of hundreds of thousands that we see going on now.

Hyndman the socialist was here yesterday. He takes a gloomy view of the future conduct of the masses, as they are called. He thinks they will never go back to their former docility, & that if something be not organized there will be anarchy. He is a most amiable man: I had never met him before.

Always sincerely
Thomas Hardy.

Text MS. Taylor.
disappeared by 1831: Harrison wrote 16 June 18 (DCM) to say that his recent reading of *Wessex Tales*, containing two episodes of capital punishment, had induced him to consult TH on the question of whether hanging in chains was still practised during Harrison's infancy in the 1830s or whether (as a clergyman friend had insisted) it ended, along with other judicial excesses, in 1831. *My grandmother*: i.e., Mary Hardy (*née* Head), his father's mother. [*Dorchester*]: TH's square brackets. *the latest I can find*: TH copied out all three examples from his 'Facts' notebook (DCM). *Hyndman*: Henry Mayers Hyndman (1842–1921), socialist leader and publicist; *D.N.B.* *most amiable man*: TH did not always speak so highly of Hyndman, though he very much liked Hyndman's second wife Rosalind, *née* Travers (d. 1923), who wrote verse; for their visit to Max Gate, see *LY*, 187.

To ALFRED POPE

MAX GATE, | DORCHESTER. | 25th. June 1918.

Dear Mr Pope:

Herewith I enclose the "Foreword" that we talked of, which I hope will suit the contents of the book. If there should be anything discordant please let me know and I can easily alter it.

I will look over the proofs if you wish me to see them.

Yours very truly,
Th: Hardy.

Text MS. (typewritten) Christopher Pope.
the "Foreword": to the privately printed *A Book of Remembrance, Being a Short Summary of the Service and Sacrifice Rendered to the Empire During the Great War by One of the Many Patriotic Families of Wessex, the Popes of Wrackleford, Co. Dorset* (London, 1919); the printed text of the Foreword is dated 'September 1918'. See letter to Pope of 28 May 15.

To SIR ROBERT PEARCE EDGCUMBE

Max Gate | July 6: 1918

My dear Edgcumbe:

I must thank the unknown young lady you bring to my notice for being the means of my getting this letter from you. Whenever she likes to call she will be welcome. I have not yet come to any conclusion about her poetry, being a slow critic as well as a very unsafe one, but I will read her book, for which I am much obliged to you.

I am glad to hear that your sons are so active. May they be spared all contingencies. The war has brought death into my family but remotely: still it has brought it, a cousin being killed at Gallipoli. And it seems to me that we are no nearer the end than we were nearly 4 years ago. Mrs Sheridan was a great loss. She used to drive over here a good deal, & at her last visit spoke to my wife in a manner & on subjects implying we might never see her again. You would find Dorchester externally much as it was, but considerably changed mentally—perhaps because strangers have settled in & near it. Up to the war it was becoming quite suburban, people from London calling on us at all sorts of hours in their cars, but this has naturally ceased now. It is pathetic enough to see on the shutters of some of the one-man shops: "Closed till the end of the war".

Your letter was almost met here by one from Charles Moule, whom you will remember. He still keeps up his interest in literature.

We do not often—in fact never—go so far West as Newquay, though I know the air of that coast very well, & have said a good deal about it first & last in prose & rhyme. But last autumn we were in Plymouth, & some summers back at Boscastle, where I went to see if a tablet in S. Juliot church, 1½ mile up the valley from that place, to the memory of my late wife, had been put up properly.

I am, with best remembrances,

Always yrs sincerely
Thomas Hardy.

I should think your son must find it congenial to be working with R. Cecil. The last time I saw him was at a country-house week-end up to his elbows in papers. Th: H.

Text MS. Texas.
Edgcumbe: Sir Robert Pearce Edgcumbe, former Dorchester banker, farmer, and politician; see I.180 and II.66. *unknown young lady*: May O'Rourke (1897–1978), poet. She subsequently acted as an occasional secretary to TH and FEH at Max Gate; see her *Thomas Hardy: His Secretary Remembers* (Beaminster, Dorset, 1965). *bring to my notice*: Edgcumbe (3 July 18, DCM) expressed the hope that TH would encourage Miss O'Rourke in her ambition to be a poet, adding that she was currently living at the old Fordington Vicarage (the former home of the Moule family) and 'worships you afar off'. *her book*: *West Wind Days* (London, 1918). *so active*: Edgcumbe reported that one of his three sons was in the navy, another in the army, and another at the Foreign Office. *Mrs Sheridan*: she had died in January 1918; see *LY*, 183. *never see her again*: FEH described this last visit in a letter to Rebekah Owen, [14 Jan 18?] (Colby). *Charles Moule*: Charles Walter Moule, younger brother of TH's friend Horace Moule, currently president of Corpus Christi College, Cambridge; see I.84. He wrote to TH 4 July 18 (DCM). *Newquay*: where Edgcumbe had been living for some years. *R. Cecil*: Lord Robert Cecil (1864–1958), third son of the Marquess of Salisbury, currently Under-Secretary of State for Foreign Affairs and Minister of Blockade; *D.N.B.*

To SIEGFRIED SASSOON

MAX GATE, | DORCHESTER. | July 8: 1918

Dear Mr Sassoon:

I am discharging this arrow at a venture into space & time, hoping it will reach you somehow, to thank you for this last little volume of your poems, "Counter Attack", of which I have read some, but not all. One cannot read poetry straight off—at least I cannot—so I look into them now & then. I like the title pieces, & "To any dead officer", so far, best.

I trust you are keeping as well as can be expected, & will have a long & safe-time in the future for carrying on your art.

Very truly yours
Th: Hardy.

Text MS. Eton College.
Attack": Sassoon's *Counter-Attack and Other Poems* (London, 1918). *title pieces*: TH appears to be linking the opening poem, 'Prelude: The Troops', with the second, 'Counter-Attack' itself.

To DOROTHY ALLHUSEN

MAX GATE, | DORCHESTER. | July 10: 1918

My dear Dorothy:

I am delighted to have the nice copy of Gray, which has better type than mine, an important matter to me nowadays, & the illustrations make it most interesting. I wonder if there are any remains of the Poet's summer house left in your grounds.

As to the shares, how prompt you have been! I think I ought to wait as your friend suggests till after the dividend. I am greatly obliged by your making the inquiry. I myself am very dilatory in such doings.

We missed you very much after you were gone. Last night, to our great relief, some rain fell—perhaps as a commendation from the skies of the Duke of Rutland's letter in the *Times* telling us to pray for it.

Your affectionate friend
Thomas Hardy.

Text MS. (with envelope) Purdy.
copy of Gray: *The Poetical Works of Thomas Gray, English and Latin,* ed. the Revd. John Moultrie (Eton, 1854); the vol., inscribed 'To Uncle Tom,/with much affection and friendship,/Dorothy Allhusen./July 8th. 1918.', is in DCM. *than mine*: also in DCM is TH's copy of the Aldine edn. of *The Poetical Works of Thomas Gray* (London, 1885). *summer house*: a steel engraving by E. Redclyffe of 'Summer House, West-End, Stoke' appears as one of the illustrations. *your grounds*: i.e., those of Stoke Court, Stoke Poges; see II.222. *the shares*: unidentified. *after you were gone*: Mrs. Allhusen stayed at Max Gate at the end of June 1918, going to Church with TH at Stinsford on the 30th (FEH diary fragment, Purdy). *pray for it*: the Duke's letter (*The Times*, 9 July 1918) urged that in view of the seriousness of the current drought the bishops should instruct the clergy to read the Prayer for Rain in their churches.

To DOROTHY HANBURY

MAX GATE, | DORCHESTER. | 12: 7: 1918

Dear Mrs Hanbury:

I am so sorry to hear that Mr Jeune has been unwell. I will call on Sunday afternoon, at whatever time weather permits (if capricious). It is not at all necessary to send, as I wd rather walk if possible. (I am writing hurriedly as the post is just going).

Sincerely yrs
Th: Hardy.

Text MS. Eton College.

To THE LORD MAYOR OF LONDON

July 23. 1918

Mr Thomas Hardy thanks the Lord Mayor for the honour of his invitation to the Luncheon at the Mansion House to meet Lord Rayleigh with the object of founding a Chair of French at Cambridge; but regrets to say that age, distance, & railway difficulties prevent his attendance to take part in a movement so commendable & necessary.

The Right Hon. the Lord Mayor.

Text MS. (pencil draft) DCM.
Lord Mayor: Sir Charles Augustin Hanson, Bt. (1846–1922), M.P. for the Bodmin Division of Cornwall for many years, Lord Mayor of London 1917–18. Sir Arthur Quiller-Couch wrote TH (25 July 18, DCM) to say that Hanson was a friend and neighbour (in Cornwall) who was promoting the French chair at his instigation. *Rayleigh*: John William Strutt, 3rd Lord Rayleigh (1842–1919), mathematician and physicist, Nobel prizeman, currently Chancellor of Cambridge University; *D.N.B.* He was in fact absent from the occasion on account of illness. *Chair of French*: the Drapers Professorship of French in the University of Cambridge was established in May 1919, the Worshipful Company of Drapers (of the City of London) having guaranteed the salary of the professor for 10 years.

To J.J. FOSTER

MAX GATE, | DORCHESTER. | 24th. July 1918.

Dear Mr Foster:

I do not myself know anything of Beach more than that he was a Dorset painter whose pictures I have occasionally seen. As to Came, I am ashamed to say that though some friends of ours rented the house for years, and I have sat there many times with them, I cannot recollect if there were any of Beach's among the paintings. The house is shut up now, but my wife can get access to it, and says she will endeavour to find out if such paintings are still there.

An illustrated account of the Came pictures was published in *The*

Sphere—possibly about 1890, but I am not sure of the date—which might help you if you were to consult a file of the paper. With kind regards from Mrs Hardy and myself, I am,

Very truly yours,
Th: Hardy.

Text MS. (typewritten) Yale.
Beach: Thomas Beach (1738–1806), Dorset-born portrait painter; *D.N.B.* *some friends of ours*: probably Charles John Cornish Browne, J.P., and his wife, who lived at Came House, near Dorchester, 1903–14. *still there*: Foster (22 July 18, Princeton) had asked if TH knew anything of 10 paintings by Beach said to have been at Came House; it appears that these, all portraits of officers of the Dorset Volunteer Rangers, are now in Australia. *about 1890*: the *Sphere* did not, however, begin publication until 1900 and the article remains untraced.

To JOHN GALSWORTHY

MAX GATE, | DORCHESTER. | July 30: 1918

My dear Galsworthy:

My wife has got hold of your book of stories, & is reading them so closely that I have not begun them as yet, but I send this line to let you know they have arrived & to thank you much for the gift. She says they are excellent, & as she is a keen critic I know they must be good.

How I should like to be on Dartmoor (where you are I imagine). But the obstacles caused by this huge tragedy created by mankind, for fun as it were, prevent my coming.

Always yrs sincerely
Thomas Hardy.

Text MS. Univ. of Birmingham.
book of stories: Galsworthy's *Five Tales* (London, 1918).

To J.S. UDAL

MAX GATE, | DORCHESTER. | August 1. 1918.

My dear Udal,

It is generous of you to send me this almost last copy of your poems, which you should not have taken the trouble to get bound so excellently for me. My best thanks for the same.

I have only just looked into them as yet, but so far as I have seen they appear to be as good as the early effusions of great poets. However perhaps it is as well that you did not attempt to make poetry your trade instead of law, for its risks, if it be indulged in further than as a hobby, are too serious to be undertaken lightly.

You will I am sure excuse the intervention of the clicking typewriter. I am compelled, sans choice, to use it largely nowadays.

Yours sincerely,
Th: Hardy.

His Hon. J. S. Udal.

Text MS. (typewritten, with envelope in FEH's hand) Princeton.
your poems: Udal's privately printed *Marriage, and Other Poems* (London, 1876).

To SYDNEY COCKERELL

[4 August 1918]

It is unfortunate for the cause of present day poetry that a fashion for obscurity rages among young poets, so that much good verse is lost by the simple inability of readers to rack their brains to solve conundrums. They should remember Spencer's remark that the brain power spent in ascertaining a meaning is so much lost to its appreciation when ascertained.

Text MS. (paragraph dictated by TH and included by FEH in her letter to Cockerell of 4 August 1918) Purdy.
young poets: Cockerell had sent TH a letter he had recently received from Wilfred Scawen Blunt (1840–1922; *D.N.B.*), with whose criticisms of Charlotte Mew (see letter of 28 Oct 19 to her) for leaving unclear 'what the situation of the lyric exactly is' TH was here expressing his agreement; the Blunt letter, of 17 July 18, appears in *Friends of a Lifetime* (see letter to Cockerell of 9 Aug 14), 202–3. *Spencer's*: Herbert Spencer, the philosopher; see III.244.

To CLEMENT SHORTER

FROM THO. HARDY, | MAX GATE, | DORCHESTER. | 12: 8: 1918

I sign the application with pleasure. Though I have never known Francillon personally, he wrote in the Cornhill when I wrote there. I think I have signed one before for him, or, it may be, have been asked to. Believe me,

Very truly yours
Th. H.

Text MS. (correspondence card) Colby.
application: to the Royal Literary Fund. *Francillon*: Robert Edward Francillon, novelist; see IV.257. *when I wrote there*: specifically, in 1874. *one before for him*: see IV.256.

To JOHN GALSWORTHY

MAX GATE, | DORCHESTER. | August 15: 1918

My dear Galsworthy:

Here are a few humble lines for *Reveille*, which may have at least the negative merit that nothing particular can be said against them. The fact is that I cannot do patriotic poems very well—seeing the other side too much.

I have read—or rather had read to me—all the Tales: & have staunchly recommended them to people. Old Heythorp is an imperishable figure—though I don't as a rule like old men—probably because I am one myself. "The Appletree" touches finer emotions, perhaps, than the rest of the stories; but they are all good.

Alas; I don't know when we shall get down into Devon. I should like to be there now: Dartmoor must be at its finest. But locomotion is so irksome in August, particularly now, that I must be content to imagine the scene.

With kindest regards to Mrs Galsworthy

Yours most sincerely
Thomas Hardy.

P.S. I could perhaps find another piece if this one is too mild. Th.H.

Text MS. Univ. of Birmingham.
for Reveille: Galsworthy, as editor of *Reveille* ('Devoted to the Disabled Sailor & Soldier') had written 30 July 18 (DCM) to ask TH for a contribution; he sent 'The Whitewashed Wall', pub. November 1918. *the Tales*: Galsworthy's *Five Tales* (see letter of 30 July 18). *Old Heythorp*: in 'A Stoic', one of the stories in the vol.; other opinions of TH's were reported by FEH to Mrs. Galsworthy, 13 Aug 18, pub. in H.V. Marrot, *The Life and Letters of John Galsworthy* (London, 1935), 481.

To THE REVD. MALCOLM VENABLES

MAX GATE, | DORCHESTER. | 18: 8: 1918

Dear Mr Venables:

I have read the Sonnet with pleasure. I do not think that a departure from the customary Italian form is at all undesirable, though that form goes on year after year among so many poets, who, I suppose, do not think much on the question why they should, or should not, follow it.

My philosophy is, I fear, of a very tentative & inconsistent pattern, so perhaps it was as well that you did not enter upon it, for your own peace of mind!

Very truly yours
Thomas Hardy.

Text MS. Eton College.
Venables: the Revd. E. Malcolm Venables (1884–1957), schoolmaster, author of *Christ and the Public Schools* (Oxford, 1917); he and his wife visited Max Gate 15 Aug 1918. *the Sonnet*: it was sent with, but no longer accompanies, Venables' letter of 16 Aug 18 (DCM).

To FLORENCE HARDY

Max Gate: | Tuesday. 4.0 p.m. [3 September 1918]

My dearest F:

When you go away things begin to happen. Mrs Logan called this morning, & was disappointed at not seeing you. However I answered the purpose partly. She wants to know if you will give the prizes at the Church of E. Temperance Society, on Wednesday the 11th—to-morrow week, at 5 in the evening. The Bishop is to be there, & he will present the banner, & the prizes are to be given immediately after. "It is felt that Mrs T.H., the author of such beautiful books for children as Baby Birds & Baby Beasts is a more appropriate lady than any to do this for the Band of Hope—all children, especially as Mrs T.H. makes such excellent speeches". The Bishop, who has been consulted about it, says he would much like to meet Mr & Mrs T.H. (He has met me already, by the way, so it must be you he wants to see.)

He is coming to Mrs Logan's to tea on the day in question, & Mrs L. proposes that we meet him there. There will be nobody else but his Right Reverence, Mr Coote, & ourselves.

I said I would send on her message, & that I thought you would not at all object, especially as you *did* make good speeches. I said you would be back at the end of the week, so that will be soon enough to let her know, I understand, & you need not trouble to write while away.

Mrs L's manner was, I thought, in the best taste as she asked—quite as if she thought it would be a great honour.

I hope you got to Enfield without much hustling. Wess was in great misery all the morning at your absence, but he eat his dinner well, & seems much as usual this afternoon.

Unless you direct me differently by telegram or letter I shall write & send, after to-night, to the Royal York Hotel Brighton.

It was fortunate you put out that brandy. The indigestion, whatever caused it, was so acute, that the inside of my stomach seemed as if it had been scalded; but the spirit helped it much. I think when I am in Dorchester I will bring home another bottle, in case of necessity. I am going out presently with Wessie.

Your affectte hub
Th:

(I sent on a letter this morning)

This moment a letter has come from Mrs Pocock to me, saying she has used my name as a reference to the Dorset Police in her request for permission to sketch at Sea Town, & hoping that I don't mind. Th.

Text MS. Purdy. *Date* From internal evidence.
go away: FEH had gone to visit relatives in London and Brighton. *Mrs Logan*: Alice Logan, the wife of a Dorchester solicitor; she was secretary of the Fordington St. George branch of the Band of Hope, the children's organization run by the Church of England Temperance Society. *give the prizes*: for a Band of Hope essay competition; FEH seems not to have been present at the parade and presentation on 11 Sept 1918 but she was publicly thanked for having entertained and addressed the members of the Fordington St. George branch at Max Gate. *The Bishop*: the Right Revd. Frederick Edward Ridgeway (1848–1921), Bishop of Salisbury since 1911. *& Baby Beasts*: FEH's *The Book of Baby Birds* (London, 1912) and *The Book of Baby Beasts* (London, 1911), both illustrated by E. J. Detmold. *Mr Coote*: the Revd. Herbert Chidley Coote (d. 1919), rector of St. Peter's, Dorchester, 1913–19. *Mrs Pocock*: Constance Pocock, *née* Osborne (d. 1942), wife of Reginald Innes Pocock, F.R.S., superintendent of the Zoological Society's Gardens, Regent's Park, 1904–23. *Sea Town*: a coastal hamlet SW of Bridport, evidently within an area of war-time restriction; see letter of 2 Oct 19.

To ARNOLD BENNETT

(Ansr) Sept 8: 1918

Dear Arnold Bennett:

I have read the Manifesto you send, but have scruples against signing it, being, too, neither a public man nor a writer on public affairs.

If it be all true that the letter prophesies I do not think a world in which such fiendishness is possible to be worth the saving. Better let Western "Civilization" perish, & the black or yellow races have a chance. Moreover I don't see how by any sort of Mutual League such nations can prevent themselves doing what they want to do.

However, I think better of the world, as a meliorist (not a pessimist as they say). The instinct of self-preservation, & an ultimate common-sense at present obscured, will I think hinder the evils foretold from arising.

I am greatly obliged to you for letting me see the document although I am found wanting.

Yours sincerely
Th— H—

Text MS. (pencil draft) DCM.
Bennett: Enoch Arnold Bennett (1867–1931), novelist, dramatist, and man of letters; *D.N.B.* *Manifesto you send*: 'What We Are Fighting For', a set of proposals for the maintenance of the post-war peace prepared but later abandoned by the 'Writers' Group', of which Bennett was a leading member; a copy accompanies TH's draft. See *LY*, 189–90.

To JOHN DRINKWATER

FROM THO. HARDY, | MAX GATE, | DORCHESTER. | Sept. 8: 1918.

Dear Mr Drinkwater:

You have my permission to include "The Oxen" in your proposed anthology for schools.

Please print it from the volume entitled "Moments of Vision" where it is quite correct.

Yours truly
Th: H.

Text MS. (correspondence card) Yale.
anthology for schools: Drinkwater's *The Way of Poetry* (London, 1921).

To SIR FREDERICK MACMILLAN

MAX GATE, | DORCHESTER. | Sept. 15th 1918

Dear Sir Frederick Macmillan:

I have received the enclosed letter from a Madrid house asking permission to publish Jude the Obscure in Spanish. I suppose they have a right to do it without asking, as more than ten years have elapsed since publication; but I imagine it to be as well to express permission.

So if you agree will you kindly send the inquirer an answer.

Yours very truly,
Thomas Hardy.

Text MS. (typewritten) BL.
a Madrid house: still accompanying this MS. is a letter to TH, 5 Sept 18, from the Spanish publisher Atenea. *in Spanish*: no such translation seems to have appeared.

To SIR FREDERICK MACMILLAN

MAX GATE, | DORCHESTER. | 18th. September 1918.

Dear Sir Frederick,

I am much obliged for your suggestion about the Spanish translation of "Jude the Obscure", and shall be glad if you will write to that effect.

Yours very truly,
Th: Hardy.

Text MS. (typewritten) BL.
Obscure": see letter of 15 Sept 18; Macmillan (17 Sept 18, Macmillan letterbooks, BL) suggested a fee of £5 for Spanish book and serial rights.

To THE REVD. HERBERT PENTIN

MAX GATE, | DORCHESTER. | 22nd. September '18

Dear Mr Pentin:

I am greatly obliged to you for kindly sending a copy of the Children's Rhymes. Reading them over revives in my mind the peculiar effect they conveyed to me and other listeners when you repeated them in the winter dusk at the museum. I remember some of them, of course, as being said by village children when I was a boy. Also Sally Water, All around the gooseberry bush, London Bridge is broken down, etc, etc. By the way, the mysterious "Green Gravel" may be a corruption of "Green Grave, O," the addition making up the number of syllables.

Yours sincerely,
Th: Hardy.

P.S. Call any time that you are in Dorchester if you are disposed to walk out here. T.H.

Text MS. (typewritten) DCM.
Pentin: the Revd. Herbert Pentin (see III.156), currently vicar of St. Peter's, Portland. *Children's Rhymes*: an off-print of Pentin's paper, 'Dorset Children's Doggerel Rhymes', *Proceedings of the Dorset Natural History and Antiquarian Field Club*, vol. 38 (1918). *at the museum*: i.e., the Dorset County Museum, although there is no indication that this paper was ever read at a meeting of the Field Club; TH may have been remembering the paper on 'Old Dorset Songs' which Pentin read in February 1905 (*Proceedings*, vol. 27, 1906).

To H. G. WELLS

MAX GATE, | DORCHESTER. | Sept. 23: 1918.

Dear Mr Wells:

I have received with much pleasure the copy you have kindly given me of "Joan & Peter." We were talking about it only the night before, & wondering what the queer reviews we had caught sight of were really meant to express.

I have read only a little way as yet, or rather have heard it read, for my eyes being not so strong as they were formerly my wife reads to me.

You have a preternatural knowledge of what people do! I believe you could go down a street a mile long & see through the house-fronts & describe the movements of every inhabitant.

With my thanks for the book believe me,

Sincerely yours
Thomas Hardy.

Text MS. Univ. of Illinois, Urbana.
Wells: Herbert George Wells (1866–1946), author; *D.N.B.* TH seems first to have met him in 1907 (*LY*, 124). *& Peter."*: Wells's *Joan and Peter: The Story of an Education* (London, 1918). *queer reviews*: TH was perhaps thinking of the highly ambivalent review in *The Times Literary Supplement*, 19 Sept 1918, which concludes, 'But if [Mr. Wells] is one of those writers who snap their fingers in the face of the future, the roar of genuine applause which salutes every new work of his more than makes up, we are sure, for the dubious silence, and possibly the unconcealed boredom, of posterity.'

To M. R. JAMES

MAX GATE, | DORCHESTER. | 27: 9: 1918

Dear Dr James:

Our best wishes for your new & important undertaking. But alas, we shall miss you at Cambridge when we go there!

Sincerely yrs
Thomas Hardy.
Florence Hardy.

Text MS. (correspondence card) Cambridge Univ. Library.
James: Montague Rhodes James, biblical scholar, antiquary, and author; see IV.321. *undertaking*: James had resigned as Provost of King's College, Cambridge, in order to become Provost of Eton. *Florence Hardy*: this signature is in TH's hand.

To J. M. BULLOCH

FROM THO. HARDY, | MAX GATE, | DORCHESTER. | Oct 6. 1918.

Dear Mr Bulloch:

Alas, I have nothing to hand, & as I write so little now I fear nothing will be forthcoming, as I have long promised one or two—whenever they may come to light.

I am glad to hear about old Aberdeen. To me it bears, & always will, a curiously romantic aspect. I suppose I shall never see it again.

Truly yours
Th: H.

Text MS. (correspondence card) Texas.
nothing to hand: Bulloch, as editor of the *Graphic*, had evidently asked TH for a poem. *old Aberdeen*: see letter of 25 Nov 17.

To ETHEL COWLEY

Max Gate | 9: 10: 1918

Dear Mrs Cowley:

The book has come at last & I enclose it herewith. I ordered one in larger type, but they sent this.

You will see an alternative tune to Psalm CI—as they sing it at St Paul's.

Always yours
Th: Hardy.

Text MS. Canon Cowley.
Cowley: Ethel Florence Cowley (d. 1961), wife of the vicar of Stinsford (see letter of 15 Jan 14). *The book*: unidentified, but evidently a hymnal or psalter.

To CECIL PALMER

FROM THO. HARDY, | MAX GATE, | DORCHESTER. | Oct 15. 1918.

Permission given to print "Jezreel" in "Air Pie".—

Text MS. (postcard, written by TH in a disguised hand) Yale.
Palmer: H. Cecil Palmer, journalist and author, the compiler of *The Thomas Hardy Calendar* (see letter of 15 June 14 to Macmillan) and currently editor of *Air Pie: The Royal Air Force Annual* (London, 1919). *"Jezreel"*: first pub. in *The Times*, 27 Sept 1918, without reservation of copyright; Palmer (12 Oct 18, DCM) had asked for a contribution to *Air Pie* but did not specify a particular poem.

To JOHN DRINKWATER

FROM THO. HARDY, | MAX GATE, | DORCHESTER. | Oct 18: 1918.

Play arrived. What a good & timely subject! Nobody, I shd think, had thought of using it before. Many thanks.

Th. H.

Text MS. (postcard) Yale.
Play: Drinkwater's *Abraham Lincoln: A Play* (London, 1918).

To LORD NORTHCLIFFE

Max Gate, | Dorchester. | October 21, 1918.

Dear Lord Northcliffe,

I must send a line to thank you for your kindly interest in my books—now, alas, getting rather old, though I may say that your interest in them shows that you do not age much mentally.

I saw to my surprise in a paper on Saturday that the heroine of *A Pair of Blue Eyes* was one of my best. Tennyson also told me the same thing as being his opinion. If you ever meet with the novel, I should like to know what you think.

Believe me, with renewed thanks,

Sincerely yours,
Thomas Hardy.

Text Reginald Pound and Geoffrey Harmsworth, *Northcliffe* (London, 1959), 665.
Northcliffe: Alfred Charles William Harmsworth, Viscount Northcliffe (1865–1922), newspaper proprietor; *D.N.B.* *interest in my books*: Northcliffe, informed by FEH that TH's books were not in great demand, had written to Sir Frederick Macmillan (with a copy to FEH) to say that he would 'be very glad to use my Press to open up to as many minds as possible the enjoyment of [TH's] genius' (*Northcliffe*, 665). *a paper*: unidentified. *what you think*: Northcliffe replied, 24 Oct 18 (*Northcliffe*, 665), that he could recite 'the story of *A Pair of Blue Eyes* backwards'.

To AMY WELLS

MAX GATE, | DORCHESTER. | 25: 10: 1918

Dear Mrs Wells:

I was very glad to sign the books, which I have done on the second page, so that the owner can put his or her name on the first. I hope they will reach you in time, but they arrived only last night, & are sent off this morning. With kind regards,

Sincerely yrs
Thomas Hardy.

Text MS. Univ. of Illinois, Urbana.
Wells: Amy Catherine Wells, *née* Robbins (d. 1927), second wife of H. G. Wells. *the books*: evidently copies of TH's own books, to be sold for some charitable cause.

To FLORENCE HENNIKER

Max Gate | Sunday. 27: 10: '18

My dear friend:

I was much gratified to hear that you liked "Jezreel", though I have not hurried to tell you so: this however you must put down to my indolence. It was written very rapidly, & was published the day after, it being just a poem for the moment. I thought people did not seem to realize that

Esdraelon & Jezreel were the same. Well, as to my having any affection for Jezebel, I don't think I can admit that: I have the same sort of admiration for her that I have for Lady Macbeth, Clytaemnestra, & such. Her courage was splendid.

I am not doing much just now. I hope the influenza has kept outside your door so far. It is creeping about down here, & appears in villages in a mysterious way. We have taken two or three short bicycle rides lately—one to the scene of that poem "The Revisitation", another to "Egdon Heath", &c. Last week Florence's sister achieved a little boy—her first baby—which she thinks a wonderful performance. Her husband is a flying man, & has rushed home to see the baby, though he is compelled to do it at his own expense—all the way from Ireland. If I were a woman I should think twice before entering into matrimony in these days of emancipation, when everything is open to the sex.

I hope your nephew has got well of his wound by this time. We have large hospitals for the wounded here & at Weymouth, & trainloads of them come in quite unexpectedly.

I think Arthur Balfour made a fool of himself in stating on his own responsibility (apparently) that we were not going to let the Germans have their colonies back. But he was always a tactless man. F. gets letters asking her to review books (since she reviewed Mrs Shorter's poems under her own name), but she does not want to, as the house is enough for her to attend to, she finds. Lady Ilchester consulted her last week about getting up a *Café Chantant* here for Xmas. I am afraid I cannot assist, except by giving advice. Let us hear again when you can.

Affly yours
Th: H.

While writing a golden-crested wren has come outside my window: also a cole-tit. Th. H.

Text MS. DCM.
"Jezreel": see letter of 15 Oct 18. *the same*: i.e., alternative names for the same Palestinian region, whose recent capture by British forces under General Allenby had provided the occasion for the poem. *Jezebel*: mentioned in the poem, which juxtaposes biblical and contemporary events; see 2 Kings 9: 30–7. *"The Revisitation"*: its principal setting is the 'ridge of Waterstone', just NE of Dorchester. *little boy*: Thomas Dugdale Soundy (b. 1918), only son of Reginald and Margaret Soundy. *your nephew*: Gerald Fitzgerald, the son of Mrs. Henniker's sister (see II.21). *Balfour*: Arthur James Balfour, philosopher and statesman (see II.185); he was currently Foreign Secretary and had made his declaration on the former German colonies in a speech delivered 23 Oct 1918. *under her own name*: FEH's review of Dora Sigerson Shorter's *The Sad Years* has not been traced. *for Xmas*: this scheme seems not to have materialized, perhaps because the end of the war reduced the need for such charitable undertakings.

To GEORGE MACMILLAN

MAX GATE, | DORCHESTER. | 30 Oct. 1918

My dear Macmillan:

Certainly let him publish it. I leave you to consider if he should be charged a fee. What do you say to a guinea.

Sincerely yours
Thomas Hardy.

Text MS. (correspondence card) BL.
publish it: Macmillan wrote 29 Oct 18 (Macmillan letterbooks, BL) to say that Clement Shorter had asked permission to print 'Valenciennes' in the *Sphere*, of which he was editor.

To WALTER DE LA MARE

Max Gate, | Dorchester. | Nov. 1. 1918

Dear Mr de la Mare:

I am writing this line for what is hardly a reason. I have been turning out papers from a cupboard where they have been lying many long years—press cuttings that were sent me in my active days—& among them I find a most generous review, such as only a poet could write, by you of The Dynasts in the Bookman. Well: better late than never, & I send my thanks. If I saw it at all at the time it came out—ten years ago—your name did not convey to me as it does now any of those delightful sensations of moonlight & forests & haunted houses which I myself seem to have visited, curiously enough; & that may be why I had no recollection of the article.

Believe me, yours truly,

(& not a stranger, though we have never met except at the ghostly places aforesaid)

Thomas Hardy.

Text MS. Eton College.
de la Mare: Walter John de la Mare (1873–1956), poet and novelist; *D.N.B.* *Bookman*: de la Mare's short article—less a review than a celebration of the completion of *The Dynasts*—appeared in the *Bookman*, June 1908. *send my thanks*: de la Mare responded to TH's initiative with a warm and admiring letter, 6 Nov 18 (typed transcript, DCM).

To J. S. UDAL

Max Gate, | Dorchester. | 9th. November 1918.

My dear Udal:

I have been searching for the mumming play of "St George" of which I had a copy many years ago, and which, as you may remember, I referred to in "The Return of the Native". I believe that you worked up the subject of Dorset mumming for the folk-lore Society, and hence it occurs to me that you may have an old copy of the play that the Dorset Dramatic Society could use in giving a short entertainment in the Corn Exchange here to raise funds for a charitable object connected with the war. I have promised the Society to enquire if you have such a copy, or could tell them where they could get one. I hope your neuritis is better, and my wife sends her kind regards.

Yours sincerely,
Thomas Hardy.

Text MS. (typewritten) Princeton.
of the Native": specifically, in Book Two, chaps. 4–6. *for the folk-lore Society*: apparently a reference to Udal's 'Christmas Mummers in Dorsetshire', *Folk-Lore Record* (1880), based on a paper delivered to the Folk-Lore Society in April 1880. *a short entertainment*: if, as appears, a performance of the mumming-play was contemplated at this date, it seems subsequently to have been abandoned, perhaps as a consequence of the Armistice. See, however, letter of 13 Nov 18.

To J. S. UDAL

Max Gate | 13: 11: '18

My dear Udal:

How unlucky of me not to have mentioned your 70th birthday. But better late than never. Congratulations from both of us now.

Thanks about the play. You may depend on my returning it as soon as one of the versions has been copied.

I hope the change is benefiting Mrs Udal. European events are bigger than can be realized.

Sincerely yours
Th: Hardy.

Text MS. (with envelope) Taylor.
one of the versions: two versions of a Dorset Mummers' Play had been given in Udal's article of 1880 (see letter of 9 Nov 18), and a note by him on the present MS. indicates that he sent both versions in response to TH's request. The single version pub. in Udal's *Dorsetshire Folk-lore* (Hertford, 1922) was reprinted in *Mumming and the Mummers' Play of St. George*, ed. J. Stevens Cox (St. Peter Port, Guernsey, 1970), together with TH's own recension—first printed, privately, as *The Play of 'Saint George'* (Cambridge, 1921)—as used in the 1920 production of *The Return of the Native* by the Dorchester Debating and Dramatic Society (see Purdy, 212–13). *European events*: an allusion chiefly to the Armistice of 11 Nov 1918.

To EDWARD MARSH

MAX GATE, | DORCHESTER. | 17 Nov. 1918

Dear Mr Marsh:

I am much honoured by your asking me about the dedication of the new volume whenever it comes out, & have of course great pleasure in accepting it.

My thanks for your letter. I hardly liked to write my poem on the first page of your book, but as there was absolutely no other place I had to do it!

Sincerely yours
Thomas Hardy.

Text MS. Berg.
Marsh: Edward Howard Marsh (1872–1953), civil servant and patron of the arts; *D.N.B.* *asking me*: in his letter of 14 Nov 18 (DCM). *new volume*: *Georgian Poetry 1918–1919*, ed. Edward Marsh (London, 1919); it is dedicated 'To / Thomas Hardy'. *your book*: Marsh's 'Little Book' in which his literary friends were asked to inscribe a sample of their work; TH's choice was 'In Time of the "Breaking of Nations"'. The book had been taken to Max Gate by Siegfried Sassoon on 6 Nov 1918. *had to do it!*: according to Christopher Hassall, *Edward Marsh: Patron of the Arts* (London, 1959), 456, there was in fact 'plenty of room'.

To DOROTHY ALLHUSEN

MAX GATE, | DORCHESTER. | 24: 11: 1918

My best thanks for the view of Cires-les Mellos, & for the previous ones. I don't think it looks dreary.

What a change in the aspect of affairs! Remembrances to H. & to the household.

Th: H.

Text MS. (postcard) Purdy.
Cires-les Mellos: correctly, Cires-lès-Mello, a village NW of Chantilly, the site of a canteen for French soldiers run by Mrs. Allhusen. *H.*: Henry Allhusen, Mrs. Allhusen's husband; see II.249.

To SIR FREDERICK MACMILLAN

MAX GATE, | DORCHESTER. | Dec 1. 1918

My dear Macmillan:

Can you let me have two or three copies of the Golden Treasury Selection of my poems? If so I shall be much obliged.

If you have, too, a copy of the "Moments of Vision" to spare, I should be glad.

I suppose that when Peace is really concluded it will begin to remove printing difficulties. I hope so.

Yours very truly
Thomas Hardy.

Text MS. BL.
of my poems: i.e., *Selected Poems of Thomas Hardy* (1916).

To SIR FREDERICK MACMILLAN

MAX GATE, | DORCHESTER. | Dec 4: 1918

Dear Sir Frederick:

Many thanks for the books. I too, noticed the difference in sales, which of course is cheering.

As I am writing I enclose a list of corrections, which I shall be obliged if you can get made whenever you may be printing another impression of either book.

Very truly yours
Thomas Hardy.

Text MS. BL.
either book: see letter of 1 Dec 18.

To ALFRED POPE

Max Gate | 18: 12: 1918

Dear Mr Pope:

I am reading the Biographies with much interest, & am marking any possible modifications, but they are quite unimportant.

I thought you might have called this afternoon, but as I have not got far on there is no hurry. If fine to-morrow (Thursday) afternoon I shall be out, but we shall both be in on Friday or Saturday, if you & Mrs Pope would come to tea. Nobody else will be here, so far as I know.

Yours very truly
Th: Hardy.

Text MS. (with envelope) Christopher Pope.
the Biographies: i.e., the several chapters of *A Book of Remembrance*; see letter of 25 June 18.

To FLORENCE HENNIKER

Max Gate | Dec 28: 1918

My dear friend:

I am aiming for this to reach you on New Year's day to wish you many happy returns, but as you are flitting I am not sure that it will. My best thanks for your nice letter. Alas, about my writing fine poems next year! I fear I am past that; though people who know seem to like some I write, & praise them. But "to what purpose cometh there to me incense from Sheba!" I often say. As it is an exceptionally mild afternoon I have been gardening a little, & had to tie up a rosebush planted by Emma a month or two before her death: it has grown luxuriantly, & she would be pleased if she could know & that I care for it.

However this is a bad beginning for a New Year's letter. I heard two or three days ago from Mr Birrell, who tells me he is going to print a little book about his father-in-law Frederick Locker, & asked if he might insert a letter of mine in it, written so long ago as 1880. Of course I did not mind.

Two evenings ago we dined at the Cecil Hanburys who now own those beautiful gardens at La Mortola near Ventimiglia & live about a mile from us here. F. enjoyed herself much, & as she did I did. An amusing naval Commander was there, who had been all through the war, & told us queer experiences.

I quite agree that people ought not to be let tear the holly trees to pieces for decoration. There used to be a good many on the heaths here, but they have all been destroyed.

You mention John Fortescue. Did I ever tell you that he met his wife for the first time at a garden party here? I hope they are happy, but the meeting was by a stone we call the Druid Stone, which sounds ominous, though perhaps it is quite the reverse.

I have received from a composer the music to "When I set out for Lyonnesse"—which seems good, but I don't know for certain yet. (The words are in the "Golden Treasury" Selection)

I don't attempt to understand how the League of Nations is to be accomplished, so can only wait. I am glad you liked Cockerell: he is a most sincere man, & devoted to his friends.

I saw that Gosse read the lessons. *I* used to read them in my brother-in-law's church, but I hardly thought that G. knew about such things—I mean such old-fashioned doings. I am sorry to hear he has had such a bad cold. We had a Christmas line or two from Lady St Helier, who seems to be well. Now where shall I direct this to find you?

Ever yours
Tho. H.

Text MS. DCM.
from Sheba!": Jer. 6: 20. *Birrell*: Augustine Birrell, author and statesman; see II.83. He wrote TH 24 Dec 18 (DCM). *as 1880*: see I.69; the letter duly appeared in Birrell's *Frederick Locker-Lampson: A Character Sketch* (London, 1920), 139–40. *from us here*: at Kingston Maurward House, clearly visible from the back of Max Gate. *naval Commander*: unidentified. *garden party here*: see letter to Mrs. Henniker of 5 June 18. *Druid Stone*: a large stone dug up at Max Gate in March 1891 (see *EL*, 306) and placed, on end, at the edge of the lawn to the east of the house. *from a composer*: see letter of 28 Dec 18 to C. A. Speyer. *read the lessons*: Gosse was reported in *The Times*, 23 Dec 1918, as having 'read the Lessons' at a service held at All Saints, Ennismore Gardens, London, on 21 Dec 1918 'in memory of the authors, men and women, who have given their lives in the war'. *brother-in-law's church*: St. Juliot, Cornwall, of which ELH's sister's husband, the Revd. Caddell Holder, was rector; see Millgate, 146.

To CHARLES SPEYER

Dec 28: 1918

My dear Sir,

I am pleased to get as a Christmas gift the music you have composed to "When I set out for Lyonnesse". It happens that I have wondered at moments if it might not melodize very well; but I was not able to judge without more special knowledge.

I assume that you think of publishing it. I need hardly say I accept the dedication willingly.

I have not yet been able to get the tune played over by an accomplished musician, so as to appreciate it properly, but I shall do so shortly.

In respect of the question you ask—the meaning of "The rime was on the spray"—it refers, if I remember, to the spray of the trees when covered with rime at dawn in winter or early spring after a white frost. The hero is supposed to be living inland, & hence would not be near the sea when setting out. "Lyonnesse" is a vague term denoting the north & west coast of Cornwall generally.

Yours very truly
T.H.

Text MS. (pencil draft) DCM.
Speyer: Charles Anthony Speyer, composer, of Kingswood, Surrey; he had written 21 Dec 18 (DCM) to ask if TH would accept the dedication of his setting of 'When I Set Out for Lyonnesse'. *publishing it*: it appeared as Speyer's *Six Selected Lyrics . . . No. 1. When I set out for Lyonnesse. (Op. 10)* (London, 1920). *on the spray"*: the third line of 'When I Set Out for Lyonnesse'.

To SIR HENRY NEWBOLT

MAX GATE, | DORCHESTER. | Dec 30: 1918

My dear Newbolt:

In an impulse (which if closely analysed might be found to have a touch of vanity in it) I send you the lines copied out, thinking you might like to have them as you have valued them, & as there were a few trifling errors in the newspaper copies. My mind goes back to the row of poor young fellows in straw hats who had fallen-in in front of our County Hall here—lit by the September sun, whom my rather despondent eye surveyed.

Well, it is all over now—at least I suppose so. I confess that I take a smaller interest in the human race since this outburst than I did before.

All good wishes for the coming year to you & your household from us both. I cannot think why you want to be in London much longer. If we do go up we will not forget your kind invitation.

Always sincerely yrs
Thomas Hardy.

Text MS. (with envelope) Texas.
the lines: TH's 'Men Who March Away', praised by Newbolt (29 Dec 18, Texas) as 'the truest & most national poem ever written of Englishmen in war'. *copied out*: this is presumably the fair copy of the poem formerly in the Bliss collection (see Purdy, 158) and now at Texas. *the September sun*: i.e., September 1914.

1919

To ALFRED POPE

8: 1: '19

Dear Mr Pope:

I had nearly finished going through it, & now, having done so send it on. I have found it highly interesting, &, as you will see, have made little comment or change. There was only one bad blunder—"intestinal" for "intestine".

Pray don't feel indebted to me in any way for looking through the typoscript. It has been no trouble.

Very truly yours
Th. Hardy.

P.S. I have been obliged to keep upstairs for the last 2 days.

Text MS. Christopher Pope.
through it: *A Book of Remembrance*; see letters of 28 June and 18 Dec 18.

To HAROLD CHILD

Max Gate | Dorchester | Jan 10: 1919.

Dear Mr Child:

We are truly sorry to hear of your bereavement, of which we were quite in ignorance. Such wrenches leave indelible scars on one's life, so far as my experience goes, & it has been rather intense in that direction of late years, unhappily.

I shall look out for your review, with interest. I am sure it will not quote only the bad lines (of which there are many enough) as so often is done by the smart young men—& alas, young women—who review my verses.

The corrections you saw in Mr Cockerell's volume of Moments of Vision I must, I suppose, have taken from the list of errors sent to the publishers. Anyhow, such a list was sent, & has been put in type for reprinting. But a rather large number of copies of the book was issued in the first place, war conditions making reprints difficult, so I imagine that the new edition embodying these corrections is not out. I will therefore either send the list to you, or correct the errata on your copy; or, if you like, will send you the second edition containing the revisions when it comes out. (They are merely of single words as a rule, & really not of much importance.)

I believe you will find in the Oxford Dictionary the words that puzzle you. "To clam" is to make clammy.

(I have looked into the Dictionary since writing the above, & find I have the authority of Milton for "clammed") "To wanze" is, I think, an old word for to waste away. "Griff" is a claw: also a griffin. I had no idea that I had used it!

I hope the sea-air & quiet will set you right soon. There is nothing like going off into "a desart place" like John the Baptist, to recuperate. (I don't mean to insult Glamorgan by calling it a "desart") We have both been unwell, but are picking up by degrees, though we have been obliged to put off engagements. My wife sends her kind remembrances, & I am

Sincerely yours
Thomas Hardy.

Text MS. Adams.
your bereavement: Child (8 Jan 19, DCM) had spoken of his wife's death in January 1918. *your review*: of *Moments of Vision*; see letter of 11 Feb 19. *sent to the publishers*: Cockerell's copy of *Moments of Vision*, which Child had been shown on a recent visit to Cambridge, contained a number of corrections in TH's own hand (Purdy, 208). *new edition . . . second edition*: a second, slightly revised, printing of the first edn. of *Moments of Vision* appeared in 1919; the vol. was also reprinted in the Wessex edn. and the Pocket edn. that same year. *"clammed"*: TH uses 'clammy' in 'At the Word "Farewell"'; *OED* cites 'clamm'd' from Milton's *Animadversions*. *"To wanze"*: TH's use of 'wanzing' in 'He Revisits His First School' is cited in *OED*. *"Griff"*: used in 'The Clock of the Years'; TH cites two of several definitions offered in *OED*. *the Baptist*: no precise source for 'desart place' has been discovered; although in the Authorized Version John the Baptist is several times associated with the wilderness (Vulgate 'deserto'), the phrase 'desert place' seems to be used only in reference to Jesus (e.g., Matt. 14: 13, Mark 6: 32). *Glamorgan*: Child wrote from Southerndown, Glamorgan, a small resort on the Bristol Channel.

To H. D. STRANGE

(Ans) Jan 19. [1919]

Happy to connect if feasible. Wd depend on the cost—& on the meaning of "joint service".

Text MS. (pencil draft) DCM. *Date* Replies to letter of 17 Jan 19.
Strange: Harman Daniel Strange, borough engineer and surveyor; he wrote 17 Jan 19 (DCM) to ask if TH would be interested in sharing a projected telephone line to the Dorchester Borough Council's depot at the Louds Mill sewage works, just SE of Max Gate. This scheme seems to have fallen through, but the Contract Manager, Post Office Telephones, wrote 13 Sept 19 (DCM) to accept TH's application of 12 Sept 19 for the hire of a telephone, and the instrument was installed before the end of the year.

To HENRY WILSON

(Ansr) Max Gate. | January 22. 1919

Dear Mr Wilson:

The information you give me in your letter received yesterday on the proposed "Pageant of Construction" is of high interest, & if the scheme be carried out it will have—so far as one can prophesy—an educative & stimulating effect upon the people of this country that can hardly be overestimated. I gather from what you say that one section of the historic pageant is to relate to the history of English Freedom, the narrative part of which is to be written in terse & vigorous prose—forming a series of labels or legends attached to the representations.

Attractive as the scheme may be I am sorry to say that I am quite unable to undertake to write this book of the words (so to call it) for several reasons. It would require a younger man than I, & one on the spot, to set about such a work & finish it in a brief time.

I regret my inability the less when I consider how many able writers there are who are fully competent to take the matter up, & apply themselves to the necessary research with thoroughness. With every wish for the success of the enterprise, & my thanks for your opening to me the opportunity of having a share in it I am,

Most truly yours
Th . . H . . .

Text MS. (pencil draft) DCM.
Wilson: Henry Wilson (1864–1934), architect and jeweller, currently president of the Arts and Crafts Exhibition Society. He wrote (n.d., DCM) to ask TH to write 'a book, a theme, a plot a synopsis of the National Epos' which could be used as the basis of 'the Masque of Freedom', proposed as part of a Pageant of Construction to be held in and around Trafalgar Square with the object of showing the importance of creative expression in human life and civilization. The scheme seems not to have materialized.

To AMY LOWELL

MAX GATE, | DORCHESTER. | 26th. January 1919.

Dear Miss Lowell:

I am truly glad to hear from you again, not only for personal reasons but because you are so staunchly zealous in the cause of poetry. The kind gift of your new book is most welcome to me, and I send warm thanks for your thought of me in presenting it.

I have not yet mastered your argument for "polyphonic prose"—(Qy: polyphonic prosody?), but I daresay I shall discover it as I go on. I don't suppose it is what, 40 years ago, we used to call "word-painting". Curiously enough, at that time, prose having the rhythm of verse concealed in it, so to speak (e.g. in the novels of R. D. Blackmore and others) was considered a fantastic affectation. Earlier still, when used by Lytton, it was nicknamed "the ever and anon style"—I suppose because of the rhythm in those words.

This however may be quite a different thing from what you mean, and if so you must consider my mention of it an irrelevant reminiscence. I am, naturally at my age, what they call old-fashioned, and having written rhymes and metred numbers nearly fifty years ago—before you were born!—you must forgive a pedagogic tone if you find it in me.

Though of course in divine poesy there is no such thing as old fashion or new. What made poetry 2000 years ago makes poetry now.

My wife has read some of your book aloud to me, and sends her kindest regards. By the way, in taking up your book I say, Let's read some more of "Cousin Amy," (after the lady in Locksley Hall). "A great liberty!" you will say, especially as she was of a faithless nature. But you must excuse it, remembering under what strange conditions we met when you were here—when the whole world seemed to be in incipient combustion.

With best wishes and hope of seeing you again, believe me

Yours most sincerely,
Thomas Hardy.

P.S. Kind regards also to Mrs Russell. T.H.

Text MS. (typewritten) Harvard.
from you again: she wrote 21 Dec 18 (DCM), sending a copy of her *Can Grande's Castle* (New York, 1918). *"polyphonic prose"*: discussed in the Preface to *Can Grande's Castle*, x–xv. *Blackmore*: Richard Doddridge Blackmore, novelist; see I.38. *Lytton*: Edward George Earle Bulwer-Lytton, 1st Lord Lytton, novelist; see I.240. *Locksley Hall*: i.e., Tennyson's poem of that title. *incipient combustion*: see letter of 6 Dec 14. *Mrs Russell*: see letter of 6 Dec 14; this postscript added in TH's hand.

To H. G. WELLS

MAX GATE, | DORCHESTER. | 27 Jan: 1919

Dear H. G. Wells:

I am glad to find you have honoured old neglected Weymouth by your presence. Certainly come & see us, & bring the lady who is as yet only a floating nebulous bright intellectuality to me. There is nobody I should like better to see, & my wife likewise. Will she be angry that I have not read The Return, although I have heard it so much & so well spoken of? But I feel sure she is one of that excellent sort (which I flatter myself I am, & I am sure you are) who don't care a d—— whether friends have read their last book or not, or any of their books. Indeed I am rather glad sometimes when they *haven't* read mine.

We suggest Wednesday afternoon—say about 4, or as trains suit. If that shd be a bad day say Friday.

Sincerely yrs.
Thomas Hardy.

Text MS. Yale.
Weymouth: Wells wrote 26 Jan 19 (DCM) from the Royal Hotel, Weymouth. *the lady*: Cicily Isabel Andrews, better known as Rebecca West (1892–1983), author, created Dame 1959. Wells said she was 'also staying' at the Royal Hotel and asked if he might bring her with him to Max Gate. *The Return*: Rebecca West's novel, *The Return of the Soldier* (London, 1918). *Wednesday afternoon*: they did visit Max Gate on 29 Jan 1919; for their responses see Gordon N. Ray, *H. G. Wells & Rebecca West* (New Haven, 1974), 94–5.

To WALTER HOUNSELL

MAX GATE, | DORCHESTER. | Jan 29: 1919

I hope Mr Hounsell understands that the slab is to be put to the *middle* one of the three tombs—that of Mrs Emma Lavinia Hardy.

T.H.

Text MS. (postcard) Adams.

To SYDNEY COCKERELL

[6 February 1919]

There is a fragment of truth in what Mr Shorter is reported as having said—though it is not all true. Crabbe was not the *most* potent influence, but was *one* of the influences that led him towards his method—in his novels not in his poetry. The report probably arose from T.H.'s saying that he owed more of his realistic style to Crabbe than to Zola. The knowing English reviewers asserted that all English realism came from Zola, but it existed in Crabbe fifty years before Zola's time. But in his other sort of writing he was influenced far more by Shakespeare, Shelley, Browning etc. than by Crabbe.

Text MS. (paragraph dictated by TH and included in FEH's typewritten letter to Cockerell of 6 Feb 19) Purdy.
as having said: perhaps in conversation, although Shorter's 'A Literary Letter', *Sphere*, 24 Oct 1903, makes a brief reference to TH's having told him 'that his earliest influence in the direction of realism was gained from Crabbe's works'. *than to Zola*: Émile Édouard Charles Antoine Zola (1840–1902), French novelist; a similar point is made in *LY*, 114.

To HAROLD CHILD

MAX GATE, | DORCHESTER. | Feb 11: 1919.

Dear Mr Child:

The pleasant apparition of your review of Moments of Vision in the Observer reminded me of what I had promised to do but had idly neglected. It is done now, & the book is sent back to you under another cover with the corrections for the second edition duly marked. They are merely those that first struck me when I looked through the pages some time ago. I notice now a good many more that might be made but probably will not be. It is vexing what a number of oversights occur in a first edition—at any rate with me.

I must thank you very warmly for what you say—lifting words that, alas, I do not feel worthy to have suggested. By the way I put my name on the title-page: & will you please ink in your own? I have discovered that odd things are done in the way of rubbing out owners' inscriptions.

A friend writes from Cambridge to say that yours is just the review he would have written if he had had the brains & literary skill. You selected quite judiciously for the scanty room you complained of. One poem that I thought critics might select (not for its supposed excellence but for the strange incident which produced it, & really happened) was "Near Lanivet"; but *nobody* did. It is curious how often writers are thus mistaken in what they think will strike readers. The explanation is, of course, that the author judges from the actual event, which he has seen & been impressed by: & the critic from the description only, which may not convey the event as it was.

Our kindest regards. I hope you don't feel the cold much. We have had no snow here to speak of, but a deal of frost.

Sincerely yours
Thomas Hardy.

Text MS. Adams.
in the Observer: of 9 Feb 1919. *promised . . . neglected*: see letter of 10 Jan 19. *the book*: Child's personal copy of *Moments of Vision* (Purdy). *from Cambridge*: presumably Cockerell.

To ALFRED POPE

Feb 14: [1919]

Dear Mr Pope:

You will observe that I suggest the omission of two or three words here & there—it is not because they are wrong, but to avoid too much repetition.

T.H.

I hope this thaw will ease your cold.

Text MS. Christopher Pope. *Date* See letter of 8 Jan 19.
here & there: TH was apparently returning a batch of the proofs of *A Book of Remembrance*.

To SIR ARTHUR QUILLER-COUCH

Max Gate | Dorchester | Feb 15: 1919

My dear Q:

We both are deeply grieved to hear of your loss, & have thought of you & Lady Quiller Couch constantly since we learnt of it.

Always sincerely
Thomas Hardy.

Text MS. Miss F. F. Quiller-Couch.
your loss: Quiller-Couch's only son, Bevil, died suddenly of pneumonia, 6 Feb 1919, while awaiting demobilization from the army.

To THE SECRETARY OF THE SOCIETY FOR THE PROTECTION OF ANCIENT BUILDINGS

MAX GATE, | DORCHESTER. | 18th. February 1919.

Dear Sir:

In reply to your inquiry I can say that I approve of Lord Crawford's suggestion that a memorial be addressed to the Foreign Secretary on the subject of preventing injury to Sta. Sophia, Constantinople by "Restoration" as practised in Western churches, which is usually the obliteration of the successive modifications in the features of a building that give continuity to its history.

I have not the detailed knowledge necessary for forming an opinion on how the essential repairs should be carried out so as to avoid such a contingency.

Yours truly,
Thomas Hardy.

The Secretary, | Society for the Protection of Ancient Buildings.

Text MS. (typewritten) Colby.
The Secretary: Albert Reginald Powys (1881–1936), architect, secretary of the SPAB at this date, younger brother of John Cowper Powys (1872–1963; *D.N.B.*). *your inquiry*: a circular letter, signed by Powys, dated February 1919 (DCM). *Lord Crawford's*: David Alexander Edward Lindsay, 27th Earl of Crawford (1871–1940), politician and art connoisseur; *D.N.B.* *a memorial*: the Annual Report of the SPAB, June 1919, prints a letter of 25 Feb 1919 written by Thackeray Turner, as chairman of the Committee of the Society, to Lord Curzon, as Foreign Secretary, warning against the dangers both of decay, if Santa Sophia remained in Turkish hands, and of 'restoration', if it were to come under Christian or international control. Ownership of the church was currently being debated at the Versailles Peace Conference. *the essential repairs*: the condition of the church was described in a letter from Thomas G. Jackson, *The Times*, 18 Feb 1919.

To ALFRED POPE

Friday. [21 February 1919?]

Dear Mr Pope:

I have gone through them, & find only a few trifling corrections to make.

By the way will the girls like their birth dates to be mentioned?—those that are mentioned. I am too old to be a judge of the modern feminine mind.

Yours truly
Th: Hardy.

Text MS. Christopher Pope. *Date* See note below.
them: the proofs of *A Book of Remembrance*; see letter of 14 Feb 19. It is just possible that TH returned two batches of proof on the same day and that the present letter should also be dated 14 Feb 19. *the girls*: the wartime services and sacrifices of Pope's four daughters are described in *A Book of Remembrance* along with those of their brothers.

To THE REVD. H.G.B. COWLEY

MAX GATE, | DORCHESTER. | Feb 22: 1919

Dear Mr Cowley:

I return the letter you kindly sent on from one of the many amusing Paul Prys who are not content with what a writer offers, but want to get behind the scenes at something he does not offer. Please answer him or not, as you are disposed. If out of civility you send him a brief reply you can remind him that "Under the Greenwood Tree" is a work of fiction, & that as in most works of fiction the scenes are invented (there is a clock, for instance, in "Mellstock" tower, but none in Stinsford), & the characters, even if they have any truth in them at all, are composite, & impossible to dissect for facts.

I may say that I never heard or saw the old choir & players, nor my grandfather, who died before I was born.

With kind regards

Yrs sincerely
Th: Hardy.

Text MS. Canon Cowley.
the letter: from D.R. Cousin, asking Cowley about the 'original' of William Dewy, the character in *Under the Greenwood Tree*; TH made a pencil copy of the letter (DCM) before returning it to Cowley. *Paul Prys*: *Paul Pry* is the title of a comedy by John Poole (1786?–1872; *D.N.B.*), first performed in 1825. *grandfather*: Thomas Hardy (1778–1837), mason and church-musician, buried at Stinsford.

To JOHN MIDDLETON MURRY

MAX GATE, | DORCHESTER. | March 2: 1919

Dear Sir:

I have been searching everywhere for some poem that would meet your views, but so far have not been able to find anything at all up to date, or quite in keeping with the first number of a review. The only verses I can light upon do not relate to a new start, & are not what is called topical. And I am not in trim for writing something special.

So I fear I must forgo the honour, as I consider it, of having room offered me in your proposed pages, being in fact not so young as I was.

I am glad to hear that there is a prospect of a review so famous coming to life again—though perhaps I ought not to be—as it gave me some hard knocks occasionally in its previous incarnation—some 40 or 50 years ago. Believe me

Very truly yours
Thomas Hardy

J. Middleton Murry Esq.

Text MS. Berg.
Murry: John Middleton Murry (1889–1957), critic and author; *D.N.B.* *of a review*: Murry wrote 20 Feb 19 (DCM) to request a poem for the 4 Apr 1919 issue of the *Athenaeum*, the first to appear under his editorship. *forgo the honour*: see, however, the letter of 9 Mar 19. *some hard knocks*: TH was perhaps thinking of the *Athenaeum* review of *The Return of the Native*, 23 Nov 1878, to which he wrote a reply; see Millgate, 198–9.

To JOHN MIDDLETON MURRY

FROM THO. HARDY, | MAX GATE, | DORCHESTER. | March 9: 1919.

Have found two verses, which can be sent when required—

Text MS. (postcard) Berg.
two verses: the two stanzas of 'According to the Mighty Working', *Athenaeum*, 4 Apr 1919; TH was responding to a renewed plea from Murry, who insisted (3 Mar 19, DCM) that the young writers who would be connected with the *Athenaeum* 'desire to sail under your flag'.

To G. HERBERT THRING

MAX GATE, | DORCHESTER. | 15th. March 1919.

Dear Mr Thring:

In reply to your letter I write for Mr Hardy (who has a trouble with his eyes just now) to say that all his books before 1891 were non-copyright in America, and pirated. By looking in "Who's Who" you can see the list of them. All these non-copyright and pirated books are inaccurate and incomplete in many ways, besides being without prefaces and notes. He therefore prefers to have nothing to do with any reprints of them, as by so doing he would be authorizing rival copies to the definitive, complete, and correct edition, published by the Messrs Harper.

I trust you will see the difficulty, and with many thanks for your calling his attention to the matter,

I am,

Yours very truly,
F. Hardy.

Text MS. (typed draft) DCM.
your letter: of 10 Mar 19 (DCM), referring to a possible American piracy of *The Mayor of Casterbridge* and to the publisher's willingness to print with TH's authorization rather than without it. *F. Hardy*: like other holograph additions and corrections to the typescript this signature is in TH's hand.

To THOMAS HUMPHRY WARD

MAX GATE, | DORCHESTER. | 15 March (Ides) 1919

Dear Mr Humphry Ward:

Many thanks. I should have been repaid as much as I deserved for the article by the receipt of the volume containing it, for we have been reading the book with great pleasure & getting all sorts of new impressions, as one does when things forgotten are recalled by accomplished writers.

I am glad to hear that Mrs Ward has got back from her third visit to the scene of desolation. Kindest regards to her.

Yours very truly
Thomas Hardy.

Text MS. Texas.
Many thanks: Ward wrote 12 Mar 19 (DCM) to send TH his fee for the article on William Barnes in vol. 5 of *The English Poets* (see letter of 11 Oct 16) and to apologize for not having sent it two years previously. *scene of desolation*: Mrs. Humphry Ward had made her third visit to the French battlefields 7–30 Jan 1919, an experience recorded in her *Fields of Victory* (London, 1919).

To SIR FREDERICK MACMILLAN

MAX GATE, | DORCHESTER. | 22nd. March 1919.

Dear Sir Frederick:

I have received the enclosed request from a Mr Bertram Lloyd. I am not keen on the matter, and will ask you to reply as you judge best.

As I am writing I may mention that in February I received a letter from the manager of W.H. Smith and Son at their Letchworth branch, stating that they were frequently asked when my *complete* works would be included in the 3/6 edition. I said I would let you know of this inquiry.

The Wessex edition could, of course, easily be made complete by adding one more volume containing Satires of Circumstance and Moments of Vision, whenever you find it convenient. I also get inquiries for a compact edition of all the poetry only. And I have thought that we might some day carry this out by making a companion volume to the one-volume Dynasts of all the rest of my verse—so that there may be an edition of the complete poetical works in two volumes. You may remember that some of the miscellaneous poems were put in type corresponding with the one-volume Dynasts, with the idea that the one volume would hold the whole. But I think two volumes would be better, the present one-volume Dynasts being one of the volumes.

These two not very extensive re-adjustments would, to some extent at any rate, be meeting the wishes of people who want complete sets. I shall be obliged if you will think the matter over.

Yours very truly,
Thomas Hardy.

Text MS. (typewritten) BL.
Lloyd: see letter of 3 Jan 18. *judge best*: Macmillan replied (27 Mar 19, Macmillan letterbooks, BL) that Lloyd's anthology seemed unlikely to prove 'a very satisfactory production' and that permission to include any of TH's poems had been refused. See, however, letter of 3 Jan 18. *The Wessex*: deleted from the beginning of this paragraph is a sentence ('I also get inquiries for a compact edition of the poetry alone') repeated almost verbatim as the present second sentence of the same paragraph. *convenient*: such a vol. was pub. later in 1919; see letter of 30 Mar 19. *in two volumes*: Macmillan also acted on this suggestion before the end of the year; see letter of 30 Mar 19.

To SYDNEY COCKERELL

Max Gate | Sunday 23: 3: 1919

My dear Cockerell:

We are both so sorry to hear that you have been pulled down by this pestilence. I daresay it is the same as that the Lord offered to David—(I have been looking into the Bible, so am scriptural). I trust your hope is well founded that you are getting to the end of it, & shall be glad to know that it is really true: or in any case how you progress.

We have been free as yet, but I wont brag, for the winter is not over. We have a few flakes of snow this morning, but have had none lie this year, & the roads have got dusty the last two days.

Is Sussex a sufficient change? I think Torquay would be better—We are expecting to see you here again when spring has really come, but at present we cannot get enough firing to keep us warm, & have to do without, downstairs, for many hours, hovering over it here in the study, where we have breakfast. By "down stairs" I don't mean in the kitchen, where they of course keep a roaring fire, cooking or no cooking.

It was a great wonder that a letter from me did not cross with yours. I was going to ask you a question (in my dream that all was well with you) which you can answer better than any other man in England. Is Thomas-a-Didymus represented in old stained glass with a black beard, or in old manuscripts? There is a jingle amongst the country folk here, to which I used to be treated when a child, to my annoyance:

". . Thomas a-Didymus had a black beard;
Kissed all the maidens & made 'em afeard,"

& I thought it might date from mediaeval times. But don't trouble to answer now.

My brother is better, but my sister has a violent cold, & ought really to be in bed. Their servant brought it into the house as usual.

Yes: that was very good in the *Times* suppt—"o'erleaps its selle"—I knew of the emendation before. Since I hit on the Keats emendation somebody else has suggested it; so I hardly think it worth while to send up mine.

Thanks for the amusing note of a painting "by T.H." Who is that T.H.? A sketch "by T.H." was sold in America some time ago on the supposition that it was mine, & a print of it circulated in the papers. A collector sent the print to me (of a subject I had never seen or heard of) to know if I had done it.

Always sincerely
Thomas Hardy.

I hope the rest of the household are well or promising. Th.H.

Text MS. Taylor.
this pestilence: the great post-war influenza epidemic. *scriptural)*: the allusion is to 2 Sam. 24: 12–15 (or to 1 Chr. 21: 10–14). *Sussex*: Cockerell had gone to visit Wilfred Scawen

Blunt (1840–1922; *D.N.B.*), traveller and poet. *Thomas-a-Didymus*: i.e., St. Thomas, as in John 11: 16, 'Thomas, which is called Didymus'; Thomas is the Aramaic word for 'twin', Didymus the Greek. *the emendation*: for 'o'erleaps itself', *Macbeth,* I.vii.27; it was mentioned in 'The Textual Criticism of English Classics', *Times Literary Supplement*, 20 Mar 1919. *Keats emendation*: unidentified. *that T.H.?*: Thomas Bush Hardy (1842–97), painter, chiefly of coastal scenes.

To JOHN MIDDLETON MURRY

FROM THO. HARDY, | MAX GATE, | DORCHESTER. | 23: 3: 1919

Dear Sir:

Many thanks for proof. If not inconvenient will you let me have back the hurried type-written copy sent: & this corrected proof with the revise.

Very truly yours
Th: H.

Text MS. (correspondence card) Berg.
proof: of 'According to the Mighty Working'; see letter of 9 Mar 19.

To SIR FREDERICK MACMILLAN

MAX GATE, | DORCHESTER. | 30th. March 1919.

Dear Sir Frederick:

There can be no objection to letting Mr Reginald Wheeler of California include the "Song of the Soldiers" in his anthology.

As to the completion of the editions, the arrangements you detail for carrying out some time this year would, I am sure, be satisfactory to buyers, and quite meet my views.

It is very possible that I may be in London the first two or three days of May, and I shall hope to call,

Yours very truly,
Thomas Hardy.

Text MS. (typewritten) BL.
anthology: Macmillan reported (27 Mar 19, Macmillan letterbooks, BL) that W. Reginald Wheeler, of Pasadena, California, had already included TH's 'Song of the Soldiers' in his *A Book of Verse of the Great War* (New Haven, 1917) but now wished to import the book into Britain. *the editions*: see letter of 22 Mar 19. Macmillan's letter undertook to complete the Wessex edn. by adding the *Satires of Circumstance/Moments of Vision* vol., the Uniform edn. by adding the last three vols. of verse, and the Pocket edn. by adding the same three vols. and *A Changed Man*; it also agreed to the pub. of a 1-vol. *Collected Poems* to accompany the 1-vol. edn. of *The Dynasts*.

To SIR JAMES BARRIE

MAX GATE, | DORCHESTER. | April 10: 1919

My dear Barrie:

I have (rather rashly) promised to be at the Academy Dinner on Saturday May 3., & we think of being in London from the 1st to the 4th partly on this account, & partly for other reasons. I fear that as the beginning of May is a crowded time in town you will be full up, but (since you were kind enough to request it) I duly let you know that we could come to you on those days, assuming that nothing happens to baulk my going.

Do not consider this suggestion of any importance if you have made other arrangements, as we can manage to go elsewhere, but for sentimental reasons should naturally like to be in your eyrie.

Always sincerely yrs
Thomas Hardy.

Text MS. (with envelope) Colby.
Academy Dinner: TH was present at the Royal Academy Dinner, 3 May 1919. *sentimental reasons*: TH had worked at 8 Adelphi Terrace in the 1860s, and Barrie now lived in another part of the same building; replying on 11 Apr 19 (DCM) Barrie suggested that they could 'reel home together' from the Academy dinner and 'ring up No 8 by mistake!'

To ALFRED POPE

MAX GATE, | DORCHESTER. | Sunday. 13. 4. 1919

Dear Mr Pope:

We have been grieved to learn of the loss you & Mrs Pope have sustained in the death of your son after his long battle for life against the malady caused by his military strains & hardships. That is the insidious evil of campaigning—what it leaves behind.

You will know, I am sure, that you have our deep sympathy in this taking of yet one more of your family by the late war.

Very truly yours
Thomas Hardy.

Text MS. (with envelope) Thomas Hardy Society.
your son: Lieutenant-Colonel Edward Alexander Pope (1875–1919), a director of the Dorchester Brewery, died 9 Apr 1919 of an illness first contracted during his wartime service; he was Pope's second son.

To HAROLD CHILD

MAX GATE, | DORCHESTER. | 23: 4: 1919

Many thanks. I do not know the writer's name, but he has written a thoughtful article, even though Ireland comes in as King Charles's head.

Your little book is wonderful for its size. I don't know any other that comes near it. I hope you keep well now you have resumed town life.

Th: H.

Text MS. (postcard) Adams.
article: not identified. *Charles's head*: see Charles Dickens, *David Copperfield*, chap. 24, etc. *Your little book*: Child's *Thomas Hardy* (see letter to Child of 1 Feb 16).

To EDMUND GOSSE

MAX GATE, | DORCHESTER. | Monday. [28 April 1919]

My dear Gosse:

We shall, D.V., be in London from Thursday to Monday next, & should like to call & see you & Mrs Gosse during the time. Will you be at home Sunday evening in the old way?

Sincerely yours
Thomas Hardy.

Text MS. Colby. *Date* From internal evidence.
Thursday to Monday next: see letter of 10 Apr 19. *in the old way?*: an allusion to the long interval since TH's last visit to London; he and FEH were at the Gosses' 4 May 1919 in company with George Moore, John Drinkwater and his wife, and a few others (Book of Gosse, Cambridge Univ. Library).

To SIR GEORGE DOUGLAS

Max Gate | May 7: 1919

My dear Douglas:

I have been in London for a few days, so that my letter is belated. There were things to be done, so I took the bull by the horns & went up, especially as some of the things were pleasant—Private-viewing the Academy for instance, in which performance we surged about in a great crowd & could see the pictures only over peoples' heads, but we had luckily been looking at them in the morning when viewers were thinner. I was told that why the crowd was so great was owing to "Bolshevism having got into the Academy"—which meant that "outsiders"—non-members allowed to exhibit—were for the first time in human history invited to join the fashionables.

Yes: the end of the war was unexpected—if it has ended, as I hope; but how it is to be prevented beginning again at some future year I do not pretend to understand. However, we will hope for the best on this point also. I was glad to know that your nephew got through without serious hurt: his gassing will enable him to appreciate Sargent's picture when he sees it.

Your turning to Spanish literature is, I think, a step of great wisdom. Very few English readers really know much about it, & you will be quite an authority on its productions. I think I told you about my having to grind up that tongue, very roughly, to get some facts about the Prince of Peace that I could not get from English books. The strange thing is that what I acquired went clean away from me afterwards. I have heard of such being the case with barristers. I hope you will keep up this line of study. Goethe has certainly sunk into neglect over here: & in fact I have heard him belittled. But that sort of thing is inevitable. I should like to see your article on him when it comes out.

I have not been doing much.—mainly destroying papers of the last 30 or

40 years, & they raise ghosts. Kipling, by the way, whom I met in London, said that we all seem ghosts nowadays. Kind regards to your brother Frank when you are writing to him. Believe me

Always yours,
Thomas Hardy.

Text MS. NLS.
belated: Douglas wrote 26 Apr 19 (DCM). *the Academy*: the Royal Academy Private View was on 2 May 1919. *your nephew*: the son of Douglas's brother Francis; see letter to Douglas of 2 Feb 18. *Sargent's picture*: John Singer Sargent's 'Gassed', lent by the Imperial War Museum, was the 'picture of the year' at the Royal Academy's Summer Exhibition. *to Spanish literature*: as Douglas (whose mother was Spanish) had reported in his letter; see letter of 22 Nov 19. *of Peace*: Manuel de Godoy (1767–1851), Duke of Alcudia and Prince of the Peace, Spanish minister during the Napoleonic period; he appears in *The Dynasts,* Part Second. *Goethe*: also mentioned in Douglas's letter; see letter of 11 Sept 19. *met in London*: at the Academy Dinner. *your brother*: TH wrote 'you brother'.

To ARTHUR SYMONS

Max Gate, Dorchester | 11th May 1919.

Dear Symons,

I am sorry to say that I was in London only four or five days, so that now your visit to Ventnor ends I am settled down here again, and unable to meet you as you kindly propose. A chance may arise later on.

London was not attractive, the crowds in the streets and trains being wearisome to one no longer young.

Very truly yours,
Thomas Hardy.

Text Typed transcript DCM.

To SIR FREDERICK MACMILLAN

MAX GATE, | DORCHESTER. | 12th. May 1919.

Dear Sir Frederick:

To-day I have chosen what I think an appropriate photograph for the frontispiece to the new volume of the Wessex Edition containing Satires of Circumstance and Moments of Vision. Mr Hermann Lea took it, and will send you the negative in a day or two for reproducing from.

Perhaps it would save labour in the proofs if you have a copy of the two books in sheets that you could send whenever convenient, so that I might combine the title pages, contents &c, into the one volume to match the others.

Yours sincerely,
Thomas Hardy.

Text MS. (typewritten) BL.
photograph: of the Higher Bockhampton cottage in which TH was born, captioned '"when I set out for Lyonnesse . . . the rime was on the spray." (page 18.)'

To SIR FREDERICK MACMILLAN

Max Gate. 14: 5: '19

My dear Macmillan:

As the order of a few of the poems is changed by combining the 2 vols. I send the list of Contents showing the correct order, that the printers may not have to alter it in proof; also showing the legend under the frontispiece.

I will read through the pages you send this morning (which are not much affected by this) & return them with corrections if any.

Yours very truly
Th: Hardy.

By the way, I have received the blank sheets, & will begin them. Th.H.

Text MS. BL.
correct order: e.g., 'Men Who March Away' was shifted from the 'Postscript' section of *Satires of Circumstance* to the 'Poems of War and Patriotism' section of *Moments of Vision*; see also letter to Macmillan of 15 May 19. *frontispiece*: see letter of 12 May 19. *blank sheets*: the 500 sheets that TH was to sign for the limited signed Mellstock Edition, pub. later in 1919.

To SAMUEL BENSUSAN

[Mid-May 1919]

Dear Mr B——

. . . . The C.B. . . . seems to have made a promising beginning. Mr H. is glad to see that it bestows a good proportion of articles upon poetry. That is as it should be. Take care of the poetry & the prose will take care of itself. These articles are very suggestive. "Free verse & the Parthenon" for instance is particularly good, as is also that of Alfred Gordon on "What is Poetry?". . . . But why does the paper stultify its earlier articles by advertising "the best sellers"? Of all marks of the unliterary journal this is the clearest. If the Canadian Bookman were to take a new line & advertise eulogistically the *worst* sellers it might do something towards its object, as they are usually the best literature. He is compelled to say this though he has occasionally been one among the guilty.

F H

Text MS. (pencil draft, begun in TH's hand, completed in FEH's) DCM. *Date* Replies to letter of 12 May 19.
Bensusan: Samuel Levy Bensusan (1872–1958), journalist and author; he had been a newspaper correspondent in Canada. *The C.B.*: the *Canadian Bookman*, of which the first number appeared in January 1919; Bensusan sent (12 May 19, DCM) a copy of the second (April) number, saying that the editors of the magazine hoped for advice from leading English men of letters. Sydney Walton, 'Two Great British Writers Speak to Canada', *Canadian Bookman*, October 1919, quotes extensively from this reply of TH's, implying that he was himself the recipient of it. *& the Parthenon*": an article by Ramsay Traquair, professor of architecture at McGill Univ., *Canadian Bookman*, April 1919. *is Poetry?*": 'What Is Poetry?—A Synthesis of Modern Criticism', *Canadian Bookman*, April 1919; its Canadian author, Arthur Gordon, had earlier sent TH a copy of his '*Vimy Ridge*', *and New Poems* (Toronto, 1918). As quoted by Walton (see above) the letter includes at this point the

additional sentence, 'Such articles directly help real literature as distinct from commercial matters'. *But why ... its object*: this passage appears, with minor variations, in *LY*, 191, attributed directly to TH.

To JAMES FITZMAURICE-KELLY

May 15. 1919

Dear Sir:

I am delighted with the idea of marking the occasion of Mr Edmund Gosse's seventieth birthday by some sort of testimonial, & have accordingly enclosed to Mr Ross the Honorary Treasurer of the Fund my subscription of £1–1–0, to which the amount has been limited.

Yours truly

James Fitzmaurice-Kelly Esq, Litt.D.

Text MS. (pencil draft) DCM.
Fitzmaurice-Kelly: James Fitzmaurice-Kelly (1857–1923), historian of Spanish literature; *D.N.B.* *seventieth birthday*: 21 Sept 1919. *Mr Ross*: Alexander Galt Ross (1860–1927), Canadian-born businessman of literary interests, former secretary of the Incorporated Society of Authors; a draft of TH's brief letter to him of 15 May 19 is in DCM.

To SIR FREDERICK MACMILLAN

MAX GATE, | DORCHESTER. | May 15th. 1919.

Dear Sir Frederick:

I am very anxious that no errors in this edition should be made by the printers, and I am therefore sending on under separate cover, in continuation of what I sent yesterday, the copy of the first half of the intended volume combining Satires of Circumstance and Moments of Vision. As you will see, the change is mainly the shifting of one section of the poems to another place. I hope to send the remainder of the copy in a day or two.

Yours sincerely,
Thomas Hardy.

Text MS. (typewritten) BL.
sent yesterday: see letter of 14 May 19. *to another place*: the 'Satires of Circumstance' poems were moved from the 'Lyrics and Reveries' section of *Satires of Circumstance* to a separate section at the end of the vol.

To ARTHUR McDOWALL

Max Gate | May 19: 1919

Dear Mr McDowall:

My thanks for the cutting from The Athenaeum—though any time would have been soon enough. It must have been more of an accident than design I imagine that the lines suited the present date, for I told the editor I had nothing "topical". That is always the difficulty when one is asked for verses for a periodical: it is easy enough to send *something* that one has lying about, possibly on the moon, stars, trees, grass, or shadowy kine; but the reader of the paper says on seeing it—"Why, what I want is the author's last word upon the world's events; not this stuff!"

My thanks also for your kind remarks on Moments of Vision, which, coming from such a good critic as yourself, are valuable, as is too the list of those you like.

Sincerely yours
Thomas Hardy.

Text MS. T.R. Creighton.
the cutting: of TH's poem 'According to the Mighty Working'; see letter of 9 Mar 19 and *L Y*, 190. *kind remarks*: in McDowall's letter of 15 May 19 (DCM).

To SIR FREDERICK MACMILLAN

MAX GATE, | DORCHESTER. | May 27: 1919

Dear Sir Frederick:

I have just received the enclosed from the Messrs Harpers' London branch, and perhaps it will be more convenient if you answer it. Whatever the offer may be worth, we are, I conclude, debarred from having anything to do with it by the previous contract—which the Harpers themselves ought to be fully aware of, as they, if I remember, arranged it for America.

Would it be worth while to say in replying that the Mr Giffen mentioned can have the film-rights of any unappropriated novel on the terms?

Yours very truly,
Th: Hardy.

Text MS. (typewritten) BL.
enclosed: a proposal for a new sale of the film rights to *Tess of the d'Urbervilles*; see letter to Macmillan of 29 May 19. *Mr Giffen*: Robert Lawrence Giffen (d. 1946), American producer and agent.

To SIR FREDERICK MACMILLAN

MAX GATE, | DORCHESTER. | 29 May 1919.

Dear Sir Frederick:

I write one line to catch the post, & to say that I agree to your going on with the Film proposals of Mr Slater, & to get free of the other agreement as you think best.

Sincerely yours
Thomas Hardy.

Text MS. (correspondence card) BL.
Mr Slater: Macmillan wrote 28 May 19 (Macmillan letterbooks, BL) to report that he had seen F.W. Slater, Harper & Brothers' London representative, and felt that TH should accept

the (Metro Pictures Corporation) offer of $5,000 for world film rights to *Tess*; the Metro-Goldwyn Pictures Corporation film of the novel was released in 1924. *other agreement*: Macmillan pointed out that the 'previous contract' referred to by TH in his 27 May letter had expired so far as the United States was concerned and that he proposed, with TH's agreement, to give the Famous Players' Film Company the required six months' notice of termination of all other rights.

To H.G. WELLS

MAX GATE, | DORCHESTER. | 29 May 1919

Dear H.G.W.:

I was going to wait till I had finished the book before writing to thank you very heartily for the kind gift of it, but as we are reading it aloud, & my wife is away temporarily, I write now.

I am quite childishly curious about that operation on poor Huss, but have been too honest to peep & learn its result.

One excellent effect has already resulted in this house from the story. Strict orders have been given in the kitchen, I find, that all lettuce must be washed most rigorously.

What an extraordinarily wide sweep over human conditions you take, & how eloquently you expound them!

Most sincerely
Th: Hardy.

Text MS. Univ. of Illinois, Urbana.
the book: Wells's *The Undying Fire: A Contemporary Novel* (London, 1919). *poor Huss*: Job Huss, the central figure in the novel; during an operation for a suspected cancer he has a vision of himself as the biblical Job. *all lettuce*: according to Huss, who sees nature as inherently cruel, 'An unwashed leaf of lettuce may be the means of planting a parasitic cyst in your brain to dethrone your reason' (103).

To EDWARD CLODD

Max Gate | June 3: 1919

My dear Clodd:

I only care for my birthday because my kind friends & acquaintances care for it, & I thank you for helping me to do this by your letter & its good thoughts of me.

I am glad to learn that you & Mrs Clodd are brisk enough to go the long (in these still difficult & crowded days for travel) journey to Cornwall. I hardly go anywhere, & doubt when I shall have the pleasure of seeing Aldeburgh again; though I had to go to London on business for a day or two a month ago.

With best wishes I am

Sincerely yours
Th: Hardy.

Text MS. Leeds.

To EDMUND GOSSE

Max Gate | June 4: 1919

My dear Gosse:

Hearty thanks for your kind remembrances: also to Mrs Gosse & the household. The only thing that makes me care for my birthday is that it is cared for by friends.

I should write more, but have just now an affection of the eyes which I get sometimes, & it makes looking at paper rather trying, if for long.

Always yours
Thomas Hardy.

Text MS. Leeds.

To FLORENCE HENNIKER

Max Gate | 5 June 1919

Sincere thanks for your good wishes, my dear friend, which I echo back towards you. I should care more for my birthdays if at each succeeding one I could see any sign of real improvement in the world—as at one time I fondly hoped there was; but I fear that what appears much more evident is that it is getting worse & worse. All development is of a material & scientific kind—& scarcely any addition to our knowledge is applied to objects philanthropic or ameliorative. I almost think that people were less pitiless towards their fellow-creatures—human & animal—under the Roman Empire than they are now: so why does not Christianity throw up the sponge & say I am beaten, & let another religion take its place.

I suddenly remember that we had a call from our Bishop & his wife two or three days ago, so that perhaps it is rather shabby of me to write as above. By a curious coincidence we had motored to Salisbury that very day, & were in his cathedral when he was in our house.

Do you mean to go to London for any length of time this summer? We are not going again till I don't know when. We squeezed a good deal into the 4 days we were there, & I got a bad throat as usual, but it has gone off. At Lady St Helier's we met the Archbishop of Dublin (English Ch:) & found him a pleasant man. We also met several young poets at Barrie's where we were staying.

We do hope you will carry out your idea of coming. We can put you up, & Anna, without trouble, & you can stay in bed half the day if you like. (I think, by the way, that Birdie will be vexed if you don't go on to her too).

I hope you are very very well—in "rude" health, as they call it. Florence sends her love, & I am

Ever affectionately
Th: H.

Text MS. DCM.
our Bishop: see letter of 3 Sept 18. *that very day*: i.e., TH's 79th birthday; see *LY*, 191. *of Dublin*: the Right Revd. John Henry Bernard (1860–1927), Archbishop of Dublin since 1915; *D.N.B.* See *LY*, 191. *poets at Barrie's*: see letter of 13 June 19 to Abercrombie. *Anna*: Anna Hirschmann, Mrs. Henniker's servant of many years; see letter to Mrs. Henniker of 25 May 15. *Birdie*: Lady Ilchester. *on to her*: at Melbury House, Dorset.

To WALTER DE LA MARE

MAX GATE, | DORCHESTER. | 6 June 1919

Dear Mr de la Mare:

Your good words were largely among the kindnesses that made me think birthdays were, perhaps, worth having. I thank you very heartily.

We sometimes look for that old haunted house of your poems when we go hither & thither: but though I have one or two of my own they don't seem so interesting as yours; so we shall go on hunting. With best wishes

I am

Sincerely yrs
Thomas Hardy.

I am in doubt about your address. T.H.

Text MS. (correspondence card) Eton College.
good words: de la Mare's congratulatory telegram of 2 June 19 (DCM). *of your poems*: de la Mare's 'The Listeners' was one of the poems TH asked to have read to him during his last illness; see *LY*, 265.

To ALFRED POPE

Max Gate. June 7. [1919]

Many thanks for kind letter: also to Mrs Pope for her good wishes.

Th: H.

Text MS. (postcard) Thomas Hardy Society. *Date* From postmark.

To DOROTHY ALLHUSEN

MAX GATE, | DORCHESTER. | June 8: 1919

My dear Dorothy:

Best thanks for your nice letter—not at all too late.

I don't suppose we shall go to London this summer on account of the crowds. It is curious that people should be all so happy on borrowed money which will have to be repaid & will impoverish us all for the next 100 years!

Have you found a country house down this way yet? I hope so, or that you will soon, if you are still in the mind to come.

I am glad to hear that the Canteen was a real success; & hope that your visit to the Péronne will be in good weather, so as to make it pleasant.

Florence sends her love, & I am always

Your affectionate friend
Th: H.

Text MS. (with envelope) Purdy.
nice letter: of 6 June 19 (DCM). *borrowed money*: a reference to Britain's heavy post-war indebtedness to the United States. *the Canteen*: for French soldiers; see letter of 24 Nov 18 and Purdy, 209. *Péronne*: a town on the Somme E. of Amiens; it was almost entirely destroyed during the Somme battles of 1916.

To LADY HOARE

MAX GATE, | DORCHESTER. | June 8: 1919.

My dear Lady Hoare:

What a beautiful bowl: how came you to think of it! I am sure I cannot thank you enough for sending it to me.

These events make birthdays tolerable & even desirable: otherwise one would not altogether jump at such anniversaries.

Florence is writing, so I will be brief. Kindest remembrances to Sir Henry.

Believe me, always yours
Thomas Hardy.

Text MS. (with envelope in FEH's hand) Wiltshire Record Office.

To J.H. MORGAN

MAX GATE, | DORCHESTER. | June 8: 1919

Dear Colonel Morgan:

I must thank you for your most interesting letter, though unfortunately I must leave my wife to answer it in detail, as I have a complaint of the eyes which makes it painful for me to look at writing paper for more than a minute or two.

I have some misgivings about the Treaty: but having no special knowledge cannot advance them positively.

Sincerely yours
Th: Hardy.

Text MS. Berg.
interesting letter: of 27 May 19, describing Morgan's experiences as a member (as Assistant Adjutant-General) of the British delegation to the Versailles peace conference. *the Treaty*: of Versailles, formally signed 28 June 1919.

To SIR FREDERICK MACMILLAN

MAX GATE, | DORCHESTER. | June 12. 1919.

Dear Sir Frederick:

I am interested to learn that you think a "Mellstock" edition can be brought out; and in respect of your proposal thereon I am quite willing to abide by it, trusting to the accuracy of your conclusions from the trade estimates, and feeling sure that you would propose nothing but what is equitable. I therefore accept the terms you mention for printing 500 copies of the edition and no more; containing 37 volumes in each set, and the retail price being 18s/- a volume, on each volume of which you pay me a royalty of 3s/-, and which would mean a sum of £2,775 for the whole edition.

I do not at all mind sitting to Mr Strang for an etching, and he can come down here at any time. He was here some years ago for a similar purpose, and we can easily put him up. I suppose a portrait would be considered more desirable by subscribers than an etching of "Mellstock."

I send herewith a copy of the map in the Wessex edition, with two or three names added which I assume can be put on the plate before the copies for the Mellstock edition are printed off. They are marked in red merely to be easily discovered by the etcher.

I also enclose a photograph by Mr Lea for the Collected Poems. He cannot find the negative, but says that the surface of the photograph being smooth will enable a good reproduction to be made from it.

Yours sincerely,
Thomas Hardy.

Text MS. (typewritten) BL.
"Mellstock" edition: the *édition de luxe* of TH's works first proposed by Macmillan in 1914 but postponed because of the outbreak of war; see letter of 15 July 14. *your proposal*: in Macmillan's letter of 10 June 19 (Macmillan letterbooks, BL). *some years ago*: in 1910; see letter of 12 Feb 14 to Strang. *more desirable*: a Strang etching of TH was used as the frontispiece to the first vol. of the edn. *Collected Poems*: a photograph of TH by Hermann Lea was used as the frontispiece to early printings of the 1-vol. *Collected Poems*.

To LASCELLES ABERCROMBIE

Max Gate | Dorchester | June 13: 1919

Dear Mr Abercrombie:

I must thank you, though late in the day, for the lines you wrote in The Daily Herald, which I wish my books were worthy of. It has crossed my mind that another volume of poems from you must be almost due. However, don't hurry.

I was in London for a few days at the beginning of May, & met there a trio you know—Turner, Squire, & Sassoon—who were very pleasant & hopeful. Believe me,

Sincerely yours
Thomas Hardy.

Text MS. (with envelope) Texas.
Daily Herald: Abercrombie's article, 'Thomas Hardy', *Daily Herald*, 4 June 1919, in which he argued that TH's experience as a novelist had liberated the poet in him. *volume of poems*: Abercrombie's *Twelve Idyls, and Other Poems* did not appear until 1928, but he pub. vols. of verse-drama in 1922 and 1923. *met there*: at Sir James Barrie's. *Turner*: Walter James Redfern Turner (1889–1946), poet and critic; *D.N.B.* He was currently reviewing music for the *New Statesman* and drama for the *London Mercury*. *Squire*: see letter of 24 Aug 19.

To JAMES MILNE

Max Gate, | Dorchester. | 13th. June 1919.

Dear Mr Milne:

I fear I cannot do anything for the Jubilee number, since, as you know, I write very little now; nor on searching can I find anything that would suit. But if I come across anything in the course of the next few days I will send it. However, as I say, I fear not.

Yours very truly,
Th: Hardy.

Text MS. (typewritten) Minnesota Historical Society.
Milne: James Milne, journalist; see III.32. *Jubilee number*: the Jubilee Xmas Number of the *Graphic*, 24 Nov 1919, to which TH contributed his poem 'The Peace Peal (After Years of Silence)' and Milne a retrospective article 'The Romance of *The Graphic*'.

To SIR FREDERICK MACMILLAN

MAX GATE, | DORCHESTER. | 15th. June 1919.

Dear Sir Frederick:

I am glad to hear that the Messrs Harper have come to terms with the cinema company for the film rights in "Tess".

The title-page for the "Collected Poems" is satisfactory.

There are a few words in one of the novels which I should like to modify for the "Mellstock" edition. I will send up the corrected words before the printers reach the novel in which they occur, that they may put them in.

Yours sincerely,
Th: Hardy.

Text MS. (typewritten) BL.
rights in "Tess": see letter of 27 May 19. *a few words*: see letter of 18 June 19.

To SIR FREDERICK MACMILLAN

(Enclo.) Max Gate, | Dorchester. | 18th. June 1919.

Dear Sir Frederick:

I am sending the corrections for the Mellstock Edition, which as you will see, are almost all in "A Pair of Blue Eyes". I do not want to read the proofs of the edition—having had enough of reading them, as you will imagine.

However it would be advisable perhaps for safety that I should see the pages of "A Pair of Blue Eyes", where the words are inserted, to make sure they are put in rightly. That is the only one I want to see, if you think the printers can be relied on against misprints.

Yours sincerely,
Th: Hardy.

Text MS. (typewritten) BL.
(*Enclo.*): added in TH's hand. *the corrections*: a list in TH's hand, headed 'Corrections for the Mellstock Edition' and annotated '[Sent to publishers for use in the Mellstock Edition. June 18, 1919]', is in DCM.

To EDGAR LEE MASTERS

MAX GATE, | DORCHESTER. | June 25. 1919.

Dear Mr Masters:

I have pleasure in receiving your letter, your book having been kindly sent me by a stranger some time ago. It did not occur to me on reading it that you were influenced in its writing by my verses, or my way of looking at things, and I do not know why other people were led to think so.

The explanation may be that as the "Satires of Circumstance" were first published a long time back (in the Fortnightly Review for April. 1911), and were immediately parodied in *Punch*, and copied and imitated in English and American papers, readers became familiar with them; so that any trifling accident of expression in "Spoon River" may have led them to imagine a resemblance in it to "Satires of Circumstance" which did not exist.

I am sorry that owing to a weakness of the eyes I am compelled to dictate this letter.

Yours very truly,
Th: Hardy.

Text MS. (typewritten, with envelope in FEH's hand) Texas.
Masters: Edgar Lee Masters (1869–1950), American poet. *your letter*: of 12 June 19 (DCM). *your book*: Masters's *Spoon River Anthology* (New York, 1915). *other people*: according to Masters, Clement Shorter (visiting Chicago) had said that TH was curious to know whether his own verse had influenced *Spoon River Anthology*. *parodied in* Punch: the *Punch* parodies, by G.H. Powell, did not in fact appear until 26 May 1915, after the pub. of the vol. entitled *Satires of Circumstance*.

To EDWARD CLODD

MAX GATE, | DORCHESTER. | Sunday: 29: 6: 1919

My dear Clodd:

Your birthday comes along, I know, either on Tuesday or Wednesday, & I am determined that it shall not escape me this time to send you best wishes & hopes for many happy returns.

I cannot say that the outlook is encouraging, though calm may last long enough for us, at any rate. But the peace seems to me far from satisfactory; & I have visions ahead of ignorance overruling intelligence, & reducing us to another Dark Age. Absit omen! Believe me always

Yours sincerely
Thomas Hardy.

Text MS. Leeds.
or Wednesday: on Tuesday, in fact; Clodd was born 1 July 1840.

To BISHOP HANDLEY MOULE

MAX GATE, | DORCHESTER. | 29 June: 1919

My dear Bishop of Durham:

You may agree with me in thinking it a curious coincidence that the evening before your letter arrived, & when it probably was just posted, we were reading a chapter in Job, & on coming to the verse: "All the days of my appointed time will I wait, till my change come," I interrupted & said: "that was the text of the Vicar of Fordington one Sunday evening about 1860." And I can hear his voice repeating the text as the sermon went on—in the way they used to repeat it in those days—just as if it were but yesterday. I wonder if you have ever preached from that text, I daresay you have. I should add that he delivered his discourse without note of any kind.

My warm thanks for your good feeling about my birthday. The thoughts of friends about one at these times take off some of the sadness they bring as one gets old.

The study of your father's life (too short, really) has interested me much. I well remember the cholera years in Fordington: you might have added many details. For instance, every morning a man used to wheel the clothing & bed linen of those who had died in the night out into the mead, where the Vicar had had a large copper set. Some was boiled there, & some burnt. He also had large fires kindled in Mill Street to carry off the infection. An excellent plan I should think.

Many thanks, too for the volume of poems which duly came. "Apollo at Pherae" seems to me remarkably well constructed in "plot", & the verse facile: I don't quite know how you could have acquired such readiness at such an early date, & the influence of Milton is not excessive—at least I think not.

I hope you will let us know when you come this way again. Our bishop tells me that he is never so happy as when he is in a cottage he has at Lulworth.

Believe me always

Sincerely yours
Thomas Hardy.

Text MS. DCM.
Moule: the Right Revd. Handley Carr Glyn Moule, Bishop of Durham; see I.70. *change come,"*: Job 14: 14. *Vicar of Fordington*: Moule's father, the Revd. Henry Moule; see I.70. *The study*: since Moule had sent TH his *Memories of a Vicarage* at the time of its

publication in 1913 (see IV.326), the reference is perhaps to the biographical notice he supplied to "*Doctrine, Manner of Life, Purpose*" (Dorchester, 1880), containing the texts of the sermons preached by Moule and two of his brothers on the occasion of their father's death. *the cholera years*: the biographical notice devotes a paragraph to the cholera visitations of 1849 and 1854. *at Pherae*": Moule's privately printed *Apollo at Pheræ: A Dramatic Poem after the Greek Model* (Cambridge, 1865). *Our bishop*: see letter of 3 Sept 18.

To WALTER HOUNSELL

MAX GATE, | DORCHESTER. | June 30. 1919.

Having been to Stinsford Mr Hardy thinks that if the tombs are scrubbed it will be sufficient for all three, so as not to destroy the weathered surface, & that the new stone will soon tone down.

Text MS. (postcard) Adams.

To SYDNEY COCKERELL

Max Gate | St Swithin [15 July] 1919.

My dear Cockerell:

Many thanks for the corrections. They are, happily, innocent misprints: not the guilty sort that make a banal sense of a passage.

We went across to Stinsford on Sunday, but the Hanburys were not at home. I have just finished reading the proofs of the "collected" Edition of my verse. The two volumes that will comprise *all* of it will be I think, in point of quantity, the cheapest books issued of late: 500 & more pages each of close print.

As for the prose, it is woefully in need of a revision that it will never get. Who cares about what he wrote from hand to mouth 40 years ago! One novel, however, & only one, I mean to look over for the "Mellstock" edition—A Pair of Blue Eyes—to correct the topography a little—the reasons which led me to disguise the spot when the book was written in 1872 no longer existing, the hand of death having taken care of that.

How you managed to squeeze £1000 out of a dinner table passes my understanding. It is, I admit, better than big game shooting.

I hope Mrs Cockerell is steadily mending & cheerful, & am

Always yours
Thomas Hardy.

Could you let us know the name of that remedy for harvesters?

Text MS. (with envelope) Adams.
corrections: Cockerell's letter of 13 July 19 (DCM) refers to an accompanying list of corrections for the Wessex edn., although TH perhaps wanted them more immediately for the Mellstock edn. (see letter of 18 June 19). *of my verse*: TH's *Collected Poems*, reprinting the contents of all vols. up to and including *Moments of Vision*, was pub. by Macmillan 10 Oct 1919 in a format matching that of the existing 1-vol. edn. of *The Dynasts*. *the spot*: St.

Juliot, Cornwall. *big game shooting*: Cockerell, describing in his letter a London dinner at which over £1,000 had been raised towards the cost of a MS. for the Fitzwilliam Museum, had observed, 'This sport has all the excitement of big game shooting without any of its brutalities' (DCM). *harvesters*: harvest-bugs; this postscript was written on the back of the envelope.

To SIEGFRIED SASSOON

Max Gate | July 19: 1919

Dear Mr Sassoon:

I have been again reading your new book "Picture Show" (excellent title) to-day, & remember that I have not written to thank you for the gift of it. Better late than never, so I do now, while the rain is coming down in torrents on the Peace celebrations.

I am unable to criticize it with due detachment as they tell us we ought to do ("they" stands for—well, you know) but merely can say that I think it your best thing yet.

The poems are also unusual in a minor feature—in being so equal in goodness, & not up & down as so many collections are. At any rate so they seem to me so far. I mean I cannot very well pick out particular ones as favourites, but choose them all.

Perhaps I shall later, for I have not done with them. If so you will hear anon. Believe me

Always yours
Thomas Hardy.

Text MS. Eton College.
"Picture Show": Sassoon's privately printed *Picture Show* (Cambridge, 1919). *Peace celebrations*: the large military parade through London on 19 July 1919 (declared a public holiday) in celebration of the formal signing of the Peace on 28 June 1919.

To H.J. MASSINGHAM

(Ansr Copy) July 20: 1919

Dear Mr Massingham:

On reading over the proposed address I find that the modification of a sentence here & there would be required before I could sign it.

par. 1. After the words "the plume trade" add "according to trustworthy reports".

par 2. For "Unless immediate action", read "Unless therefore immediate action"

par 3. For "It is known for instance" read "It has been shown for instance"

par 4. For "are used merely" read "are used mainly".

par 7. For "demand that a bill" read "urge that a bill".

If the above changes are made I shall have pleasure in adding my name.

Yours very truly

Text MS. (pencil draft) DCM.
Massingham: Harold John Massingham (1888–1952), author of books on the English countryside; *D.N.B.* He was the son of Henry William Massingham (see I.250). *proposed address*: Massingham had sent TH a typescript copy (DCM) of a projected public statement on 'The Plumage Trade', protesting against the widespread killing of exotic birds to provide feathers for the decoration of women's hats; TH has marked the typescript to incorporate the changes here recommended, despite a note in Massingham's hand to the effect that the letter was 'in its final, revised form'. *adding my name*: Massingham replied 21 July 19 (DCM) that it was too late to adopt TH's suggestions, so many people having signed the letter as it stood; he added that the letter was to be delivered 'almost immediately' by a deputation to the Board of Trade.

To JOHN MIDDLETON MURRY

MAX GATE, | DORCHESTER. | July 29: 1919

Dear Mr Murry:

I have just received your beautifully printed sheaf of poems, & as I shall read them but slowly I write now. I am sure they will be as good inside as out, from glimpses I have taken. The very kind inscription I have certainly not earned. Believe me always

Yours sincerely
Thomas Hardy.

Text MS. Berg.
sheaf of poems: Murry's *Poems: 1917–18* (Hampstead, 1918). *inscription*: 'To Thomas Hardy as a mark of devotion and gratitude from John Middleton Murry. July, 1919.' (Maggs Bros. Cat. 664).

To ROBERT LYND

MAX GATE, | DORCHESTER. | July 30: 1919

Dear Mr Lynd:

We have been reading your essays—"Old & New Masters", & to my disappointment the article on "Moments of Vision" which appeared in The Nation, & is now reprinted, turns out to have been written by you. This has reminded me of a curious error I noticed in it when it came out anononymously in that paper, & which at the time I let pass in silence, thinking it to be not an oversight, but an evidence of the ignorance of my critic, wondering why the editor put me into such incompetent hands!!

You will be surprised probably when I mention it. The lines you quoted, & now reprint, of the poem "On Sturminster Foot-Bridge" as being as musical as a "milk-cart" are an attempt (& I am told by poets a not unsuccessful one) at *Onomatopoeia*, in which the words are made to reflect the clucking sound of water when blown up-stream into holes on the bank; so that, to those who know, your ridicule of them must have been of a reflected kind.

I write this line on the point merely because the review is recalled to me by the reprint, & not with any feeling about it (for, alas, all feeling at being misrepresented is long past for one who has been misrepresented so much as I.)

I will not dwell upon other statements in the review: e.g. that Browning invented short stories in verse. He invented the name "Dramatic Lyrics", but not the thing, which has existed for centuries.

You may resent this criticism of a brilliant professional critic; & I used to be told never to offend one, as he always take it out of you later. That I cannot help, & after all one survives these things.

Yours very truly
Th: Hardy.

Text MS. the Executors of Robert Lynd.
Lynd: Robert Wilson Lynd (1879–1949), journalist and essayist; *D.N.B.* *& New Masters*": Lynd's *Old and New Masters* (London, 1919). *in The Nation*: 'Mr. Hardy in Winter', *Nation*, 22 Dec 1917. *anononymously*: so spelled by TH. *in that paper*: see, however, *LY*, 193, where it is said that TH's attention was first drawn to the review by a reference to it 'in an Australian paper'.

To ROBERT NICHOLS

(Ansr) [Early August 1919]

.... I am quite pleased that he [Mr Kent] should do what I imagine he proposes: Select a dramatic paragraph or sentence from any novel or poem, & make a drawing to it—collecting these drawings together into a book. But he wd perhaps produce a greater effect if he were to take one complete dramatic piece in verse—say "A Trampwoman's Tragedy" & illustrate that throughout. He has my permission to quote it all—& the publishers (who have certain rights in it) would be content if he were to pay them a fee of, say, a guinea ....

Text MS. (pencil draft) DCM. *Date* Replies to letter of 29 July 19.
Nichols: Robert Malise Bowyer Nichols (1893–1944), poet; *D.N.B.* His vol. *Ardours and Endurances* (London, 1917) had attracted much attention both in Britain and in the United States. [*Mr Kent*]: TH's square brackets; Nichols (29 July 19, DCM) had reported that his American artist friend Rockwell Kent (1882–1971) would like to illustrate some of TH's works. Kent himself wrote (12 Sept 19, DCM) to thank TH for his encouragement and an illustration by Kent to TH's 'An Ancient to Ancients' appeared in *Century Magazine*, May 1922.

To ROBERT LYND

MAX GATE, | DORCHESTER. | August 10: 1919.

Dear Mr Lynd:

I must thank you for your letter, & its interesting analysis of the mood forced upon critics by rash young bloods.

I hope you will be able to stay a long time by the sea this hot weather—London being, they tell me, fagging & dusty just now.

Yours very truly
Th: Hardy.

Text MS. Gordon N. Ray.
your letter: it has not survived but would have responded to TH's critical letter of 30 July 19.

To FLORENCE HARDY

Max Gate. | Wedny morning. [13 August 1919]

My dearest F:

I hope you got to Enfield without trouble. I went to Talbothays yesterday, & found Henry all alone, the others having gone to picnic in Knighton Wood. I sent on two letters to you.

If you find it desirable to stay another day & return Friday please don't mind doing so, as I would rather put up with your being away than that you should not finish your jobs.

Nobody has called, & it is just as hot here as ever—I don't think of going out to day at all—as Wessex had plenty of exercise yesterday—& panted with the heat.

I hope you found them all well.

Ever yr affectte
Th.

Text MS. (pencil, with envelope) Purdy. *Date* From postmark.
Enfield: where FEH's parents still lived. *Talbothays*: see letter to FEH of 30 May 15. *the others*: TH's sister Kate, their cousin Mary Antell (see I.232), and a neighbour, Mrs. Clara Marsh (Kate Hardy's diary, Lock Collection, Dorset County Library). *your jobs*: one of these was a visit to Claybury Asylum, in Essex, to visit ELH's niece Lilian Gifford (see Millgate, 527–8) and consult with the medical superintendent about her condition (FEH to Cockerell, 19 Aug 19, Purdy).

To CLEMENT SHORTER

MAX GATE, | DORCHESTER. | August 20: 1919

My dear Shorter:

Your return from America is first made known to me by your interesting letter, for though doubtless many were aware that you had come back, I was supposing you still in the west amid the scenes you describe weekly in *The Sphere*.

My thanks for your good wishes. I sincerely hope you will feel more cheerful when you have settled down. Reentering old haunts is inevitably depressing when you have shared them with another who is no longer there.

Yours very truly
Thomas Hardy.

Text MS. David Holmes.
in The Sphere: Shorter's 'A Literary Letter', *Sphere*, 16 Aug 1919, described visits to San Francisco and Seattle during the final stages of a trip to the United States which he had also chronicled in previous 'Literary Letters'. *no longer there*: a reference to the death of Shorter's wife; see letter of 7 Jan 18.

To MACMILLAN & CO.

Max Gate, | Dorchester. | August 23. 1919.

Dear Sirs:

I have just returned to you the second batch of the sheets you forwarded for me to sign for the Mellstock edition,—the first half of them having been sent back in, I think, June last. The total number seems to be about 540, which will allow a margin for spoilt sheets etc. over the 500.

Yours very truly,
Thomas Hardy.
per F.E.

Text MS. (all except FEH's initials typewritten) BL.
the sheets: see letter of 14 May 19.

To W. J. MALDEN

August 23. 1919.

Dear Sir;

I must thank you for your attention in sending me particulars of the Wessex Saddleback Pig Society, & the Herd Book.

I do not know much about breeding such stock, & am more bent on humane methods of slaughtering than on anything else in relation to it. So that in accepting with appreciation Honorary Membership of the Society I add a suggestion that the question of slaughtering, & transit before slaughtering, should be among the matters that the Society takes up; with a view to causing as little suffering as possible to an animal so intelligent. This worthy object would, I think, add distinction to the Society.

I am not aware if the stupid custom still prevails of having pork well bled. This impoverishment of the meat for the sake of a temporary appearance should, I feel, be discouraged by the Society.

Yours very truly
(Signed) T.H.

W.J. Malden Esq. | [Chairman]

Text MS. (pencil draft) DCM.
Malden: Walter James Malden, agricultural and land agency expert, responsible for introducing the Wessex Saddleback breed of pig. *Pig Society*: Malden (12 Aug 19, DCM) invited TH to become the first Honorary Member of the Society and thus add to the 'many helps' he had already given to Wessex. *discouraged by the Society*: a typed version (DCM) of this draft, prepared for inclusion in *LY* but later omitted, carries the additional statement, 'It is satisfactory to know that Hardy's suggestions were acted upon by the Society'. [*Chairman*]: TH's square brackets.

To J. C. SQUIRE

MAX GATE, | DORCHESTER. | August 24. 1919.

Dear Mr Squire:

It makes me feel rather uneasy when you tell me of this project of a literary monthly, and ask me to send something for the first number,—for I am not up to date nowadays, and as a contributor should probably disappoint everybody. I daresay I could find some small poem of an inoffensive kind; but that would hardly be sufficiently striking, to my mind, and would have no connection with a new enterprise. However, please let me know if nothing better turns up for your purpose, and such would serve.

Yours sincerely,
Thomas Hardy.

P.S. I hope you will forgive machine writing. My wife sends kind regards. Th.H.

Text MS. (typewritten) Taylor.
Squire: John Collings Squire (1884–1958), poet and man of letters; *D.N.B.* *first number*: of the *London Mercury*, ed. by Squire, November 1919; see letter of 29 Aug 19.

To J. C. SQUIRE

MAX GATE, | DORCHESTER. | 29th. August 1919.

Dear Mr Squire:

I am sending this little poem of only two verses, as the nearest I can find to what might pass as proper for a new review. At the same time, as "The London Mercury" (excellent title) seems threatening to be of a flash-of-lightning kind, the poem is decidedly not up to that level.

The only other I can lay hands on is livelier than the one I send, entitled "The Fiddler's Story". So if you fancy something would be better with no philosophy in it, please return this and I will send the other. (By the way it has been printed by my wife in a limited private edition of 25 copies—I suppose this would not matter.) The present one has not been printed anywhere.

Yours sincerely,
Th: Hardy.

P.S. I am honoured by being the first to have the new notepaper.

Text MS. (typewritten) Taylor.
little poem: 'Going and Staying', *London Mercury*, November 1919; a third stanza was added when the poem was collected in *Late Lyrics and Earlier*. *Story"*: subsequently retitled 'The Country Wedding'. *of 25 copies*: this pamphlet, containing 'The Fiddler's Story' and 'A Jingle on the Times', was privately printed at the Chiswick Press in 1917; see Purdy, 192-3. *not matter:* Squire (1 Sept 19, DCM) agreed that this previous publication was unimportant and asked for 'The Fiddler's Story' as well as 'Going and Staying'; it seems not to have appeared in the *London Mercury*, however.

To MACMILLAN & CO.

Max Gate | Dorchester 4 Sept 1919.

The Dynasts.

—There are a few corrections: a word here & there—which will not overrun.

Will send them in a post or two.

Th: H.

Text MS. (postcard printed with Macmillan address) BL.
The Dynasts: the 1-vol. edn. of 1910 was about to be reissued as the second vol. of the 2-vol. edn. of TH's poems; see letter of 15 July 19.

To MACMILLAN & CO.

MAX GATE, | DORCHESTER. | 5th. September 1919.

Dear Sirs:

I send the corrections to the Dynasts.

I also send the Contents-list for the same, which was accidentally omitted from the first edition. When I was speaking to Sir F. Macmillan on the subject he told me it should be inserted in the next edition.

Yours truly,
Thomas Hardy.
per. F.E.

Text MS. (all except FEH's initials typewritten) BL.
corrections: see letter of 4 Sept 19. *from the first edition*: and not incorporated in the printings of 1915 and 1918.

To SIR GEORGE DOUGLAS

MAX GATE, | DORCHESTER. | 11 Sept. 1919

My dear Douglas:

At last I am writing to let you know that I duly received the Hibbert Journal & the welcome letter from you. I did not know till I read the article from your pen that you were so well acquainted with the writings of Goethe—you have kept that light under a bushel hitherto, anyhow. I wish writing were not too irksome to let me enter into the many interesting points you raise. I will only remark on his tendency to moralize, to which you rightly draw attention, as being a defect. Don't you think it was their way in those days? Just along at that time they seem to have forgotten that a writer can be more emphatic without pointing a moral, & by leaving the reader to draw it for himself, than by stating it. However I am such a poor critic of bygone authors—I mean dead authors—that I may be wrong. As to *Werther*, I have always had a sneaking liking for the tale, though that is morbidity, I suppose.

I hope you are not wasting this fine weather—that is, if yours is the same as ours—but are going romantically about your neighbourhood. This afternoon a friend called whom you may have known in years past—Dampier-Whetham, Fellow of Trinity, & writer on eugenics. He is a Dorset man, & a breeder of Devon cows. He has a farm & dairy near here, & comes here in vacation-times.

I had nearly forgotten to reply to the most important thing you tell me—most interesting rather—your doings in Spanish. You will remember I used to have great faith in your possibilities in that direction. I shall be looking out for the article on the Picaresque novel. Both that subject & Don Juan are exceedingly *fresh* ones.

I have been occupied in the dismal work of destroying all sorts of papers which were absolutely of no use for any purpose, God's or man's. I am glad to hear about your nephew & where he is—I love the Rhine as much as any German can. As you say nothing about your health I conclude you are well—as I am, except for a semi-sore throat I have had for a few days, caught I think in the late rain.

Always yours,
Thomas Hardy.

Text MS. NLS.
Hibbert Journal: Douglas's 'Goethe Restudied', *Hibbert Journal*, July 1919. *letter from you*: of 19 Aug 19 (DCM). *a defect*: Douglas wrote, 'A further defect in Goethe, and one which grew on him insidiously, is his tendency to moralise' (685). Werther: TH owned the Bohn's Standard Library edn. of Goethe's novels and tales (London, 1875). *Dampier-Whetham*: William Cecil Dampier Whetham (1867-1952), scientist and agriculturalist, fellow of Trinity College, Cambridge; *D.N.B.* During the years 1918-26 he farmed a family estate at Hilfield St. Nicholas, Dorset, specializing in the making of cheese. *in Spanish*: see letter of 7 May 19. *Picaresque novel . . . Don Juan*: mentioned in Douglas's letter as topics in which he was currently interested; his essay 'The Picaresque Novel' appeared in *Cornhill*, November 1920. *the Rhine*: Douglas's nephew (see letter to Douglas of 2 Feb 18) was serving with the Army of the Rhine.

To EDMUND GOSSE

Max Gate | Sept 22. 1919

My dear Gosse:

As I appear in the list of conspirators against the repose of your 70th birthday you will know that the date was not forgotten by me, even though you get only a belated letter, to express the great pleasure it gives me, &, I may add, my wife, to feel that you have accomplished those years almost without knowing it; for it is really not a compliment, but a bald statement of fact with which even your enemies, if you have any, would agree, to say that age cannot wither him nor custom stale his infinite variety.

As you will be getting or have already got heaps of letters I will not say another word, except of that parental kind which a really old man may use towards a comparatively young one, videlicet, that you are to take care of your health & keep early hours, so as to go on being as you have been.

Always your sincere friend

Thomas Hardy.

Our kindest regards to Mrs Gosse, & the children (as they seem to me.) Th: H.

Text MS. Adams.
list of conspirators: TH's name is appended, along with many others, to a letter of congratulation to Gosse on his 70th birthday, 21 Sept 1919, pub. in *The Times* 22 Sept 1919; see also letter of 15 May 19 to Fitzmaurice-Kelly. *infinite variety*: adapted from *Antony and Cleopatra*, II.ii.235.

To LADY ST. HELIER

MAX GATE, | DORCHESTER. | Thursday | 25 Sept. 1919.

My dear friend:

Florence has to be in London for a night next week, to see the surgeon who is attending to her displaced toe. But on writing to two or three hotels she cannot get a room anywhere. Can you let her have a bed for Wednesday night next, or any other? A telegram form is enclosed to save time & trouble.

I don't know whether you are in London or not, but I send this at a venture. In any case you will, I know, believe that I hope you are well & thriving & that I am

Yours affectionately
Thomas Hardy.

Text MS. Purdy.
displaced toe: this condition was not serious enough for FEH to mention it in any of her letters to Cockerell of this period.

To FLORENCE HARDY

Thursday. 12-30. [2 October 1919]

My dearest F.

Mrs Pocock, & Mr, & Constantine, have called, in conformity with the enclosed telegram—& we have let her have the rug that was in the hall. They drove up to our gate, on their way to London, in a huge van, the one they fetch the animals in. On the outside was painted "Zoological Society"—& it had come for them, driven by 2 of the Zooll Socs men. It smells so of lions, tigers, wolves, &c inside, that Mrs P. said it nearly made her sick, so how she will bear the smell all the way to London I don't know. It was a 10 hours journey to London from Sea Town, & as she wasted an hour by coming round here they will not get back till late. She says people stare as they go by, thinking there are wild animals inside.

Everything is all right here. Eva is gone to get some butter. I have not yet seen to-day's paper. We think of going to Talbothays to-day as it was too wet yesterday. Lily is trying the fire in the Store room.

Every affectly
Th.

I am so glad that you are feeling better—Don't hurry away.

Text MS. (pencil, with envelope) Purdy. *Date* From postmark.
Mrs Pocock, & Mr: see letter of 3 Sept 18. *Constantine*: evidently the Pococks' son. *telegram*: it has not survived and the destination of the rug is therefore unknown. *Sea Town*: where she had been staying; see letter of 3 Sept 18. *Eva*: Eva Dugdale, FEH's sister. *not yet seen*: TH wrote 'not yet see'. *Talbothays*: see letter to FEH of 30 May 15. *Lily*: one of the Max Gate maids. *hurry away*: the envelope is addressed to FEH c/o Mrs. Hanbury at Kingston Maurward House; FEH was apparently there to nurse her foot (see letter of 25 Sept 19) and enjoy the few days rest, away from TH, that had been ordered by her doctor (FEH to Cockerell, 14 Sept 19, Purdy).

To SYDNEY COCKERELL

Max Gate | Oct 12. 1919

My dear Cockerell:

You should not have given yourself trouble about the legend, or otherwise, of Napoleon's landing to reconnoitre. It would certainly be very strange if an invented story should turn out to have already existed. If it would amuse you to send a letter to the Literary Suppt you might do so, but I leave it for you to judge. What you may be sure of is that I never heard of any such tradition. It may be that my having, with the licence of a storyteller to tell lies, *pretended* there was such an account in being, led people to think there was. Of course I did it to give verisimilitude to *my* story.

Young Siegfried Sassoon is here for the week end, & has gone off for a walk in the rain without a hat. He has brought the book from the poets. I really don't deserve their tribute, being as a matter of fact quite unworthy of it. We went for a car-ride on Friday, to the top of Blackdon, & could see all down into Devonshire.

Always yrs
Th:H.

Text MS. Adams.
already existed: according to a note of Cockerell's (Adams), Herbert Trench's play *Napoleon* (London, 1919) had taken as factual the central episode of TH's story 'A Tradition of Eighteen Hundred and Four' (first pub. 1882), in which Napoleon personally lands on the Dorset coast to inspect the site of his projected invasion; Cockerell wrote 9 Oct 19 (DCM) to report that he could find no historical basis for the episode. *might do so*: Cockerell seems not to have acted on this suggestion. *book from the poets*: the 'Poets' Tribute', a bound vol. of poems inscribed in holograph by 43 poets on the occasion of TH's 79th birthday; see *LY*, 192–3, where the impression is given that Sassoon brought the vol. to Max Gate in the early summer of 1919.

To LASCELLES ABERCROMBIE

MAX GATE, | DORCHESTER. | October 13: 1919

Dear Mr Abercrombie:

This book of verses from poet-friends has just come. I knew nothing about any intention of sending such a thing, & I must thank you so much, yet so inadequately, for taking part in it by inscribing those beautiful verses of yours. I shall always value the MS. & think of you as the writer of it. Believe me always

Sincerely yours
Thomas Hardy.

Text MS. (with envelope) Texas.
book of verses: see letter of 12 Oct 19. *verses of yours*: Abercrombie chose to inscribe his 'Love and War'.

To MAURICE BARING

MAX GATE, | DORCHESTER. | October 13: 1919.

Dear Mr Baring:

I discover, to my pleasure, a poem of yours, in your own writing, in this book of verses from poet-friends that has just arrived. I knew nothing about its compilation, & must thank you very heartily for contributing the moving ballad you inscribe. I shall aways prize the MS., & so I hope will others do who come after me.

Yours most sincerely
Thomas Hardy.

Text MS. Harvard.
Baring: Maurice Baring (1874–1945), poet and man of letters; *D.N.B.* *moving ballad*: Baring's 'Song' ('From the bleak sand and the grey sand').

To ROBERT BRIDGES

MAX GATE, | DORCHESTER. | Oct 13: 1919.

Dear Mr Bridges:

I have just received the book of verses from poet-friends, which has been got up quite without my knowledge. To my pleasure I find at the very beginning some striking lines by yourself in your own writing. I cannot express in a brief note my feelings at the discovery, or say how much I value the manuscript.

I often wonder when you are going to give us some more short poems like "The wood is bare". I hope soon. Believe me with warmest thanks & good wishes

Yours sincerely
Thomas Hardy.

Text MS. Lord Bridges.
Bridges: Robert Seymour Bridges (see II.50), poet, Poet Laureate since 1913. *striking lines*: Bridges' 'Trafalgar Square: September, 1917'. *is bare"*: 'The wood is bare: a river-mist is steeping', first pub. in Bridges' *Poems* (London, 1873).

To MACMILLAN & CO.

MAX GATE, | DORCHESTER. | 13th. October 1919.

Dear Sirs:

Miss Mary C. Sturgeon is preparing a new edition of her "Studies of Contemporary Poets," and she wants to include an account of my work, and to make about 60 lines of quotation. I have thought that permission might be given her, charging her, say, a guinea for the extracts. If you agree will you kindly write to her to that effect.

Yours very truly,
Thomas Hardy.
per F.E.

P.S. Her address is Melford Lodge, 159 Stamford Hill, N.16.

Text MS. (all except FEH's initials typewritten) BL.
Sturgeon: Mary C. Sturgeon, literary critic, wrote to TH 1 Oct 19 (DCM). Her *Studies of Contemporary Poets* (London, 1916) did not include TH, but his work was discussed in the revised and enlarged edn. of 1920.

To SIR HENRY NEWBOLT

MAX GATE, | DORCHESTER. | October 13: 1919

My dear Newbolt:

Within the last 48 hours I have been surprised at receiving a book of verses from poet-friends, & to my pleasure an extra degree is added by my finding a poem of yours to be one of those inscribed. I thank you very warmly for writing it, & shall value the MS. greatly. I really don't deserve anything of this sort, particularly now that I am merely a dusty figure on a shelf. However, with renewed thanks & good wishes I am,

Always sincerely yours
Thomas Hardy.

Text MS. Texas.
poem of yours: 'The War Films'.

To SIR ARTHUR QUILLER-COUCH

MAX GATE, | DORCHESTER. | Oct 13. 1919.

My dear Q:

I have had a pleasant surprise in the shape of a book of verses all written out by my poet-friends, & the pleasure was increased when I found a beautiful pastoral poem of yours in its pages. I thank you very warmly, though I am unworthy of such a delightful tribute, being a cracked old pot at the best.

When the strike was on I thought of you frequently, & of how you would get up to Cambridge; but I think it finished before you had occasion to go. I wonder how dear old Cornwall is looking: I don't know when I shall see it again: perhaps never, for I seldom go anywhere now.

With renewed thanks believe me

Always sincerely yours
Thomas Hardy.

Text MS. Miss F.F. Quiller-Couch.
poem of yours: 'Upon Eckington Bridge, River Avon'. *the strike*: a national railway strike, 26 Sept–5 Oct 1919.

To EDMUND GOSSE

MAX GATE, | DORCHESTER. | October 14: 1919.

My dear Gosse:

I had no idea when I wrote my last letter to you that the next I should be sending would be one to thank you for the transcript in your own writing of those verses of yours I have liked so long, which now greet me with those of so many poet-friends. The whole thing has been got up without my knowledge, & I feel unworthy of such a distinction, piping but a feeble reed now & then. However you & the rest have thought it worth while to send these charming pages, & I can only thank you again, & ask you to believe me

Always sincerely yours
Thomas Hardy.

Text MS. (with envelope) Leeds.
liked so long: Gosse's 'Two Points of View'; see III.11.

To ARTHUR McDOWALL

FROM THO. HARDY, | MAX GATE, | DORCHESTER. | Tuesday.
[14 October 1919]

What a pity that I shd have missed you! Had just gone to Froom Hill for Wessex's sake, & must have got back to where the roads part after you had passed. Hope to see you soon.

Th. H.

Text MS. (postcard) T.R. Creighton. *Date* From postmark.
for Wessex's sake: i.e., to take the dog for a walk; for Wessex, see letter of 29 Jan 14. *see you soon*: McDowall was living in the Dorset village of Broadmayne, not far from Dorchester.

To GILBERT MURRAY

MAX GATE, | DORCHESTER. | October 14: 1919

Dear Dr Murray:

I have been reading your fine rendering of the faun-chorus in The Bacchae, which I found—to my added pleasure—in the book of their verses that poet friends have kindly sent me & that I am quite unworthy of. I value the lines too as being in your own hand, & thank you warmly for inscribing them.

It is a relief in these days of rhymeless, rhythmless poets to come across one who still holds that poetry is an art.

Believe me to be

Sincerely yours
Thomas Hardy.

Text MS. Bodleian Library.
Murray: George Gilbert Aimé Murray, classical scholar; see IV.144. *The Bacchae*: Murray's verse trans. of Euripides' play, first pub. 1902.

To J. C. SQUIRE

MAX GATE, | DORCHESTER. | Oct 14: 1919.

Dear Mr Squire:

(I. Editor.) I am taking rather a liberty, but as the poem seems rather grey for a new & hopeful magazine I have annexed another, of quite a frivolous kind, as you will see enclosed. Please do as you like about printing it of course. But I mention my reason.

(II. Poet.) Just one word on another matter. It has been a surprise to me to receive, as I have done within the last day or two, a kind tribute from poet-friends in the form of a book of their verses, in which, to my extra pleasure, I find one from yourself. Accept my very warm thanks, & believe me,

Sincerely yours
Thomas Hardy.

Text MS. Taylor.
annexed another: TH, returning the corrected proof of 'Going and Staying' (see letter of 29 Aug 19), had pasted on the MS. of 'A Glimpse from the Train' (later retitled 'Faintheart in a Railway Train'), which Squire pub. in the *London Mercury*, January 1920. *one from yourself*: Squire's 'The Stronghold'.

To WALTER DE LA MARE

MAX GATE, | DORCHESTER. | October 15: 1919

Dear Mr de la Mare:

This tribute I have just received from my poet-friends is made delightfully satisfactory by your verses, "The Song of the Mad Prince" being among those inscribed. My wife says that it is her favourite among all your poems; while to myself it has a meaning almost too intense to speak of. Many real thanks for sending it, & my best wishes for future poems of yours, which I hope will soon be coming along.

Believe me,

Sincerely yours
Thomas Hardy.

Text MS. Eton College.
Mad Prince": first collected in de la Mare's *Peacock Pie: A Book of Rhymes* (London, 1913). *to speak of*: TH seems to have associated it with the death of ELH.

To ALFRED NOYES

MAX GATE, | DORCHESTER. | October 16: 1919

Dear Mr Noyes:

Among the poems in the collection written by poet-friends for me, that reached me only a few days ago (there having been some delay in binding it I believe) I find a beautiful one by yourself, & must warmly thank you for inscribing it. I did not know that any such gift was in preparation, & value it highly.

I gather that you have wandered far from these shores since we met, & hope you gained much in all ways by your experience.

With renewed thanks I am

Sincerely yours
Thomas Hardy.

Text MS. Univ. of Kentucky.
Noyes: Alfred Noyes, poet; see III.296. *one by yourself*: 'After Victory' ('Love, that still holds us with immortal power'), pub. as part V of Noyes's 7-part poem 'Victory'. *wandered far*: Noyes spent much of the 1914–18 war period in the United States, where he was an active propagandist for the Allied cause.

To SIR FREDERICK MACMILLAN

MAX GATE, | DORCHESTER. | October 17. 1919.

My dear Macmillan:

Many thanks for Cheque. The receipt on back of it is I suppose enough. I did not count upon that American Company being so prompt.

My wife has got back safely. I am glad she mentioned to you what she is doing, which I should never have done myself, though I don't mind her doing it.

Sincerely yours
Thomas Hardy.

Text MS. BL.
for Cheque: Macmillan's letter of 16 Oct 19 (Macmillan letterbooks, BL) forwards a cheque for £1,000 from the American film company which had purchased the rights to *Tess*; see letter to

him of 29 May 19. *back safely*: from a short visit to London; Macmillan speaks of her having visited him on 15 October. *what she is doing*: a reference to the secret composition of 'The Life and Work of Thomas Hardy', largely written by TH himself but pub. after his death, as *Early Life* and *Later Years*, over FEH's name; see Purdy, 265–7, and Millgate, 516–19.

To ROBERT NICHOLS

MAX GATE, | DORCHESTER. | October 17: 1919

Dear Mr Nichols:

Within the last week I have received the volume of poems written out by my poet-friends—there having been some delay, I believe, in getting it bound—& I find in it to my extra pleasure that beautiful poem beginning "Was there love once?" from you. Accept my warmest thanks for the MS. which will always be kept & much valued. Believe me

Sincerely yours
Thomas Hardy.

Text MS. (with envelope) Texas.
beautiful poem: Nichols's 'Fulfilment'; see letter of 8 Jan 18.

To HAROLD MONRO

MAX GATE, | DORCHESTER. | October 18: 1919

Dear Mr Monro:

I have within this week received the sheaf of MS. poems that my poet-friends have taken the trouble to write out & get bound, & my pleasure is increased when I find one among them is by you. Your lines make me wish that Spring would hasten along again; but alas we have some chills to undergo before she reappears. With my sincere thanks for the poem believe me

Always yours truly
Thomas Hardy.

Text MS. Eton College.
Monro: Harold Edward Monro (1879–1932), poet and editor; *D.N.B.* *Your lines*: Monro's 'Spring'.

To JAMES STEPHENS

MAX GATE, | DORCHESTER. | October 18: 1919

Dear Mr Stephens:

In the book of MS. poems that have been bound up & sent me this last week by my poet friends I find some by yourself—three charmingly imaginative, & one more realistic. Please accept my sincere thanks for this unexpected tribute, inadequate as they are, & my assurance that I shall always prize the verses. Believe me,

Ever truly yours
Thomas Hardy.

Text MS. Mrs. Iris Wise.
Stephens: James Stephens (1882–1950), Irish writer; *D.N.B.* *by yourself*: Stephens inscribed his 'Mary Hynes', 'The Voice of God', 'The Rivals', and 'The Tinker's Brat'.

To ROBERT BRIDGES

Max Gate | Dorchester | 19:10:1919

Dear Mr Bridges:

Many thanks for your letter. Alas, I fear I am past the time at which I could write anything for the S.P.E., though never was pure English in more need of help—owing to the influence of American journalism, I suppose. Even in our leading newspapers the head-lines are appalling. It is curious that there seems to be no good *English Grammar* in existence. I wish one of the Society wd take that up.

Sincerely yours
Th: Hardy.

Text MS. Lord Bridges.
S.P.E.: Society for Pure English, of which Bridges was one of the founders (in 1913) and most active members; in his letter of 15 Oct 19 (DCM) he expressed the hope that TH would continue his own support of the Society (see IV.305).

To G. K. CHESTERTON

MAX GATE, | DORCHESTER. | October 19: 1919

Dear Mr Chesterton:

I have had a pleasant surprise within the last few days in receiving a lot of MS. verse bound together, & written by my poet-friends. I must heartily thank you for being one of the number, & shall always value the gift you have sent. Believe me

Sincerely yours
Thomas Hardy.

Text MS. Dorothy Collins.
Chesterton: Gilbert Keith Chesterton (1874–1936), critic, essayist, poet, and novelist; *D.N.B.* *one of the number*: Chesterton inscribed his 'Ecclesiastes'. *always value*: though TH dictated from his deathbed a savage 'Epitaph' on Chesterton; see Millgate, 571.

To AUSTIN DOBSON

Max Gate | Dorchester | Oct. 20. '19.

Dear Austin Dobson:

They have sent me—by "they" I mean a lot of poet-friends—a volume made up of their poems: & among these I find to my extra pleasure one of yours, written in that well-known hand which must insure you against misprints. (I wonder if it does, by the way). I did not expect any such attention, & thank you sincerely for your MS. which I value much.

I hardly ever am in London now, & should like to meet you again at the Athm. Believe me,

Always yours truly
Thomas Hardy.

Text MS. Univ. of London.
Dobson: Austin Dobson, poet and man of letters; see I.288. *one of yours*: Dobson's 'More Poets Yet'. *Athm*: the Athenaeum Club; see I.235.

To SIR WILLIAM WATSON

MAX GATE, | DORCHESTER. | October 20: 1919

Dear Sir William Watson:

Within the last few days I have had the pleasure of receiving a volume made up of poems by my poet-friends, & among them I find a beautiful lyric of yours—made more valuable by being in your own writing. I thank you very sincerely for the gift which I shall always prize.

I don't know where you may be just now, but hope this will get to you by the route of your publisher's office.

Believe me

Ever yours truly
Thomas Hardy.

Text MS. (with envelope) Texas.
lyric of yours: Watson's 'Whither Afar?' *publisher's office*: the envelope is addressed to Watson c/o Mr. John Murray.

To SIR FREDERICK MACMILLAN

MAX GATE, | DORCHESTER. | 24th. October '19.

Dear Sir Frederick Macmillan:

I have received the enclosed letter asking about film-rights in any of my novels not yet appropriated. Do you think it is worth while to go on with the Company inquiring? I know nothing of them.

So far as I remember, the only novels of which the cinema-rights are not open are Tess of the D'Urbervilles and Far from the Madding Crowd. I vaguely recollect people inquiring before this time, and my answering that certain ones were available; but I can find no agreements on the subject, and probably nothing came of their request. So that there are plenty that the Master Films Co. might have.

Of these, two have an American copyright, Jude and the Well-Beloved. Also two volumes of Short stories (but I suppose these latter are not worth considering.)

We corresponded on this point in May 1915, as you will find.

I suppose The Dynasts (on which I had a discussion with Mr Drinkwater in November 1915, and he came and consulted with you, and apparently did not carry out his idea of filming it) would be too big a thing for the Master Films?

Anyhow, The Mayor of Casterbridge, The Trumpet Major, and (if they want sensation) Desperate Remedies, would film very well, I should think, so that if you are willing to offer them either of these I would agree.

I am sorry to trouble you about this, but if it comes to anything please deduct a sufficient percentage to cover the trouble.

Yours sincerely
Thomas Hardy.

Text MS. (typewritten) BL.
enclosed letter: although the letter itself has disappeared, Macmillan's reply to TH (27 Oct 19, Macmillan letterbooks, BL) indicates that it was an enquiry about film rights in TH's novels from The Master Films, Ltd., a short-lived British film company which produced a version of George Eliot's *Daniel Deronda* but not, apparently, any films based on TH's works. *in May 1915*: see letters to Macmillan of 19 and 30 May 15. *in November 1915*: see letter of 6 Nov 15, in which TH discouraged Albert Drinkwater from pursuing his idea. *sufficient percentage*: Macmillan replied that he would be glad to act without charging a percentage or indeed any kind of fee.

To T. STURGE MOORE

Max Gate | Dorchester [Late October 1919]

Dear Mr Sturge Moore:

I am writing just one line of thanks to you for so kindly transcribing your fine sonnet on Shakespeare into the book my poet friends have made up & sent me within the last ten days, to my surprise & pleasure.

Believe me

Yours always truly
Thomas Hardy.

Text MS. NYU. *Date* From internal evidence.
Moore: Thomas Sturge Moore (1870–1944), poet, critic, and wood engraver. *on Shakespeare*: Moore's 'On Shakespeare's Sonnets', subsequently collected as 'Before Rereading Shakespeare's Sonnets'. *the last ten days*: compare letter of 28 Oct 19 to Charlotte Mew.

To CHARLOTTE MEW

MAX GATE, | DORCHESTER. | Oct. 28: 1919

Dear Miss Mew:

I am sending a brief line to thank you for the beautiful poem you wrote in the volume made up by my poet friends, without my knowledge, which reached me about 10 days ago, having been delayed I believe by the binder. I shall always value the MS. & keep it for your sake, as will my wife also.

Believe me

Ever yours sincerely
Thomas Hardy.

Text MS. Univ. of Virginia.
Mew: Charlotte Mary Mew (1869–1928), poet; *D.N.B.* TH was much interested in her work and she had visited Max Gate in December 1918 (see Millgate, 525). *beautiful poem*: her 'Love Love Today'. *about 10 days ago*: TH had of course received the vol. earlier than this; see letter of 12 Oct 19.

To JOHN MIDDLETON MURRY

MAX GATE, | DORCHESTER. | October 28: 1919.

Dear Mr Murry:

I write a line of acknowledgement, little as I write now. The verses are very striking I think, & they will keep. It will be for others to judge of their content. I must limit myself to admiring their form.

Their arrival was of the nature of a coincidence. I had just unearthed a drawing of the tomb in Stinsford Churchyard under which my wife lies & where I suppose I shall be laid—I hope so at any rate—& I was thinking of matters connected therewith, when lo, there enters your letter with the verses. I am glad you did not alter them.

With best thanks I am

Always yours
Thomas Hardy.

Text MS. Berg.
The verses: tipped on to a blank leaf of the 'Poets' Tribute' vol., and on different paper from that used by the other contributors, is Murry's poem 'To T.H.', dated 25 Oct 1919. *they will keep*: the poem begins 'He is gone' and amounts to a lament for TH's death. *alter them*: Murry apparently asked TH's forgiveness for 'writing as though you were no longer among us', saying that he had thought of altering the verses but decided he 'could not do otherwise than be honest. It is a virtue which you compel' (letter of 26 Oct 19, quoted *Journal of Modern Literature*, February 1973, 39).

To SIR FREDERICK MACMILLAN

MAX GATE, | DORCHESTER. | 29th. October 1919.

Dear Sir Frederick:

Many thanks for your agreeing to see the Master Films Co. about the novels. As I do not myself know what the films are worth I will ask you to settle for me about a price, and your suggestion of a sum down is certainly the best, as their performances cannot be watched. £500 would be quite satisfactory, but I leave terms to you, if it gets so far as that.

Believe me,

Very truly yours,
Thomas Hardy.

Text MS. (typewritten) BL.
about the novels: see letter of 24 Oct 19.

To W.H. DAVIES

MAX GATE, | DORCHESTER. | Nov. 2: 1919

Dear Sir:

Please accept my sincere thanks for the beautiful verses on "The Kingfisher" which I find in the book of contributions by poet-friends. I shall always prize the MS.

Very truly yours
Thomas Hardy.

W.H. Davies Esq.

Text MS. Texas.
Davies: William Henry Davies (1871–1940), poet and author; *D.N.B.* *"The Kingfisher"*: first collected in Davies' *Farewell to Poesy and Other Pieces* (London, 1910).

To J. J. FOSTER

MAX GATE, | DORCHESTER. | 2nd. November 1919.

Dear Mr Foster:

The paper is returned signed. As to the first Earl of Salisbury, I should not think him a Dorset worthy, and I should even more positively exclude Jane Austen and Wordsworth. Hoping you are well I am,

Very truly yours
Th: Hardy.

P.S. Kind regards from F.E.H.

Text MS. (typewritten) Princeton.
signed: Foster (30 Oct 19, DCM) had asked if TH would propose him for membership in the Incorporated Society of Authors, of which TH was president. *and Wordsworth*: all three

figures are in fact mentioned in Foster's *Wessex Worthies*, the 1st Earl of Salisbury (1563?-1612; *D.N.B.*) for his occasional visits to Cranborne Manor, Jane Austen for her connection with Lyme Regis, and Wordsworth for the period he spent at Racedown Lodge, near Pilsdon; they are not, however, included in the 'Classified List' of Worthies.

To J. C. SQUIRE

Max Gate | Dorchester. | Nov. 2: 1919

Many thanks for first number. Please do what you like with the other little poem—

Th: H.

Text MS. (postcard) Taylor.
first number: of the *London Mercury*. *other little poem*: see letter to Squire of 14 Oct 19.

To CHARLES GIFFORD

MAX GATE, | DORCHESTER. | Nov 3: 1919

Dear Mr Gifford:

Many thanks for your congratulations. But it is rather amusing that, though I have been 80 in America for several years, & am now called 80 in England, I shall not be really 80 till the middle of next year, when people will doubtless begin to say: "How many more times is that Hardy going to be fourscore!"

We are glad to find that you are a little nearer than you were. If the railways are ever rational again we may get a glimpse of you or of Léonie. The sound of grandchildren is cheerful. I am at the fag end of my family. Your son's connection with electricity, which is so much to the fore in everything, must be promising. We are still in the Dark ages here, so to speak, using lamps & candles.

Yes: we have been very well this year till last week, when though I had a slight cold we fulfilled a promise to a friend, Mr Symons-Jeune, & his daughter who lives near, to go to the opening of a hospital at Swanage, where, in a north-east wind, I had to make a speech proposing a vote of thanks to the Bishop; & my cold is pretty bad now in consequence.

Our kindest regards to both your girls & yourself. I hope the rheumatism does not trouble you much.

Sincerely yours
Thomas Hardy.

Text MS. C. H. Gifford.
congratulations: Gifford, misled by newspaper reports of the 'Poets' Tribute' (which is dedicated to TH 'On this birthday of your eightieth year'), wrote 2 Nov 19 (DCM) to congratulate TH on his 80th birthday. *nearer than you were*: Gifford had moved during the war from Blackheath, SE of London, to West Byfleet, near Woking, Surrey. *rational again*: a reference to the recent railway strike; see letter of 13 Oct 19 to Quiller-Couch. *Léonie*: see letter to Gifford of 4 Oct 15. *with electricity*: Walter Stanley Gifford (see letter to Gifford of 4 Oct 15) was co-founder of the Electric Furnace Company. *his daughter*:

Mrs. Hanbury; see letter of 13 Oct 15 for her connection with the Giffords. *at Swanage*: TH and FEH were present at the opening of the Dorset Red Cross Memorial Children's Hospital at Swanage, Dorset, 31 Oct 1919; Mrs. Hanbury was Secretary of the Dorset Red Cross Society. *the Bishop*: of Salisbury (see letter of 3 Sept 18); TH in fact seconded the vote of thanks (see letter of 7 Nov 19).

To LORD BLYTH

MAX GATE, | DORCHESTER. | Nov. 4. 1919.

Dear Lord Blyth:

Many thanks for the Portuguese Onions that you so kindly send. My garden produce is limited for various reasons, & in the case of this particular vegetable because we are on the chalk, which seems not to agree with onions altogether.

These are beautifully spherical. Such perfect shapes one seldom sees.

Yours very truly
Thomas Hardy.

Text MS. NYU.
Blyth: James Blyth, 1st Lord Blyth (1841–1925), authority on agriculture; his home was in Essex and the occasion of his gift to TH is not known.

To GEORGE RUSSELL

MAX GATE, | DORCHESTER. | Nov. 4: 1919

Dear Mr Russell:

It was so kind of you to write those beautiful lines in the MS. volume my poet-friends have sent me that I would have thanked you sooner if I had known it was coming; but I have received it only just lately, quite as a surprise. I shall always value your contribution highly, & I hope others will after me.

With renewed thanks believe me

Sincerely yours
Thomas Hardy.

Text MS. University College, Dublin.
Russell: George William Russell (1867–1935), better known as 'AE', Irish literary and political figure; *D.N.B.* *beautiful lines*: Russell's 'Continuity'.

To FLORENCE HENNIKER

Max Gate | Nov. 7: 1919

My dear friend:

Your welcome letter came when I was keeping in bed for a day or two with a bad cold—well, rather bad—& now I am about the house again. It was developed, if not caught, by a visit we paid to Swanage a week ago to assist at the opening of a Children's Hospital by the Bishop. He is a very nice man, & you should have seen & heard me making a speech of thanks to him for coming. All went off very well, but Florence has now the cold—I knew she would get it. We got there & back (about 25 miles each way) with our neighbours the Hanburys—who have a big car. Lady Ilchester is the President, & she made a very good speech. She asked F. affectionately about you, & was on her way to Holland House.

Those three & forty took me by surprise. It seems that the "tribute", as they call it, has been in preparation for some time. I fear I shall not be able to live up to it with due dignity. Some of them are charming poems. I hope you will see the collection some day.

Yes: I am a strange member of the Wessex Pig Society. I accepted the nomination entirely in the hope of helping to popularize the "killer". I have seen so much cruelty practised on those poor animals.

I regret to hear of Anna's cold; but it is impossible to go to London at this time of the year without getting one. We are much struck by Milner's hospital treatment: he would hold up his head to Wessex, whose life is of a wild sort, though he has several bedrooms, & goes from one to another.

I thought the letters you allude to very charming & graceful. Gerrie as an explorer is a new idea, & rather attractive. By the way those youngsters—I mean the poets—have made me a year older than I am, but it has this convenience, that if I ever do get to be 80 I shall be able to slip by the date without much notice, it having been discounted (I think that is the commercial word) already.

Emma will have been in Stinsford Churchyard seven years this month. It does not seem so long. I am sending a short poem to the Fortnightly which they asked me for a year ago. Believe me

Always affectionately
Tho. H.

Florence sends love, & is going to write.

Text MS. DCM.
welcome letter: of 1 Nov 19 (typed transcript, DCM). *by the Bishop*: see letter of 3 Nov 19. *the President*: of the British Red Cross Society, which had established the hospital. *Holland House*: see letter of 3 June 15 to FEH. *the "killer"*: see letter of 23 Aug 19 to Malden; Mrs. Henniker had expressed the hope that TH's advocacy had been effective. *Anna's*: see letter of 5 June 19. *Milner's*: Mrs. Henniker reported that her dog (see letter of 11 June 14) was receiving 'massage and electric treatment'. *the letters*: the letter on Gosse's 70th birthday (see letter of 22 Sept 19), and Gosse's reply, pub. in *The Times* 18 Oct 19. *Gerrie*: Gerald Fitzgerald; see letter to Mrs. Henniker of 22 Dec 16. *an explorer*: Mrs. Henniker said that her nephew was studying archaeology at Cambridge 'with a view to doing explorations later on'. *a year older*: see letter of 3 Nov 19. *short poem*: 'By Mellstock Cross at the Year's End', *Fortnightly Review*, December 1919; TH later revised the title to 'By Henstridge Cross at the Year's End'.

To JOHN MIDDLETON MURRY

Max Gate | Nov 8: 1919.

Dear Mr Murry:

I have just read the review, & must thank you for it; but as you will recognize I am precluded from weighing it. I must leave that process for other scales.

In going through it (I have not read it carefully yet) I have been struck with some of your casual remarks. One is: "There is no necessary connection between poetic apprehension & poetic method." You could throw a flood of light on the history & art of poetry by using that as the text for a long article (though parsons don't usually *make* their own texts!) There are many others.

I forget if I told you that the second poem you quote really happened, which now gives it a peculiar quality to myself—the white clothed form having long escaped all further possibility of crucifixion.

These are notes I am making over the fire during a bad cold—you will excuse their disjointedness, I am sure.

Sincerely yours
Thomas Hardy.

Text MS. Berg.
the review: Murry's 'The Poetry of Mr. Hardy' (a review of the 1-vol. *Collected Poems*), *Athenaeum*, 7 Nov 1919. *second poem*: TH's 'Near Lanivet, 1872'; see letter of 28 Jan 18.

To LORD SANDHURST

18 Nov. 1919.

Dear Lord Sandhurst:

I fear I must not at present write a special appeal for Barts, much as I sympathize. Our County Hospital here, of wh. I am one of the Governors is deeply in debt, & we are at our wit's end as to how it is to be cleared off. We try all sorts of methods—among others that of plays based on my novels—with more or less success. I helped arrange one of these for an entertainment given a few days ago.

So what little I can do specially must be limited to home, & I must to my regret leave St. Bartholomew's to writers living more in its vicinity.

But I would, with pleasure, be one amongst other signatories to a general letter drawn up by yourself or another. It is strange that three weeks ago, in making a short speech for a Children's Hospital just established in this county, I gave some details of Bart's as the oldest hospital.

Yours very truly
(Signed) Th. H——y

Text MS. (pencil draft) DCM.
Sandhurst: William Mansfield, Viscount Sandhurst (1855–1921), Governor of Bombay 1895–1900. *Barts*: St. Bartholomew's Hospital, London; Lord Sandhurst, as Treasurer, had

asked TH (17 Nov 19, DCM) to write a letter supporting the hospital's appeal for funds which could be pub. in a forthcoming special issue of the *Daily Mirror*. *entertainment*: dramatic sketches from *Far from the Madding Crowd* performed in the Dorchester Corn Exchange, 6 Nov 1919, in aid of the St. Mary's Church Building Fund. *short speech*: see letter of 3 Nov 19. *oldest hospital*: TH spoke of it as 'the first modern hospital' in England (*Dorset County Chronicle*, 6 Nov 19).

To SIR FREDERICK MACMILLAN

MAX GATE, | DORCHESTER. | 22nd. November 1919.

Dear Sir Frederick:

Certainly. I don't see any help for it—if the prices of paper, printing, binding, &c, have gone up as you say. I had heard about the large increase in binding prices, but only vaguely of the others. I am sure you and your partners will do what is the just thing all round in the matter.

I am reminded to send a small list of errata that I and other people have noted in the Collected Poems. Could they be printed on a slip of paper and dropped into bound copies opposite the first page. In the case of unbound ones I suppose they could be stitched in when they come to the binding. I am assuming that this is a small matter, but if troublesome it can stand over, as it is not of vital importance.

Many thanks for the Spanish translation of "A Pair of Blue Eyes". I am sending one copy to my friend Sir George Douglas, whose mother was a Spanish lady, and to whom the language is half-native, for his opinion on the work.

I am glad to hear of the good prospects of the 'Mellstock' edition. As you will remember, the only proofs I should like to glance through are those of "A Pair of Blue Eyes", of which I sent a list of corrections for the printers' copy that it would be well I should verify.

Yours sincerely,
Thomas Hardy.

Text MS. (typewritten) BL.
Certainly: Macmillan (21 Nov 19, Macmillan letterbooks, BL) had asked if, in view of rising production costs, TH would sanction an increase in the retail prices of his books. *opposite the first page*: Macmillan (26 Nov 19, Macmillan letterbooks, BL) replied that the slips would be printed immediately and inserted in all unsold copies of *Collected Poems*. *Blue Eyes*": sent by Macmillan 20 Nov 19 (Macmillan letterbooks, BL); see letter of 18 Mar 17. *will remember*: see letter of 18 June 19.

To NEWMAN FLOWER

MAX GATE, | DORCHESTER. | 23rd. November 1919.

Dear Mr Flower:

I would willingly let you have early next year first serial use of a new poem for 30 guineas, but I have some doubts whether the kind of poem I could send would suit your purpose. Any poem I write now, which is not often, is almost sure to be of a domestic kind, and not "topical", or of public interest. Please therefore consider whether you still think it would be worth while to have such verses. My wife has replied, I know, concerning the use of poem in the Dorset Year Book.

With kind regards,

Yours very sincerely,
Thomas Hardy.

Text MS. (typewritten) Texas.
suit your purpose: Flower (17 Nov 19, DCM) asked TH for a contribution to an ambitious new magazine, printed largely in colour, which Cassells were projecting; the scheme seems not to have materialized, although an enlarged version of TH's 'The Fiddler's Story' (see letter of 29 Aug 19) did appear, as 'The Country Wedding', in *Cassell's Winter Annual*, 1921–22, with 2 illustrations in colour by C. E. Brock. *Year Book*: of which Flower was editor; TH's 'Autumn in King's Hintock Park' was pub., under its original title 'Autumn in the Park', in the 1919–20 number.

To SIR HAMO THORNYCROFT

Max Gate | Nov 23: 1919

My dear Thornycroft:

I am reminded that I have not replied to your letter by seeing in a London Evening paper that though there is a good portrait of me in my "Collected Poems", "*the Thornycroft Bust*, of which a photograph is given in the Golden Treasury Selection", is the best—or words to that effect.

Yes, indeed. I wish I could have been present at the performance of "The Trojan Maidens"—Years & years ago I used to wonder why translations of Greek plays were not put on the English stage—and now perhaps they are going to be—though I doubt if they will oust the *Revues*.

I am sorry to hear that such wretched drawings as you describe should be so eulogized. I wish I could see them & form an opinion. But London in the winter is not for me. If there are a dozen germs of influenza in the whole city they go for us people who come from fresh air, though they leave immune the people who live there—Kindest regards to Lady Thornycroft from us both.

Always sincerely
Thomas Hardy.

Text MS. DCM.
your letter: of 19 Nov 19 (DCM). *the best*: for the bust and vignette see letter to Thornycroft of 24 Feb 15 and letter of 27 July 16 to Macmillan. *Trojan Maidens*": Thornycroft described in glowing terms a performance at the Alhambra Theatre of Gilbert Murray's translation of *The Trojan Women* of Euripides. *why translations*: TH first wrote 'why more translations'. *wretched drawings*: Thornycroft expressed annoyance at the positive review in *The Times*, 18 Nov 1919, of a Matisse and Maillol exhibition at one of the London galleries.

To FRANCIS BRETT YOUNG

MAX GATE, | DORCHESTER. | Nov. 24: 1919

Dear Mr Brett-Young:

I must write a line of thanks, though a late one, & though I don't know where you are, for the striking song you have been so good as to put into the book sent me by poet-friends. The last verse of it comes as a strange surprise. I shall always value the MS., & I need not say that it will be taken care of by me, & others after me.

Yours sincerely
Thomas Hardy.

Text MS. Univ. of Birmingham.
Young: Francis Brett Young (1884–1954), novelist and poet; *D.N.B.* *striking song*: Young's 'Song', beginning 'I made a song in my love's likeness'.

To HELEN GIFFORD

MAX GATE, | DORCHESTER. | Nov. 25: 1919.

Dear Miss Gifford:

Yes: I remember hearing from your father about the school & that it was becoming a success. Many congratulations. As one of the Governors of our Grammar School here I have an inkling of what teaching is nowadays. I think I also recollect your coming to our London flat in 1910. I hope some day to see you again & your sister. I tell your father that now he is on this side of London we shall be more accessible to each other. That bit of journey beyond London used to be troublesome.

We have been amused at looking over your pupils' list of the poets who contributed. We find that they are right as to *33* out of the 43—a remarkably high proportion I think, & a credit to your girls' acquaintance with current verse, considering the crowd of young poets now writing. We have been requested not to make known the actual list, or I would send it. Believe me

Sincerely yours
Thomas Hardy.

Text MS. C. H. Gifford.
Gifford: Helen Gifford (1887–1964), schoolteacher, younger daughter of ELH's cousin Charles Gifford. *the school*: Miss Gifford was currently joint-headmistress of Allenswood School, Wimbledon, of which Marie Souvestre (see Michael Holroyd, *Lytton Strachey: A Critical Biography*, Vol. I, London, 1967, 34–41) had been the principal until her death in 1905. *this side of London*: see letter of 3 Nov 19. *who contributed*: Miss Gifford's pupils had evidently been asked to guess the names of the 43 contributors to the 'Poets' Tribute'.

To SIR FREDERICK MACMILLAN

MAX GATE, | DORCHESTER. | 27: 11: 1919

My dear Macmillan:

I shall be pleased for you to do for the Scandinavian rights of "F.M. Crowd" as you did for the Spanish translation of "A Pair of Blue Eyes", which was quite satisfactory.

Sincerely yrs
Thomas Hardy.

Text MS. (correspondence card) BL.
"F.M. Crowd": Macmillan reported (26 Nov 19, Macmillan letterbooks, BL) a request for Scandinavian rights to TH's *Far from the Madding Crowd*; the translation, *Fjärran fran vimlets yra* (Helsingfors, 1920), was by Nino Runeberg. *Blue Eyes"*: see letter of 18 Mar 17.

To AN UNIDENTIFIED CORRESPONDENT

[December 1919?]

The only practical advice I can give, and I give that with great diffidence, is to begin with *imitative* poetry, adopting the manner and views of any recent poet—say Wordsworth or Tennyson—You will thus attract the praises of the critical papers, and escape the satire and censure which they are sure to bestow on anything that strikes them as unfamiliar. Having won them by good imitations you can introduce your originalities by degrees. For if you want your book to sell it is fatal to begin with any original vein you may be blest with—to hear "some new thing", which so fascinated the Athenians, being a red rag to the English reviewer.

Be also very careful about the mechanical part of your verse—rhythms, rhymes, &c. They do not know that dissonances, and other irregularities can be produced advisedly, as art, and worked as to give more charm than strict conformities, to the mind and ear of those trained and steeped in poetry; but they assume that a poet who commits one of these irregularities does so because of his ignorance, and the inferiority of his ear to that of the critic himself. *Ars est celare artem* they have never heard of or forget it.

Text Typed transcript DCM. *Date* See note below.
Unidentified: this item, headed 'To an unnamed young poet— / (about December 1919.)', appears among the materials once considered for inclusion in *Later Years* ('Memoranda & Notes towards completing the remainder of Vol. II'); it seems possible, however, that the young poet was imaginary and the letter a polemical exercise, never sent. *to hear . . . reviewer*: TH later revised the typescript to read, 'the hearing of "some new thing", which so fascinated the Athenians, being to the English reviewer as a red rag to a bull'. *"some new thing"*: Acts 17: 21.

To A.E. DRINKWATER

MAX GATE, | DORCHESTER. | December 6th. 1919.

Dear Mr Drinkwater:

I was glad to hear from Oxford some time ago that you were to arrange the production of the scenes from "The Dynasts" for the Dramatic Society—your experience not only in general, but in that particular representation, being invaluable.

As you already know what I think about the giving of out-door scenes—conventionally only, of course,—by a green-gray floorcloth and a back-cloth modulating from greyish where it touches the floor to bluish at the top, I will quite leave it to you. These two cloths would do for *every* outdoor scene I should think; but you will know best as I have no practical experience.

In respect of your question about the Prologue, I would suggest either omitting it altogether, or (if you really want a prologue) making it merely the few lines from

"We'll close up Time, as a bird its van"

down to

"Close to the rearward of its Cause".

These lines are in the volume itself, but the earlier part of the Prologue you used in London were lines written for the nonce, in the middle of the war-struggle, and were not a part of the drama.

For the same reason I would omit the Epilogue entirely, that being quite a temporary addition that applied only to the moment.

Believe me,

Sincerely yours,
Th: Hardy.

P.S. It is, of course, distinctly understood, as on the former occasion, that this selection of scenes for the stage is not to be printed. Th: H.

Text MS. (typewritten) Colby.
Dramatic Society: the Oxford University Dramatic Society; Drinkwater had written (4 Dec 19, DCM) to seek TH's advice. The production, staged 10–14 Feb 1920, used the Granville Barker version of 1914, for which Drinkwater had been stage-manager (see letter of 27 Sept 14 and letter of 10 Nov 14 to Macmillan).

To SYDNEY COCKERELL

[7 December 1919]

It is most generous of Mr. Johnson to write the letter: yet he may hardly have perceived what was most flagrant in the Saturday Review criticism—that, of the only two of my husband's poems the reviewer quoted as samples from which to judge of his work, one was written in 1866, more than fifty years ago, when he had just begun writing, and the other was a piece of intentional doggerel, from the "Fifteen Glimpses"—all written as doggerel satire in a periodical, which he would never have reprinted if he had not been compelled to by its having been so imitated. It would be as honest to quote the "Epitaph on John Adams the Carrier" as a specimen of Byron's poetry, or "The Devil's Thoughts" as a specimen of Coleridge's, as to do what the reviewer did. It seems extraordinary that such trickery should be practised nowadays, which would, I should think, damage any review, since, if discovered, it would set people against the review.

Text MS. (typewritten; passage dictated by TH included in FEH's letter to Cockerell of 7 Dec 19) Purdy.
the letter: as FEH made clear to Cockerell in her opening paragraph, a letter from an Austen H. Johnson pub. in the *Saturday Review*, 29 Nov 1919, had revived TH's irritation at the anonymous review ('The Poetry of Thomas Hardy', *Saturday Review*, 15 Nov 1919) against which Johnson sought to defend him; TH's dictation of these comments was acknowledged in FEH's letter to Cockerell of 18 Dec 19 (Purdy). See Viola Meynell, ed., *Friends of a Lifetime: Letters to Sydney Carlyle Cockerell* (London, 1940), 304–5.

To JOHN FREEMAN

MAX GATE, | DORCHESTER. | Dec. 7: 1919

Dear Mr Freeman:

Your poem "The Herd", that you so kindly inscribed in the book of MS. verses sent me by contemporary poets & friends, so appealed to me—one who knows that sort of thing—that I ought to have thanked you for it long ago. However, I do so now, & assure you I shall always value the lines, & your handwriting of them.

Very truly yours,
Thomas Hardy.

Text MS. (correspondence card) Univ. of British Columbia.
Freeman: John Freeman (1880–1929), poet and critic; *D.N.B.*

To MAURICE COLBOURNE

MAX GATE, | DORCHESTER. | 11th. December 1919.

My dear Mr Colbourne:

Your plan for out-of-doors is very ingenious and attractive—and more elaborate than I imagined, my idea having been just a back-cloth coloured greyish-blue, and a floor cloth coloured greenish grey—a purely conventional representation for all open-air scenes. But if the roller-scheme can be carried out I, of course, quite agree to it.

My feeling was the same as yours about the Strophe and Antistrophe—that they should be unseen, and as it were speaking from the sky. But it is, as you hint, doubtful if the two ladies will like to have their charms hidden. Would boys do instead, or ugly ladies with good voices?

Mr Drinkwater also wrote to me about the Prologue and Epilogue; and I have suggested to him to omit either all the former, or all except the lines beginning "We'll close up Time as a bird its van."—which are in the original book. The Epilogue, having been so entirely temporary, should I think be quite left out. If you really need an Epilogue the Choruses beginning "Last as first the question rings" might do.

But I do not wish to influence largely your methods of presentation. It will be of the greatest interest to me, whether I can get to Oxford for the performance or not, to see how the questions that arise in doing the thing have been grappled with by younger brains than mine.

Believe me,

Yours sincerely,
Th: Hardy.

Text MS. (typewritten) Purdy. *Date* The erroneous date, 11 Nov 19, assigned to this letter in *LY*, 196–7, was derived from TH's draft (DCM).
Colbourne: Maurice Colbourne (1894–1965), actor, manager, and director; he was currently president of the O.U.D.S. and director of its production of *The Dynasts* (see letter of 6 Dec 19). *Your plan*: described in Colbourne's letter of 8 Dec 19 (DCM). *wrote to me*: see letter of 6 Dec 19.

To CHARLES MORGAN

MAX GATE, | DORCHESTER. | 11th. December 1919.

Dear Mr Morgan:

I have great pleasure in hearing from you on your plans for materializing "The Dynasts", or a part of it. As to my being present on one or two of the days I by no means would say that it is impossible: merely that I don't like to promise to attend; so that there is not the slightest harm in your stating that I hope to be there (on whichever night you like to fix). Indeed on looking at the map by the light of the suggestion to go by road I find the distance to be not so formidable as I thought—about 95 miles I make it—a distance I have been accustomed to do by car in one day. Hence to break the journey would be unnecessary.

As to your sending a car, I don't like to trouble the Society to do that—yet if they would *like* to do it, I am quite willing. Suppose we let it be that you will fetch me and my wife, if all is well; but that we will get home independently.

I assume there would be no necessity for a speech or anything of that kind? I am quite unable to make one, or the tenth part of one: and the imminence of it would keep me away more than winter weather. Please inform your President of these things.

As to the details of representation. Rather than impose any conditions of method, what I should prefer would be that you and your committee exercise your own judgment thereon: it would greatly interest me to see what younger and more vigorous minds than my own had decided to do in the various problems that arise. So please consider yourselves quite free-handed in any questions that occur. Certainly give more of the choral passages if you think the audience will stand them without being bored. Those given at the Kingsway were not selected by me. I like too the idea of concealing the Reader as well as Strophe and Antistrophe. But it will be advisable to try the effect of all this before deciding.

There is, by the way, one more point I may mention. Mr Barker after a few representations, omitted two (I think) scenes of his stage selection, because of the distress they seemed to cause those among the spectators who had just lost relatives in the war. The scenes were two of the best—the Burial of Moore, and another, I am not sure which;—and by so doing he brought other scenes together that should have been kept apart. This I should advise you not to do.

Believe me,

Yours very truly,
Th: Hardy.

Text MS. (typewritten, with envelope in FEH's hand) Roger Morgan.
Morgan: Charles Langbridge Morgan (1894–1958), novelist, dramatic critic, and playwright; *D.N.B.* He was currently stage-manager of the O.U.D.S. production of *The Dynasts*. *hearing from you*: Morgan wrote 9 Dec 19 (DCM), mentioning a letter of introduction which Mrs. Crackanthorpe (see IV.89) had already sent TH on his behalf (5 Dec 19, DCM). *your President*: Maurice Colbourne.

To ELIZABETH ROBINS

MAX GATE, | DORCHESTER. | 12th. December 1919.

Dear Miss Robins:

I am sending to you, care of Dr Edmonds, a book for the Hospital, with my signature, as you request. I wish I could send more; but I have already two local hospitals to do what I can for. I do not remember the meeting at Rossetti's house, but I very well remember meeting you on other occasions; and I am glad, by receiving your application for help to this Hospital, to be able to conclude that you are well and active.

I am compelled nowadays to have recourse to the typewriter, which I hope you will excuse.

Yours most truly,
Th: Hardy.

Text MS. (typewritten) NYU.
Robins: Elizabeth Robins, actress and author; see II.109. *Dr Edmonds*: Florence Mary Edmonds, house surgeon, Royal Alexandra Hospital for Children, Brighton. *as you request*: Miss Robins, as chairman of the Board of Management of the New Sussex Hospital for Women and Children, had asked TH (4 Dec 19, DCM) to send a signed copy of one of his books for sale at a fund-raising bazaar. *at Rossetti's house*: Tudor House, Cheyne Walk, Chelsea, where Dante Gabriel Rossetti lived from 1869 until his death in 1882. Miss Robins had recalled meeting TH at a luncheon there in 1894, at which date the house was occupied by the Revd. Hugh Reginald Haweis and his wife Mary (see II.37, 59).

To HAROLD CHILD

MAX GATE, | DORCHESTER. | December 15: 1919

Dear Mr Child:

I thought I would read the book before writing, & as I don't care to hurry through a volume of poetry I am rather late in my acknowledgment. The verses interested me much, though they would have to drift a few years into the past before I could coolly criticize them.

I will just say that I like "In the Minster", "For her birthday", "Her laugh", "Pastiche", & "Wind in the Corn". Also "Time", & "Wild Roses" (both of the kind best described as "charming"—the latter Waller-ish). Also "Wind in the Night" "The Yellow Rock", "Wind & Wave" & "Real & Ideal". Then, too, I rather like "The Woman", "A Dream", & "Before her Portrait." I may shift my preferences later on, or may include more. Meanwhile with many thanks I am

Sincerely yours
Thomas Hardy.

P.S. I fear that verses of mine in the periodicals is not good evidence of my being at work. One is asked, & one goes to a drawer, & hunts up old effusions! Th: H.

Text MS. Adams.
the book: TH's copy of Child's *The Yellow Rock and Other Poems of Love* (London, 1919) is now in the Adams collection. *"Wild Roses"*: the title of this poem is in fact 'Song', but the first line reads, 'Wild roses in her hair'. *Waller-ish*: i.e., reminiscent of the verse of Edmund Waller (1606–87; *D.N.B.*). *at work*: as Child had suggested in his letter of 9 Dec 19 (DCM).

To SYDNEY COCKERELL

Max Gate | Dec. 15: 1919.

My dear Cockerell:

Your interesting letter would have been answered sooner if I had consulted my feelings & not submitted to be occupied with innumerable little matters of no real account.

"She wore a wreath of roses"—an immensely popular song by T. Haynes Bayly, has always had an attraction for me—not for any poetical merit that it shows, but because it appeals to tender memories, having been sung by so many of the generation now dead & gone. The sentiment is of a sort now despised, but for which I have a weakness, &, I think, a good many more people if they had honesty enough to own it. Knight, who wrote the tune, set many of Bayly's songs to music. Bayly was also the author of "Isle of Beauty" "Gaily the Troubadour", "O no, we never mention her", "I'd be a butterfly", &c., &c.,—all songs that my mother used to sing, my late wife's mother, & my late wife from her mother's old music. All these pieces of torn & yellow old music have descended to me—a sad heritage enough.

My dreams are not so coherent as yours. They are more like cubist paintings & generally end by my falling down the turret stairs of an old church owing to steps being missing.

Purcell's Fairy Queen will give Mrs Cockerell a lot of labour, but if she likes doing it it will not hurt her. It will, I suppose, come on just about the time that The Dynasts—or rather scenes from it—is to be done by the Oxford U.D.C. They want us to go to the latter, but it is doubtful if I shall, even if my wife does. February is an uncertain month. Believe me, with kind regards to the household,

Always yours
Thomas Hardy.

Text MS. Adams; envelope Purdy.
interesting letter: of 30 Nov 19 (DCM). *Bayly*: Thomas Haynes Bayly (1797–1839), prolific writer of songs, plays, and novels; *D.N.B.* *Knight*: Joseph Philip Knight (1812–87), clergyman and composer of popular songs; *D.N.B.* Cockerell, remembering TH's fondness for 'She wore a wreath of roses', had copied out of Samuel Butler's notebooks a reference to Knight's obituary in *The Times*. *not so coherent as yours*: Cockerell had dreamed about visiting Max Gate and seeing 'all the county' bow before a very grandly dressed TH. *Fairy Queen*: Mrs. Cockerell designed the costumes for the Cambridge University Musical Society production of Henry Purcell's opera *The Fairy Queen*, 10–14 Feb 1920. *doubtful if I shall*: TH did in fact see the performance in February 1920 when he went to Oxford to receive an honorary degree; see *LY*, 201–7.

To JOHN DRINKWATER

MAX GATE, | DORCHESTER. | Dec: 15: 1919

Dear Mr Drinkwater:

I believe I never thanked you for those charming lines, that bring up a vision & sense of wide open space, which you inscribed in the book sent me so kindly by poet-friends. Anyhow I thank you now, & can assure you that I shall always value the MS.

Sincerely yours
Thomas Hardy.

Text MS. Yale.
charming lines: Drinkwater's poem 'Reciprocity'.

To DOROTHY ALLHUSEN

MAX GATE, | DORCHESTER. | Dec. 23: 1919

My dear Dorothy:

I am so glad to hear from you, & trust you will be having a happy time this Christmas & New Year—as happy as is possible, that is to say, in the queer state of worldly affairs into which we have drifted.

Florence, who sends her love, is going to London the first week in

January, but I don't suppose I shall appear there till late spring, if then. She only runs up for a day or two. Let us know when there is a chance of your being near here.

Affectionately yours,
Th: H.

Text MS. Purdy.
hear from you: she wrote 21 Dec 19 (DCM). *worldly affairs*: TH perhaps had in mind the outbreak of violence in Ireland, the continuing civil war in Russia, and a report in that day's *Times* that Christmas in Berlin would be celebrated with as much gaiety as in any other European capital.

To WILLIAM LYON PHELPS

December 26. 1919

Dear Professor Phelps:

I am much honoured by the request of the Governing body of Yale University & yourself that I should deliver the first of the lectures instituted as a memorial to Francis Bergen. It is however quite out of my power to entertain the notion of such an undertaking; & this for more than one reason. I have never practised lecturing, or had any inclination to do so, & the time of life has now come to me at which, even if I had practised it, I should be compelled to leave off for physical reasons. All the same I thank the University for sending the suggestion to me, & including my wife in the welcome that is offered.

Believe me to be

Yours very truly
T—— H——

Text MS. (pencil draft) DCM.
Phelps: William Lyon Phelps (1865–1943), American critic and professor; he had called on TH at Max Gate in 1900 (see his *Autobiography with Letters*, New York, 1939, 390–5). *& yourself*: Phelps wrote 9 Dec 19 (DCM). *Bergen*: as Phelps explained in his letter, Francis Bergen was a member of the Yale class of 1914 who had been killed during the war.

To ANITA DUDLEY

Dec. 30. 1919

Dear Mrs Ambrose Dudley:

I am sorry to say that your appeal for a poem for the War Commemoration Book, that should be worthy of the event of the 8th August 1918, reaches me at too late a time of life for me to be able to attempt it.—The spirit truly is willing, but the flesh is weak. The outline of such a poem, which you very cleverly sketch, is striking, & ought to result at the hands of somebody or other who may undertake it, in a literary parallel to the Battle of Prague—a piece of music which ceased to be known long before your time, but was extraordinarily popular in its day—

reproducing the crashing of guns nearer & nearer, the groans of the wounded, & the final fulfilment with great fidelity.

The length of the late war exhausted me of all my impromptu poems dealing with that tragedy, the number of which you may not be aware of unless you are familiar with the volume of my collected verses. I quite think that one of our young poets would rise to the occasion if you were to give him the opportunity. With many regrets I am

Very truly yours

Text MS. (pencil draft) DCM.
Dudley: Anita Dudley, poet, wife of Ambrose Dudley, portrait painter and illustrator. *your appeal*: she wrote 27 Dec 19 (DCM) asking TH to write for inclusion in *The Royal Artillery War Commemoration Book* (London, 1920) a poem celebrating the artillery barrage of 8 Aug 1918, preceding the Allied attack which eventually led to victory in November 1918. *Battle of Prague*: a once-famous piece of programme music by the Bohemian composer František Kočzwara (probably known to TH as Kotzwara), who died in London 1791.

To J. McT.E. McTAGGART

Dec 31. 1919

Dear Dr McTaggart:

It is a pleasure to get your kind letter, & we send on best wishes for the imminent New Year to you & Mrs McTaggart. I am glad to hear that your Magnum Opus (for such I take it to be) is at any rate well under way, though whether I shall live to see the end of it published is doubtful.

I have of late been getting out of patience, if not with philosophers, with men of science. You probably, or I shd say certainly, have grasped with ease all that Einstein has been telling us, which is more than I have done. Really after what he says the universe seems to be getting too comic for words. However, though one may think queerly of time & space I can see that *motion* is merely relative, & long have done so; & I feel that it is just as true to assert that the earth stands still & the rest of the universe moves as to assert the opposite: & who knows if we may not get to despise Galileo & applaud the views of the Holy Inquisition! . . . .

Text MS. (pencil draft) DCM.
McTaggart: John McTaggart Ellis McTaggart, the philosopher; see III.208 and *LY*, 159. *kind letter*: of 28 Dec 19 (DCM). *Magnum Opus*: McTaggart had told TH he hoped soon to pub. 'the first volume of my system'—i.e., vol. 1 of his *The Nature of Existence* (Cambridge, 1921). *Einstein*: Albert Einstein (1879–1955), mathematician, physicist, and astronomer; TH's copy of his *Relativity*: *The Special and the General Theory. A Popular Exposition*, trans. Robert W. Lawson (3rd edn., London, 1920) is in DCM.

INDEX OF RECIPIENTS

A General Index will be included in the last volume of the edition.